STRANGERS, GODS AND MONSTERS

Strangers, Gods and Monsters is a fascinating look at how human identity is shaped by three powerful but enigmatic forces. Often overlooked in accounts of how we think about ourselves and others, Richard Kearney skilfully shows, with the help of vivid illustrations, how the human outlook on the world is formed by the mysterious triumvirate of strangers, gods and monsters.

The first part of the book shows how the figure of the stranger – the 'barbarian' for ancient Greece, the 'savage' for imperial Europe – defines our own identity by the very idea that it is the Other, not we, who is unknown. Kearney then goes on to examine the image of the monster, and with the aid of powerful examples from ancient Minotaurs to medieval demons and postmodern enemies, argues that human selfhood itself frequently contains a monstrous element. In the final part of the book he explores how some gods are still alive for people today, testifying to the human psyche's yearning to slip the shackles of our finitude and death.

Throughout, Richard Kearney shows how strangers, gods and monsters do not merely reside in myths or fantasies but constitute a central part of our cultural unconscious. Above all, he argues that until we better understand how the Other resonates deep within ourselves, we can have little hope of understanding how our most basic fears and desires manifest themselves in the external world and how we can learn to live with them.

Richard Kearney is Professor of Philosophy at Boston College and University College Dublin. His publications include *On Stories*, *Wake of Imagination* and *Postnationalist Ireland* (all published by Routledge), and *Sam's Fall* (a novel).

STRANGERS, GODS AND MONSTERS

Interpreting otherness

Richard Kearney

London and New York

First published 2003
by Routledge
11 New Fetter Lane, London EC4P 4EE

Simultaneously published in the USA and Canada
by Routledge
29 West 35th Street, New York, NY 10001
Reprinted 2004

Routledge is an imprint of the Taylor & Francis Group

Typeset in Joanna by Keystroke, Jacaranda Lodge, Wolverhampton
Printed and bound in Great Britain by
The Cromwell Press, Trowbridge, Wiltshire

British Library Cataloguing in Publication Data
A catalogue record for this book is available from the British Library

Library of Congress Cataloging in Publication Data
A catalog record for this book has been requested

ISBN 0–415–27257–2 (hbk)
ISBN 0–415–27258–0 (pbk)

CONTENTS

ILLUSTRATIONS

ACKNOWLEDGEMENTS

I wish to thank all those – and they were many – who were part of the dialogue which brought this book through a long process of conception, gestation and labour to its present published state.

In particular I wish to acknowledge the help and guidance I received from a number of colleagues at various universities and conferences where I delivered earlier versions of the chapters in this book as papers or discussions over the years. These include: David Wood at Vanderbilt; Patrick Burke, James Risser at Seattle University; Merold Westphal at Fordham; David Tracey and Chris Shepherd at the University of Chicago; Regina Swartz and Tom McCarthy at Northwestern; Simon Critchley, Robert Bernasconi and Françoise Dastur at the Collegium Phenomenologicum, Perugia; William Desmond at Leuven; Jack Caputo, Timothy Beal, Kevin Hart, Jacques Derrida, John Milbank, Clayton Crockett, and Jeffrey Bennington at the Villanova conferences; Jean Greisch and Stanislas Breton at L'Institut Catholique, Paris; Rene Girard, Monique Schneider and Olivier Mongin at the Cerisy-La-Salle decades; Paul Ricoeur, Emmanuel Levinas, Jacques Colette and Julia Kristeva at the University of Paris; Noam Chomsky at MIT; John McNamara and Charles Taylor at McGill; Jim Olthuis at the Institute for Christian Studies, Toronto; Stephen Daniel and John McDermott at Texas A and M University; Georgia Warnke and Jeff Pettigrove at UC Riverside; Paul Muldoon at Princeton; John and Laura McCourt at the University of Trieste; Marina Warner at the International Artists Conference in Belfast; Marek Toman, Erazim Kohak and Hindrich Pokorny at Charles University Seminar, Prague; Eileen Rizo-Patron and Martin Dillon at SUNY Binghampton; Hugh Silverman and Ed Casey at SUNY Stoneybrook; David Carr and Thomas Flynn at Emory; Jennifer Geddes at the University of Virginia; Michael Dillon and Paul Fletcher at the University of Lancaster; Dominique Janicaud at the University of Nice; Patrick Masterson, Bo Strath and James Kaye at the European University Institute in Florence; Denis Donoghue at NYU; Kevin Whelan and Luke Gibbons, Notre Dame Keogh Centre for Irish Studies; Dominico Jervolino and Maria Petit at the Hermeneutics Conference, University of Halle; Lisa Schnell and Charles Guignon at the University of Vermont; Gev Harvey at the University of Jerusalem; Jeffrey Barash of the University of Picardy; Joseph O'Leary of the University of Sophia, Tokyo; John Cleary at Maynooth University; Jean-Francois Courtine and Peter Kemp at the Hermeneutics Conference, Naples; Kalpana Seshadri-Crooks of the Post-Colonial Studies Seminar, Harvard; Paul Sheehan at the University of London; Martha Nussbaum at the Irish Philosophical Society conference, Dublin; Stephen Houlgate and Andrew Benjamin at Warwick.

I also owe a great debt to my colleagues and friends, closer to home as it were, at both Boston College and University College Dublin where I have had the good fortune to teach and research for most of my academic career.

Finally to my assistants at BC, John Manoussakis and Matt Pelletier, I owe an enormous thanks for their unrelenting assistance, inspiration and encouragement during the writing and editing of this book. As I do to Tony Bruce and Muna Khogali at Routledge whose faith, hope and charity made this book not only possible but actual.

I wish to dedicate this work to the three most important people in my life: my wife, Anne, and my daughters, Simone and Sarah.

Earlier versions of several of the chapters below have appeared in different publications. Sections of Chapters 1 to 3 have appeared as 'Others and Aliens: Between Good and Evil' in *Evil after Postmodernism: Histories, Narratives, Ethics*, ed. Jennifer Geddes, Routledge, London and New York, 2001; 'L'Autre et L'Etranger: Entre Derrida et Ricoeur' in *Philosopher en Français*, ed. Jean-François Mattéi, PUF, Paris, 2001; 'Strangers and Others: From Deconstruction to Hermeneutics' in *Critical Horizons*, vol. 3, no. 1, 2002; 'Aliens and Others: Between Girard and Ricoeur' in *Cultural Values*, vol. 3, no. 3, 1999. An extended version of the Appendix to Chapter 1 has appeared as 'Le mythe comme bouc émissaire chez Girard' in *Violence et Vérité*, ed. P. Dumouchel and J.-P. Dupuy, Grasset, Paris, 1985. Shorter and partial versions of Chapter 4 appeared as 'Evil, Monstrosity and the Sublime' in *Revista Portuguesa de Filosofia*, vol. 58, no. 3, 2001, and as 'Evil and Others' in *The Hedgehog Review*, vol. 2, no. 2, 2000.

A section of Chapter 5 appeared in *Philosophy and Social Criticism*, vol. 29, no. 1, 2002. Part of Chapter 9 was published, with a reply by John Caputo, in *The Passion for the Impossible: John D. Caputo in Focus*, ed. Mark Dooley, SUNY, Albany, New York, 2002. An edited version of the section entitled 'Joyce's Hamlet' in Chapter 6 appeared as 'Fathers and Sons: What Hamlet Meant to Shakespeare and Joyce' in *Bullan*, vol. 6, no. 2, 2002. Earlier and partial versions of Chapter 10 appeared as 'Faith or Philosophy?' in *Yearbook of the Irish Philosophical Society*, ed. Thomas Kelly, National University of Ireland, Maynooth 2002, and as 'Poetics of a Possible God' in *Hermeneutic Philosophy of Science, Van Gogh's Eyes, and God*, ed. Babette Babich, Kluwer Academic Publishers, Dordrecht, 2002.

INTRODUCTION

Strangers, gods and monsters

Uncharted Waters.
Late Medieval Print – anonymous

Strangers, gods and monsters are the central characters of my story. Their favourite haunts are those phantasmal boundaries where maps run out, ships slip moorings and navigators click their compasses shut. No man's land. Land's end. Out there, as the story goes, 'where the wild things are'. These figures of Otherness occupy the frontier zone where reason falters and fantasies flourish.

Strangers, gods and monsters represent experiences of extremity which bring us to the edge. They subvert our established categories and challenge us to think again. And because they threaten the known with the unknown, they are often set apart in fear and trembling. Exiled to hell or heaven; or simply ostracized from the human community into a land of aliens.

The figure of the 'stranger' – ranging from the ancient notion of 'foreigner' (*xenos*) to the contemporary category of alien invader – frequently operates as a limit-experience for humans trying to identify themselves over and against others. Greeks had their 'barbarians', Romans their Etruscans, Europeans their exotic overseas 'savages'. The western myth of the frontier epitomizes this, for example, when Pilgrim encounters Pequot on the shores of Massachusetts and asks 'Who is this stranger?' Not realizing, of course, that the native Pequot is asking exactly the same question of the arrivals from Plymouth. Strangers are almost always other to each other.

'Monsters' also signal borderline experiences of uncontainable excess, reminding the ego that it is never wholly sovereign. Many great myths and tales bear witness to this. Oedipus and the Sphinx. Theseus and the Minotaur. Job and Leviathan. Saint George and the Dragon. Beowulf and Grendel. Ahab and the Whale. Lucy and the Vampire. Ripley and the Alien. Each monster narrative recalls that the self is never secure in itself. 'There are monsters on the prowl', as Michel Foucault writes, 'whose form changes with the history of knowledge'.[1] For as our ideas of self-identity alter so do our ideas of what menaces this identity. Liminal creatures of the unknown shift and slide, change masks. We are of the earth, they whisper, autochthonous. We are carriers of the mark of Cain, hobbled by the Achilles heel of a primal unconscious. Monsters show us that if our aims are celestial, our origins are terrestrial. They ghost the margins of what can be legitimately thought and said. By definition unrecognizable, they defy our accredited norms of identification. Unnatural, transgressive, obscene, contradictory, heterogeneous, mad. Monsters are what keep us awake at night and make us nervous during the day. And even when they claim as in *Monsters Inc.* that 'they only scare because they care', they still scare.

And what of 'gods'? Gods are the names given by most mythologies and religions to those beings whose numinous power and mystery exceed our grasp and bid us kneel and worship. Sometimes they are benign, at other times cruel and capricious. But whatever their character they refuse to be reduced to the bidding of mortals. Transcending laws of time and space, they readily take on immortal or protean status. Gods' ways are not our ways. They bedazzle and surprise us. It is not ours to reason why. But where monsters arise from underworlds, and strangers intrude from hinterworlds, gods generally reside in otherworlds beyond us. Whether it be Jehovah, Zeus or Jupiter, deities inhabit sublime heights. We look up to them, if we dare look at all.

*

Most strangers, gods and monsters – along with various ghosts, phantoms and doubles who bear a family resemblance – are, deep down, tokens of fracture within the human psyche. They speak to us of how we are split between conscious and unconscious, familiar and unfamiliar, same and other. And they remind us that we have a choice: (a) to try to understand and accommodate our experience of strangeness, or (b) to repudiate it by projecting it exclusively onto outsiders. All too often, humans have chosen the latter option, allowing paranoid illusions to serve the purpose of making sense of our confused emotions by externalizing them into black-and-white scenarios – a strategy found again and again from ancient tales of knights and demons to contemporary war rhetorics of Good versus Evil. When menaced by terror or war, as Anthony Storr observes:

Many people resort to the so-called paranoid–schizoid stage of development, in which they will follow a guru-like leader whom they invest with magical powers for good, and at the same time find scapegoats whom they blame for the disaster and regard as wholly evil.[2]

This volume is an attempt to reinvestigate practices of defining ourselves in terms of otherness. In an age crippled by crises of identity and legitimation, it would seem particularly urgent to challenge the polarization between Us and Them. What new forms do the emblematic figures of otherness take, we may ask, in a society increasingly dominated by simulation and spectacle? And what critical means might we deploy to differentiate between diverse kinds of otherness in a culture where everything has become more and more undecidable – sometimes to the point where we have difficulty distinguishing Self from Other in the first place? Clearly some kind of philosophical questioning is called for if we are to try to understand the enigma of self and other or to explore modes of discerning between different kinds of self and different kinds of other.

*

One of my guiding hypotheses in this work will be that we often project onto others those unconscious fears from which we recoil in ourselves. Rather than acknowledge that we are deep down answerable to an alterity which unsettles us, we devise all kinds of evasion strategies. Primary amongst these is the attempt to simplify our existence by scapegoating others as 'aliens'. So doing we contrive to transmute the sacrificial alien into a monster, or into a fetish-god. But either way, we refuse to recognize the stranger before us as a singular other who responds, in turn, to the singular otherness in each of us. We refuse to acknowledge ourselves-as-others.

Sometimes, in our confusion, we have been known to turn the Other into a monster *and* a god. Hierophanies – where the unshowable deity shows itself – are often terrifying. Hence the double etymology of *monstrare*, to show and to warn. Zeus' mutations into a plundering bull or rapacious swan epitomize this paradox. And Kali certainly knew how to scare mortals. Even the generally 'good' biblical God could resort to horror on occasion, as Job realized; or Abraham when commanded to kill Isaac, or Jacob when he found himself maimed at the hip after wrestling with the dark angel of Israel. Or Zechariah struck dumb by the angel Gabriel. Not to mention the tales of floods and plagues and conflagrations sent by a jealous God to fill his people with fear. Divine monstrance was not infrequently an occasion of terror. *Fascinans et tremendum*, as the mystics said.

Poets too have attested to this enigma of the monstrous God. W.B. Yeats captured this disturbing ambiguity of the sacred, for example, in his apocalyptic image of the 'rough beast slouching towards Bethlehem to be born'. A sentiment echoed by Rilke in his famous opening apostrophe to the *Duino Elegies*: 'Every angel is terrible'. And one might also recall here Herman Melville's chilling evocation of the quasi-divine, quasi-demonic whiteness of the whale, recalling at once the horror of Leviathan and the transcendence of Yahweh:

> But not yet have we solved the incantation of this whiteness, and learned why it appeals with such power to the soul; and more strange and more portentous – why, as we have seen, it is at once the most meaning symbol of spiritual things, nay, the very veil of the Christian's Deity; and yet should be as it is, the intensifying agent in things the most appalling to mankind.
>
> (*Moby Dick*, Modern Library, New York, p. 42)

We will be investigating this fundamental paradox of the sacred-savage Other in various chapters of this volume, with examples ranging from ancient myths and religions to contemporary sacrificial narratives such as *Apocalypse Now Redux* and the symbolism of 11 September.

*

My purpose in this book is more than the investigation of certain formative archives in the Western genealogy of the stranger. My main task is actually to explore possibilities of responding to the problem of the stranger in terms of some kind of philosophical understanding. Julia Kristeva has suggested that there are three main ways in which we might respond to our fundamental experience of estrangement: *art, religion* and *psychoanalysis*. I will be looking at each of these during the course of this study. But I will also be suggesting a fourth way of response: *philosophy*. For if art offers therapy in terms of images, religion in terms of faith, and psychoanalysis in terms of a 'talking cure', philosophy has something extra (though not necessarily better) to offer. And that something extra, which may usefully supplement the other three, is a certain kind of *understanding*. During the course of these studies I will be referring to various moments in the history of philosophy which might help us in our search for ways of understanding the Other – from Aristotle's practical wisdom (*phronesis*) and Kant's 'reflective judgement' to more contemporary hermeneutic models of narrative comprehension (Ricoeur, Arendt, Taylor). My wager is that if the enigma of the Other has been largely ignored by the mainstream metaphysical tradition – going back to Parmenides and Plato who defined the Other in relation to the Same – it resurfaces again and again throughout our western cultural history in the guise of strangers, gods and monsters who will not go away and continue to command our attention. Preoccupied with the Rule of Reason, most western philosophers since Parmenides have banished the puzzlements provoked by 'strangeness' to the realm of Unreason, namely the cultural unconscious of myth, art and religion. And in the process of this estrangement, the Other passed from the horizon of reflective understanding into the invisible, unspeakable, unthinkable dark.

It is my conviction that the Other may be brought back onto the horizon of philosophical understanding again in light of a number of recent explorations of the Self–Other relation in psychoanalytic theory, deconstruction, anthropology and phenomenological hermeneutics. It is also my conviction that the project of enlightenment will remain unenlightened until it comes to terms with the strangers, gods and monsters that it has all too often ostracized or ignored. And it is here that I will also be proposing a second movement from philosophy back to its others (art, religion, psychoanalysis). Understanding and pre-understanding need to get back into dialogue with each other. That is one of the guiding hypotheses of this work.

*

One example of how this might be achieved is, I suggest, a new hermeneutic understanding of 'melancholy'. If melancholic dread and anxiety is indeed one of the characteristic maladies of humanity, it is incumbent on philosophers to take this seriously. One of the best ways in which this may be done is by looking at the formative myths which epitomize this fundamental experience of alienation. Foremost here is the myth of Saturn, the monster who castrates his father and seeks to devour his own children. Though ignored by mainstream philosophy and metaphysics for centuries, certain thinkers in our own time – from Klibansky and Heidegger to Kristeva and Ricoeur – have sought to revisit the hidden meanings of this mythic monster and remind us how dread before death and loss can veer manically between abjection and elation unless we come to terms with it. Such reckoning implies both an acknowledgement and a working-through of this estranging mood, so that we may tame the monster and be less 'driven' by it. Once again, art, religion and psychoanalysis offer indispensable means of achieving this task. But so, I submit, does philosophy. To go on evading the monster of *angst* within us is a recipe for obsessional neurosis and existential inauthenticity. To face the Saturnine monster and acknowledge that it is an intregral part of us is to accept the truth that we are strangers-to-ourselves and that we need not fear such strangeness or 'act it out' by projecting such fear onto Others.

The story of Hamlet, which we explore below in both its Shakespearean and Joycean retellings, dramatizes the options faced by the melancholic soul. Confronting the terrors of death – triggered by the untimely loss of his father – the tortured Dane finds himself vacillating between mania and despair. One moment he apotheosizes his dead father as a demi-god (Hyperion), the next he recoils in horror from his ghostly apparition. The anguished Prince is a well-seasoned traveller on the peaks and troughs of strangeness. But what every melancholic – from heroic Danes to existential Daseins – must ultimately accept is this: the lost thing is really lost and the only cure lies in true mourning, that is, in the readiness to let go of the other we hold captive within or scapegoat without. The key is to let the other be other so that the self may be itself again. I will be suggesting that one of the best aids in this task is *narrative understanding*: a working-through of loss and fear by means of cathartic imagination and mindful acknowledgement.

*

Letting the other be other in the right way is, of course, no easy task. Our contemporary culture in particular exploits our deep ambiguity towards the death instinct, displacing our fearful fascination onto spectacular stories of horror, monstrosity and violence. Julia Kristeva captures this point well in a dialogue we conducted on the subject in Paris in 1991:

> The media propagate the death instinct. Look at the films people like to watch after a long tiring day: a thriller or a horror film, anything less is considered boring. We are attracted to this violence. So the

great moral work which grapples with the problem of identity also grapples with this contemporary experience of death, violence and hate.

And Kristeva goes on to suggest, quite correctly in my view, that this expresses itself in extremist forms of identity politics:

> Nationalisms, like fundamentalisms, are screens in front of this violence, fragile screens, see-through screens, because they only displace that hatred, sending it to the other, to the neighbour, to the rival ethnic group. The big work of our civilization is to try to fight this hatred.[3]

Indeed, it could be said that the history of modern Western philosophy reads like a litany of refusals to let go. Hegel explores the violent conflict between self and other in his famous master–slave dialectic, Freud in his writings on the uncanny and death-drive, Marx in his analysis of fetishism and false consciousness, and existentialists like Sartre and Heidegger in their detailed phenomenological descriptions of inauthentic existence and bad faith.

With the emergence of a distinctly postmodern preoccupation with *alterity* and the *sublime*, we confront new tasks of thinking about the opposition between self and other. The challenge now is to acknowledge a difference between self and other without separating them so schismatically that *no* relation at all is possible. This is a genuine difficulty for some post-phenomenological thinkers who externalize the category of alterity to the point that any contact with the self smacks of betrayal or contamination. The attempt to build hermeneutic bridges between us and 'others' (human, divine or whatever) should not, I will argue, be denounced as ontology, onto-theology or logocentrism – that is to say, as some form of totalizing reduction bordering on violence. For such denunciation ultimately denies any form of dialogical interbeing between self and other. Hence, in a thinker like Levinas, we find that the experience of irreducible alterity (divine *Illeity*) is at bottom indistinguishable from the experience of irreducible abjection (atheistic *Il y a*). The high becomes so high and the low so low that they slip over the edge and begin to converge – sometimes to the point of indifferenciation. The God beyond being becomes an abyss beneath being. The Other becomes Alien.

These dialectical conflations – or deconstructive inversions – will merit distinct treatments in the studies below. But they do share a common symptom of radical undecidability which, I contend, needs to be addressed by a critical hermeneutics of self-and-other. This, I will argue, calls for a practice of narrative interpretation capable of tracing interconnections between the poles of sameness and strangeness. Faced with the postmodern fixation with inaccessible alterity we need to build paths between the worlds of *autos* and *heteros*. We need to chart a course between the extremes of tautology and heterology. For in this way philosophy might help us to discover the other in our self and our self in the other – without abjuring either.

*

Hence my proposal in this work of a hermeneutic model of narrative, resolved in spite of all to say something about the unsayable, to imagine images of the unimaginable, to tell tales of the untellable, respecting all the while the border limits that defer all Final Answers. I am not, let me make clear at the outset, sponsoring a return to Master Narratives of totality or closure. Nor am I interested in espousing redundant ontologies of the *ens causa sui* or *cogito sum*. On the contrary, I am largely persuaded by the Heideggerean critique of the metaphysics of presence. And I fully appreciate the ethical spin given this by recent exposures of the 'appropriating' tendencies of human thought (Levinas, Derrida, Caputo, Kristeva, etc). But I am equally convinced that some hermeneutic stitching and weaving needs to be sustained if we are to keep alive the practice of responsible judgement and justice. For how are we to address otherness at all if it becomes totally *unrecognizable* to us? Faced with such putative indetermination, how could we tell the difference between one kind of other and another – between (a) those aliens and strangers that need our care and hospitality, no matter how monstrous they might first appear, and (b) those others that really do seek to destroy and exterminate (as evidenced in genocidal slaughters from Belsen to Bosnia where certain 'enemies' are indeed murderous adversaries). Or to take one of the most ancient examples of ethical discernment, how are we to differentiate between the voice that bade Abraham kill Isaac and the voice that forbade him to do so? These are urgent hermeneutic matters. For they determine how cultures take the side of murder or compassion.

Not all 'selves' are evil and not all 'others' are angelic. That is why, I suggest, it is wise to supplement the critique of the *self* with an equally indispensable critique of the *other*. Without such a double critique – which exposes illusory categories of ego *and* alien – we can no longer speak of any real relation between humans, or indeed between humans and non-humans (animal or divine). Only by means of such an ambidexterous move, I believe, can we hope to de-alienate some of the forces which pervade our global consumerist culture.[4]

This double critique requires a delicate balance. On one hand, if others become *too transcendent*, they disappear off our radar screen and we lose all contact. We then not only stop seeing them directly but even stop seeing them indirectly *as* this or that other. The possibility of imagining, narrating or interpreting alterity becomes impossible; and in the field of philosophy, we witness the demise of phenomenological and hermeneutic inquiry. The silent dark of sublime unthinkability reigns supreme. We wait in paralytic fear for the return of the faceless repressed. Kratophany replaces epiphany.[5]

On the other hand, if others become too *immanent*, they become equally exempt from ethical relation. In this instance, they become indistinguishable from our own totalizing selves (conscious or unconscious). The trick is therefore, I suggest, not to let the foreign become *too* foreign or the familiar *too* familiar. If certain kinds of apophatic mysticism and deconstruction run the former risk, certain forms of psychoanalytic and New Age immanentism run the latter.

Postmodernism is a contentious and somewhat confused term, but it is, I suggest, a sufficiently capacious umbrella to cover both contemporary extremes – and still have room for alternatives which eschew this polarity. The balance I seek to strike in this volume involves an effort to discern the *juste milieu* where a valid sense of selfhood and strangeness might coexist. The goal of the diacritical hermeneutic I explore below is to make the foreign more familiar and the familiar more foreign. Or to rehearse the metaphor of altitude, my task is to let the self walk at sea level with its other, avoiding the inhospitable extremities of vertiginous heights and abyssal depths. My aim, in short, is to open up itineraries between elation and dejection – itineraries both multiple and traversible. So doing, it is hoped that the self might achieve a more discerning readiness to welcome strangers, respect gods and acknowledge monsters.

With this goal in mind, I will be seeking guidance and assistance from a number of contemporary debates on the fundamental dialectic of identification and alienation which lies at the root of the human obsession with strangers, gods and monsters – an obsession which is symptomatic of the wound inflicted by the refusal to acknowledge oneself-as-another. The main debates on the enigma of the Other which I will be exploring below range from religious anthropology (Eliade/Girard/Lévi-Strauss) and psychoanalysis (Freud/Lacan/Kristeva) to deconstruction (Derrida/Lyotard/Caputo), phenomenology (Husserl/Heidegger/Levinas) and hermeneutics (Gadamer/Greisch/Ricoeur).

*

My basic suggestion throughout this book is that philosophy today needs a narrative understanding capable of casting rope ladders and swing bridges across opposing extremes. This requires various kinds of image, analogy and symbol to address the challenge of *intersignification*. I am suggesting that philosophy might help relocate the subtle chiasmus linking but not conflating self and other. That a new hermeneutics of understanding might help us learn to knit together again the weaves of transcendent and incarnate existence – an exercise which John Donne called 'interanimation', and which he described so movingly in his poem, *The Extasie*:

> As our blood labours to beget
> Spirits, as like souls as it can,
> Because such fingers need to knit
> That subtile knot, which makes us man.
>
> So must pure lovers soules descend
> To th'affections, and to faculties,
> That sense may reach and apprehend,
> Else a great Prince in prison lies.

One can find prefigurings of this kind of hermeneutic translation in that labour of 'symbolic imagination' which, as the poet Allen Tate has it, 'conducts an action through analogy, of the human to the divine, of the natural and the supernatural, of the low to the high, of time to eternity'.[6] This is less a question of Hegelian synthesis than of multiple traversals between seeming incompatibles. It does not signal recourse to some speculative metaphysical system that would wrap opposites into some happy ending. Nor does it summon us to the call of a 'Last God', as Heidegger might have us believe. Nor, finally, need such translation revert to a model of scholastic compromise, setting out middle-range rules and then settling for the median mark. It is more a matter of gracious affinities. Constellations. Interlacings of alterities.

*

The quest is not new. It did not begin with Hegel or Levinas or Derrida. The conundrum of the Other goes back to the beginnings of western metaphysics in Parmenides and Plato. And in a way we might say that the three figures of our title – strangers, gods and monsters – are three colloquial names for the experience of alterity.

Plato approaches this alterity in terms of wonderment (*thaumazein*) and terror (*deinon*). While he and other Greek philosophers acknowledge such experience as the very source of philosophizing, there is a deep ambivalence from the outset. As Socrates suggests in the *Phaedrus*, strangers, gods and monsters belong to the realm of myth, not philosophy. Philosophy proper should be able to transcend mythic imaginings in favour of more rational pursuits. 'I look not into them (myths)', says Socrates, 'but into my own self: Am I a beast more complicated and savage than Typhon, or am I a tamer, simpler animal with a share in a divine and gentle nature?' (*Phaedrus*, 230e). The question is doubtless rhetorical. Socrates, in spite of his modest doubts, has clearly decided for the latter option. But the either/or is telling; as is the specific mention of Typhon as an alternative to the 'divine and gentle' philosopher.

Typhon, Hesiod tells us, was a 'fearful dragon' (*deinos drakon*) with a 'hundred heads' (*Theogony*, 823–5). The child of Earth and Tartarus, born after Zeus had driven the Titans out of heaven, Typhon stayed on as a reminder of our wild terrestrial origins. Mad voices sounded from his multiple heads, his serpent eyes flashed fire which shook mountains and his breath produced whirlwinds that destroyed ships and sailors. But while some of his voices cried like savage animals, others were so 'wonderful to hear' (*thauma akouein*) that they were immediately understood by the gods and seduced both mortals and immortals alike. The power of this dark creature soon came to threaten the gods themselves however, until Zeus waged a mighty battle against Typhon and cast him into Tartarus, the abyss below Hades where the other Titans and giants had been banished from the world of light. (Typhon was also used as a name for the Egyptian evil divinity Set.)

The fact that Typhon is the particular beast that Socrates chooses to define himself against qua philosopher is, I believe, highly significant. It implies that it is only by exorcising this last and most atavistic of monsters that one can 'know oneself' according to the light of reason. Moreover, the fact that this creature is, as the adjective *deinoteron* suggests, wonderful *and* terrible betrays the fact that it is both akin to the gods (who readily comprehend its speech) and uncanny, strange and fearful to men. Not surprisingly therefore, Socrates is full of puzzlement about his double origins – as quasi-terrestrial and

13

quasi-divine. And he seems determined to follow Zeus in combatting mythic and chthonic forces in order to ascend to the higher realms of metaphysical insight and civility.

Plato, like Parmenides before him, can generally be said to mark a transition from the mythology of monsters to the metaphysics of reason. But just as Typhon survived the initial expulsion of Titans from Olympus, so too it seems he is wont to somehow linger on in the world of humans, revisiting even enlightened sages like Socrates. The eternal return of reason's repressed. Perhaps this accounts for the curious ambiguity witnessed in *The Symposium* where Socrates is compared by Alcibiades to a Silenus or Satyr (strange monstrous figures) even as he is hailed as the most rational of beings![7]

By thus linking the origin of philosophising to a certain *pathos* of wonder and awe (*thaumazein/deinon*), Plato appears to acknowledge that if Reason is predicated upon the expulsion of its monstrous Other, it is never wholly rid of it. Indeed the very notion that the contemplative quietude of metaphysical reasoning might be provoked in the first place by something as turbulent as a *pathos* reminds the logic of the Same that it always carries traces of its spectral origin and that this origin can never be fully purged or controlled. In short, Socrates can never step entirely out of his shadow. Anymore than he can escape his daimon. Which accounts for the fact, as Arendt reminds us, that philosophy always begins and ends in speechlessness.[8]

This is one good reason why, if philosophers are indeed enjoined to *know themselves*, they do well to continue concerning themselves with this inaugural and abiding enigma of the monster within.

*

But Socrates' reckoning with the spectre of Typhon in the *Phaedrus*, and subsequent preference for metaphysics over myth, is not the only moment when Plato confronts the problem of the Other.

It is no accident that in *The Sophist* Plato puts the interrogation of otherness into the mouth of the Eleatic stranger (*xenos*). This involves establishing the existence of an 'other category' (*heteros genos*) beyond being. For if being is all that exists and there is nothing other than being – e.g. a non-being in which words, images and things might also have some part – then one cannot explain the possibility of falsehood or error (which confounds what is and what is not). Nor, if this be the case, could strangers or foreigners justify their own right to exist in so far as they are *other* than the self-identical order of being itself. In the Parmenidean regime, non-resident aliens need not apply. The Stranger argues accordingly, against Parmenides, that

> The kinds blend with each other and that what-is and the other run through each and every kind, that the other shares in that which is and, because of that sharing (*methexis*), is; but (since) the other is different from that in which it shares, being other than what-is, it is most clear and necessary that what-is-not is.
>
> (*Soph.* 259a–b)

Moreover, in order for being to have its own being, the Stranger insists, it must, for its part, share in the other so that it can be itself and, therefore, other than everything else.

Whence the conclusion of the Stranger that discourse, as the statement of truth or falsehood – i.e. a confection of being and non-being – is only made possible by the splicing of one form with the other (*ton eidon symploken*) (*Soph.*259). The implications are wide-ranging. The complete separation of same (*autos*) and other (*heteron*), of being and what is other than being, would be the obliteration (*apophansis*) of all speech (*Soph.* 259e). Nothing less. And, consequently, it would eliminate any means of distinguishing between true and false. It would make the Other, quite literally, unspeakable. And, by extension, unrecognizable.

For the Eleatic stranger the other is other, finally, only *in relation to the same*. The Other as a distinct class is not comprehensible unless it is considered *relative* to some Other (*pros heteron*) (255d). In so far as it differs from the known order of being, the Other is always relative. Or more simply put, any relation with the Absolute makes the Absolute relative (*Parmenides* 133–5; 141–2).[9] It is this fundamental distinction between what is absolute (*kath'auto*) and what is relative (*pros alla*) (255c) that proves decisive for subsequent controversies in western philosophy.

*

This definition of alterity in relation to sameness is revisited by the modern movement of phenomenology, as noted above. In *The Phenomenology of Spirit*, Hegel historicizes the problem in terms of a master–slave dialectic. Here, he argues, the self only expresses itself as a sovereign subject in so far as it struggles with, and is eventually recognized by, its Other (*das Andere*). But it is

Husserl who brings the phenomenological dialectic to its logical conclusion in the Fifth *Cartesian Meditation* when he claims that the other is never absolutely alien but is always and everywhere recognized as other precisely as other-than-me, that is, by analogy and appresentation. Here the other manifests itself as *alter ego*. And this position is further radicalized by Heidegger in his portrayal of the other in terms of the being-with (*Mitsein*) of ontological self-existence (*Dasein*). Otherness is a horizon of selfhood.

Now it is just this notion of relative otherness which Levinas and certain other contemporary thinkers resist. Levinas himself rejects such a notion unambiguously in *Totality and Infinity*. The Other, he states, does not manifest itself in relation to the ego's horizons of consciousness or subjectivity but 'expresses itself'.[10] In this phenomenological turnaround, the Stranger is at root *kath'auto*, not *pros heteron*. Absolutely not relatively other.

Absolute versus relative otherness. This problematic informs, I am suggesting, the entire metaphysical paradigm of self-and-other running from Plato and Aristotle to Hegel and the modern philosophy of consciousness. The rejection of relative otherness in favour of absolute otherness, by Levinas and other thinkers of radical alterity, marks a decisive 'break' between thought and language. At the last minute, Levinas opts for what Derrida calls the 'unthinkable-impossible-unutterable beyond Being and Logos'.[11] By this reasoning, the positive plenitude of infinity can only translate into language by 'betraying' itself in a negative term (in-finity). Though often ambiguous on this complex issue, Derrida seems to side with the Eleatic stranger when he criticizes Levinas for trying to keep the infinite Other absolutely separate from the ontological order of phenomena, that is, for refusing to mix beyond-being with being. Levinas' idea of absolute alterity presupposes the very phenomenology of speech and appearance it seeks to transcend.[12] But, to be fair, Levinas is aware of this; and he is perfectly capable of retorting that Derrida has a similar predicament with his own notion of the other. A point well taken, and one to which we will return in Chapter 3 below.

For now, however, suffice it to say that to Plato's Eleatic stranger who argues for the mixing of being and non-being, Levinas would doubtless oppose the 'ethical' stranger of the Torah: the Other of Psalm 119 who declares, 'I am a stranger on earth, hide not thy commandments from me'. My response will be that the two strangers are not mutually exclusive. They need to negotiate a new alliance.

*

16

In this volume I endeavour to steer a winding path between ontological and ethical categories of Otherness. I attempt to re-establish some kind of congress between Eleatic and Biblical strangers. Not by resorting to metaphysical fusion, but by trying out a variety of crossings between same and other. I am not proposing speculative flyovers or viaducts but tentative footbridges and rope-ladders reaching across the chasms separating old ontologies from new heterologies.

The method I propose is a *diacritical hermeneutics*. This I distinguish from both *romantic* and *radical hermeneutics*. Romantic hermeneutics sponsors the view – endorsed by Schleiermacher, Dilthey and Gadamer – that the purpose of philosophical interpretation is to unite the consciousness of one subject with that of the other. This process is called 'appropriation' which in the German, *Aneignung*, means *becoming one with*. Schleiermacher explored this retrieval of estranged consciousness in terms of a theological reappropriation of the original message of the Kerygma. Dilthey, for his part, analysed it in terms of the historical resolve to reach some kind of 'objective' knowledge about the past; even though he distinguished sharply between the objectivity of the natural sciences (*Naturwissenschaften*) and that of the human sciences (*Geisteswissenschaften*) where hermeneutic understanding properly applies.[13] Gadamer, finally, pursued the idea of a reconciliation between our own understanding and that of strangers in terms of a 'fusion of horizons'. For all three, the purpose of hermeneutic understanding was to recover some lost original consciousness by way of rendering what is past contemporaneous with our present modes of comprehension.

By contrast, the 'radical' hermeneutics of Caputo – inspired by the deconstructive turn of Derrida, Blanchot and Lyotard – rejects the model of appropriation, insisting on the unmediatable and ultimately 'sublime' nature of alterity. In defiance of a community of minds, this uncompromising stance holds out for irreducible difference and separation. To this end Caputo promotes the 'hyperbolic hypothesis' of Levinas and Derrida, defined as an 'unphenomenological model' in which 'an invisible infinity comes over me and demands everything of me, the food out of my mouth' – a new model 'for the friend and for politics, which have always been understood in *egalitarian* terms'.[14] In this light, radical hermeneutics invokes an irreducible dissymmetry of self and other. It proposes that human friendship should not be conceived according to the Greek and metaphysical paradigm of intimacy, comparison and consensus but rather in terms of infinite alterity. The friend is no longer to be taken as the 'other' of the 'same': one who is of an analogous mind or soul, as in Aristotle's *homonoia* or Husserl's *Paarung* and *Einfühling*. The hyperbolic hypothesis resists the idea of a community of similars. It flouts the virtue of equality. The friend is always *more* than my fellow, which effectively means that 'friendship is caught up in the infinite disproportion of a gift without exchange, in which the other, appearing without appearing, comes from a place of structural superiority and invisible imminence'.[15] So friendship between oneself and another is, Derrida insists, not yet actually possible but is something – like democracy or justice – that is always still to come. Friendship-to-come will not, we are told, be signalled by the 'good sense' of equal, autonomous selves but by the 'madness and nonsense of heteronomy'.[16]

The *diacritical* hermeneutics I propose, by contrast, is committed to a third way beyond these romantic and radical options. It is my contention that this middle way (*metaxu*) is in fact more radical and challenging than either. Obviating both the congenial communion of fused horizons and the apocalyptic rupture of non-communion, I will endeavour to explore possibilities of intercommunion between distinct but not incomparable selves. The diacritical approach holds that friendship begins by welcoming difference (*dia-legein*). It champions the practice of dialogue between self and other, while refusing to submit to the reductionist dialectics of egology governed by the *logos* of the Same. Between the *logos* of the One and the anti-*logos* of the Other, falls the *dia-logos* of oneself-as-another.

The basic aim of diacritical hermeneutics is, I suggest, to make us more hospitable to strangers, gods and monsters without succumbing to mystique or madness. We have too often demonized the 'other' in western culture out of fear. But if we can become more mindful of who the other is – and is it not a primary task of philosophy to foster such mindfulness? – we will, I am convinced, be less likely to live in horror of the dark. For the dark is all too frequently a mask for the alterity of our own death and a screen against the advent of strangers unbeknownst and still unknown to us.

Perfect love casts out fear. A sentiment echoed in many wisdom traditions East and West, including this Tibetan verse:

> If this elephant of mind is held on all sides
> by the cord of mindfulness,
> All fear disappears and happiness comes.
> All enemies: all the tigers, lions, bears,
> serpents, elephants . . .

and all the keepers of hell; the demons and the horrors,
All of these are contained by the attention of your mind,
and by the calming of that mind all are calmed,
Because from the mind are derived all fears and unmeasurable
  sorrows.

A final advantage of the diacritical hermeneutics I am endorsing in this volume is its hospitality to other disciplines. Thus while striving to remain loyal to the demands of philosophical lucidity and coherence, our dialogue proposes to also reach across strict disciplinary divides and engage in a cross-hatching of intellectual horizons. And in this respect I fully approve the generous definition of hermeneutics offered by Rudiger Bubner:

> Hermeneutics has become more and more of a key word in philosophical discussions of the most varied kind. It seems as if hermeneutics creates cross-connections between problems of different origin. In linguistics and sociology, in history and literary studies, in theology, jurisprudence and aesthetics, and finally in the general theory of science, hermeneutic perspectives have been successfully brought to bear. In this way, the traditional philosophical claim to universality is renewed under another name.[17]

I would simply want to preface the term 'universality' with the qualifier 'quasi', thereby retaining the claim as a wager rather than a presumption. And to add that if hermeneutics extends horizontally across disciplines it also extends historically across temporal horizons, reinterpreting the myths and memories of our past in the light of future hopes for a more mindful and compassionate understanding of our Others.

*

The present volume is the third part of a philosophical trilogy exploring the role of 'Philosophy at the Limit'. The companion volumes – On Stories and The God who May Be – deal respectively with the enigmas of the narrative imaginary and the task of naming the unnameable. This last volume tackles diverse experiences of human estrangement by means of a hermeneutic retrieval of selfhoood through the odyssey of otherness. During the course of the journey, several of our frontier maps may have to be revised. We may even have to abandon some cherished baggage and belongings on the wayside. But our basic wager is this: by sounding out certain borderlands separating Us from Others we may become more ready to acknowledge strangers in ourselves and ourselves in strangers.

Part I

1

STRANGERS AND SCAPEGOATS

Limbo.
Detail from the Chapel of St Lorenzo, Florence. (Photo by Richard Kearney)

Mosaic of the Devil.
Detail from the Chapel of St Lorenzo, Florence. (Photo by Richard Kearney)

> She walks with him as a stranger, and at first she puts him to the
> test; fear and dread she brings upon him and tries him with her
> discipline . . . Then she comes back to bring him happiness and
> reveal her secrets to him.
>
> (On Wisdom, Sirach 4)

Most human cultures have been known to deploy myths of sacrifice to scapegoat strangers. Holding certain aliens responsible for the ills of society, the scapegoaters proceed to isolate or eliminate them. This sacrificial strategy furnishes communities with a binding identity, that is, with the basic sense of who is included (us) and who is excluded (them). So the price to be paid for the construction of the happy tribe is often the ostracizing of some outsider: the immolation of the 'other' on the altar of the 'alien'.

This scapegoating practice is evidenced in many different cultures, but I will focus my remarks here on the Western treatment of this phenomenon. More specifically, I will trace the genealogy of sacrificial purgation from ancient mythic and religious narratives up to recent controversies surrounding the whole practice of scapegoating. I will conclude by suggesting how the theme of the ritual scapegoat continues to preoccupy the contemporary cultural imaginary in such films as *Apocalypse Now* and the *Alien* series.

Genealogy of the scapegoat

Cultic practices of scapegoating are common in early Greco-Roman society. One thinks of Prometheus bound to his sacrificial rock, Dionysius dismembered by the Maeneds, Iphigenia exposed to the sword, Remus cut down by Romulus. By contrast, the whole notion of sacrifice was to assume highly problematic proportions in Judaeo-Christian thinking.

A formative text here is Leviticus 16. Entitled 'The great day of expiation', it describes an annual rite of purification by means of which the chosen people of God cleanse themselves through the expulsion of a 'scapegoat', thereby setting themselves off from what is unholy. The passage most relevant for our purposes records a series of procedures revealed by Yahweh to Moses. Though a number of animals are involved in the sacrificial rite – lambs, bulls and goats – it is the last of these which particularly concern us. With a view to expiating his community of all sin, the sacrificial priest (in this instance, Moses' brother, Aaron) adorned himself in consecrated linen tunic before taking 'two he-goats for a sacrifice for sin' (Lev. 16, 5). Drawing lots, the priest then marked off one of the goats for Yahweh (the Holy one) and the other for Azazel (the Unholy one). The former he slaughtered, scattering its blood inside the curtain of the sanctuary as a 'rite of expiation for the sanctuary for the uncleanness of the Israelites' (Lev. 16, 16). And before the altar of Yahweh he performed an act of similar expiation using the blood and horns of the goat: 'He will take some of . . . the goat's blood and put it on the horns at the corners of the altar all around it . . . thus purifying it and setting it apart' (Lev. 16, 19).

The ritual bloodletting of the first goat completed, the second sacrificial goat comes into play: the scapegoat proper. Here is the decisive account for our inquiry:

> Aaron will then lay both his hands on the head (of the scapegoat) and over it confess all the guilt of the Israelites, all their acts of rebellion and all their sins. Having thus laid them on the goat's head, he will send it out into the desert . . . and the goat will bear all their guilt away into some desolate place.
>
> (Lev. 16, 20–2)

In this wise, the demarcation of pure from impure is realized; and it only remains for the sacrificial priest to return to the sanctuary, now purified, and engage in ritual ablutions, before going out again to his people and performing the final rite of burning the 'fat of the sacrifice for sin on the altar' (Lev. 16, 23). The text ends with the injunction from the Holy One himself, Yahweh, that this 'rite of expiation will be performed for you to purify you' on the tenth day of the seventh month of every year, an annual holy day of sabbatical prayer, fasting and purgation (Lev. 16, 30).

The message could not be clearer. The people of God remain holy by casting from their midst what is unholy, thus propitiating the Lord and removing all traces of evil from their community. By means of such purging they become one Holy Nation in the service of the Lord. Several things emerge from this passage. First, the goat is the animal figure which stands – and stands in – for evil. This association is not, of course, particular to Leviticus: it recurs throughout the Bible up to the sin-laden goats who serve as proverbial counterparts of sinless lambs in the New Testament, to the horned and bearded devils of medieval religious art (especially scenes of the Last Judgement, as we shall see below). In this sense, Leviticus could be said to mark the sublimation of human sacrifice into animal sacrifice – the human scapegoat of ancient pagan sacrifice, being replaced by a vicarious non-human one. Lambs too were sacrificial beasts, of course, in the Bible; but the unique role of the scapegoat is that it is invested with the internal malice of the community and then expelled into the wilderness, eradicating all peril of contagion.

The tradition of sacrificing animals as surrogates for humans runs from the story of Abraham and Isaac to the charged symbolism of Isaiah and the Crucifixion accounts. These recurring scenes are interpreted by some as signalling a progressive movement *beyond* the primitive rites of scapegoating. This reading of biblical and Christian revelation as a deeply anti-sacrificial and anti-scapegoating religion is one offered by contemporary commentators like Bultmann, Moltmann and Girard. And it is certainly the case that the Judaeo-Christian sublation of human into animal sacrifice means that one does not witness the same Dionysiac rites of human bloodletting in the biblical tradition that one finds, for example, in the myths of ancient Greek tragedy, where (as Nietzsche amongst others has shown) all too human figures like Dionysius, Pentheus and Oedipus bear the brunt of sacrificial purgation. In sum, this reading – to which we shall return below – argues that Judaeo-Christian revelation signals an *ethical* step beyond the old pagan rites of human blood sacrifice which sought to fuse with the immanent universe and propitiate mercurial gods.[1]

*

But the matter is not so simple. Even if it is true that the biblical tradition transferred the scapegoating mechanism from humans to animals, this did not, I submit, prevent repeated reversals throughout history. Time after time, one witnesses the role of scapegoats reverting to human figures known variously as Canaanites, Gentiles, Jews, heretics, witches, infidels and – after the discovery of new continents by colonial empires – unregenerate 'savages'.[2] This should hardly surprise us when we consider the way in which the sacrificial rites of expiation, powerfully laid down in Leviticus as 'Perpetual

Law' (Lev. 16: 29, 31), were later to find their way into the dramatic imaginary of Western religious culture. One thinks of the iconographic proliferation of demons and devils in medieval frescoes, murals, mosaics, paintings, illuminated manuscripts or liturgical furnishings. Here saints are tempted by satanic strangers. Holy prophets and priests are tortured by fiendish monsters. The unredeemed are ushered to their hellish fate by hirsute demoniacs going by such names as Lucifer, Beelzebub and Legion. Even the Messiah Himself is confronted by the Devil Himself. And in all these scenes, the demon figures are almost invariably attributed *goatish* characteristics (horns, thick hair, beard, snout, hooves).

Such inhuman features cannot, for all that, mask the fact that the demons are also at least *half-human* in appearance. The Florence Baptistery scene of the Last Judgment is a case in point. The octagonal mosaic, dating from 1260, is dominated by the struggle between the Christ the Pantocrator and a most unholy Lucifer who possesses the features of both a human being *and* a goat with serpents protruding from his goat-ears and buttocks. This dramatic portrayal of demonic monsters constitutes a veritable *corpus maleficorum* of late medieval iconography. Straddling a pool of fire, this Prince of Darkness re-enacts the apocalyptic scene of lambs being separated from goats as hideous throngs of subdemons torture nearby sinners.

Giotto's thirteenth-century mosiac in Florence, and many other depictions of devils which followed it in Pisa, Padua and San Gimignano, are even less indirect in their allusions to humans. They cover a wide variety of 'undesirables' considered damned under the Holy Roman Empire: *heretics* (Arius and the Simoniacs); *infidels* (Mahomet and Averroes); *sodomites* (skewered by furry goatish devils); *transsexuals* (in the Pisa and San Gimignano portraits of hell Lucifer is depicted with *both* the horns, beard and hairy chest of a goat-man *and* a vagina expelling hideous offspring); *seducers* (phallic-horned he-goats); *temptresses* (usually serpentine bodies with the face of Eve, as in Ucello's Original Sin in the Convent of Santa Maria Novella in Florence); and *Jews* (portrayed as membranous goat-bat fiends 'who hate daylight and love shadows').[3] As Lorenzo Lorenzi puts it in his study of demons in religious art: 'Goats' horns in Christian symbolism represent the iniquitous sin that is transformed into impotence' (Psalm 75; Revelation 12: 3).[4] But in addition to representing the *homo selvaticus*, enslaved to lascivious and bestial instincts, this symbolism also served as iconographic material for anti-Semitic scape-goating. Writing of the portrait of Limbo by Andrea Bonaiuto in the Spanish Chapel in Florence (1366–8), Lorenzi observes

All the devils have animals' faces and brutish expressions, reflecting their evil natures and their eternal separation from Paradise, the place of all loveliness. Their hairy pelts, beards and goatish horns represent the principal attributes of that animal – the goat – which because of its complaining was perceived as being far from divine grace, unlike the lamb who patiently accepted the terrible sacrifice; the devil-goat therefore represents the Jewish people, who rejected the Messiah.[5]

The fact that the most horrific demon in the tableau is painted yellow – the colour of Jews – compounds the association.

In most of these images the diabolic creatures conjoin features of the human head and face with bestial or reptilian characteristics. In her Introduction to Devils in Art, Maria Dal Pogetto claims that each of such portraits can be read as a microcosm of the collective unconscious, combining a whole set of religious and cultural mutations. Foremost among these were the three traditional images of the scapegoat in (1) Leviticus (outlined above), (2) the serpent of the Fall of Adam and Eve, and (3) Satan (from the Hebrew he-satan, meaning the 'enemy' or 'accuser', one who brings disunity, conflict and temptation). In the Old Testament, the Satanic figure could even play the role of prosecutor in the heavenly court, citing charges against individuals and tempting God himself – as in the Book of Job. In Christian tradition, Satan was reinterpreted in terms of the snake in the Garden of Eden and the terrifying beasts of the Apocalypse. The devil was thus partially 'bestialized' at the same time as he became more 'personalized' in the form of whatever particular heretic or dissenter threatened the unity of Christendom at the time.

In this manner, the demonic was located within the heretical movements of Christendom as well as in the diabolical infidel without (e.g. during the Crusades).

In the Christian tradition, he-Satan, the adversary, is no longer a common noun but becomes the personal name of that being who seeks by every means to damage mankind, impede salvation, and transfer to the spirit world the corruption already present in the body. The assaults of the Devil in the early centuries of the Church led to . . . persecutions, to the rise of Gnosticism (which posited a devil who had created matter and was coeternal with the Good and in constant conflict with it), and to the great Trinitarian and Christological heresies.[6]

Augustine tried to resolve these heretical controversies by declaring that whatever *is* has been created by God and is therefore good, which means that the demonic is logically consigned to the *non-being* of evil. But devils did not always conform to Augustinian ontology. More often than not, the demonic would continue to blur such boundaries until *what is* became contaminated with *what-is-not.*

The monsters that adorn the tableaux of late medieval and Renaissance art may thus be seen as carrying this double status of the demonic as insider *and* outsider, a hybrid creature at once animal and anthropological, a fiend fallen into the deepest abyss of hell yet capable of holding forth in the Heavenly Tribunals of the Most High. Indeed the idea of the demon as adversarial mirror-image of God is succinctly captured in Dante's portrait of the Devil's head with three faces (*Divine Comedy*, Canto 34): a startling image intended as an antithetical parody of the triune God (Inferno III). It is also present in the juxtaposing of the evil monster, Rahab, and the divine Lion of Judah, on the sacristy lavabo of the Church of San Lorenzo in Florence, the font where the priest washed his hands of impurities before he approached the sacrificial altar. Lorenzi notes:

> A Demon . . . was any supernatural being who appeared suddenly and unexpectedly: it was the fantastical personification of the irrational, the frightening, the unforseen . . . The demon was an indeterminate power, whereas a god was a completed individual. Demons are bearers of the numen, and as such are *ambivalent.*[7]

*

My point in detailing these iconographic examples of religious eschatology is to suggest that if such hybrid creatures could inhabit the popular unconscious of the Holy Roman Empire, it is not so surprising to witness examples of surrogate demonic creatures serving as sacrificial scapegoats in *real life* – both then and subsequently. The countless instances of heretic burning, witch-hunting, Jew-baiting, persecution, torture and other inquisitorial rites of purgation speak for themselves. For the Church to stay pure it needed to expel those deemed impure. Only by ridding itself of unholy ones could it guarantee

Judas hanging.
Detail from a fresco in Notre Dame des Fontaines, La Brigue, France. (Photo by Richard Kearney)

Slave hanging.
Period poster – anonymous

its holiness. And if the Church Triumphant did indeed believe that Heaven had come on Earth, then its sovereignty (one and indivisible) had perforce to be guaranteed by the attendant assurance that Hell too had come on Earth – i.e. in the guise of that out-of-bounds 'wilderness' to which demonic scapegoats were mercilessly dispatched. This was especially true in times of plague or ecclesiastical crisis. The Black Death, or bubonic plague, that brought many European cities to their knees in the fourteenth century coincided, tellingly, with the largest number of devil-in-hell scenes ever recorded. (Fourteenth-century Florence, let us not forget, also witnessed the manic period of Savonarola puritanism with its brimstone sermons and 'Bonfires of the vanities'.) One only has to peer at Buffalmacco's horrific depiction of the Inferno in Pisa to realize just how deep the apocalyptic fears of retribution ran. In sum, for saints to remain saintly, strangers had to be scapegoated.

As the need for expiation grew, in the face of growing corruption and chaos, the range of eligible aliens (xenos, alienus, gast, étranger) became more disturbingly generous. In times of most acute ecclesiastical conflict – during the Medici reign in Italy or the terrible religious wars in Europe – almost any old 'sinner' would do, and this recurring need to resort to scapegoating did not end with the rise of secular nation-states. One thinks of the Terror after the French Revolution; the continuation of slavery and racism after the American Revolution; the mushrooming of Moscow Show Trials after the Russian Revolution; and the Holocaust and subsequent genocides – all chilling instances of the seemingly ineradicable lust to purify saints by purging scapegoats.

Demythologizing monsters

The mythical imaginary of sacrifice has its intellectual exponents and opponents. I will now consider some of the contemporary debates on sacrificial scapegoating, broadly dividing them into anthropological and theological.

Anthropological readings

The anthropologists usually confine themselves to descriptions of the primordial structure of sacrifice without apportioning praise or blame. Mircea Eliade, for example, describes it as a means of segregating the 'sacred' from the 'profane' (originally by means of cogmogenic myths of order and chaos). Georges Dumézil sees it as an expression of the structural institution of sovereignty functions. Georges Bataille deems it to be a violent means of returning from the world of utilitarian things to an 'unreal' mythic world of fusion and immanence. While, for his part, Lévi-Strauss regards it as a fundamental expression of an unconscious 'savage mind' bent on dividing up the world into a series of binary oppositions: culture and nature, edible and inedible, cooked and raw, marriagable and non-marriagable, vertical and horizontal, good and evil. A key function of mythologies of the sacricial monster was to separate the sacredness of the cosmos from a perilous nether world – 'a foreign, chaotic space, peopled by ghosts, demons, foreigners'. As Eliade put it: 'The sacred reveals absolute reality and at the same time makes orientation possible; hence it founds the world in the sense that it fixes the limits and establishes the very order of the world'.[8]

In *Religion and Its Monsters*, Timothy Beal radically amplifies the critique of the monstrous. He analyses the fundamental role played by mythic monsters, ranging from biblical and Near Eastern religions to modern horror and vampire movies. These monsters, he argues, often disclose an experience of the sacred that, like many of our religions, is 'caught in endless, irreducible tensions between order and chaos, orientation and disorientation, self and other, foundation and abyss'.[9] Religion is rarely without its monsters, he surmises. No matter how many times we demonize, divinize or simply kill off our monsters, they keep returning for more. Not just Dracula. Not just the Devil. Nor the extraterrestrial of *Alien Resurrection*. All monsters are 'undead'. And maybe they keep coming back because, as Beal suggests, they still have 'something to say or show us about ourselves'.[10] The irrepressible return of the monstrous has reasons that Reason may not always understand.

The interrogation of sacrificial monsters reveals the paradox that the monster is not only a portent of impurity (the root of *monstrum* in *monere*, to warn) but also an apparition of something utterly other and numinous (from the root *monstrare*, to show). In this double sense the monstrous can fill us with both awe and awfulness.

> A *monstrum* is a message that breaks into this world from the realm of the sacred, even in the ancient and extremely cruel notion of 'monstrous births' as revelations of divine judgement, the otherness of the monster is considered not only horrifically *unnatural* but also horrifically *supernatural*, charged with religious import. Likewise, the *experience* of horror in relation to the monstrous is often described in terms reminiscent of religious experience.[11]

Both of these experiences signal a mode of contact with mysterious alterity that provokes a vertiginous blend of fear and fascination.

This line of argument develops the view canvassed by Rudolph Otto in his influential work, *The Idea of the Holy*, that even biblical monsters – e.g. Leviathan and Behemoth in Job, Rahab in Psalm 73 or the dragon in the Apocalpyse – are typical manifestations of the 'wholly Other'. As such they serve as dark counterparts of the utterly transcendent Yahweh. The monstrous (*das Ungeheuere*), Otto maintained, is a 'fairly exact expression for the numinous in its aspects of mystery, awefulness, augustness and "energy"; nay, even the fascination is dimly felt in it'.[12] For Otto, as for Freud before him, the coincidence of representation and horror marks a specific experience of the 'uncanny' (*das Unheimliche*). But the differences between the two approaches here are, I think, most revealing. Otto construes the uncanny as a sign of the utterly transcendent numen, 'a completely unhomely experience of the *mysterium* that has broken into the home from a wholly other realm'.[13] By contrast, Freud sees no suggestion of radical transcendence here, only traces of repressed unconscious trauma. For Freud:

> The *unheimlich* encounter with the monstrous is a revelation not of the wholly other but of a repressed otherness within the self. The monster, as personification of the *unheimlich*, stands for that which has broken out of the subterranean basement or the locked closet where it has been hidden and largely forgotten.[14]

The studies in this volume are, one might say, committed to the unravelling of certain consequences of this interpretive conflict. My own view throughout this book is that Otto and Freud represent two extreme positions – absolute transcendence or absolute immanence – both of which need to be surpassed and hermeneutically negotiated.

Theological readings

Against the so-called 'neutral' readings of anthropology and psychology, a number of modern thinkers, of mainly Jewish and Christian persuasion, offer a sustained demythologizing of the functions of sacrifice. This I call the *theological* approach. Jewish thinkers like Levinas and Jonas, for example, make a radical distinction between what they call the monotheistic rectitude of the 'saint' and the pagan practices of the 'sacré' (characterized by irrational nature worship, orgiastic sacrificial rites and the totalizing reduction of the 'other' to the violent economy of the 'same'). Many Christian thinkers also endorse this monotheistic distrust of sacrificial paganism, from Bultmann, Barth and Bonhoeffer to Moltmann and Girard. These theologians are committed to a *double* critique: (a) of the perverse use of sacrificial practices in non-monotheistic religion and culture; and (b) of the internal perversions of sacrificial mystery rites *within* the monotheistic legacy itself.

Two of the most vocal practitioners of this double (external/internal) critique are Rudolf Bultmann and Jürgen Moltmann. These theologians call for a radical 'demythologization' of the biblical tradition which they believe has been infiltrated by magico-mystery rites of saviour cults, epitomized in myths of pagan deities (Hellenic, Orphic, Germanic etc.). In his seminal *Theology of the New Testament*, Bultmann argued that:

> To understand Jesus' fate as the basis for a mythic cult and to understand such a cult as the celebration which sacramentally brings the celebrant into such fellowship with the cult-divinity that the latter's fate avail for the former as if it were his own – that is the Hellenic idea.[15]

For his part, Moltmann extends the demythicizing project into a more precise critique of the sacrificial cult of martyrdom properly speaking, a complex process where scapegoating and sanctification go hand in hand. He writes:

> The influence of cultic piety shows itself not only as a formal event in the self-preservation of Christianity on Hellenistic soil, but quite certainly extends also to the understanding of the event of Christ. The Christ event is here understood as an epiphany of the eternal (past) in the form of a dying and rising *Kyrios* of the *cultus* . . . Initiation into the death and resurrection of Christ then means that the goal of redemption is already determined, for in this baptism eternity is sacramentally present.

This results in turn in the Cross being magically invoked as a 'timeless sacrament of martyrdom which perfects the martyr and unites him with the heavenly Christ'.[16] This mythology of martyrdom is, for Moltmann, a betrayal of the true Judaeo-Christian message, ignoring the involvement of the Lord in the struggle of history proper as a quest for justice and redemption.

*

In more recent times, however, it has probably been René Girard who has done most to bring the ethico-religious critique of sacrificial scapegoating to the fore of intellectual debate. In a series of controversial writings beginning in the 1970s and 1980s – from *Violence and the Sacred* (1972) and *Things Hidden since the Foundation of the World* (1978) to *The Scapegoat* (1982) – Girard has endeavoured to expose the scapegoat mechanisms at work not only in myths of cultic sacrifice but also in such diverse areas as politics, law, literature and ethnology. Though not a professional theologian, Girard is resolved to interpret the masked operations of our social imaginary in light of a religious ethics of transcendence.

Girard begins by subjecting ideologies of scapegoating to a critical hermeneutics of suspicion, exposing concealed meanings behind apparent ones. His core hypothesis goes something like this. Most societies are based on the ritual sacrifice of a maligned other. The foundational consensus needed for social coexistence is provided by a collective projection wherein some victimized outsider becomes the alleged carrier of all the aggression, guilt and violence that sets one neighbour against another within the tribe. This victimization of the scapegoat–stranger serves to engender a sense of solidarity amongst 'the people' (*gens, natio*), now reunited in a shared act of persecution. In this manner, harmony is restored to the community which conveniently forgets its initial hatred for the alien and may even come to revere it (retrospectively); it was, after all, the alien's ritual oblation which saved the community from itself in the first place. The scapegoat thus becomes the one who – *mirabile dictu* – enabled the internally divided society to turn away from its own internecine rivalry and focus its hatred on someone outside the tribe.

In this respect at least, Girard would agree with Bataille's thesis that 'empire is a diversion of violence to the outside'.[17] In our companion volume, *On Stories*, I already remarked how several imperial nations were founded upon myths of sacrificial violence. One particular example I cited was that of the Anglo-Saxon narrative of Beowulf slaying the monster and thereby purging the community of evil and chaos. Beowulf's hall represents a refuge from the 'huge marauders from other worlds' who prowl the moors. In particular, the scaled monster, Grendel, haunts the unstable borders of the struggling nation divided as it is between Geats, Norse, Swedes, Saxons and Celts. This alien stranger (*ellor gast*) is described as a 'fiend out of hell', haunting the misty marshes, an obscene ghost hailing from a hinterworld of banished beasts – 'Cain's clan, whom the creator had outlawed and condemned as outcast'.[18]

The allusion here is of course to the murderous Cain who killed his twin brother, Abel, in the biblical equivalent of the Roman story of Romulus and Remus. In time, the genealogical descendents of Grendel become the colonial enemies of the conquering British empire, both overseas (Africa, Asia and the Americas) and closer to home in Ireland, where the 'natives' were caricatured as simian-like, mindless savages: the *degens* serving as dialectical foil to the *gens* (English gentlemen). 'To see white chimpanzees is dreadful', remarked the English commentator, Charles Kingsley. 'If they were black, one would not feel it so much, but their skins are as white as ours.'[19]

But the scapegoat was not always reviled. As noted above, the sacrificial victim sometimes came to be *revered* after the event – even to the point of becoming over time a founding hero for the community. The Greeks celebrated Prometheus as a sacred *pharmakos* (scapegoat) after he had met with his sacrificial fate,[20] and we witness a similarly retrospective apotheosis of scapegoats across a variety of foundational myths – Osiris, Romulus, Christ, Orpheus, Socrates, Cuchulain. Such figures, though invariably ostracized or excoriated by their contemporaries, became hallowed over the ages until they were eventually remembered as saviour gods who restored their community from chaos to order. They re-emerge out of the mists of time as miraculous deities who managed to transmute conflict into law. But this alteration of sacrificed 'aliens' into sacred 'others' is, of course, predicated upon a strategic forgetfulness of their initial stigmatization, that is, the fact that they were originally victims of ritual bloodletting.

Sacrificial myths of alienation are not confined to ancient times. They continue, as both Girard and Mircea Eliade argue, to operate today even though the mechanisms for demonizing the other have become more sophisticated and surreptitious.[21] Indeed, Girard goes so far as to claim that no modern society is entirely free from scapegoating tendencies – informed as every society is with mimetic rivalry for scarce resources, periodically resolved by making common cause against an agreed 'enemy'. Thus may be explained the recurring phenomena of witch-hunting, xenophobia, racism and anti-Semitism, often in the name of 'national security'. Such persecutionary strategies operate on the fantasy that it is the evil adversary outside/inside the *Volk* who is poisoning the wells, contaminating the body politic, corrupting the unsuspecting youth, eroding the economy, sabotaging peace and destroying the general moral fabric of society. Moreover, the popular media in modern societies often play a pivotal role in ostracizing some commonly identified 'alien' (individual or minority group).

But scapegoating myths fail. A society can only pretend to believe in the lie because it is that same society which is lying to itself! Hence the ultimately self-defeating nature of ideological persecution. This is borne out in the need for constant renewal of the sacrificial act. The reliance on an alien–scapegoat never subsides – at least not until such time as we renounce our desire to always covet what the other has, and to accept one's other as oneself, thereby overcoming the condition of mimetic strife which gave rise to scapegoating in the first place. A genuinely peaceful community would be one which, Girard contends, exposes its own strategies of sacrificial alienation and enters the light of 'true fraternity'. It would be a society without need of scapegoats. Having freed itself from myths of fratricide, based on conflicts of desire and fear of strangers, such a community would commit itself instead to principles of 'transcendence' beyond time and history. It would take its lead from the exemplary action of Christ, who underwent death on the Cross in order to expose the sacrificial lie for once and for all by revealing the innocence of the victim. The sacrifice to end all sacrifice.

In short, peace requires nothing less than the decoupling of the stranger and the scapegoat. And this means acknowledging that the genuine 'other' is always guaranteed by a radically divine Other – an asymmetrical, vertical alterity irreducible to the envious ploys of mimetic desire. Girard, like Levinas, calls this ethical alterity – even if it addresses us through the face of the other – God.[22]

*

A paradigmatic example of this redemptive response to scapegoating is the story of the forgiveness of Judas by Christ. In Canevesio's vivid fifteenth-century mural in Notre Dame des Fontaines in La Brigue, France, we witness Judas hanging from an olive tree after the betrayal of Jesus (see p. 32). While a demon is shown extracting a miniature replica of Judas from the entrails of the suspended body of the betrayer – epitomizing the eternal recurrence of the same – the olive tree symbolizes the tree of the crucifix from which Jesus simultaneously hangs in redemptive death, holding out the offer of pardon and salvation to Judas. The fact that Judas' entrails are depicted in the form of a Ourobouros further highlights the plight of endless circular return from which the redemptive grace of Christ promises to deliver the sinner. The location of this Renaissance church mural just ten miles beneath Mount Bego where human–animal sacrifice – evidenced in Indo-European stone carvings of bull-horns – was practised in prehistoric times, signals a stark contrast with the anti-sacrificial ethic portrayed in Canevesio's paintings. Here we have a powerful image of salvation as answer to scapegoating.

Or to return to the story of Beowulf, Girard would surely concur with Seamus Heaney's view that the Christian ethos of redemption ultimately loosens the pagan grip of sacrificial purgation which informs much of the saga. In the end, it is his *inner* monster that Beowulf must confront, the terrifying shadow of his own death. The dragon which the hero finally faces is not, like Grendel, a monster from without but a monster from his home ground – a beast 'abiding in his *underearth* as in his understanding' and against which Beowulf must ultimately measure himself. 'Dragon equals shadow-line', concludes Heaney, 'the Psalmist's valley of the shadow of death'.[23] The hero signs off not with bellicose virtuosity but with a sense of transcendent wisdom. The last note is less one of sacrificial rivalry than of resignation to a higher will.

Such stories vividly convey the biblical wisdom that only by confronting the serpent can we ultimately overcome it; as Moses demonstrated when he conjured a bronze serpent as antidote to the deadly serpent (Numbers 21, 4), or as Jesus suggested when he declared that his disciples would speak 'entirely new languages and be able to handle serpents' (Mark 16, 17). For as John wrote, 'Just as Moses lifted up the serpent in the wilderness, so must the Son of Man be lifted up' (John 3, 11).

Conclusion

Girard's Christian critique of scapegoating as a practice of social purgation and persecution is not, I believe, without its problems. These become particularly evident in his treatment of the *monstrous* per se. By describing his own theory of the scapegoat as the 'Ariadne's thread' which guides us through the labyrinth of sacrificial myth, Girard appears to imply that myths are themselves somehow inherently monstrous – menacing Minotaurs of the mind that need to be expelled. The frequent slippage from the nominal form (*mythical* monster) to the adjectival (monstrous *myth*) betrays a tendency in Girard to scapegoat myth itself. In such readings, Girard treats myth as a textual monster to be expurgated by his own demythologizing critique. Mythic narrative comes to function, thus, as a new scapegoat, inherently alienating in so far as it contrives to negate reality. So we might ask: if Girard rebukes ethnology for masking the scapegoating function of myth, might he himself not be accused of scapegoating the mythic function? Is he not, unbeknownst to himself, assuming the role of some evangelical exorcist?

If this be so, a radically self-critical gesture might, I suggest, be usefully deployed by Girard against himself. For monotheist ethics, it seems, is not exempt from exclusivist or absolutist tendencies. In other words, it is here that a moral culture's purging of 'monsters' might recall its own potential excesses when pushed to inquisitorial extremes.

So, while agreeing with much in the above critiques of sacrifice, I believe they are often too confessionally partisan in their claim that only one religious tradition – usually Judaeo-Christian monotheism – can redeem us from the myths of scapegoating. I have as much difficulty accepting that a single confessional theology has the remedy to the enigma of otherness as I would accepting similar claims for a positivist, Marxist, Freudian or any other interpretive model. Each has its unique light to shed on the puzzle, but none possesses the absolute answer. The question I would put to Girard and the other demythologizers, therefore, is whether all non Judaeo-Christian religious myths are necessarily scapegoating? Are there not at least some which might not be so, that is, which might not be based on the need to project false accusations onto innocent victims? Might not certain Buddhist, Taoist or native American myths, for example, also express a genuinely open impulse to imagine other possibilities of existence which challenge the status quo and embrace peace and justice over dualist agonistics? Or to put it in terms of Ricoeur's critical hermeneutics: might not some non-monotheistic narratives serve a utopian function of symbolic innovation rather than an exclusively ideological one of dissimulation and domination? If this be so, I would suggest that Girard's blanket equation of all non-biblical mythologizing with sacrificial scapegoating is itself, at times, an exercise in scapegoating – an effort to introject hidden sacrificial motives into the very poetics of myth itself (see Appendix, pp. 43–6).[24]

In this light we might reconsider the cogent arguments offered by Edward Said in Orientalism and Partha Mitter in Maligned Monsters to the effect that Western monotheistic culture demonized what it considered to be 'excessive' characteristics of alterity; and that this amounted to an ethnocentric reaction against what was deemed 'different' and 'alien'.[25] But we equally need to recall that such demonizing also took place within the occidental Judaeo-Christian culture itself, as well as in reaction to its Oriental Other. As our brief genealogy of scapegoating indicates, certain aspects of biblical culture were already exemplifying the maxim – demonizing monsters keeps God on our side![26] Read in this way, we may see how Bible narratives sometimes served to stigmatize the monster as menace to the divine order. As Tim Beal explains:

> The monstrous other who threatens 'us' and 'our world' is represented as an enemy of God and then is exorcised from the right order of things and sent to some sort of hell. 'Our' order is identified with the sacred over against a diabolically monstrous chaos. Such is the fate of . . . the sea monster Leviathan in Psalm 74 and Isaiah 27.[27]

But another way of responding to the monster as personification of otherness-in-sameness is to *deify* it in some way, and this tendency to construe the demonic as a necessary dialectical counterpart of the divine is, I believe, equally problematic. One witnesses examples of this in several Gnostic accounts of the biblical God as well as in numerous myths of non-biblical deities (e.g. Hindu and other Near Eastern religions). Occasionally, the Godhead itself is actually *identified* with the monstrous. Opposite extremes merge, becoming indistinguishable in their respective *strangeness* and *uncanniness*. In such instances, we find the demon being divinized as a manifestation of sacral alterity.

> Its coming into the world is represented as *hierophany*, that is, an epiphany of the holy. Here the monster is an envoy of the divine or the sacred as radically other than 'our' established order of things. It is an invasion of what we might call *sacred chaos* and disorientation within self, society and world.[28]

Classic examples of this phenomenon include Tiamat in the Babylonian Enuma Elish, or Behemoth who features in the divine speech of the whirlwind in the Book of Job.

In short, if demonizing monsters (as impure) keeps God on our side (as pure), deifying them brings us into a zone of 'religious horror'. We here enter that ambivalent world of the magico-mystical Holy (*das Heilige*) which Rudolf Otto linked with the long tradition of sacred 'terror and awe' running from Old Testament hierophanies and certain mystical notions of the *mysterium tremendum* right down to postmodern theories of the 'hysterical sublime'. I shall return to this critical point in below chapters.

Suffice it to say for now that what is needed, when confronted with extreme tendencies to demonize or deify monsters, is to look into our own psyches and examine our consciences in the mirror of our gods and monsters. We need, I suggest, to explore further the spaces between polarities, to dwell on the thresholds which mediate between the vertical and the abject. We need to look to the middle way.

APPENDIX:
MYTHS, MONSTERS AND SCAPEGOATS

In a chapter of The Scapegoat entitled 'What is myth?' Girard enumerates four essential characteristics of narratives of collective persecution: (a) a social or cultural crisis ('generalized indifferentiation'); (b) a crime considered to be the cause of this crisis; (c) a culprit accused not because of direct involvement in the crime but because of some association with it (the scapegoat–alien); and finally (d) a violence frequently assigned a sacred character.[29]

The basic aim of persecution texts is to attribute responsibility for the social crisis to the culprit and then to restore social order (differentiation) by expelling the alleged culprit–alien from the body politic. Girard treats as myth any narrative which contains these sacrificial characteristics. Every text which tells of sacrificial violence against a victim while seeking to cover up its own persecution mechanism qualifies. Moreover, Girard goes so far as to declare that sacrificial myths refer not just to unconscious desires to persecute but to real events. We are not dealing here with symbolic or imaginary acts of violence, but with narratives rooted in repressed historical facts. ('All myths are rooted in real acts of violence'.)[30] Girard resists any suggestion that sacrificial myths are reducible to some 'intertextual' play of linguistic relations, as certain post-structuralists or deconstructionists might hold. Nor do they relate to mere 'structures' of mind, as structural anthropologists like Lévi-Strauss or Dumézil claim. They refer, insists Girard, to events of historical victimization.[31] They are less matters of fantasy than of flesh and blood.

*

Girard opens his analysis by concentrating on the 'exemplary myth' of Oedipus, which he believes 'contains all of the persecution stereotypes'.[32] Then moving from this explicit myth of persecution to other less evident ones, Girard proposes to show that all myths are rooted, in the first and last analysis, in actual persecutions of actual scapegoats. He offers the following paradigmatic reading of Sophocles' Oedipus Rex:

> Thebes is ravaged by plague: the first stereotype of persecution. Oedipus is responsible because he has killed his father and married his mother: the second stereotype of persecution. In order to put an end to the epidemic, the Oracle announces, the guilty criminal must be found and hunted out. The persecutionary intent is evident. Parricide and incest serve openly as intermediaries between the individual and the collective; these crimes are so undifferentiated that their influence contaminates the entire society. In the text by Sophocles, one notes that the

43

undifferentiated (i.e. the disordered) is equated with the contaminated. This brings in the third stereotype: the signs or stigmata of victimization. First there is infirmity, Oedipus limps. The hero moreover has arrived in Thebes unknown to all, an outsider in fact if not in essence. Finally, he is the king's son and the king himself – the legitimate heir of Laios. Like all other mythic characters, Oedipus manages to accumulate both the marginality of the outside and the inside. Similar to Ulysses at the end of the *Odyssey*, he is sometimes a mendicant stranger, sometimes an omnipotent monarch . . . The infirmity of Oedipus, his wounded childhood, his status of outsider, of stranger, of king, make him a veritable conglomerate of victim-signs.[33]

Comparing the Oedipus myth to the medieval documents of Guillaume de Machaut on the persecution of Jews, Girard notes that both texts bear traces of 'persecution drawn up from the perspective of naive persecutors'.[34] In the Oedipus myth, as in Guillaume de Machaut or the witch trials of the Inquisition, Girard finds 'mythological accusations of parricide, incest and the physical or moral corruption of the community'.[35] Likewise, he finds in the historical narratives of persecution that the annihilation of the 'guilty one' arises in circumstances of acute social crisis and is carried out by a paranoid mob.

In short, Girard repudiates the view that myths are neutral entities to be revered as antique signifiers of some *pensée sauvage*. Every society, he argues, is based on an empirical act of sacrifice – the only difference between 'ancient' and 'advanced' cultures is that the function of sacrificial mythology is more obvious in the former. In primitive myths, as Girard notes:

> The stereotypes are more complete and conspicuous than in the Guillaume text. How is one to pretend that they are somehow thrown together by accident, or by some gratuitous act of poetic imagination or fantasy, utterly removed from the mentality and reality of persecution? And yet that is precisely what our research experts are asking us to believe, and they consider my arguments extravagant when I claim the contrary.[36]

Girard makes no apologies and no exceptions. He throws down the gauntlet to the romantic nostalgia of modern ethnologists who think of myths as imaginary tales referring to nothing outside of their own linguistic structures. The 'mythicality' of myth, retorts Girard, 'is not some kind of vapourous literary perfume but a persecutor's interpretation of persecution'.[37] If myths are indeed fictional in some respect, it is in their formal capacity to camouflage the genesis of sacrificial signs in historical acts of persecution.

Girard claims that his analysis of the alien is ethical, therefore, precisely because it is realist. In contrast to the denial of myth's reference to reality, Girard insists that the symbolic aspects of myth are no more than representational cover-ups of actual sacrificial events. One of the obsessions of romantic poetics is, he argues, to construe mythological monsters as pure inventions, thereby occluding what they really are: combinations of elements borrowed from real forms. The Minotaur, for example, is a mixture of man and bull. Identifying the monstrous as an expression of indifferentiation and chaos, Girard demonstrates how monsters bear signs of persecution stereotypes – especially those of physical and moral deformity (equated in myth) and of the 'stranger' allegedly responsible for the crisis in the community. By portraying the Minotaur as a criminal alien of unspeakable bestiality, the persecutors contrived to project the moral culpability for a particular crisis onto an outsider whose physical infirmity suggested an affinity with the monstrous.[38]

The imaginary character of myth, in sum, makes the so-called 'guilty one' consubstantial with the crime. The monstrous character of the 'criminal' and the direct causal connection between his monstrosity and the collective crisis itself, appears so immediate at the level of narrative fantasy that one scarcely notices the accusatory process behind it. 'We assume that we are secure in mythic illusion because we only see it as so much fancy . . . The most effective and definitive alibi remains that abstract disbelief which denies the reality of violence reflected by the myth'.[39] This is why Girard was so adamant in his repudiation of those who persist in construing mythological monsters as fabulous poetic creations. And it was in order to disclose the victimizing motivation behind myth that Girard proposed his own hermeneutic of suspicion – the theory of the scapegoat.

*

This Girardian analysis of sacrificial myths and monsters is, as mentioned above, largely based on a monotheistic critique of blood sacrifice. It would seem to take its inspiration from the biblical denunciation of sacrificial rites, typically expressed in Psalm 40: 'Sacrifice or oblation you wished not . . . Holocausts or sin-offerings you sought not . . . To do your will, O my God, is my delight, And your law is within my heart!'. Girard sees a progressive radicalizing of this anti-sacrificial ethic from the Abraham-Isaac episode on Mount Moriah to the Crucifixion of Christ as the wholly blameless victim (the God-Man without sin) who exposes the entire scapegoating mechanism for the violent and deceitful practice that it is. But I return here to the reservation expressed above: Girard has little or no time for ethical response to monsters and scapegoats in other religious traditions. He says nothing, for example, of the Taoist virtues of *Chih* (wisdom), *Jen* (compassion), *Li* (correct understanding), *Ying Ning* (tranquillity) and *Yi* (justice and responsibility to others), so powerfully translated and presented by Thomas Merton in *The Way of Chuang Tzu*.[40] Nor does Girard appear attentive to the wise ways of dealing with scapegoats in the Buddhist tradition, which calls not only for the acknowledgement of our monsters but for their integration into a higher wisdom of loving kindness and mindfulness.

Does biblical monotheism, we might ask, necessarily have exclusive or superior insight into the hidden ways of dealing with our demons? Might it not have something to learn from a dialogue with the non-monotheist wisdoms of Tao and the Buddha, as Thomas Merton suggests in his ground-breaking meeting with the Dalai Lama in 1968? Might it not be a good thing for Christians, Jews and Muslims to listen to the words of some of their Eastern brethren at the same time as they worship their absolute God? For just as Martin Luther King was able to invoke the Bible to argue that 'war is a nightmare for victims of our nation and for those it calls its enemies', so too he was able to nominate a Vietnamese Buddhist master like Thich Nhat Hanh for the Nobel Peace Prize and learn from his wisdom of non-violence.[41] The following words of Thich Nhat Hanh have, I would suggest, much to teach every believer in Absolutes – secular or religious:

When you have the insight of non-duality and interbeing, you take care of your body in the most non-violent way possible. You take care of your mental formations, including your anger, with non-violence. You take care of your brother, your sister, your father, your mother, your community, and your society, with utmost tenderness. You won't regard anyone as an enemy when you have penetrated the reality of interbeing.[42]

In short, if Western monotheism has much to teach us about the virtues of ethical judgement (when it comes to sacrifice and scapegoating), Eastern wisdom traditions are there to remind us that judgement must be ever wary of lapsing into judgementalism. For if Jerusalem is indeed one way to peace, it is not the only one. The religions of Abraham have much to give *and* to receive in dialogue with the religions of Tao and the Buddha (and others). Interbeing is the way between.

2

RIGHTS OF SACRIFICE

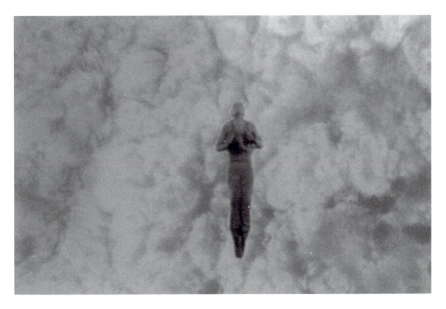

Agent Ripley's last sacrifice. *Alien* 3 © 1992 20th Century Fox Film. Reproduced courtesy of the Roland Grant Archive.

The scapegoating function is not, of course, confined to mythological and theological discourses. There is, in our contemporary popular unconscious, a pervasive obsession with the monstrous which is symptomatic of the perduring role of sacrificial scapegoats in our culture.[1] By way of amplifying our range of investigation, and taking a cue from our discussion of monsters in Part 3 of our companion volume *On Stories*, I propose to look now at some dramatic reapparitions of the sacrificial demon in recent cinema: (1) the extraterrestrial monster of the *Alien* series; and (2) the figure of Kurtz in *Apocalypse Now Redux*.

The *Alien* series

My mummy always said that there were no monsters, no real ones
– but there are.

(First words of Agent Ripley in *Alien Resurrection*,
echoing her adopted girl, Newt, in *Alien 3*)

The *Alien* series consists of four films directed by Ridley Scott, James Cameron, David Fincher and Jean-Pierre Jeunet over the two decades leading up to the third millennium. One of the most intriguing features of the quadrology is that it not only screens alien monsters but actually reflects the very process by which such screening takes place. This self-reflexive gesture is accentuated by the fact that the four directors quote each other's works – held together by the same, self-replicating protagonist (Ellen Ripley played by Sigourney Weaver). But this mirror-play recurs within the films themselves, as well as between them, to the extent that various exchanges between the characters focus on the *monstration* of sacrificial scapegoating, thereby exposing the ways in which our most feared monsters can serve as uncanny doubles for our all-too-human selves. The series has already been critically analysed in my own *On Stories* and, more extensively, in Stephen's Mulhall's *On Film*,[2] so I confine myself here to a few remarks which I consider especially relevant to my present argument.

I think it telling that throughout the series allusions are made to the interchangeability of human and extraterrestrial aliens. Human space travellers actually find themselves playing 'host' to the hostile monster from outer space, thus discovering (to their horror) that the monster is not just 'out there' but 'in here'. The dragon-shaped alien, recalling portraits of the satanic beast of the apocalypse, is capable of invading our most intimate being. So that the thing these human astronauts consider most foreign is in fact the most familiar.[3] What really terrifies them is the alien *within*, already inscribed in the homely but such that it cannot be integrated or named. The extraterrestrials in the series thus serve, I am suggesting, as imaginary personifications of our inner alienation, reminding us that we are not at home with ourselves, even at home. They are, we might say, postmodern replicas of the old religious demons: figures of chaos and disorientation within order and orientation.[4]

Stephen Mulhall argues convincingly that the monsters symbolize our fear of our own carnality – e.g. sexual difference, phallic penetration, genital violation, pregnancy, generativity, reproduction, labour, birth-death. The alien, he writes, 'represents the return of the repressed human body, of our ineluctable participation in the realm of nature – of life'.[5] More specifically, for the androgenous Lieutenant Ripley, maternal fecundity represents her 'monstrous other'. But the monstrosity of the alien represents more than just life. It stems also from a deeper fear that nature may itself be reduced to the out of control and invasive culture of biotechnology. The alien's body, as Mulhall notes, *is* its technology; an unnerving phenomenon which suggests that science is amoral and inhuman, and terrifyingly 'sublime'. Indeed in the last film in the series, *Alien Resurrection*, Ripley herself is replicated as a cloned, posthumous hybrid who behaves like an android but possesses the racial memory and flair of the alien who invaded her. Here Ripley embodies the saint and the stranger in one!

The sentiment that the monstrous nature of the alien is not in fact that alien to humanity at all is vividly captured in the scene in Ridley Scott's *Alien* (the opening film in the series) where the android Ash describes the monster-foetus that has exploded through Kane's chest as 'Kane's son' – an allusion to the evil inherited from the original Cain of Genesis. Even Agent Ripley comes to resemble the alien in terms of physiognomic features by *Alien* 3, and at one point finds herself impregnated by the extraterrestrial beast whose offspring bursts through her torso in the final sequence. What most deeply defines Ripley is that she is so irrevocably obsessed by the Alien that she becomes incapable of recalling almost anything else.[6] In this sense, Ripley is not just one of the alien family, 'she *is* the alien; it incarnates the nightmare that makes her who she is, and that she has been incubating'. On this reading, Ripley's encounter with the impregnating alien is paralleled by her sexual intercourse with Clemens, marking the decisive point where she overcomes her deep antipathy towards human embodiedness. For Ripley, 'the sexual body is ultimately the long repressed and sublimated *das Ding* from which she has sought to flee'.[7] Mulhall offers this reading of the final graphic scene:

> As she descends into the flames, the alien queen bursts out; Ripley holds it gently in her cupped hands, and lays its crowned head on her breast, as if to suckle it. The logic of the Alien universe, and of Ripley's own nature, is here finally consummated. Since the alien itself originates from within her, since it is an incarnate projection of her deepest fears, she can succeed in eliminating it only by eliminating herself.[8]

This uneasy sense that we humans are in fact the *real* aliens – or at least just as alien as the 'others somewhere out there' – is further reinforced by a number of revealing puns and allusions. One of the Hispanic women officers preparing to do battle with the monsters in the first sequel refers to herself as an 'illegal alien'. The heinous criminals exiled in the outer space prison, Fiorina 161, in *Alien* 3 are themselves so alienated from all humanity that some try to rape Ripley (just as the monster does). And they can only be saved by following their Christian-apocalyptic leader, Dillon, into the ultimate sacrificial encounter with their own 'in-human' double, the facehugging, chestbursting monster itself. Moreover, the suggestion of collusion between robotic clones and galactic aliens in the first film of the series – where the android Ash is conspiring with *Nostromo*'s central computer, Mother, to divert the ship to the alien-infested planet – is cleverly transposed in the second and third movies into a realization that the worst monsters are not: (a) the extraterrestrials who are simply following their nature (like their Alien Queen protecting her nursery); nor are they (b) the robotic clones and androids (Bishop actually saves Agent Ripley and her adopted daughter, Newt, from the exploding planet). The ultimate monsters turn out, in the final analysis, to be the all-too-*terrestrial* humans of The Company who have employed Ripley to hunt the outer-space monster with a view to bringing it back to earth as a deadly addition to their bio-weapons programme.

This reversibility between human and inhuman orders of monstrosity is underlined by James Cameron's own avowal that his depiction of the Marine mission to LV 426 is a replay of the Vietnam War. In short, while the *Alien* movie series could be said to dramatize the rite of scapegoating, there is a radical religious inversion of this mechanism when Ripley finally chooses to transcend the mimetic order of sacrificial violence and offer herself up for the sake of the human race. In the final scene of *Alien 3*, Ripley defies the Company's plans to extract the monster-foetus from her womb, falling in cruciform position into a pit of molten lead (see p. 47).[9] Only, of course, to be miraculously reborn in the next sequel, *Alien Resurrection*!

*

This final reversal is, I think, key to the message of the series regarding the sacrificial phenomenon. For while ostensibly scapegoating monsters from other planets, the series actually suggests that the primary source of death and destruction is to be found in humanity's own will-to-power. The real culprits of the piece are the *human* manipulators of war technology and biogenetic engineering back on earth. In sum, the most alienating and alien-making forces of all are shown to reside not out there in intergalactic space but within the human species itself. Left alone, the aliens would have just done their own survival thing: reproduce their biological species in their 'natural' way. It is humanity's tampering with this different order of being that causes havoc and carnage. It is *we* who have turned these strangers into scapegoats.

There is, one might say, nothing particularly new about this. Human interference with monsters goes back to Greeks myths of the Minotaur, Kabbalistic stories of Golems and Gothic tales of vampires, ghouls and Frankensteins. Indeed, Dr Pretorius sounds the typically apocalyptic note on this score when he makes his famous toast in *The Bride of Frankenstein*: 'To a new world of gods and monsters!' But what sets the *Alien* series off from such prototypical versions of the human–inhuman monster is the fact that today we actually possess the technology that can travel into outer space and bring the *imaginary* world of aliens into contact with the *real* earth. The boundary separating science from science fiction has become blurred. Hence the inflation of our horror before the undecidability of the monstrous. As Stanley Cavell so astutely reasons:

> Isn't it the case that not the human horrifies me, but the inhuman, the monstrous? Very well. But only what is human can be inhuman. – Can only the human be monstrous? If something is monstrous, and we do not believe that there are monsters, then only the human is a candidate for the monstrous.

Horror, Cavell deduces, is the name we give to the experience of the

> precariousness of human identity, to the perception that it may be lost or invaded, that we may be, or may become, something other than we are, or take ourselves for; that our origins as human beings need accounting for, and are unaccountable.[10]

Though he is not speaking of the *Alien* series as such, Cavell's deduction bears directly on our thesis. We will return to it in our conclusion.

Apocalypse Now Redux: hearts of darkness

> Horror may have a face, and you must make a friend of horror. Horror and moral terror are your friends. If they are not then they are an enemy to be feared.
>
> (Colonel Kurtz)

'The Horror, the Horror'. A phrase made immortal by Conrad's *Heart of Darkness*, and given contemporary celebrity by Coppola's film version *Apocalypse Now Redux*. By way of offering an alternative look at the theme of strangers and scapegoats I will conclude this chapter with a brief account of this film.

Apocalypse Now transposes the characters of *Heart of Darkness* to Vietnam. It tells the story of a US Special Forces officer, Lieutenant Willard, sent up the rivers of North Vietnam in search of a renegade Colonel, Walter Kurtz. Kurtz has gone AWOL after returning to Vietnam. He has forfeited a high-ranking job in the Joint Chiefs of Staff in Washington to counter a threat by double agents endangering the lives of hundreds of American soldiers. Operating deep within Cambodian territory – then legally off-limits to US troops – Kurtz disobeys orders and eliminates the threat. Faced with disciplinary action, he escapes deeper into the jungle and starts carrying out

Faces merging.
Final sequence of *Apocalypse Now Redux*. (With kind permission of Zoetrope)

Portals of sacrifice

Before the sacrifice.
Final sequence of *Apocalypse Now Redux*. (With kind permission of Zoetrope)

After the sacrifice.
Final sequence of *Apocalypse Now Redux*. (With kind permission of Zoetrope)

indiscriminate raids against military stations and villages. His methods are ruthless and utterly effective, but the US Command judges that he has gone too far. Willard is called in to terminate Kurtz's command, and to do so 'with extreme prejudice'.

This summary expression betrays how US war policy mirrors the 'illegal' activities of Kurtz. The mirroring becomes more and more alarming as the film unfolds, charting Willard's journey towards the heart of darkness that is Kurtz's hideout. The parallel between righteous executioner and evil criminal is signposted from the opening scene of the film: Willard admits that his narrative and Kurtz's are inextricably bound up with each other. 'There is really no way of telling his story without telling mine', says Willard, 'if his is a confession, then so is mine'. As he leafs further through his dossier, Willard discovers that Kurtz was once just like him. He reads one of Kurtz's letters to his son in which Kurtz claims that the charges levelled against him by the High Command are 'quite simply insane' (the very term used by the High Command to describe Kurtz's behaviour). In this same letter, Kurtz explains to his son that he is beyond the Army's 'lying timid morality' − a morality which Willard has plenty of opportunity to realize is only skin deep. The photograph in the dossier is a shadowy silhouette marked 'Believed to be Col. Walter Kurtz': a signal that as we approach the heart of darkness the Minotaur lurking in wait becomes more undecidable. The question of whether we are dealing with a neo-Nietzschean hero or a psychopathic monster grows problematic. Who is the real demon? we find ourselves asking. This out of bounds unknown reprobate or his sanctimonious accusers back in Washington and Saigon? Should Willard embrace this estranged being, or execute him? How, in short, is he to make the right call? How, in this night of fear and trembling, is he to judge?

The narrator's odyssey to the heart of the labyrinthine jungle serves to retrace Kurtz's own itinerary. From the sententious briefing with top brass at home base, to the various detours through one horrifying US Army outpost after the next, Willard begins to realize that Kurtz's horrific acts are no more than efficient enactments of so-called 'legitimate' military behaviour. Kurtz, he finally acknowledges, is playing out the role of a sacrificial scapegoat as the High Command keeps its hands clean. The final scene where the execution of Kurtz is juxtaposed with graphic shots of animal sacrifice (a caribou cleft in two by a sword) aptly captures this.

*

There are several premonitory scenes which anticipate this sacrificial denouement. At the opening military briefing, Willard is told by his Senior Officer that Kurtz has crossed the line between 'us' and 'them'. The General in question describes Kurtz as being 'out there . . . with the natives . . . operating beyond the pale of any human decency'. He tells how Kurtz, once a prized first-ranking Colonel, has supped with the devil beyond the point of return, traversing the border between civilians and barbarians. Kurtz has broken with the norms of civilized, reasonable behaviour. He has gone 'insane', ultimately yielding to the temptation 'to be a god'. He has become the Other, the Monster, one of the pure who has passed over to the Hades of the impure. A friend turned enemy. He is damned.

The irony of these demonizing sentiments is breathtaking, of course, in light of what we soon discover the 'civilized, reasonable behaviour' of the officially approved US troops to be.

But the discovery is gradual, as Willard steers his gunboat up the river leading from North Vietnam to Cambodia. His nightmare encounter with two military commands says it all. The first of these is led by Colonel Kilgore, a Cavalry officer who shares the same rank as Kurtz but seems more brutal in his bloodlust. He distributes 'death cards' to his victims, orders his troops to surf on the river during military manoeuvres and plays Wagner – the chosen music of Nazi machismo and *Birth of the Nation* suprematism – to accompany his helicopter gun missions. In contradistinction to Kurtz's crystalline logic of terminating war by whatever means, Kilgore just wants to keep it going for the heck of it. The banality of evil could hardly be more lucidly illustrated than in these surreal scenes of gratuitous violence. If we are talking 'insanity', this is it; though Kilgore is considered 'legitimate' while Kurtz is not. Compared to this hellish mayhem, Kurtz's description of his incisive actions as 'moments of clarity' begins to sound more convincing than the Army's dismissal of them as 'unsound methods'. (As if the actual *aim* of 'exterminating the brutes' is quite acceptable!) The Army objects to the means, not the end.

The confusion of friend and foe, ally and alien, is compounded as Willard visits the US frontier outposts. At the first we see GIs debauching themselves at an officially sponsored show of Playboy bunnies, while the second displays an inferno of military inefficiency, cowardice and drug abuse. The US myth of the noble frontiersman takes a last dive here as one of Kilgore's super surfers collapses in a hail of shrapnel. Could Kurtz possibly be worse than this?

*

As Willard arrives at his final destination – Kurtz's hideout – the enigma deepens further. Willard is met by an American photographer who proclaims Kurtz to be a 'poet warrior'. He hails Kurtz as the prophet of a new 'dialectic' which, far from making him mad, brings him beyond conventional categories of good and evil. 'No maybes, no supposes, no fractions'. Willard appears to vacillate yet one more time. He eventually meets Kurtz himself and is invited into his den.

So the pursuer confronts the monster. They talk for days without guard. Kurtz expounds his reasoning. He recounts how he learned from the Vietcong 'enemy' the uncompromising logic of war. He tells the story of how he and his troops had vaccinated children in a certain village only to discover that, after they had left, the Vietcong had returned and cut off each inoculated arm. This enemy act struck Kurtz 'like a diamond bullet through his forehead', revealing to him the inner truth of military action: pure will to power without judgement. These were 'not monsters but men', he learnt. These were 'geniuses . . . perfect, genuine, complete, crystalline, pure of act'. These were men who could both love and kill: love their own families with total passion and kill their enemies 'without passion . . . without judgement'. Why? 'Because it is judgement that defeats us'. And Kurtz ultimately confesses to Willard that if he had ten divisions of men like that he could have dispensed with all hypocrisy and terminated the war in no time. Even the corpses strewn on Kurtz's compound serve a specific purpose – to instil enough horror to bring the war to an end. What looks like madness is in fact a (perverse) obsession with peace, the desire to win the war as effectively and rapidly as possible. Here we have a morality of immorality.[11] Kurtz's speech culminates with the observation: 'You can kill me but you cannot judge me'.

Having listened to Kurtz's razor-sharp reasoning and witnessed the result of his new im/morality – a camp inhabited by crazed warriors and strewn with body-parts and decapitated heads – Willard *does* eventually judge. He kills Kurtz. Coppola does not explain what criteria Willard deploys to differentiate between Kurtz the neo-Nietzschean hero and Kurtz the manic monster. We are not told how Willard decides. Nor how we might judge his decision in turn. Coppola, after all, is a movie-maker, not a philosopher. It is his business to screen this age-old conundrum, not to solve it. But in dramatizing this fundamental question of discernment for a contemporary audience, Coppola has performed a great intellectual service.

*

From the perspective of our scapegoating thesis this film raises key questions. Amongst these are: How do we judge the horror? How do we distinguish between one kind of monstrosity and another? How does one differentiate between 'normal' and 'abnormal' actions, especially in a war like Vietnam where, in Willard's words, 'charging a man with murder was like handing out speeding tickets at the Indy 500'? How is Willard to know who is on the 'right' side in a war where even the Americans have changed sides, as he learns from French colonials on a lost plantation (he also learns from a French widow that 'men love and kill')? And if it is true that Kurtz has welcomed his potential executioner, Willard, in an act of unconditional hospitality, has Willard been entirely just in responding to this hospitality with an act of summary execution? And, what is more, an execution without trial, in seeming defiance of Willard's own prolonged scruples about High Command's order to 'exterminate without prejudice'.

Morever, the fact that his host, Kurtz, hangs out in a Buddhist temple and is an avid reader of Eliot's *Hollow Men* – not to mention Frazer's *The Golden Bough* and the Bible – sharpens the enigma by suggesting how deeply resolved Kurtz is to prosecute the chilling logic of war. Even if it means succumbing to its 'horror'. 'After such knowledge what forgiveness?' as Eliot says. So, even if the demands of absolute hospitality seem impossible here, one is left wondering if the only alternative is the sacrificial killing of the monster at the heart of the labyrinth. Willard obeys his command. Theseus rules OK. But does it have to be like this?

*

There are two key scenes towards the close of the film which put these questions into sharp relief. The first shows one of Willard's troops, Chef, being terrified by a tiger as they patrol the jungle. They are on the lookout for the 'enemy'. But what actually surprises them is an animal who is perfectly at home in his local environment. Because they are estranged from this 'foreign' place the US Marines mistake one 'monster' for another, confusing human and animal adversaries. At least one implication of this scene is that the 'monster' Kurtz, who has gone over to the other side and assumed the mores of the natives who revere him, may also be a case of mistaken identity. A suspicion deepened by the fact that when Kurtz and Willard eventually encounter each other at the heart of darkness, their semi-naked, sleeked figures have become almost indistinguishable. The question of who is the hunter and who the hunted accentuates the problem of prejudice and judgement.

The second image, also at the film's finale, shows the statue of a Buddha in Kurtz's Cambodian hideaway just before the latter's execution. We see the veiled statue facing Kurtz as he recites his terminal reflections on war onto a tape recorder. (He is railing against the hypocrisy of the US Army which trains troops to drop napalm on innocents but refuses to allow the word 'fuck' to be written on its planes.) In the preceding scene Kurtz was seen entering the doorway of the Buddhist temple as a caribou passes him on its way to its own ritual sacrifice. Both will be offered as scapegoats to purge the community. It is significant that the twin sacrificial rites which follow – the slaughtering of the caribou being juxtaposed with the killing of Kurtz in graphic montage – give rise to a scene where the 'purged' Willard re-emerges through the same temple door, his bare, dark figure almost identical to Kurtz's (see p. 54). But with this difference: it is Willard who now wields the executioner's axe and possesses the manuscript of Kurtz's memoirs.

So here again the question is raised as to whether one is justified in executing an enemy deemed inhuman? With Kurtz's closing statement to Willard – 'You have a right to kill me but not to judge me' – still ringing in our ears, the calm visage of the bald Buddha which closes the film gives us pause. This is all the more so if one is mindful of the Buddhist doctrine of non-judgement. Could Willard have executed Kurtz had he heeded this ancient Buddhist prayer?

> When I encounter beings of wicked nature
> Overwhelmed by violent negative actions and suffering,
> I shall hold such rare ones dear,
> As if I had found a precious treasure.
> When someone gives me terrible harm
> I shall regard him as my holy spiritual friend.[12]

What, in short, if Willard had forgiven Kurtz and tried to save him from this inferno, acknowledging that Kurtz was not only the ultimate expression of US military involvement in Vietnam but also a scapegoat serving to preserve the illusion of a clean conscience? A man who, for all his killing, was still capable of loving (his wife and son, and even, arguably, Willard, whom he refuses to slay). A man who, in his own words, hated the 'stench of lies'.

And yet, there is one mitigating factor in Willard's role: the confessional narrative of these events. These events are related retrospectively, to be sure, but they are no less cathartic for that. In acknowledging that (1) there was no way to 'tell his (Kurtz's) story without telling my own' and (2) that 'if his (Kurtz's) story is really a confession then so is mine', Willard admits to a deep identification with the monster he has slain. He openly acknowledges his role as testimonial witness to Kurtz's life, before the world but most especially before Kurtz's son. 'It was no accident that I got to be the caretaker of Colonel Walter E. Kurtz's memory', he concedes. Both Willard and Kurtz expose the mendacities of US military practice in Vietnam. Willard does so by telling the whole story in direct response to Kurtz's final request: 'I worry that my son might not understand what I have tried to be. I want someone to tell him everything . . . There is nothing that I hate more than lies . . . If you understand me, you'll do this for me.'

These are hardly the words of an irredeemable monster. They are those of someone who was ultimately subsumed by the horror. Someone for whom the truth of war won out over the truth of poetry. Someone who could not survive to tell the tale. In this he differs from Willard who in spite of his collusion with sacrificial killing, manages to transcend the logic of scapegoating in favour of narrative testimony and wisdom: he tells the story of Kurtz which he carries in his hand as he exits the temple and merges finally with the face of the Buddha (see p. 54).

Willard refuses to be divinized by Kurtz's followers after he has killed the demon. As the throngs of warriors kneel before him in their bandoleers and bloodied loincloths, Willard passes through them to his waiting boat. Having defeated the Minotaur, Theseus declines the sacrificial role of replacement deity. He escapes the cycle of bloodletting. And in resisting the lure of false gods, he appears to choose the option of poetic catharsis so well described by Eliot himself when he writes:

> (The storyteller) is haunted by a demon against which he feels powerless, because in its first manifestation it has no face, no name, nothing; and the words, the poem he makes, are a kind of form of exorcism of this demon.[13]

Apocalypse Now Redux is such a poem. As were *Heart of Darkness* and *The Hollow Men* before it.

Yet the tragedy for Kurtz himself is that redemption comes, if it comes at all, *posthumously*, through the confessional voice of the film's narrator. The catharsis by pity and fear comes to Willard the narrator, and perhaps also to us viewers, but not it seems to the crazed colonial. Willard's narrative testifies to the hidden root of the alienation in Kurtz which, it transpires, is symptomatic of the war itself. When Willard finally departs from the heart of darkness, refusing the nihilism of the 'Horror', he takes Kurtz's story back with him. He carries the typed pages of testimony in his trembling hand. And in the retelling that is *Apocalypse Now Redux* the Horror becomes that bit less horrible, the monster that bit less monstrous.

Conclusion

If it is the sleep of reason that produces monsters, as Goya says, it is, I would suggest, the perversion of reason in a certain sacrificial mood. If we are to put an end to the cycle of scapegoating, might we not begin by trying to understand our own monsters? And so doing, might we not transform some of them into creatures of passionate peace? Might we not even (who knows?) help one or two of those real persons who behave monstrously 'out there' – tyrants, torturers, rapists, murderers – to come to terms with their own internal monsters, and thereby put an end to homicidal and genocidal practices of scapegoating? As Willard almost does in the final confrontation with Kurtz. Or as Ellen Ripley and the prisoners of Fiorina do at the end of *Alien* 3. Indeed is this not the very meaning of Ripley's crucifical act as she cradles her alien offspring and holds it to her breast? But we do not have to send our Ripleys and Willards to the darkest reaches of Asia or outer space to find our monsters. They are lurking within us here at home – often in the depths of our own selves.

The notion of the stranger within is as old as civilization itself. Almost every wisdom tradition attests to it. We find it in the story of Jacob struggling with his dark double through the night before transmuting his monster into an angel of God. We see it in the testimony of Jesus confronting his demons in the desert before giving himself in an act of ultimate *caritas*. And we encounter a similar lesson being offered by the Buddha when he takes the monster of violent hatred to his heart and meditates on it for so many years that it eventually mutates into compassionate calm. A disciple of the Tibetan Buddhist school, Milarepa, learned this truth the hard way when one day he discovered his cave taken over by a demon. After fighting with the beast for many years to no avail, he finally put himself into its jaws saying, 'eat me if you want to'. It was only then the demon left.[14] When violent fears go, so do monsters. Love is the casting out of fear.

61

The key, perhaps, is not to kill our monsters but to learn to live with them. For that way there is hope that monsters may eventually learn to live with themselves and cease to scapegoat others. Or as Nietzsche put it in his own aphoristic way: 'Whoever fights monsters should see to it that in the process he does not become a monster'.[15] Agreed. Yet at the same time, embracing monsters doesn't mean you have to invite them to dinner – or set up house. Some monsters need to be welcomed, others struggled with. The important thing – as we argue in our studies below – is to try to tell the difference.

3

ALIENS AND OTHERS

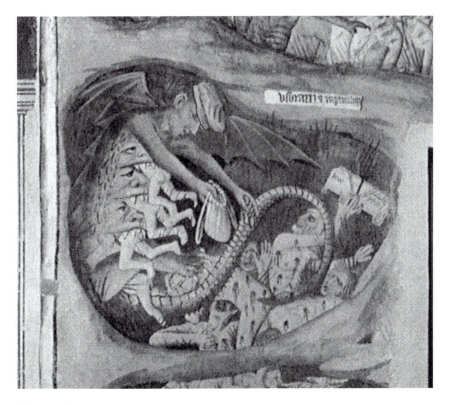

The Jew dragon.
Detail from a fourteenth-century fresco in Notre Dame des Fontaines, La Brigue, France. (Photo by Richard Kearney)

Ever since early Western thought equated the Good with notions of self-identity and sameness, the experience of evil has often been linked with notions of exteriority. Almost invariably, otherness was considered in terms of an estrangement which contaminates the pure unity of the soul. Strangeness was thought to possess our most intimate being until, as Macbeth's witches put it, 'nothing is but what is not'. Evil was alienation and the evil one was the alien. One of the oldest stories in the book.

The prejudice against exteriority has by no means disappeared in our contemporary world. We find many popular media narratives promoting paranoia by anathemizing what is unfamiliar as 'evil'. Such tales reinforce, once again, the idea that the other is an adversary, the stranger a scapegoat, the dissenter a devil. It is this proclivity to demonize alterity as a menace to our collective identity which so easily issues in hysterical stories about invading enemies (what Elaine Showalter terms *hystories*). Any threat to National Security is met with hostility. This is a recurring phenomenon of modern history. One thinks of Kristallnacht and Auschwitz, the Soviet show trials and gulags, Mao's cultural revolution and Tiananmen Square, McCarthy's blacklists and Reagan's Starwars, the embargo of Cuba and bombing of Cambodia, Sarajevo and Kosovo, Jerusalem and the West Bank, the Twin Towers and Afghanistan. The list is interminable.

Most nation-states bent on preserving their body politic from 'alien viruses' seek to pathologize their adversaries. Faced with a threatening outsider the best mode of defence is attack. Again and again the national *We* is defined over and against the foreign *Them*. Borders are policed to keep nationals in and aliens out. You can of course cross these borders with the right passport and become an alien resident. But to be truly nationalized, you need more, and this something more is not always readily available if you happen to be arriving from the wrong country. National security draws a cordon sanitaire around the nation-state, protecting it from trespassers. Like the line drawn in sand at the Alamo, or along the banks of the Rio Grande. Or like other borders separating north and south – in Vietnam, Korea, Lebanon, Ireland.

Most ideas of identity, in short, have been constructed in relation to some notion of alterity. Contemporary thinkers like Levinas and Derrida have made much of the fact that the Western metaphysical heritage, grounded in Greco-Roman thought, has generally discriminated against the Other in favour of the Same, variously understood as Logos, Being, Substance, Reason or Ego. This prejudice is called the 'ontology of Sameness' by Levinas, and 'logocentrism' by Derrida. But both share the view – one canvassed by a wide variety of continental thinkers – that justice demands a redressing of the balance so as to arrive at a more ethical appreciation of otherness. Such an

The Irish Frankenstein.
Punch, 20 May, 1882

appreciation reminds us that the human stranger before us always escapes our egological schemas and defies our efforts to treat him/her as a scapegoated 'alien' or, at best, an alter ego. Openness to the Other beyond the Same is called justice. For Levinas this relation to otherness establishes an infinite responsibility; for Derrida it establishes a summons to absolute hospitality.

But since, according to this reading, the Other surpasses all our categories of interpretation and representation, we are left with a problem – the problem of discernment. How can we tell the difference between benign and malign others? How do we know, to rehearse the query of our opening study, when the other is truly an enemy who seeks to destroy us or an innocent scapegoat projected by our phobias? Or a mixture of both? How do we account for the fact that not every other is innocent and not every self is an egoistic emperor? The basic undecidability on this issue bequeathed by Levinas and the deconstructionists requires, I believe, to be supplemented by some kind of critical hermeneutic capable of distinguishing – however tentatively – between enabling and disabling forms of alterity. I will begin with Derrida's recent attempts to deal with this question before then moving on to some alternative responses to the enigma of the other, in particular the responses of psychoanalysis and phenomenological hermeneutics.

But first a word on terminology and context. I take the term 'other' here, as frequently invoked by contemporary Continental theory, to refer to an alterity worthy of reverence and hospitality. I take the term 'alien', by contrast, to refer to that experience of strangers associated with: (a) discrimination (as in certain immigration policies or acts of separating natives from foreigners); (b) suspicion (as in UFOs, extraterrestials or other unwelcome invaders); and (c) scapegoating (as in xenophobic, racist or anti-Semitic practices). I will argue that what is needed – if we are to engage properly with the human obsession with strangers and enemies – is a critical hermeneutic capable of addressing the dialectic of others and aliens. Such a hermeneutic would have the task of soliciting ethical decisions without rushing to judgement, that is, without succumbing to overhasty acts of binary exclusion. In short, I am suggesting that we need to be able to critically discriminate between different kinds of otherness, while remaining alert to the deconstructive resistance to black and white judgements of Us versus Them. We need, at crucial moments, to discern the other in the alien and the alien in the other.

Between hostility and hospitality:
deconstruction and otherness

It is in the context of global practices of polarization that deconstructionists like Derrida, Caputo, Lacoue-Labarthe, Nancy and others have pursued the question of justice in recent years. Every nation-state is logocentric to the extent that it excludes those who do not conform (non-a) to its identity logic (a is a). This is necessary up to a point, as even the cosmopolitan Kant recognized when he accepted the need to issue conditions for refugee visitors to a state – e.g. that their sojourn be temporary, law-abiding, non-divisive.[1] The world belongs to everyone. But within the borders of nation-states it belongs to some more than others. Granted, some form of immigration law is inevitable. That's the law and deconstructionists accept this. But they go on to argue that there's something beyond the law. Namely, justice. And justice demands more: namely, unconditional hospitality to the alien.

Hospitality is only truly just, this argument goes, when it resists the temptation to discriminate between good and evil others, that is, between the hostile enemy (hostis) and the benign host (hostis). The Latin root for both hostility and hospitality is the same. And the term 'host' may in fact be used to designate one who welcomes or one who invades.[2] This paradox is illustrated, as noted in our first chapter, in the Alien series where the heroine, Agent Ripley, is at once the mother of the alien-child in her womb and the host of the alien-monster that invaded her. A paradox which provokes very mixed feelings indeed.

*

Derrida has much to say about such alien matters in On Hospitality.[3] Generally understood, the subject of hospitality is a generous host who decides, as master chez lui, who to invite into his home. But it is precisely because of such sovereign self-possession that the host comes to fear certain others who threaten to invade his house, transforming him from a host into a hostage. The laws of hospitality thus reserve the right of each host to evaluate, select and choose those he/she wishes to include or exclude – that is, the right to discriminate. Such discrimination requires that each visitor identifies him or herself before entering one's home. And this identification process – indispensable to the 'law of hospitality' (hospitalité en droit) – involves at least some degree of violence. Derrida comments astutely on this paradox:

There can be no sovereignty in the classic sense without the sovereignty of the self in its own home, but since there is no hospitality without finitude, sovereignty can only operate by filtering, choosing and therefore excluding and doing violence. A certain injustice . . . is present from the outset, at the very threshold of the right to hospitality. This collusion between the violence of power or the force of law (Gewalt) on the one hand, and hospitality on the other, seems to be radically integral to the very inscription of hospitality as a right. . . .[4]

Derrida goes on to link this inclusive/exclusive law of hospitality with ethics in the more general sense. The paradox of the stranger (xenos/hostis/gast), he writes, as either invader-alien or welcome-other:

extends from the circumscribed field of ethos or ethics, of habitation or visitation as ethos, of Sittlichkeit, of objective morality as specifically identified in Hegel's threefold determination of right and the philosophy of right: family, society (civil or bourgeois) and state (or nation-state).[5]

Derrida sums up the aporia of the alien-other thus: 'the outsider (hostis) received as host or as enemy. Hospitality, hostility, hostipitality'.[6] Fully cognisant of the way this undecidable dialectic confounds our ethical conventions, Derrida affirms the priority of a hospitality of justice – open to the absolute other as another without name. Here we supersede the hospitality of law. What distinguishes the absolute other is that it is without distinction, i.e. without name or proper name. And the absolute, unconditional hospitality which this other deserves marks a break with everyday conventions of hospitality governed by rights, contracts, duties and pacts. Absolute hospitality, argues Derrida:

requires that I open my home and that I give not only to the stranger (furnished with a family name and the social status of a stranger etc.) but to the absolute other, unknown and anonymous; and that I give place (donne lieu), let come, arrive, let him take his place in the place that I offer him, without demanding that he give his name or enter into some reciprocal pact.[7]

If absolute hospitality requires us to break with the accredited hospitality of right, this does not necessarily mean repudiating the latter out of hand.

It may sometimes mean preserving it in a state of perpetual process and mutation. But either way, for Derrida, *absolute* hospitality is as heterogeneous to *conditional* hospitality as justice is to the law of right with which it is tied.

But Derrida adds a telling coda to this reading of the right of hospitality. The other is not just the alien stranger, utterly external to home, family or state. For that would be to relegate the other to total exteriority – barbarous, savage, precultural and prejuridical. No, in order that hospitality be just we must allow some way for the absolute other to enter our 'home'. And that is why justice can never dispense with the law of right: 'The relation to the alien/stranger (l'étranger) is regulated by the law of right (le droit), by the becoming-right of justice'.[8]

*

The problem with this analysis of hospitality is, I fear, that it undervalues our need to differentiate not just legally but *ethically* between good and evil aliens. It downgrades – without denying – our legitimate duty to try to distinguish between benign and malign strangers, between saints and psychopaths (though admittedly most of us fall somewhere between the two). And it does this, in the final instance, by relegating the requirement of ethical judgement to a matter of selective and calculating legislation invariably compromised by injustice and violence. After all, if hospitality were to be absolutely just, *all* incoming others without exception would be *undecidable* – and as such worthy of welcome. Derrida appears to accept as much when he declares that 'for pure hospitality or pure gift to occur there must be absolute surprise . . . an opening without horizon of expectation . . . to the newcomer *whoever that may be*'. And he goes further: 'The newcomer may be good or evil, but if you exclude the possibility that the newcomer is coming to destroy your house, if you want to control this and exclude this terrible possibility in advance, there is no hospitality'. The other, he concludes, 'like the Messiah, must arrive wherever he or she wants'.[9]

For deconstruction, in sum, aliens only come in the dark; and we are always in the dark when they come. We are never sure who or what they are; we cannot even be sure if we are hallucinating. The absolute other is without name and without face. It is, as Jack Caputo insists, an 'impossible, unimaginable, un-forseeable, un-believable, ab-solute surprise'.[10] The best we can do then is try to read between the lines and make a leap of faith, an impossible leap of faith, like Abraham, like Kierkegaard. But why not add –

and here's my difficulty with the undecidable – like Jim Jones or David Koresh or other figures of mystical madness who believe they are recipients of messianic messages from some Other they call God? In short, if all reading is reading in the dark how can we even begin to discern between holy and unholy spirits, between bringers of peace and bringers of destruction?

In Levinas, one of Derrida's most influential mentors, we already find a tendency to conflate the irrepresentable horrors of the 'there is' (il y a) with the equally irrepresentable strangeness of the absolute Other (illéité). In both cases, the self finds itself traumatically persecuted. Indeed in certain passages of his later work, *Otherwise than Being*, Levinas will go so far as to claim that my responsibility for the other is so limitless that I am even 'responsible for the persecuting by the persecutor'.[11] Before both the highest of the high (Illeity) and the lowest of the low (il y a), the self empties itself of itself, like a haemorrhaging haemophiliac helpless to stem the outward flow. This self-emptying in pain and holocaust – epitomized in the phrase 'I am ashes and dust' – goes well beyond humility to a form of abject humiliation: what Levinas calls a 'passivity beneath all passivity'. At times the hyperbolic language borders, in my view, on masochism and paranoia: 'the one is exposed to the other as a skin is exposed to what wounds it . . .'.[12] In so far as we can talk of self at all at this ground zero of suffering, it can only be in terms of a subjectivity that is 'obsessed', 'accused', 'expulsed' and 'hostaged'. Levinas speaks accordingly of the 'shudder of subjectivity', as my inwardness breaks up and I experience myself as 'the abandon of all shelter, exposure to traumas'.[13]

This self-abjection before the wounding other is taken to such extremes at times that I find myself agreeing with Simon Critchley's claim that *Otherwise than Being* could feature on a list of horror literature. The suggestion is that Levinas' reduction of selfhood to subjectivity-as-substitution – a structure of being haunted by an alterity that can be neither comprehended nor refused – ultimately makes evil a more valid basis for ethical experience than good. 'Does not the trauma occasioned in the subject possessed by evil more adequately describe the ethical subject than possession by the good?' asks Critchley.

> Is it not in the excessive experience of evil and horror . . . that the ethical subject first assumes its shape? Does this not begin to explain why the royal road to ethical metaphysics must begin by making Levinas a master of the literature of horror? But if this is the case, why is radical otherness goodness? Why is alterity ethical? Why is it not, we may wonder, 'rather evil or an-ethical or neutral'?[14]

To be absolutely hospitable to the other is, it appears, to suspend all criteria of ethical discrimination. And in such non-discriminate openness to alterity we find ourselves unable to differentiate between good and evil. A fine lesson in tolerance, to be sure, but not necessarily in moral judgement. If there is a difference between Jesus and Jim Jones, between Saint Francis and Stalin, between Melena and Mengele, between Siddartha and de Sade – and I think most of us would want to say there is – then some further philosophical reflections are needed to supplement the deconstructive scruple of absolute hospitality. Deconstructive non-judgementalism needs to be supplemented, I suggest, with a hermeneutics of practical wisdom which might help us better discern between justice and injustice. For if we need a logic of undecidability to keep us tolerant – preventing us from setting ourselves up as Chief High Executioners – we need an ethics of judgement to commit us, as much as possible, to right action.

But before proceeding to outline such a hermeneutic approach, I wish to briefly explore another important contribution to our contemporary understanding of otherness, namely, psychoanalytic critique.

Strangers to ourselves: psychoanalysis and otherness

Most Western discourses of identity, as noted, are predicated upon some unconscious projection of an Other who is not 'us'. At the collective level of politics, this assumes the guise of an elect 'nation' or 'people' defining itself over against an alien adversary. Witness the old enmities between Greek and Barbarian, Gentile and Jew, Crusader and Infidel, Aryan and non-Aryan. Even modern 'civilized' nations have not always been immune to such stigmatizing practices. For example, the English defined themselves for colonial purposes as an elect people (*gens*) over against the Irish considered as a 'non-people' (*de-gens*). And this strategy of separating pure from impure was subsequently employed with regard to the subject races of overseas colonies in Africa, Asia and the Americas.[15] The English also opposed the abstract rights of the French and American revolutions with the 'inalienable heritage' of the 'rights of the English inherited from (their) ancestors'.[16] But independent America, in spite of its emancipatory rhetoric, was in turn capable of branding slaves and native Americans – and later again, 'communists' – as new-found scapegoats. While Revolutionary France had recourse to Us-versus-Them thinking as soon as the initial enthusiasm for foreigners (*étrangers*) at the outset of the Revolution turned, by the time of the Terror, to a campaign of suspicion and persecution. In 1793, the Committee of Public Safety demanded that all 'foreigners be obliged to leave French territory'; and within years of the Declaration of the Rights of Man and of the Citizen, hundreds of *étrangers* were proclaimed non-citizens and guillotined as 'enemy agents' (*agents de l'étranger*).[17] Far worse again, reactionary German nationalists, from the time of Bismarck to Hitler, claimed that only the Germanic Volk had – qua master race surrounded by subraces – inalienable rights to territorial and cultural dominance: *Deutschland über alles!* Nor did the need to discriminate between 'us' and 'them' disappear with the rise to world power of multi-ethnic states like the USSR – as the Stalinist campaigns against 'foreign enemy agents' remind us. In short, from ancient to modern times, the inalienable Rights of Man were not to be afforded to *aliens*. For as nations consolidated themselves into sovereign and homogenous territories, the alien was deemed an 'intruder who demolished consensus'.[18]

In *Strangers to Ourselves*, Julia Kristeva relates this recurring xenophobic drive to a basic unconscious process whereby we externalize what is 'strange' within us onto an external 'stranger'. The result is a denial of the fact that we are strangers to ourselves, a denial which takes the form of negating aliens. To the extent that we exclude the outsider we deceive ourselves into thinking that we have exempted ourselves from estrangement. We fool ourselves into believing that we have purged that singular sense of anxiety which Freud calls the 'uncanny' (*das Unheimliche*).

*

In his landmark essay, 'The Uncanny', Freud explored the paradox that the '*Unheimliche* is the name for everything that ought to have remained hidden and secret and has become visible'.[19] While the term refers ostensibly to what is unfamiliar and unknown, it also carries the very opposite sense of what is intimately interior and familiar. Freud goes on to note that the *Unheimliche* is that phenomenon of strangeness which curiously re-evokes what is 'known of old and long familiar'; a phenomenon already intimated by the etymological links between the terms, *Geheim* (secret), *heimisch* (native) and *heimlich* (homely). In short, what we witness here, in both the term and the phenomenon it describes, is a slippage between two ostensibly contrary meanings – the homely and the unhomely. And this double meaning basically signals how certain things can become so discreet as to become secretive – 'concealed, kept from sight, so that others do not get to know of or about it, withheld from others'.[20] In other words, *das Unheimliche* is the obverse of *das Heimlich*, arising when the latter becomes so privy or surreptitious that it disappears from consciousness altogether, slipping beneath the bar of the unconscious. The intimate becomes so intimate that it becomes strange. The 'uncanny' comes to mean, then, something 'secret or untrustworthy', finding its equivalents in the Latin *occultus* or *mysticus*.

Freudian hermeneutics decrypts the signs of the unconscious to disclose this process of estrangement. The 'alien' is revealed accordingly as that most occluded part of ourselves, considered so unspeakable that we externalize it onto others. The more foreign someone is the more eligible to carry the shadow cast by our unconscious. Strangers become perfect foils since we can act out on them the hostility we feel towards our own strangers within. Or as Freud puts it, the *heimlich* becomes so hidden from others and from ouselves that it

> comes to have the meaning actually ascribed to *unheimlich* . . . Thus *heimlich* is a word the meaning of which develops in the direction of ambivalence until it finally coincides with its opposite, *unheimlich*. *Unheimlich* is in some way or other a sub-species of *heimlich*.[21]

Relating this reversible dyad *heimlich/unheimlich* to the split between the conscious and unconscious, psychoanalytic thinkers have argued that in the realm of the imaginary (which blurs the distinction) we find creatures of our own repressed unconscious returning to haunt us as phantom 'doubles' – *frères ennemis*. The divided self seeks to protect itself against its own inner division by projecting its 'other self' onto someone other than itself. But the foreigner thus scapegoated is, of course, nothing other than our own estranged self coming back to ghost us. Freud thus proposes an 'archaeological hermeneutic' (to borrow Ricoeur's term in *Freud and Philosophy*) to account for the genesis of this doubling phenomenon. When all is said and done

> The quality of uncanniness can only come from the fact of the 'double' being a creation dating back to a very early mental stage, long since surmounted – a stage, incidentally, at which it wore a more friendly aspect. The double has become a thing of terror, just as, after the collapse of their religion, the gods turned into demons.[22]

Indeed, this perhaps explains why so many horror movies, from *Dr Jekyll and Mr Hyde* to *Dead Ringers* and *Face Off*, play on this phenomenon of estranged doubles.

The demonizing of 'strangers' by individuals or nations may thus be interpreted as a harking back to past repressed materials which recur in the present – often with obsessive compulsion – in the guise of something threatening and terrifying. But, ironically, what we most fear in the demonized other is our own mirror image: our othered self. 'The uncanny', concludes Freud, 'is in reality nothing new or alien, but something which is familiar and of old established in the mind and which has become alienated from it only through the process of repression'.[23]

The prefix un- in *unheimlich* is, in short, to be understood less as a logical opposition than as a dialectical reversal. The adversary I love to hate is often nothing less than myself in disguise. Taking our cue from Freud we might conclude, accordingly, that dreaded aliens are most dreaded not because they are other than us but because they are *more like us than our own selves*. There is nothing really alien about the alien.

*

Kristeva develops this psychoanaltytic reading of the uncanny in a number of suggestive ways. In the second part of *Strangers to Ourselves*, she endeavours to tease out its specifically political implications. On foot of Freud, she writes: 'disquieting strangeness (l'étrangeté) enters into the quietude of reason itself . . . Henceforth we realize that we are strangers to ourselves, and it is on this very basis that we can try to exist with others'.[24] Kristeva promotes the Kantian idea of a cosmopolitan Universal Republic where aliens (étrangers) would be respected as others, acknowledged in their right to difference. This cosmopolitan federation of states would fully honour the diversity of cultures, languages, confessions and peoples who inhabit the globe, safeguarding the right of hospitality to 'strangers' on the basis that the world is round, belongs to everyone, and that 'originally no one (people) has more right than another to its territory'.[25] From this consideration of practical reason, Kant had deduced the following definition of hospitality towards others, also noted by Derrida: 'Hospitality means therefore the right of each foreigner (étranger) not to be treated as an enemy in the land in which he arrives'.[26] A tolerant moral cosmopolitanism thus becomes, for our time, the secular equivalent of the old religious vision – originating in the biblical celebration of the 'stranger', so vigorously promoted by the Prophets and Saint Paul, of a community of peoples and tongues.

I believe that this psychoanalytic disclosure of the uncanny as an alterity-within-identity offers a useful means of *depathologizing* the alien. A gap is now located within the presumed homogeneity of human consciousness, the other at long last being admitted as an integral inhabitant of the self. Henceforth, argues Kristeva, 'the stranger is neither a race nor a nation . . . we are our own strangers – we are divided selves'.[27] This whole discovery may well, Kristeva suggests, have something to do with Freud's own biography as an insider–outsider – the nomadic Jew wandering through various parts of Europe from Galicia and Venice to Paris, New York, Rome and London. But, more funda-mentally, it expresses the universal experience of a deep unconscious malaise with 'others' arising from our repressed rapport with the internally housed 'primal scene' that informs our psyche. 'My malaise in living with the other', explains Kristeva, 'my strangeness, his/her strangeness, rests upon a vexed logic which governs the strange cluster of drive and language, of nature and symbol, which is the unconscious always already informed by the other'.[28] Kristeva proffers this therapeutic response to the conundrum of the self–other relation:

> It is the unravelling of the transfer – the great dynamic of alterity, of our love/hate for the other, of the otherness constitutive of our very psyche – which enables me, based on the other, to become reconciled with my own strangeness/alterity, to play with it and live with it. Psychoanalysis thus experiences itself as a journey into the other and into oneself, towards an ethic of respect for the irreconcilable. For how can we tolerate strangers if we do not know that we are strangers to ourselves?[29]

Finally, in a coupling of Heideggerian and Freudian perspectives, Kristeva makes the intriguing point that the ultimate stranger of strangers is the shadow of our own finitude. The phantasmatic double which returns to haunt us again and again, through the mists of troubling strangeness (l'*inquiétante étrangété*), is ultimately nothing other than our fear of death. This spectre of our own mortality, inscribed within us as our *Sein-zum-Tode*, is something we cannot bear. And so unbearable does it become that many of us choose to transfer it onto unsuspecting strangers whom we call our worst enemies.

Already in Section 40 of *Being and Time* Heidegger had offered a deft analysis of how our existential anguish before death is experienced as radical

Unheimlichkeit: a sense of deep disorientation, of not-being-at-home in ourselves. '*In der Angst ist einem "unheimlich"*', his phrase went.[30] And it is on the basis of this ontological model that Kristeva, like Lacan, seeks to redefine the Freudian take on the Uncanny.

To truly embrace the other as our stranger is to accept a certain decentring of the ego which opens the self to the novel, the incongruous and the unexpected. Once our defence mechanisms against alterity are thus suspended we either fall into psychotic breakdown or rise to a poetics of new images and an ethics of new practices. While such a poetics invites us to sublimate the alien into imaginary play (thereby preventing the *acting out* of scapegoating and war), a correlative psychoanalytic ethics might solicit, however indirectly, a new politics of cosmopolitanism whose solidarity is founded on the 'conscience of the unconscious'.[31] For if each of us can accept that we are the strangers, then there are no strangers – only others like ourselves.

But perhaps this psychoanalytic approach is too quick in its tendency to reduce alterity to a dialectic of the unconscious psyche? For however subtle and complex such a reading may be, it tells only half of the story. To put it another way, if deconstruction too rapidly subordinates the Same to the Other, psychoanalysis may too rapidly subordinate the Other to the Same. And so doing, it risks subsuming the exteriority of transcendence into the language games of psychic immanence. If these suspicions are correct, the trick would be to try to steer a path somewhere between the polar extremes of alterity and immanence. It is with this in mind that we proceed to our third model of interpretation: a critical hermeneutics of oneself-as-another.

Oneself-as-another: hermeneutics and otherness

While both deconstruction and psychoanalysis offer significant accounts of our ethical awareness of others I do not believe that either provides a *sufficient* account. Something crucial is lacking. And I suggest that this lacuna may best be filled by what I call a *diacriticial* hermeneutics of action. For if (a) deconstruction discloses the interchangeable character of others and aliens, alerting us to the irreducible alterity of all incomers, and if (b) psychoanalysis reveals the role of the other as a psychic projection of the self – it remains for hermeneutics to address the additional need for critically informed judgements. It is not enough to be simply *open* to the other beyond us or within us; though this is essential. One must also be careful to discern, in some provisional fashion at least, between different kinds of otherness.

Extraterrestrials are the True Face of God.
Cult religious circular found in North American cities

BY PERMISSION
Of the Worshipful the Mayor of Leeds.

WILD INDIAN
Savages,

From the Borders of Lake Erie,
In the Western Wilds of North-America, who arrived at Liverpool in the Brig Sally, on the
31st Day of January, 1818; THE

Chief & Six Warriors,

Of the Seneca Nation, will continue to exhibit their interesting Performances,

At the Concert-Room, in Albion-Street,
This PRESENT MONDAY EVENING, APRIL 20th, 1818,

And every Evening during the present Week:

And at the particular Request of Ladies and Gentlemen presiding over Seminaries, there will be a

Day Exhibition on Tuesday and Saturday, in the present Week,

Doors to be opened at One and to commence precisely at Two o'Clock.

Monday Evening, April 27th,
WILL POSITIVELY BE THE

LAST NIGHT.

THE PERFORMANCES WILL CONSIST OF A FAITHFUL AND
Correct Representation of their Native Manners and Customs.
For Particulars see Hand-Bills.

EDWARD BAINES, PRINTER, LEEDS.

Wild Indian savages.
Period poster – anonymous

Hermeneutics suggests that the other is neither absolutely transcendent nor absolutely immanent, but somewhere between the two. It suggests that, for the most part, others are intimately bound up with selves in ways which constitute ethical relations in their own right. Human discourse involves *someone saying something to someone about something*. It is a matter of one self communicating to another self, recognizing that if there is no perfect symmetry between the two, this does not necessarily mark a total dissymmetry. Not all selves are irreparably sundered or shattered.

A minimal quotient of self-esteem is, I would argue, indispensable to ethics. For without it I could not be a moral agent capable of keeping my promises to others. If I did not possess some sense of self-identity and self-constancy, I would be unable to recollect myself from my past memories or project myself into a future such that my pledges to the other (made in the past) might be realized (in the future). Narrative identity should not therefore be summarily dismissed as an illusion of mastery (for it is such in the breach rather than the observance). On the contrary, narrative identity which sustains some notion of selfhood over the passage of time, can serve as guarantor for one's fidelity to the other. How is one to be faithful to the other, after all, if there is no *self* to be faithful?

Levinas, I believe, underestimates this indispensable role of selfhood in the relation with alterity. His main critique of Western philosophy, from Plato's *Parmenides* to Husserl's *Cartesian Meditations* and Heidegger's *Being and Time*, is that it excludes the possibility of relating to the other as other (*kath'auto*, to cite the Platonic term used by Levinas). In most philosophies the other is reduced to the ego's horizon of consciousness.[32] This is most emphatically demonstrated in Husserl's formative analysis of the constitution of otherness in the Fifth Cartesian Meditation, where the Other is always an alter ego analogically 'appresented' or 'apperceived' as *other than mine*. As such, the Other is never given in itself or directly (*in direkter Weise zugänglich*) but only through some mediation (*Mittelbarkeit*) – that is, through a mirroring or modifying of my ego.[33] This phenomenological move towards transcendental idealism is, for Levinas, symptomatic of the entire Western metaphysical tendency to see the Other as a mere duplication of the same. Only a complete *subversion* of this intentionality of 'objectifying cognition' can, Levinas retorts, safeguard the irreducible alterity of the Other.[34]

But as Ricoeur has remarked, there can be no relation to the other that does not in some respect transform the absolute other into a relative other – an other for another self (*pros heteros*). The notion of an absolute manifestation of the other qua absolute (kath'auto) is impossible. There is no way for the other to find its way into the hermeneutic circle without entering the web of figuration, however 'passive' or pre-conscious.[35]

I conclude accordingly that one of the best ways to de-alienate the other is to recognize (a) oneself as another and (b) the other as (in part) another self. For if ethics rightly requires me to respect the singularity of the other person, it equally requires me to recognize the other as another self bearing universal rights and responsibilities, that is, as someone capable of recognizing me in turn as a self capable of recognition and esteem. To declare with the prophets of alterity that the other is so absolutely other that it defies all narrative acts of rememoration or anticipation is not only to compromise the basic practice of promise-keeping but to threaten the equally ethical practice of testimony. As Ricoeur puts it in answer to Levinas: 'With justice may we not hope for the return of memory, beyond the condemnation of the memorable? Otherwise, how could Emmanuel Levinas write the sober exergue: "To the memory of those who are closest"?'[36]

Narrative memory seeks to preserve some trace of those others – especially victims of history – who would, if unremembered, be lost to the injustice of non-existence. And this ethical task of narrative remembrance is perfectly in keeping with the biblical exhortation to 'remember' – zakhor! – while refusing any notion that the lost other could be restored in the form of some fantasy 'presence'. Testimony is a voice of record, not a reliquary. That is why I endorse the hermeneutic model of memory, advanced by thinkers like Ricoeur and Gadamer, which construes otherness less in opposition to selfhood than as a partner engaged in the constitution of its intrinsic meaning.[37] Indeed is it not this sense of the other as, in part, a stranger in myself, keeping me a stranger to myself, which serves the crucial function of moral 'conscience' (Gewissen)? And is it not possible to grant this without explaining away moral conscience, as Freudians and Lacanians sometimes do, as a mere 'effect' of unconscious repression or sublimation?[38]

We might also note here, in conclusion, the phenomenological experience of deep 'passivity' or 'receptivity' before the call of conscience: it is the other within who is calling us to act on behalf of the other without. If one closes off the other's passing in and out of the self, condemning the subject to a cloistered, autistic ego, then the other becomes so other as to remain utterly alienating – an absolutely separate alterity which torments, persecutes and ultimately paralyses. In this Levinasian scenario, as noted above, the self can only become ethical against its own nature and will; one finds oneself radically

80

assaulted and denuded, stripped of one's interpretations in exposure to an absolute Other who demands expiation.

Resisting this option of self-ruin, a complex phenomenology of the self–other dyad prompts us to espouse a hermeneutic pluralism of otherness, a sort of 'polysemy of alterity' – ranging from our experiences of conscience and the body to those of other persons, living or dead (our ancestors), or to a divine Other, living or absent.[39] There is no otherness so exterior or so unconscious, on this reading, that it cannot be at least minimally interpreted by a self, and interpreted in a variety of different ways – albeit none of them absolute, adequate or exhaustive. The other is not so traumatically estranging as to hold me hostage. Nor is it so miserably abject as to make me imperious. In ethical relation, I am neither master nor slave. I am a self before another self – brother, sister, neighbour, citizen, stranger, widow, orphan: another self who seeks to be loved as it loves itself. Which does not, I insist, mean regression to some Hegelian dialectic of self-doubling. Nor to the Husserlian model of appresentation which reduces the other to an alter ego (i.e. me over there).[40]

For critical hermeneutics, the self–other relation resists the *égoisme-à-deux* of mutual admiration societies. Instead it reveals a practice of ethical 'conscience' which is the other inscribed within me as an uncontainable call from beyond. And it is precisely this summons of conscience which breaks the closed circle of the ego–cogito and reminds us of our debts to others. Here the very ipseity of the self expresses itself, paradoxically and marvellously, as openness to otherness. Real hospitality.

By refusing to treat the other as so exterior or estranged that it becomes utterly alien, hermeneutics not only alters the ego into a self-as-another but guarantees that the other, for its part, retains a basic fluidity and equivocity. The other is neither too close nor too far, neither too familiar nor too foreign, to escape my attention. By thus ensuring that the other does not collapse into sameness or exile itself into some inaccessible alterity, hermeneutics *keeps in contact with* the other. Indeed I would argue that it is because of this ethical contact, always striving to make the other that little less alien, that we can tender (however provisionally) different interpretations of this or that other. And it is ultimately, I believe, in tune with such discernments that we may offer some tentative judgements about what *kinds* of others we have before us.

*

What our three readings – deconstructive, psychoanalytic and hermeneutic – teach us is, I submit, that moral critique should not be pushed to moralistic extremes. Each serves to remind us that judgement is, de facto, informed by an unavoidable conflict of interpretations. We need to acknowledge, then, that if ethical critique is an indispensable component in the discernment of others and aliens, it is never above the hermeneutic imperative of a plurality of interpretations – an imperative invoked by thinkers as diverse as Derrida, Kristeva and Ricoeur. The vigilance of justice demands no less. An ethics of otherness is not a matter of black and white, but of grey and grey. This is no call for relativism. On the contrary, it is an invitation to judge more judiciously so that we may, wherever possible, judge more justly.

4

EVIL, MONSTROSITY
AND THE SUBLIME

One of the oldest conundrums of human thought is *unde malum?* Where does evil come from? What are the origins of evil – human, natural, supernatural? And what, by implication, is the character and content of evil – sin, suffering, catastrophe, death? I open this chapter with a brief history of evil from early myths to the modern theories of Leibniz and Kant, before proceeding in the second part to a critical discussion of the postmodern notion of the monstrous sublime. I will conclude with an outline of some 'ethical' responses to the enigma of evil in terms of narrative understanding and action.

A genealogy of evil

The human mind has endeavoured to think the unthinkable experience of evil in a variety of ways. Confining ourselves here to the history of Western discursive genres, we find four main categories at work: *mythological, scriptural, metaphysical* and *anthropological.*

Mythological

The first discursive genre – myth – allows for the incorporation of evil into 'great narratives of origin' (Mircea Eliade). These genealogical narratives, epitomized by ancient Greek myths, for example, seek to explain the origin of evil in terms of the genesis of the cosmos – cosmogeny. They offer a 'plot' which configures the monstrosity of evil, explaining the source of the obscene and thereby taking some of the shock out of it. Such mythic spectacles make the unbearable somehow bearable, the outrageous accessible. As Aristotle noted in his *Poetics*, Book III, paragraph 4–iv, 3: 'There is the enjoyment people always get from representations . . . we enjoy looking at accurate like- nesses of things which are themselves painful to see, such as obscene beasts and corpses' . In mythological dramas, considerations of moral choice are inextricably linked to cosmological cycles of fate and destiny. Evil is basically *alienation* – something predetermined by forces beyond us. And since evil is not of our own doing, many myths seek to account for it in terms of the sacrifice of some scapegoat. Such ritual oblation, as noted in our opening chapters, is considered necessary to propitiate the gods and restore a sense of unity to the stricken community.[1]

Scriptural

The second discursive genre – the *scriptural* or *biblical* – differentiates between evil as suffering and evil as wrongdoing. While lament protests against evil that befalls us, blame locates evil within a moral agent. The former relates to something passively endured, the latter to something actively committed. Or as Paul Ricoeur puts it, if lament sees us as victims, blame makes culprits of us.[2] The fact is, of course, that these twin categories are almost always intertwined in biblical accounts: in Genesis the serpent symbolizes an *external* focus of seduction but the Fall signals Adam's own sense of *inner* culpability. Adam feels guilty for committing a forbidden act while simultaneously experiencing invasion by an overwhelming force from without. But in both instances, explanation in terms of cosmology is replaced by a genre of deliberative questioning. In biblical discourse, humans ask questions of the divine; and frequently answer back. There is a sense in which the creature described in Scripture, unlike the mere mortal of ancient myth, is a subject *of* evil in addition to being subject *to* evil.

The biblical genre of lament and blame proceeds towards *wisdom*, to the extent that the Scriptures not only recount the origins of evil but also seek to justify why such is the case for each one of us. In short, while myth recounts and lament protests, wisdom argues and deliberates.[3] It seeks to address the question not only of *why* but *why me?* The scriptural genre of wisdom literature turns lament into a question of legitimacy and justice. It tries to make moral sense of the monstrous. An example here is the Book of Job, where God and man engage in dialogue about the nature of creation and covenant. With such wisdom literature, the enigma of evil becomes less a matter of cosmological givenness, as in myth, than of interpersonal relations (human–human or human–divine). In the conclusion to Job, arguments about retribution and fairness are ultimately turned to contemplative wisdom: Job learns to love Yahweh 'for nought' in defiance of Satan's wager at the outset of the story.

Metaphysical

Wisdom discourse gives way to 'speculative' discourse with the emergence of our third discursive genre – namely, *metaphysical* theology. Augustine is one of the most articulate advocates of this position in his answer to the gnostics. In order to show that evil is not a substance implanted in the universe but a punishment (*poena*) for human sin (*peccatum*), Augustine invents a new category, 'nothingness' (*nihil*). Evil is now construed as a deficiency in being which amounts to a privation of goodness (*privatio boni*). If there is evil in the world, therefore, it can only be the result of human action – that is, an act of turning away from the good being of God towards a lack of being. Augustine thus proposes a radically *moral* vision of evil that replaces the genealogical question *Unde malum?* with the question of wilful human wrongdoing, *Unde malum faciamus?* The cause of evil is not to be found in cosmogeny but in some form of willed action – the sins of the 'bad will'. This more existential account leads in turn, of course, to a penal view of history where no one suffers unjustly. Everyone gets his/her reward and all pain is a recompense for sin. Responsibility must be commensurate with accountability.

The difficulty for Augustine and subsequent theology was how to reconcile this extreme hypothesis of moral evil with the need to give sin a 'supra-individual' and generic account in order to explain how suffering is not always justly apportioned as retribution for individual sins. In countless cases it is clearly excessive. In other words, if evil is something we as humans *do*, it is also *done to us*: something we inherit, something already there. Augustine thus sought to reinterpret the Genesis tale of original sin in order to rationalize this apparently irrational paradox: namely, we are responsible but not *entirely* responsible for the evil we commit or endure. 'By conjoining within the concept of a sinful nature the two heterogeneous notions of a biological transmission through generation and an individual imputation of guilt, the notion of original sin appears as a quasi-concept . . .'[4] In this account, which held considerable sway throughout the middle ages, sin is both a collective inheritance and an individual act.

It was not a huge step from such Augustinian speculations on original sin to full-scale *theodicy*. Leibniz offers one of the most explicit formulations of this approach when he invokes the principle of Sufficient Reason to explain the judicious balancing of good with evil in the 'best of all possible worlds'. This balancing act of punition and compensation, attributed to the infinite mind of God by Leibniz, is dialectically historicized by Hegel and the German Idealists. Hegel's 'cunning of reason' silences the scandal of suffering by subsuming the tragic into a triumphant logic where all that is real is rational. Here the hubris of systematic speculation reaches its untenable conclusion. 'The more the system flourishes, the more its victims are marginalized. The success of the system is its failure. Suffering, as what is expressed by the voices of lamentation, is what the system excludes'.[5] The explanations of speculative reason are utterly insensitive to the particular agony of evil. They ignore the horror suffered. Or as William Desmond succinctly observes, the Hegelian system does not weep.[6]

In this respect, Hegelian theodicy might be said to mark the extreme not only of speculative rationalism, promoted by the Enlightenment, but also of a certain mystical theology dear to a number of romantics. The latter deemed questions of good and evil to be the lower concerns of a radically transcendent Godhead who resides *beyond* both – and by implication well beyond our finite human understanding. A particular version of romantic mystical theodicy thus emerges which subordinates individuals to the providential will of a deity who knows better than we ever can why evil is visited on our unsuspecting world. Since God is really a super-essential transcendence beyond the opposites of good and evil, it is impossible to attribute *anything* to him – even goodness, wisdom or eternity – in any proper sense. Indeed, the mystical ascent sometimes brings us so far into the nothingness of the *via negativa* that we are struck dumb before the sublimity of the absolute. In this respect German romantics like Hegel or Schelling could be said to draw much of their dialectical mysticism from the long Christian tradition of apophatic theology, going back to the Pseudo-Dionysius.

> My argument [as this later held] now rises from what is below up to the transcendent, and the more it climbs, the more language falters, and when it has passed up and beyond the ascent, it will turn silent completely, since it will finally be at one with him who is indescribable.[7]

Commenting on this apophatic way which goes 'beyond the Good', Derrida offers this curious remark: 'Evil is even more devoid of essence than the Good. Let us draw, if possible, all the implications of this strange axiom'.[8]

Anthropological

No version of theodicy – rationalist or mystical – can, it seems to me, provide a convincing answer to the protest of unjust suffering: *Why me? Why this particular victim?* This protestation rightly continues to echo through the testimonies against evil from Job and Gethsemane to Auschwitz and Hiroshima. It is the agonizing question of Ivan Karamazov – why does this innocent child have to suffer this evil? And it ultimately calls, it would appear, for a more anthropological and ethical account. No brand of theodicy can reasonably resist the debunking of 'rational theology' in part three of Kant's *Critique of Pure Reason*. Indeed the greatness of Kant was to recognize the need to pass from a purely 'theoretical' explanation of evil to a more 'practical' one. This move from speculative explanation, in terms of some metaphysical system, to moral action rooted in human decision, delivers the insight that evil is something which *ought not to be* and needs to be struggled against. By de-alienating evil and making it a matter of contingency rather than necessity (cosmogenic, theological, metaphysical or historical), Kant brought us face to face with human responsibility.

I might add here, however, that if Kant freed us from excessive metaphysical speculation on evil, he also warned against the opposite extreme of drunken irrationalism (what he called *Schwärmerei*). Kant was deeply suspicious of any kind of mystical madness which submits to evil as an alien power that overwhelms us at a whim. This latter view typified not only belief in demonic possession but also the mystical profession of the 'dark side of God' running from the gnostics to Boehme and Schelling – and taken up again by Jung in his *Answer to Job*. By taking the mystique out of evil, Kant removed some of its captivating power. He enabled us to see that evil is not a property of some external demon or deity but a phenomenon deeply bound up with the anthropological condition. With the arrival of Kantian ethics evil ceases to be a matter of abstract metaphysical accounting and becomes instead an affair of human practice and judgement.

But even Kant, it has to be conceded, could not totally ignore the aporetic character of evil. For if he called for a response within the limits of practical human reason, he could never completely deny some residual inscrutability (*Unerforschlichkeit*) in the matter. This he called 'radical evil'. At one point indeed Kant even concedes that there may be 'no conceivable ground from which the moral evil in us could originally have come'.[9] The lament of *Why? Why me? Why my beloved child?* remains as troublingly enigmatic as ever. Victims of evil cannot be silenced with either rational explanation (theodicy) or irrational submission (mysticism). Their stories cry out for other responses capable of addressing both the *alterity* and the *humanity* of evil.

The postmodern sublime

But in addition to the speculative and mystical movements cited above, I would identify a more recent and widespread tendency to remove evil from the realm of a properly human interpretation: what I call a postmodern *teratology of the sublime*. This third movement focuses on the monstrous character of evil, variously associating it with horror, unspeakability, abjection and nothingness.

In this version of the sublime, the upwardly transcendent finds its mirror image in the downwardly monstrous. Both extremes are so marked by the experience of radical alterity that they transgress the limits of representation. For several postmodern authors like Lyotard, Kristeva and Žižek, the two sometimes become virtually *indistinguishable*.[10] By this account, horror is just as 'ineffable' as the vertical transcendence of God (invoked by Levinas and the negative theologians). There is, in short, an apophasis of the monstrous analogous to an apophasis of the divine.

To render these two apophatic extremes interchangeable, as certain postmoderns do, is to revert to a primordial indistinction which, I will argue, negates any ethical notion of the divine as unequivocally good. In 'The Dialectics of Unspeakability', Peter Haidu applies this kind of argument to the limit-case of contemporary evil – the Holocaust. The impossibility of representing the Shoah, he suggests, as well as its designation with a special status of 'exceptionality', bears similarities to the initial stage of the institutionalization of the divine. Such an unspeakable divinity is very close to the notion of the 'holy' which Otto and Eliade relate back to the experience of primordial awe – the experience of the divine as *tremendum et fascinans*. For Haidu, this is unlike anything we inherit as Jews, as Christians, or as atheists. 'The unspeakability of the Event', he goes on to claim, 'enters into a tradition of the ineffability which attends appearances of the divine . . . associated both with the experience of horror and with that of the sublime'. His real anxiety here is with those

> irruptions into human life of the divine as that which is awesome, that which strikes us with terror, inexplicable because of the

unpredictability of its violence as well as the force of that violence. Divinity here might be the name given that violence Walter Benjamin considered constitutive.[11]

This, claims Haidu, is a notion of divinity which pre-exists the moralization of God under the sign of monotheism. It is a concept, he concludes

> that is pre-Judaic, intractable in moral terms, in which divinity bypasses human understanding . . . as an object of profound repugnance. It is a concept of divinity which culture and civilization as we know them, hold at bay, rendering it also 'unspeakable'.[12]

Himmler and his Nazi acolytes endorsed such an ominous apophasis of the monstrous when they spoke of the Holocaust as a sublime and sacred glory that could never be written, spoken or represented (*ein niemals geschriebenes und niemals zu schreibendes Ruhmesblatt unserer Geschichte*). The order to exterminate the Jews, Himmler maintained, partakes of an 'unspeakable sacred order' (*Heiligkeit des Befehls*).[13] According to this perverse claim, the exemption of the Holocaust from the experience of human historicity, and its absolution from all limits of human comprehension and context, make it a 'sacred' event – an absolute secret whose very strangeness and uncanniness (*Unheimlichkeit*) constitute its glorious monstrosity.[14] One shudders before such logic.

Postmodern thinkers like Žižek, Kristeva or Lyotard could not, of course, be further removed, politically, from National Socialism. My point is rather that their versions of the sublime are sometimes such as to leave one *speechless* before the horror of evil. By way of unpacking some unsettling consequences of such speechlessness, let me say a word about each in turn.

Kristeva and the horrific sublime

'The abject is edged with the sublime', writes Kristeva in *Powers of Horror*.[15] Abjection is defined by Kristeva as an experience of the 'abominable real' prior to any sense of identifiable ego or object. As such it signals that borderline experience of something monstrously disturbing which fills us with both repulsion and attraction. This admixture of disgust and ecstasy is typical of our uncanny response to the abject. And our response is uncannily contradictory in this manner precisely because the abject refers to *no-thing*, that is, to an archaic and unnameable non-object that defies language.

The symptom of abjection is described accordingly as 'a language that gives up, a structure within the body, a non-assimilable alien'; or again, 'a monster . . . that the listening devices of the unconscious do not hear'.[16]

Though Kristeva is borrowing largely from Freud and Lacan here, her invocation of the sublime reaches back to a long tradition of usage ranging from Longinus to Burke and Kant. It is probably Kant, however, who exerted the most pervasive influence on our contemporary understanding of the subject. Where the aesthetic of beauty dealt with purposive form and limit, promising a harmonious unity between nature and the human subject, the sublime exposes a counter-aesthetic of denatured limitlessness and form-lessness. As such, the sublime strikes us as something utterly aporetic and anarchic. Kant defines it thus in the *Critique of Judgment*:

> If something arouses in us . . . a feeling of the sublime, then it may indeed appear, in its form, contra-purposive for our power of judgment, incommensurate with our power of exhibition, and, as it were violent to our imagination, and yet we judge it all the more sublime for that.[17]

Kristeva appears to be drawing much from this formative definition when she describes the sublime as 'objectless' – or at best a kind of pseudo-object that dissolves into bottomless (and archaically repressed) memories striking us with a sense of both loss and bedazzlement, of alienation and exaltation.[18] But she goes well beyond Kant when she then proceeds to link this sublime experience of the abject to the experience of that which we are forbidden to experience by the incest taboo: namely, the repressed maternal body. The primordial receptacle of fusion with the indeterminable (m)Other. *Khora*. Pre-being. Death. 'The abject shatters the wall of repression and its judgments', writes Kristeva. It returns the ego to its genesis 'on the abominable limits from which, in order to be, the ego has broken away – it assigns it a source in the non-ego, drive, and death'.[19] That is why abjection is intrinsically related to *perversion* and *transgression*. It repudiates morality and law, enhancing (as its social equivalents) the allure of criminality and corruption. What we witness in the sublime cult of the abject – epitomized for instance in popular culture's fascination with outlaws, serial killers and psychopaths – is the 'crossing over of the dichotomous categories of Pure and Impure, Prohibition and Sin, Morality and Immorality'.[20] Or we might add, without wishing to be moralistic, good and evil. We need only recall here the almost obsessional cults built up around such famous felons as Al Capone, Jack the Ripper, Dracula or Bluebeard; not to mention the more contemporary fascination with cult horror movies like Scream, Hannibal or the Alien monster series.

In the religious domain, as we saw in our opening chapters, the abject takes the form of that which is defiled and needs to be purified. According to Freud and Kristeva, abjection is associated with that moment of originary sacrificial violence integral to all religious foundations. But it remains masked by the laws and liturgies of these religions, only re-emerging in its estranging monstrosity when these same begin to fall apart. The collapse of religion – and the Law of the Father which inscribes it – marks the collapse of the Self/Other as such. And it thereby triggers a return to the primordial fusion and confusion of the abject, prior to the emergence of subject and object. For the abject is really nothing other than the repressed 'lost object' itself – the 'abominable real', the unnameable 'thing' (das Ding) which is the other face of that paradise we lost when we entered the world of egos and others.

We cannot understand social or ethical attitudes to evil unless we grasp the archaic process of abjection and sublimation that lies at the unconscious root of the Law as such. Taking as example the nihilistic 'possessed' of Dostoyevsky's famous novel, Kristeva writes:

> Abjection then wavers between the fading away of all meaning and all humanity, burnt as by the flames of a conflagration, and the ecstasy of an ego that, having lost its Other and its objects, reaches, at the precise moment of this suicide, the height of harmony with the promised land.[21]

Once again, we encounter evil portrayed as a sublime admixture of horror and exuberance. That which is beneath being rises up from its abyssal depths so high, so manic, so excessive and transgressive that it passes beyond being altogether. From non-being (which precedes being qua abyss) to non-being (which exceeds being qua excess). Privatio boni as a manic-depressive dialectic. The very core of modern nihilism.

The danger here is, however, that this approach may render us overly in thrall to the mantic suasions of the unconscious. And in the process, our ethical and political question – what is to be done? – may all too easily become neglected, if not ignored. But I will return to this critical question later in this chapter.

Lyotard and the aesthetic sublime

Lyotard's approach to the sublime is more aesthetic than psychoanalytic. It tackles the enigma head on and also has the advantage of offering an historical perspective which culminates in the celebration of a specifically *postmodern* paradigm. Starting with Burke and Kant, Lyotard's argument goes something like this. The 'sublime' is a category for dealing with experiences which are beyond categories. It is a sort of self-negating name for the experience of an alterity so 'unnameable' that it may be ascribed to either absolute terror or absolute divinity. (Lyotard cites the example of the Hebrew *makom*, which he tells us is 'one of the names given by the Torah to the Lord, the Unnameable'.[22]) As such the sublime tells us nothing about *what* happens but only *that* something happened, that some inexplicable and inconceivable 'event' took place. It has more to do with the *quod* than with the *quid*. The sublime is indeterminate and indeterminable and inspires in us the peculiarly contradictory feelings of 'pleasure and pain, joy and anxiety, exaltation and depression'.[23] In short, the sublime is that mark of the unforeseeable and incommensurable which flouts our rules of reason, and ultimately reduces us to silence – that 'most indeterminate of figures'.[24]

Parting company with the celebrated criteria of 'beauty' – namely harmony, purposiveness, taste and meaning – the one who bears witness to the sublime becomes what Kant and the romantics called a *genius*: the 'involuntary addressee' of some inspiration come to him/her from an 'I know not what'.[25] While nature and the subject were reconciled under the category of beauty, they are radically opposed under the category of the sublime. Thus the latter opens up for Lyotard a specifically postmodern aesthetic to the extent that it explodes the natural unity of the beautiful and frustrates imagination's powers of form and presentation. Nature is deprived of its sense of finality and the subject finds itself thrown back upon itself in a paroxysm of bottom-less disorientation provoking in turn a certain 'painful' pleasure. Under the name of the sublime, comments Lyotard in *Lessons on the Analytic of the Sublime*, 'a denatured aesthetic , or better, an aesthetic of denaturing, breaks the proper order of the natural aesthetic and suspends the function it assumes in the project of unification'.[26] In this light, postmodern art is understood as the event of an unidentifiable subject which endeavours to 'present the fact that the unpresentable exists'.[27] The postmodern artist, by extension, is one who bears witness to the indeterminable, operating at the limit of the imagination's own dissolution, where all one's senses are subverted. Lyotard's postmodern reading of Kant prompts one critic to retort that 'the modern subject, asserted in a postmodernist avant-gardism, is empty'.[28]

But Lyotard does not confine his postmodern reading of the sublime to Kant. He also revisits several other theorists. Citing the claim in Boileau's formative treatise Du Sublime (1674) that the sublime is not that which can be demonstated but a 'marvel which seizes and strikes one', Lyotard cannot resist this specifically avant-gardist top-spin:

> The very imperfections, the distortions of taste, even ugliness, have their share in the shock-effect. Art does not imitate nature, it creates a world apart . . . eine Nebenwelt, one might say, in which the monstrous and the formless have their rights because they can be sublime.[29]

Before such sublimity, the human self finds itself reduced to nothing, exposed to the inhuman feeling of being 'dumb, immobilized, as good as dead'.[30]

And lastly, from Burke's Philosophical Inquiry into the Origin of our Ideas of the Sublime and the Beautiful (1757), Lyotard retrieves the curious association of sublimity with 'terror' – a terror which is in turn linked with the danger of impending destruction. He rehearses the following inventory of examples: 'privation of light, terror of darkness; privation of others, terror of solitude; privation of objects, terror of emptiness; privation of life, terror of death'.[31] And one cannot help adding the most obvious of all privations – the privation of good (privatio boni), terror of evil! What is most terrifying, in short, is that things would cease to be: that events might not be. A prospect that echoes Augustine's equation of evil with radical non-being or nothingness. It is surely no accident, in this regard, that Lyotard cites Burke's religious allusion to the evil 'universe of death' where ends the journey of fallen angels in Milton's Paradise Lost. Though it has to be said that Lyotard fails to sufficiently address the troubling ethical implications of his aesthetic analysis of the sublime.

While the postmodern sublime shares with Burke, Kant and the romantics a sense of ontological dislocation, frustrating our powers to comprehend, there is something different about it. For where romanticism still held to the idea that the rupturing character of the sublime might occasionally be rendered in 'sublime objects' which mitigate some of the terror and offer cathartic compensation (however 'intense' and 'agitated'), the postmodern avant-garde offers no such solace. Today sublime aesthetics prides itself on its sheer incomprehensibility to the public. Postmodern works appear in museums or galleries as 'traces of offensives that bear witness to the . . . privation of the spirit'.[32] The postmodern sublime testifies to an increasingly 'objectless' aesthetic, be it performance art, minimalism, happenings, fluxus, immaterialism or arte povera. In each case we are confronted with a negative dialectic of privation.

Lyotard seems aware of how such an aesthetics of sublime shock can be converted into a cult of the monstrous. He even alludes at one point to the infamous cult of the Führer, presiding like a Messianic demi-god beyond good and evil. 'The aesthetics of the sublime', he concedes, '. . . converted into a politics of myth, was able to come and build its architectures of human "formations" on the Zeppelin Feld in Nuremberg'.[33] Lyotard also acknowledges a certain perverse alliance between the aesthetics of the sublime and the immaterializing tendencies of global capitalism today – tendencies which (a) make 'reality increasingly ungraspable, subject to doubt, unsteady', and (b) replace historical generational experience with short-lived, rupturing information–data.[34] In such a postmodern culture, eclecticism, pastiche and simulation prevail.

But, once again, what Lyotard neglects to protest, in all this, is that the same postmodern cult of the sublime which can degenerate into the inhuman artifices of fascism or capitalist consumerism can also deprive us of any access – imaginative or intellectual – to the reality of evil which concrete human beings, in Auschwitz or elsewhere, actually suffer. Lyotard fails to appreciate, it seems, that in a postmodern society where shock, scandal and outrageousness are themselves perfect fodder for capitalist commodification and media hype, the radical character of avant-gardist art is often co-opted into commercial cults of the sublime; and our sense of the ethical is suspended. What is more, such a co-opted avant-gardism can all too easily slide into a new extremity of 'narcissicism' to the extent that it finds itself cut off from any 'other' external to it in the intersubjective lived world.[35] (We shall return to this objection in our next chapter, 'On Terror'.)

Because Lyotard's postmodern reading of the sublime is almost exclusively aesthetic it aims 'not to supply reality but to invent allusions to (that) which cannot be presented'.[36] And this leaves us, in my view, helpless before the genuinely moral claims of certain historical realities. For example, it is because the terror of the Holocaust has become absolutized, by virtue of its incomparable singularity, that it cannot, for Lyotard, be said or represented. Qua unspeakable trauma, it warrants not a 'talking cure', nor a language of protest, but silence. Such an imperative of silence returns us, in my view, to a postmodern aesthetic of the sublime. Lyotard's post-Holocaust poetics thus ultimately does little more than radicalize Adorno's dictum that after Auschwitz poetry is impossible. His impossible poetics signals an uncompromising avant-garde refractory to referential discourse or communication. What we might call a post-poetics of silence.[37] But, as Levinas once remarked, if we remain silent about the Holocaust, the SS have won.

Finally, let me say that I find it somewhat disquieting that Lyotard can attribute the same model of the sublime to the unspeakable horror of the Holocaust *and* the equally unspeakable alterity of the Hebrew Lord. Citing Kant's famous allusion to the biblical prohibition on images, Lyotard writes:

> The dislocation of the faculties among themselves gives rise to the extreme tension (Kant calls it agitation) that characterizes the pathos of the sublime . . . At the edge of the break, infinity, or the absoluteness of the Idea can be revealed in what Kant calls a negative presentation, or even a non-presentation. He cites the Jewish law banning images as an eminent example of negative presentation: optical pleasure when reduced to near nothingness promotes an infinite contemplation of infinity.

From which he concludes that avant-gardism is thus 'present in germ in the Kantian aesthetic of the sublime'.[38] But any implication of equivalence between the unspeakability of the Most High Lord (*makom*) and the unspeakability of abyssal evil (*privatio boni*) must, I suggest, give room for pause. If the divine becomes sublime to the point of becoming sadism it has, in my view, ceased to be divine.

Žižek and the monstrous sublime

Žižek, for his part, drives the postmodern aesthetic of the sublime further still.[39] There are few equivocations here. Žižek puts his wild cards on the table. Observing that for Kant both the monstrous (*das Ungeheure*) and the suprasensible realm of the good/law belong to the domain of the noumenal, Žižek surmises that they are in essence the *same*. As soon as we come too close to the Law, 'its sublime majesty turns into obscene abhorrent monstrosity'.[40] That which appears as good from our subjective humanist perspective is in reality evil. 'What our finite mind perceives as the sublime majesty of the moral Law is in itself', claims Žižek, 'the monstrosity of a crazy sadistic God'.[41] Which is perhaps one reason why Lacan, Žižek's mentor, was so obsessed with the relation between Kant and de Sade.

Žižek radicalizes Lyotard's reading of Kant, turning implications into assertions. In Kant, he argues, the sublime Law comes to occupy the place of the noumenal God of Exodus. We know *that* the Law is but not *what* it is, for Law somehow withdraws from its various temporal incarnations, leaving us guilty and often terrified.[42] Citing Kant's equation of 'diabolical evil' with the monstrous sublime in the Third Critique, Žižek claims that 'the impossible content of the moral Law as pure form is "diabolical evil"'.[43] In other words, in the highest instance of noumenal experience – contact with the Law – the human subject finds itself obliterated in a sort of Kafkaesque confusion of sublime proportions. For what it encounters here is nothing other than the 'unconscious' of the Good: that is, the monstrous. 'The subject disintegrates, obliterates itself, the moment it comes too close to the impossible Thing whose symbolic stand-in is in the empty Law'.[44] Exposure to the noumenal God leads to madness. For if we were to secure direct access to the thing-in-itself of the noumenal sphere, Žižek contends, 'we would be confronted with the "terrible majesty" of God in his *Ungeheure, horrifying real*'.[45] Here we discover that 'Sade is the truth of Kant', since Kant is compelled to formulate the 'hypothesis of a perverse, diabolical God' and to make 'the ethical Good and Evil *indistinguishable*'.

By this alarming account, the logic of Kant's monstrous sublime follows that of several apocalyptic anti-heroes. One thinks of Milton's Satan declaring: 'Evil be thou my good'.[46] Or of Conrad's Kurtz succumbing to the horror. Or of Melville's Pip in *Moby Dick* who, cast to the bottom of the ocean, spied the demon God:

> Carried down alive to wondrous depths, where strange shapes of the unwarped primal world glided to and fro before his passive eyes . . . Pip saw the multitudinous, God-omnipresent, coral insects, that out of the firmament of waters heaved the colossal orbs. He saw God's foot upon the treadle of the loom, and spoke it; and therefore his shipmates called him mad.
>
> (*Moby Dick*, Modern Library, New York)

Admittedly, Žižek's examples of the monstrous sublime are drawn more from popular consumer culture than from high art or literature, but the point is more or less the same: Sade is the truth of the Kantian sublime in that he explicitly acknowledged the monstrous as a morbid excess which sabotages all universalizing representation and subverts the control of the conscious will. As such, the monstrous signals the eruption of the unpredictable into the economy of the modern self, expressing itself in a series of pathological phenomena which for Žižek are symptomatic of the peculiarly postmodern obsession with the Other as alien. What characterizes postmodernism, he explains in *Enjoy Your Symptom*, is a fascination with

> the Thing, with a foreign body within the social texture, in all its dimensions that range from woman *qua* the unfathomable element that undermines the rule of the 'reality principle' (*Blue Velvet*), through science-fiction monsters (*Alien*) and autistic aliens (*Elephant Man*), up to the paranoiac vision of social totality itself as the ultimate fascinating Thing, a vampire-like spectre which marks even the most idyllic everyday surface with signs of latent corruption.[47]

But I think the figure that best captures Žižek's sense of the postmodern sublime is that of the cyborg: that hybrid creature which epitomizes the way in which the controlling causality of modern humanist technology collapses into its opposite – namely, a post-humanist thing whose very robotic impersonality marks the victory of the death instinct (*thanatos*) over the life instinct (*eros*). It is, in other words:

> precisely because the tools of modernist representation cannot do justice to the 'Thing' created by modernity . . . that the 'postmodern' is the realm of monstrosity, of invading monsters, whether those of fiction (*Alien*, among others) or of political reality (Hitler, Stalin), who enforce the principle of modernity as symptom.[48]

Postmodern monsters thus emerge as self-fulfilling prophecies of modernity. The return of the repressed.

Kant, as high priest of the modern, himself stopped short of the 'abyss of the Monstrous'. He seems to have realized that to suspend the limit separating good and evil would be to embrace a form of amoral nihilism. But Žižek has no such compunctions. Mixing a postmodern cocktail of Lacan, Sade and Hegel, he follows the logic of the monstrous sublime through to its uncompromisingly dark conclusion. What Kant called radical or diabolical evil is just another word, in Žižek's psychoanalytic reading, for the death drive – a drive which embraces the negative horror of the Real. Lacan already made a move beyond the ethics of good and evil; as did Hegel before him when his dialectics of the negative reverted to the 'pagan fascination with a dark God who demands sacrifices'.[49] But Žižek's conclusion is more unblinking in its audacity. Both Hegel and Lacan, he contends, believed it is possible to move

> beyond good and evil, beyond the horizon of . . . constitutive guilt, into drive (which is the Freudian term for the Hegelian 'infinite play of the Idea with itself'). (The) implicit thesis is that diabolical Evil is another name for the Good itself; for the concept 'in itself', the two are indistinguishable; the difference is purely formal, and concerns only the point of view of the perceiving subject.[50]

In sum, the representational and interpretative space of the subject is exploded by the eruption of the death drive, an eruption which recurs with obsessional compulsion in our postmodern imaginary of aliens and monsters – which are in fact no more than figures of that unthematizable thing: the Real itself.

But I find much that is deeply puzzling in this account. As soon as the human subject dissolves into the void of the Monstrous Real are we not condemned to the indifferentiation of pure drive? Do we not thus regress to the mute traumatism of tohu bohu: the condition of the Real before the ethical God spoke the symbolic Word and the world divided into good and evil?[51] By contrast, we might take some courage from the fact that someone like Moses – and there are many such selves before and after him – did not dissolve into a void when he confronted the Real in the burning bush (as Lacan admits). Instead he came before a deity who called his people to an ethical task – the eschatological quest of a promised land, the struggle for justice. So that if Kant can be said to have one foot suspended over the monstrous void, as Žižek insists, he has his other foot firmly planted on the path of ethical justice.

The danger of Žižek's approach, as I see it, is that in spite of its dialectical dexterity it continues to operate a dualist system of death versus life instinct, sublime (incongruity) versus beauty (unity), self-erasing jouissance versus self-centring pleasure, postmodern void versus modern spatialized ego. These are useful distinctions, of course. But if elevated to the rank of ultimates and ultimatums, as tends to happen in Žižek, the risk is that our entire culture becomes little more than a *symptom* of an incurable postmodern pathology. All very arresting but too alarmist.

The trick is rather, I suggest, to explore alternative possibilities of hermeneutic discernment capable of negotiating such distinctions without lapsing into apocalyptic dualism. Such a diacritical hermeneutics would seek to respond to the postmodern obsession with the monstrous – so brilliantly described by Žižek from a sociological and psychoanalytic perspective – while retaining some measure of critical judgement. To do less, I submit, is to abandon the task of ethical praxis. It is to embrace the immobile condition of Wallace Stevens' Snowman who 'nothing himself, beholds, nothing that is there and the nothing that is'.

There must be other ways.

The New Age sublime

Dialectical conflations of the sacred and the monstrous are not, however, the prerogative of a few avant-garde academics. One finds similar evocations of the sublime transgression of good and evil in the neo-Gnostic best-sellers of several New Age authors. This represents what we might call a fourth, more populist approach to the monstrous God. Joseph Campbell, one of the leading theorists of New Age myth and mysticism, epitomizes this conflation of the unknowable deity with the Monstrous. He writes:

> By monster I mean some horrendous presence or apparition that explodes all your standards for harmony, order and ethical conduct . . . That's God in the role of destroyer. Such experiences go past ethical judgements. Ethics is wiped out . . . God is horrific.[52]

The book in which this statement appears, The Power of Myth, was not some occult curiosity but the number one best seller in North America for three years and the basis of a popular TV series, broadcast internationally in the late 1980s and 90s. Its author, Campbell, advanced a typology of mythic archetypes used by Hollywood screen writers from George Lucas (Star Wars) to the Wachowski brothers (The Matrix), both cult blockbusters on a global scale.

Such a return to the mythic indistinction of monstrosity is exacerbated, as noted in our opening study, by the growing obsession of Hollywood and the

Internet with 'aliens' – a high-tech breed of extraterrestrials who confound the boundaries of good and evil, exploiting our fascination with the hysterical sublime and blurring distinctions between Gods and demons.[53] There is much work to be done to formulate new hermeneutic discernments here, however modestly and provisionally.

What is to be done?

The postmodern cult of the sublime is not the only contemporary 'continental' response to the challenge of evil. There is also the critical philosophy of action proposed by hermeneutic thinkers like Ricoeur, Habermas, Taylor and others; and this hermeneutic approach is, I believe, crucial to the whole debate. For if certain kinds of psychoanalytic postmodernism, inspired by Freud's pivotal notion of the 'uncanny' (*das Unheimliche*), make us more attentive to the complex and often interchangeable nature of strangers and selves, sublimity and normality – thereby reminding us of the enduringly enigmatic character of evil – hermeneutics addresses the need for critical practical judgements. It is not enough to be open to radical alterity – though this too is essential to ethics. One must also be careful to discern, in some provisional fashion at least, between good and evil. Without such discernment, it seems nigh impossible to take considered ethical action.

But how might such a hermeneutics of action respond to the aporias of evil encountered above? How might we acknowledge the enigma of evil, laid bare by our detour through Western genres of thought from myth to postmodernity, while addressing the unavoidable question: *what is to be done?* Taking a further hint from Ricoeur's hermeneutic reading, I will propose a threefold approach: (a) practical understanding (*phronesis-praxis*); (b) working-through (*catharsis-Durcharbeitung*); and (c) pardon.

Practical understanding

Practical understanding is the name I give to that limited capacity of the human mind to deliberate about the enigma of evil. I draw here from such varied models as biblical 'wisdom' (discussed above), Aristotle's 'practical wisdom' (*phronesis*), Kant's 'reflective judgement', and Ricoeur's 'narrative understanding'. What these models share is an ability to transfer the aporia of evil from the sphere of theory (*theoria*) – proper to the exact knowledge criteria of logic, science and speculative metaphysics – to the sphere of a more practical art of understanding (*techne/praxis*). This move allows for an approximative grasp of phenomena: what Aristotle calls 'the flexible ruler of the architect'.

Where speculative theory, epitomized by theodicy, explained evil in terms of ultimate causal origins, practical understanding is geared towards a more hermeneutic comprehension of the contingent and singular characteristics of evil – while not abandoning all claim to quasi-universal criteria (that would account for at least a minimally shared sense of evil). Such practical understanding operates on the conviction that evil is something that must be actively *contested*. In that sense, it resists the fatalist archaeologies of evil – mythical and theodical – in favour of a future-oriented praxis. The ultimate response (though by no means solution) offered by practical understanding is to *act against evil*. Instead of acquiescing in the fate of an origin that precedes us, action turns our understanding towards the future in view of a *task* to be accomplished. The moral–political requirement to act does not therefore abandon the legitimate quest for some model (however limited) of reasonable discernment; it in fact solicits it. For how could we *act against* evil if we could not *identify* it, that is, if we could not *in some way* discern between good and evil. In this respect, the genuine struggle against evil presupposes a critical hermeneutics of suspicion. And such hermeneutic understanding fully respects, I believe, Kant's insistence on a practical reason which seeks to somehow think the unthinkable. This kind of understanding is committed to the 'sobriety of a thinking always careful not to transgress the limits of knowledge'.[54]

Our critical understanding of evil may never surpass the provisional nature of Kant's indeterminate ('aesthetic reflective') judgement. But it at least judges; and it does so in a manner alert both to the singular alterity of evil and to its quasi-universal character as grasped by the *sensus communis*. Not exact or adequate judgement, therefore, but a form of judgement for all that. Judgement based on the practical wisdom conveyed by narratives and driven by moral justice. We may say, accordingly, that practical judgement is not only 'phronetic' but 'narrative' in character. Endorsing an ethical role for narrative, Ricoeur wisely conjoins *phronesis* (Aristotle) and *Urteilung* (Kant). While morality often speaks abstractly of the relation between virtue and the pursuit of happiness, it is the task of narrative imagination to propose various fictional figures that comprise so many *thought experiments* which may help us see connections between the ethical aspects of human conduct and fortune/misfortune. Literary and artistic expressions can dramatically illustrate how reversals of fortune result from a specific kind of behaviour, as this is re-enacted by a plot. It is thanks to our familiarity with the particular types of emplotment, inherited from our culture or civilization, that we may come to better relate virtues, or forms of excellence, with happiness or misfortune.[55] These 'lessons' of poetry, as Ricoeur calls them, constitute the 'universals' of which Aristotle spoke, and which we might call approximate or quasi universals since they operate at a lower degree than the abstract universals of purely theoretical thought and logic. We are still speaking here of understanding in the sense that Aristotle gave to *phronesis*. And it is in this sense that we are prepared with Ricoeur to speak of a 'phronetic understanding' where narrative and interpretation have their proper place, in contrast to purely theoretical reason which is the domain of science proper.

Now some might argue against this that the postmodern models of the sublime have put paid to such 'interpretative' endeavours. But I disagree. To take the analogy of sublime art, for example, it seems to me that no matter how avant-gardist the text or work may be – from Warhol's electric chairs to Offilis' Madonna-Dung – none of them is completely *closed* to hermeneutic response. Indeed, just as the ostensible verbal chaos of *Finnegans Wake* only makes sense because we continue to read some sense (however minimal) into it, so too the sublime 'shock' provoked by certain anti-art experiments only achieves its impact because these experiments are reacting against, and therefore still presupposing, the inherited paradigms of 'art'. In short, we can run rings around the hermeneutic circle but we can never escape it entirely. The idea of absolute aesthetic rupture seems to me impossible. Indeed, if we were to put this in Kantian terms, I would suggest that the majority of modern and postmodern works fall somewhere *between* the formal universality of the beautiful and the unspeakable singularity of the sublime.

Relating this back to the sublime shock of evil, we might say that no experience is so utterly alien or alienating that it removes all possibility of human response. This response may be in terms of protest, praxis, imagination, judgement or even 'understanding' (in the phronetic sense noted above); but to rule out such possibilities, however tentative or partial, is, it seems to me, to condemn oneself to the paralysis of total incomprehension and, worse, inaction. Irrationalism is no more appropriate a response to evil than rationalism. And to eliminate the option of just response is to remove the option of responsibility *tout court*. That is why I agree with William Desmond when he argues that the greatness of philosophy is to confront its own limits, and subject its thinking to the challenge of its unmastered others.

The estranging phenomena of evil, monstrosity and the sublime occur at this limit and it is the task of philosophers to attend to this enigma, neither underestimating nor overestimating the power of estrangement. Referring to certain agonizing stories, Desmond makes this argument for testimonial understanding:

> The fact that I have to tell a story to make a philosophical point is relevant to the (ethical) mode of naming the happening of evil. As philosophers, we cannot escape from the truth of the story in its representational particularity into the impersonal universal. The story keeps us mindful of the intimate truth of particularity that the philosophical concept is tempted to subordinate or supersede or forget.[56]

Such a naming response involves both imagining and thinking, while acknowledging that the story can never be replaced by the concept (e.g. in some kind of Hegelian *Aufhebung*). The kind of moral mindfulness needed here is one which tries to remain faithful to the testimony which the story of evil relates. For such testimonial understanding must 'bear in itself the traces of its own origin, the originating story'.[57]

Working-through

If practical understanding addresses the *action* response to evil, it sometimes neglects the *suffering* response. Evil is not just something we *struggle against*. It is also (as noted above) something we *undergo*. Something that 'befalls' us. To ignore this passivity of evil endured is to ignore the extent to which evil strikes us as shockingly strange and disempowering. It is also to understate that irreducible alterity of evil which influential accounts from ancient mythology to postmodernism often overstate. One of the wisest responses to evil is, on this count, to acknowledge its traumatizing effects and work them through (*durcharbeiten*) as best we can. Practical understanding can only redirect us towards action if it has already recognized that some element of alterity almost always attaches to evil, especially when it concerns illness, horror, catastrophe or death. No matter how prepared we are to make sense of evil we are never prepared enough. That is why the 'work of mourning' is so important as a way of not allowing the inhuman nature of suffering to result in a complete 'loss of self' (what Freud called 'melancholia'). Some kind of catharsis is necessary to prevent the slide into fatalism which all too often issues in despair. The critical detachment brought about by cathartic mourning elicits a wisdom which turns *passive lament* into possibilities of *active complaint*. The task is to transform paralysis into protest.[58]

The role played by narrative testimonies is, once again, crucial here; whether it be those of political victims generally or of specific survivors of the Holocaust and other extreme traumas. For such narrative rememberings invite the victim to resist the alienation of evil, that is, to move from a position of mute helplessness to acts of revolt and self-renewal. Some kind of narrative working-through is necessary, it seems to me, for survivors of evil not to feel crippled by guilt (about the death of others and their own survival), or to succumb to the syndrome of the 'expiatory victim'. What the catharsis of mourning narrative allows is the realization that new actions are still possible *in spite of evil suffered*. Narrative catharsis detaches us from the obsessional repetitions of the past and frees us for a less repressed future. For only thus may we escape the disabling cycles of retribution, fate and destiny: cycles which estrange us from our power to act by instilling the view that evil is overpoweringly alien, that is, irresistible.

This is not to say that evil can be magicked away. It can never be cordoned off into some hinterland from which we, finally purged and purified, could remain forever immune. Mourning is not a way of instituting a new sacrificial dialectic of us-versus-them. On the contrary, it is a way of learning to live with the monsters in our midst so that by revisiting and renaming them we might outlive them. If monsters arise when reason sleeps, then cathartic narrative might be seen as a certain kind of reasoning with – in the sense of reckoning with – unjust and unmerited suffering (as in Job). Not that it can ever prove a solution. The evil of suffering can never be explained away by narrative; for that would be to return to the 'rationalization' of theodicy and its dialectical equivalents in latter-day ideologies (think of Koestler's *Darkness at Noon*). At best, narrative serves as a necessary, but not sufficient, condition for ethical resistance to evil.

There are, of course, many *non-narrative* criteria of judgement indispensable for a more complete response. These might be said to include a phenomenology of the face à la Levinas, discourse ethics à la Habermas, existential pragmatics à la Dewey or Sartre, religious intuitionism à la Bergson, procedural reasoning à la Kant and Rawls, or a deconstructive desire for justice à la Derrida and Caputo. To name but some. I do not for a moment deny the importance of these ethical models. All I am claiming for narrative catharsis here is that it offers one way, amongst others, to resist the lure of evil: a lure before which

I believe certain postmodern advocates of the 'hysterical sublime' remain mesmerized. In sum, working through the experience of evil – narratively, practically, cathartically – may enable us to take some of the allure out of evil so that we can begin to distinguish between possible and impossible modes of protest. In this sense, working-through is central to a hermeneutics of action for it helps make evil *resistible*.

Let me cite, in passing, some emblematic cases. If Moses had not compelled the sublime numen of the burning bush to say its name and recite its pledge to history, Moses might have perished on the spot. If Christ had not wrestled for forty days with the demons in the desert, he might not have survived his three posthumous days in hell after he was crucified. If Milarepa, in Buddhist legend, had not confronted his monster and spoken to him face to face, he might never have left his cave. Or to rehearse the example of *Apocalypse Now*, cited in Chapter 2: without the narrative catharsis brought about by Willard's final exchange with the sacrificial monster, Kurtz, he might not have been able to resist evil. It is only by listening patiently and acknowledging the horror for what it is, that Willard can eventually decline Kurtz's offer to replace him, and walk on.

Pardon

Finally, there is the difficult issue of forgiveness. Against the Never of evil, which makes pardon impossible, we are asked to think the 'marvel of a once again' which makes it possible.[59] But the possibility of forgiveness is a marvel precisely because it surpasses the limits of rational calculation and explanation. There is a certain gratuitousness about pardon due to the very fact that the evil it addresses is not part of some dialectical necessity. Pardon is something that makes little sense before we give it but much sense once we do. *Before* it occurs it seems impossible, unpredictable, incalculable in terms of an economy of exchange. There is no science of forgiveness.[60] And this is where phronetic understanding, attentive to the particularity of specific evil events, joins forces with the practice of patient working-through – their joint aim being to ensure that past evils might be prevented from recurring. Such prevention often requires pardon as well as protest in order that the cycles of repetition and revenge give way to future possibilities of non-evil. A good example of Ricoeur's claim that forgiveness gives a future to the past.

Cathartic narration can, I conclude, help to make the impossible task of pardon that bit more possible. That is why amnesty is never amnesia: the past must be recollected, reimagined, rethought and worked-through so that we can identify, *grosso modo*, what it is that we are forgiving. The cult of the 'immemorial' sublime should, I suggest, be challenged (see Chapter 8 below). For if pardon is beyond reason, it is not completely blind. Or to put it in Pascal's terms, pardon has its reasons that reason cannot comprehend. Perhaps only a divinity could forgive indiscriminately. And there may indeed be some crimes that God alone is able to pardon. Even Christ had to ask his Father to forgive his crucifiers: 'Father forgive them for they know not what they do'. As man alone he could not do it. Impossible for us, possible for God.[61] But here ethics approaches the threshold of religious hermeneutics.

For now let me tender this summary hypothesis. By transforming the discourse of sublime disorientation, alienation and victimization into practices of just struggle and forgiveness, might not a hermeneutics of action offer some kind of response (if by no means a solution) to the challenge of evil?

APPENDIX:
DECONSTRUCTION AND THE SUBLIME

Several postmodern thinkers celebrate the transgressive character of the sublime as a catalyst of avant-garde art and thought. This is true, as argued above, of Lyotard and Žižek.[62] And it is also true, on occasion, of the deconstructionists. In *The Truth of Painting*, for instance, Derrida displays great interest in the links between the category of the monstrous and the incommensurable character of the sublime. These links are teased out in section 4 of his work, entitled 'The Colossal', where Derrida revisits Kant's analytic of the sublime in *The Critique of Judgement*. Here he explores Kant's definition of the 'monstrous' (*ungeheuer*) as anything incalculable and incomparable whose size 'defeats the end that forms its concept'. The related notion of the 'colossal' (*kolossalisch*) is understood as 'the mere presentation of a concept which is almost too great for presentation, i.e. borders on the relatively monstrous'. Derrida also notes the basic ambivalence of the monstrous – observed several times above – as a double moment of attraction/recoil. The colossal is sublime in that it signals a superabundant 'excess' *and* a negative implosive 'abyss'. In struggling to apprehend what is uncontainable and unpresentable by our minds, we collapse before the monstrous sublime.

But it is here, curiously, at the very limit of perception, comprehension and imagination, that Derrida appears to recognize a certain demand for *narrative*. 'Does not the distance required for the experience of the sublime', he asks, 'open up perception to the space of narrative?'[63] This opens a door to a possible dialogue, I would suggest, between a deconstructive approach to the sublime and the hermeneutic approach to narrative I am exploring in this work. But Derrida has not, to my knowledge, yet elaborated on what precise kinds of narrative this might entail, nor suggested that deconstructive rupture might need to be supplemented by hermeneutic healing.

*

Without naming it as 'sublime', Derrida's mentor, Levinas, approaches the monstrous in an essay entitled 'There is'. This text may be read as a thinly disguised critique of Heidegger's equation of abyssal Being (Es Gibt) with Nothingness (das Nichts). And, I believe, it has exerted a considerable if neglected influence on deconstructionist thinking about Khora and the sublime. Levinas talks of the 'there is' (il y a) as a 'mute, absolutely indeterminate menace', a noctornal space without exit or response. And it is, he insists, utterly impervious to God. 'Rather than to a God the notion of the *there is* leads us to the absence of God, the absence of any being . . . before the light comes'.[64] Derrida's discussion of the nameless name and *khora* (see Chapter 9 below) sometimes reads as a radicalization of Levinas's notions of atheistic Il y a and theistic *Illéité*, rendering these two poles of sublime experience virtually undecidable. In *On the Name*, for example, Derrida confronts us with the utterly unidentifiable character of alterity, beyond all horizons of human or historical anticipation:

> The other, that is; God and no matter who . . . as soon as every other is wholly other. For the most difficult, indeed the impossible, dwells there: there where the other loses his name or is able to change it in order to become no matter what other.[65]

At this point, I fear that the divine becomes so unrecognizable in its irreducible otherness as to become indistinguishable from anything else. There is simply no way of telling. So in the last analysis, there seems no possibility of discerning between monsters and Messiahs. In the name of pure openness towards the other, deconstruction argues that 'the newcomer may be good or evil'.[66] Indiscriminately. Some commentators, notably Simon Critchley, push this logic to the ropes, suggesting that for deconstruction the border dividing the 'Illeity' of divine transcendence from the 'Il y a' of abyssal immanence disappears altogether. 'Does the impossible experience of the *es spukt*, the spectrality of the messianic', he asks, 'look upwards to a divinity, divine justice, or even the starry heaven that frames the moral law?' Or does it not rather 'look into the radically atheistic transcendence of the il y a, the absence, dis-aster and pure energy of the night that is beyond law?' To put this question another way: is there anything to prevent the face of the other in Levinas from becoming *das Ding* – a source of horror and obsession rather than of love and healing?[67]

I believe such indistinction between God and horror poses a real problem for ethical judgement. For how can we tell the difference between (1) a God of justice, memory and promise and (2) the sheer indifference of the il y a, unless the divine is in *some way* present or quasi-present in its absence, and so able to disclose itself *as* a God of justice, memory and promise? In short, can a deity be narratively recorded and remembered in scriptures, parables and psalms if it is not *somehow* capable of being *seen* (e.g. as a burning bush), *heard* (e.g. as a call to freedom) and *believed* (e.g. as a promise of the kingdom)? If the God of Exodus and Elijah – so dear to Levinas and Derrida – were to remain as anonymous as the il y a of primordial confusion (the *tohu bohu* of Genesis), surely Moses would never have been mobilized to go and free his people from slavery and lead them towards a place of justice? To overemphasize the unspeakable and ultimately 'impossible' character of transcendence may lead, I fear, less to praxis than to paralysis, less towards new tasks of communal emancipation than to a certain bedazzlement before the mystical sublimity of the event itself (as non-event *ici et maintenant sans présence*). In that case, we may be approaching the night in which all gods are black.

Was it not by way of steering us away from such unrelieved indeterminacy and emptiness, that Plotinus responded to the Gnostics: 'It does no good at all to say, "Look to God", unless one also teaches how one is to look'? (*Enneads* II 9, 15). And do the Scriptures not remind us that if the divine is indeed 'hidden' it is also 'merciful'? 'Wonder, not terror, is the keynote in this awareness of a God who lovingly and preveniently encompasses us'.[68]

*

For the most part, Levinas' and Derrida's readings of the eschatological *a-dieu* are highly elliptical and fall short, in my view, of the demands of hermeneutic narrative and judgement. Such readings too rapidly submit to the logic of the 'impossible'. And they are even liable at times to induce a pathos of dis-aster analogous to that provoked by the monstrous sublime. Writing of the 'open circumcised word' in Paul Celan's poetry, Derrida, for example, offers the following intriguing remarks on the complex and often disturbing relation between alterity, monstrosity and the one he calls the 'messianic or eschatological prophet', Elijah. These remarks give one pause. The passage in question reads:

> first of all like a door: open to the stranger, to the other, to the guest, to whomever. To whomever no doubt in the figure of the monstrous creature – and I am passing over here what the figure of Rabbi Loew may recall of the Golem . . . A word open to whomever in the figure as well, perhaps, of some prophet Elijah, of his phantom or double. He can be mistaken, but one must know how to recognize him, for Elijah is also the one to whom hospitality is owed. He may come, as we know, at any moment . . . Here in this very place, in the poem, the monster or Elijah, the host or other who stands before the door . . .[69]

A basic problem with the approach of Levinas and Derrida, as I see it, is that it fails to distinguish adequately between different *kinds* of otherness. (A poetic licence perfectly fitting for poets but somehow ill-befitting philosophers.) By thus neglecting to differentiate adequately the *relative* alterity of other humans and things from the *absolute* alterity of God, and this again from *khora* or *il y a*, such an approach seems to compromise our efforts to acknowledge a radical plurality of otherness.

The 'hyberbolic hypothesis' underestimates, I believe, the legitimate human need for recognition and reciprocity and renders virtually impossible any attempt to develop a critical hermeneutics of narrative imagination and judgement. For Levinas or Derrida, to represent the alterity of the other is a betrayal – a reabsorbtion of its unconditional difference into the Logos. Against this, we offer the wager that it may be possible to honour the 'breach of totality', that is, bear witness to the infinite other within the finite limits of certain reciprocal relations of love and justice. How else, indeed, might one honour Levinas' own call to ethical goodness? Or heed Derrida's injunction to try to *identify* Elijah? 'One must know how to *recognize* him', insists Derrida. Yes. But *how*?

5

ON TERROR

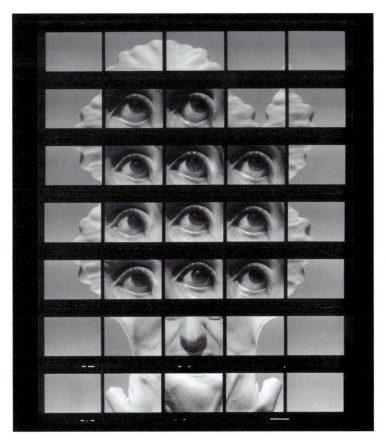

Untitled from the *Contact Sheet Self* series (negative 1980) by Karl Baden, 2001.
From the exhibition *Terrors and Wonders: Monsters in Contemporary Art*, DeCordova Museum
and Sculpture Park, Lincoln, Massachusetts

How can we understand the 'terror' of 11 September 2001 (9/11)? Three days after the event, on 14 September, I visited an exhibition in the DeCordova Museum in Lincoln Massachusetts entitled *Terrors and Wonders: Monsters in Contemporary Art*. Almost one week later again, on 19 September, I gave a graduate seminar in Boston College on a number of tentative philosophical approaches to this limit-experience which for so many split our world into 'before' and 'after'. On 10 October I visited Ground Zero in New York. Combining some reflections that emerged during those days of puzzlement, I will try to suggest here some ways in which we might begin, however provisionally, to address the radical challenge to our understanding posed by 9/11. I make this attempt with Spinoza's maxim in mind: 'Do not complain, do not rejoice, try to understand'.[1]

In the wake of terror

First let me situate the event in the context of some immediate reactions by those who suffered the attack – the Americans – and those who allegedly perpetrated it – Al Qaeda.

The initial response of President Bush was to divide the world into good and evil. In the days immediately following the terror, he declared a 'crusade' against the evil scourge of terrorism. He cited his Second World War predecessor, President Roosevelt, invoking the 'warm courage of unity' that possesses a nation at war. And reaching further back into the history of American warfare, Bush quoted the famous Wild West phrase that the outlaw (Bin Laden) should be brought in 'dead or alive'. There was much use of religious idioms of apocalypse and purgation. The term 'sacrifice' was frequently heard and the military campaign launched against the enemy was initially called 'Campaign Infinite Justice' (later altered, because offensive to Muslims, to 'Enduring Freedom'). War had been declared and everyone, as Bush made plain, had to 'take sides'. For the 'civilized' or the 'barbarians'; for the innocent or the damned; for the courageous or the 'cowards'.

Most mainstream media responded in kind. Images of apocalypse were commonplace. One commentator spoke of the attackers as many-headed beasts whose tentacles were threatening to violate every secure space in the nation. Another invoked the image of a fearsome incubus invading the free world. Idioms of virus, poison, disease and contamination were variously deployed to express the sense of an omnipresent menace – especially when the terror from the air was accompanied by terror in the air: the fear of anthrax, smallpox and other agents of biochemical destruction. Fear filtered through the nation. Yet the flip side of this was a phenomenal upsurge of patriotic fervour evidenced in the proliferation of star-spangled banners and typified in the 24 September cover headline of Time magazine – 'One Nation, Indivisible'. This sentiment was emotively evoked in an anonymous street poem written over a picture of the US Flag which I saw posted to a store window situated right beside Ground Zero in New York. Entitled, 'We Are One', it read:

> We've seen the devastation
> We know what has been done
> And yet we've come together
> To STAND UP AND BE ONE.
>
> We stand behind our Country
> We stand behind our Faith
> And Pray that in our Future
> Our Flag will stand and Wave.

President Bush reinforced this notion of a war between civilization and its enemies when he delivered a broadcast address on 8 November, wrapping with this rousing military summons: 'We wage a war to save civilization itself . . . We have our marching orders. Fellow Americans, let's roll!' (The fact that the final phrase cites the last words of the heroic passenger who took on the terrorists before the fourth hijacked plane crashed in Pennsylvania on 9/11, speaks volumes.)

Al Qaeda responded in even more emphatically apocalyptic terms. The issue was not in doubt – religious war. In messages broadcast on Al-Jazeera satellite television, Bin Laden summoned all Muslims to embrace the ultimate battle between good and evil, demonizing America as the Great Satan and Israel as the Little Satan. He called on the Islamic faithful throughout the world to join a Jihad or holy war (the traditional Islamic counter-term to 'Crusade') and denounced the American campaign against the Taliban as a 'terrorist Christian crusade'. Bin Laden went on to castigate the Pakistan government for 'standing beneath the Christian banner', provoking wide-scale riots in that country and prompting thousands of Pakistani tribesman to cross over the border to join the Taliban. Al Qaeda insisted that any Muslim who supported the US-led military alliance in any way was 'an apostate of Islam'. And one found many propaganda statements replete with references to the US and its allies as monsters, dragons and other demonic beasts who need to be purged from the earth through acts of sacrificial violence, so that the world may be made holy again.

In both these rhetorics – though I am not proposing a moral equivalency here – we witness a disturbing tendency to endorse the dualist thesis that divides the world schismatically into West and East. This echoes the 'Clash of Civilizations' scenario, famously outlined by Samuel Huntington in the summer 1993 issue of *Foreign Affairs*, subsequently developed and republished as a best-selling book in 1996. Here one finds a personification of the West versus Islam dichotomy, making for what Edward Said has called a 'cartoonlike world where Popeye and Bluto bash each other mercilessly, with one always more virtuous pugilist getting the upper hand over his adversary'. Such caricature totally ignores the plurality, complexity and interdependence of each civilization.[2] A crude mythico-religious terminology of pure versus impure takes precedence over a more reasoned discourse about justice and injustice. (It must be said, of course, that in spite of the dualist metaphors, the US government went to considerable lengths after Bush's 'Crusade' gaffe to make clear that this was not a war against Islam. In so doing they were concurring with the wise counsel of intellectuals like Alan Wolfe that 'The more we think that what is at stake is a clash of civilizations, the more like our enemy we become'.)[3]

But to the extent that such rhetorics promulgate the notion of religious war, it has to be admitted that this is religious war with a *difference*. That is to say, it is a postmodern religious war. First, as even Secretary Rumsfeld himself admitted, this would not be just a conventional war fought with tanks and bombs but a cyberwar fought with computers and information flows. In short, it would be a credit war: a war of credit cards, credit transfers and above all credibility in the sense of belief and persuasion. A war of psycho-propaganda (Psy-Ops). 'The uniforms of this conflict will be bankers' pinstripes and programmers' grunge just as assuredly as desert camouflage', said Rumsfeld. 'Even the vocabulary of this war will be different. When we "invade the enemy's territory", we may well be invading his cyberspace. There may not be as many beachheads stormed as opportunities denied.' (Echoes here, curiously, of Jean Baudrillard's thesis that contemporary war is TV war.)

But if the battle was shifting from hardware to software, as it increasingly virtualized and immaterialized the weapons of engagement, it was also shifting from a battle conducted exclusively on foreign territory – like all of American's interstate wars since 1812 – to one also fought *within* US national territory. With the alarming introduction of so-called 'weaponized' anthrax, an almost invisible toxin of corrosion and death, the Pentagon was compelled to 'shuffle its command' (as a front page headline in the *Boston Globe* put it on 27 October). The military spotlight was now on 'home soil'. This division of the battle into 'overseas' and 'domestic' had radical repercussions. Once again, Secretary Rumsfeld had to change gears, appointing a pair of military commanders with additional responsibilities for defending US territory and considering the option of a permanent 'homeland' defence command. Until this point, the US military's defence focus was on guarding the borders and protecting the country from *external* threats. But this response to the unprecedented threat of bioterrorism sparked a nervous debate in Washington over the extent to which the active-duty military should be involved in domestic 'civil defence'.

In short, war against terror was now being fought both inside and outside the national borders. And in the process borderlines themselves were becoming blurred and undecidable. The Minotaur, the horror, evil itself, was now within 'US' – inhaled like imperceptible spores of anthrax into the body politic – as well as 'somewhere out there', in THEM. Moreover, the difficulty of tracking down the culprits in their cellars or caves – due to the continuing elusiveness of the enemy – was further exacerbating the sense of uncanny anxiety. Al Queda was proving to be as invasive as anthrax itself – with hijacked planes sliding into buildings like 'letters into postboxes'. This was a war (in significant part) of disturbingly protean substances: a deadly game of smoke and mirrors. Nightly TV images showed grey fumes still smouldering from the subterranean bowels of Ground Zero (one famous shot even suggesting a demonic visage in the smoke) or rising up from the bombarded front lines of the Taliban. While the mirrors became the Bush–Bin Laden game of satellite images and counter-images, bouncing back and forth across the airwaves. The war of terror had indeed entered the digital realms of cyberspace.

In a curious echo of the choral ode of *Antigone* on uncanniness, the post-modern warrior had found himself trapped in a labyrinthine web: 'with no way out (*aporos*) he comes to nothing'.[4]

Monstrous arts

So how does this sense of uncanny terror relate, if at all, to the *Terrors and Wonders* exhibition featuring different representations of monsters in contemporary art? One of the first things that struck me as I wandered through the corridors of the DeCordova museum in New England was that Bin Laden had many prototypes, stretching back to the very beginning of time and continuing to obsess the human imagination in our own age. Some of these were 'real' and some 'imaginary'.

Real monsters, as several exhibits revealed, were generally regarded as 'freaks of nature' (*lusus naturae*), examples of nature gone wrong, as in congenital mutants, human dwarfs and giants, conjoined twins, hermaphrodites, hydrocephalics, children born with deformities such as two heads or three eyes, and so on. This category of 'real' monsters also included examples of psychically impaired 'madmen'. And in most of these cases, the so-called deviants were wont to provoke sentiments of both revulsion and fascination. For, as Michel Foucault demonstrated in his celebrated example of the Ship of Fools in *Madness and Civilization*, 'civilized' society could confirm its own sense of unitary consensus by virtue of its contemplation of outcasts. Men were men because they were *not* monsters.[5]

Where real monsters were neither proficient nor sufficient, *imaginary* ones were invented. The latter ones, the exhibition suggested, were far more common in that human imagination has a propensity to create hybrid perversions of nature. The most fascinating kind of monster is that which confuses nature's categories by mixing up body parts or crossing human with animal features. (Exhibits at DeCordova included chimeras with lion heads and goat bodies, centaurs with human faces and stag-like torsos, or Frankensteins and Golems constructed with organs from different beings.) Imaginary monsters are also constructed by grotesquely mutating certain human or animal features as in the Cyclops or the many-headed Hydra, King

Restrained by an Imposing Anchor by Aida Laleian, 2000.
From the exhibition *Terrors and Wonders: Monsters in Contemporary Art*, DeCordova Museum and Sculpture Park, Lincoln, Massachusetts

Gate Gargoyle #2 by Megumi Naitoh, 1999–2000.
From the exhibition *Terrors and Wonders: Monsters in Contemporary Art*, DeCordova Museum and Sculpture Park, Lincoln, Massachusetts

Kong or the dinosaurs of Jurassic Park. And, finally, there are monsters that are explicitly unreal and unearthly – namely, aliens and extraterrestrials of various kinds.[6]

What the DeCordova exhibition graphically brought home is that monsters are metaphors of our anxiety. They correspond to our confusion about our genesis – the fact that we derive from autochthonous origins, regardless of how much we have evolved. Our rational consciousness is forever haunted by unconscious demons. Which may explain why most great mythologies invoke some foundational story of a struggle with a monster – Theseus and the Minotaur, Herakles and Hydra, Yahweh and Leviathan, Christ and Satan. But the atavistic demon we disinherit is also the double we never fully leave behind; and as writers, film makers, TV producers, toy manufacturers and cyber designers have all realized – monsters make for good business. Whether it is Godzilla, Dracula, Gremlins or the extraterrestrial Dragons who battle with Ellen Ripley in the *Alien* series, monsters are never far from our screens, both posing (*monstrare*) and transposing our most secret phobias.

But monsters terrify and intrigue for another reason too: they defy borders. Monsters are liminal creatures who can go where we can't go. They can travel with undiplomatic immunity to those undiscovered countries from whose bourne no human travellers – only monsters – return. Transgressing the conventional frontiers separating good from evil, human from inhuman, natural from cultural, monsters scare the hell out of us and remind us that we don't know who we are. They bring us to no man's land and fill us with fear and trembling. In that sense we may say that monsters are our *Others* par excellence. Without them we know not what we are. With them we are not what we know.

*

This was always the case in fact: from the stag-men of Paleolithic cave drawings to the satyrs and devils of classical and medieval art (see Chapter 1), right down to the grotesque phantasmagorias of a painter like Hieronymus Bosch in the sixteenth century. But with the Enlightenment attempt to banish monsters to the unconscious, to make them completely invisible, it is arguable that the experience of terror took on more prolific proportions. Monsters did not go away. They merely changed their habitation and their name and returned with a vengeance. The Shadow struck back.

The main difference now, however, was that images of monstrosity tended to gravitate around a human rather than a supra- or infra-human mind.

A modern sentiment powerfully depicted in Goya's famous etching of 1799, *El sueño de la razón produce monstros.*[7] So, as the Age of Reason progresses we find the gargoyles and griffins of the ancient cathedrals flying off from their parapets and entering the dream works of the human unconscious. Nick Capasso explains:

> With the intellectual illumination of the Enlightenment came shadows. The more we understood the world around us, the less we seemed to understand our own selves. Monsters crept into the dark void left by the increasingly questionable notion of an eternal soul. The Romantic writers and artists grasped this notion immediately, and monsters became a favorite metaphor to express new anxieties surrounding the self, and its conjoined twin, the other. Monsters also appeared as the obverse of the now common coin of Reason, and as catalysts for stimulating strong emotions in readers or viewers.[8]

By the twentieth century, it is the imaginary worlds of popular culture, cinema and art that become the privileged abodes of Unreason. One recalls here the cults surrounding figures like Dracula (the seducer fiend), Frankenstein (the mechanical beast) or the Alien Invader (hybrid of within and without). Whether it be gothic, surrealist or postmodern in genre, the monster continues to hold the subconscious in thrall. And for this reason, the monster remains a personification of our repressed Other. It functions as that negative mirror image of ourselves which we project onto a fantasy world. 'Flawed beings, scapegoats, the enemy, the unknown, and the damned must all be willed into being as foils to our own inherent beauty, virtue, integrity, truth.'[9] At times, indeed, monsters can appear even *more* monstrous by dint of their hiding horror beneath a mask of beauty. One thinks of the typical seducer-vampire, or Dr Jekyll, or the lady bombers in the *Battle of Algiers* (dressed literally to kill). Or Bin Laden himself – a handsome man in spite of his death-dealing rhetoric. Released from their preset moulds in ancient religion and cosmic hierarchy, the monsters of modernity take on a heightened sense of unpredictability. In an age of secular Reason, unreason appears all the more disturbing.

We have already noted how the monstrous Other provokes contradictory feelings of anxiety *and* attraction, and this very ambivalence is greatly exacerbated in the growing cult of the sublime which pointedly mocks Enlightenment rationalism (see our discussion of Kant below). Whether we are dealing with hideous blood-sucking vampires or the domesticated creatures of *Shrek* and

Early impressions of New World inhabitants by arriving European colonists. Sixteenth-century prints reproduced in *Le Théâtre du Nouveau Monde*, Gallimard, Paris

Monsters Inc., there can be little doubt that human beings remain utterly fascinated, as much as appalled, by hybridized creatures which flout the distinction between human and non-human. Indeed, a thinker like Lévi-Strauss will argue that myths of monsters are tokens of a universal primordial mind (*pensée sauvage*) which exists in the unconscious of each one of us – myths whose purpose it is to resolve at the level of symbolic expression contradictions which remain insoluble at the level of everyday empirical reality.

Gods and monsters

The hunger for horror stories did not abate in the wake of 9/11. It actually increased. The main reason for this, I suspect, is that the terror of the Twin Towers was *so* terrible that surrogates were needed to put some kind of mask on it. Analogous or alternative horrors were desperately sought in the guise of images or stories that might take some of the harm out of the *actual* horror. Fictionalized terror could be experienced vicariously, thereby giving us a certain distance from the real. As if the narrative framing of horror, that Hollywood horror stories allowed, could afford relief from the unbearable immediacy of the event by putting it into relief. Horror movies as a kind of Gestalt therapy.

Theologian Timothy Beal has remarked on this *renewed* appeal of horror fantasies after the events of 9/11. Noting the extraordinary enthusiasm for revivals of famous monsters on TV and cinema, the author cites the much-hyped reissuing of Universal's 'Classic Monster Collection', revampings of the Dracula story (*Shadow of the Monster, Gods and Monsters*) and such big box-office movies as *Blood and Gold, Thirteen Ghosts, From Hell*, or in a lighter vein, *Monsters Inc.* and *Harry Potter and the Sorcerer's Stone* (with dragons or basilisks in almost every scene). Not to mention *The Lord of the Rings* trilogy with its Golems, Vaids and Orcs. Because monsters are essentially 'undead', notes Beal, they keep coming back. And 9/11 was a stark reminder of this. The more horrific the real world becomes the more people feel the need to re-experience the horrible in unreal worlds. Why? Because the imaginary can furnish access to the heart of darkness which remains intolerable in the flesh. Hence our fascination with monster myths from the great classic sagas of Minotaurs and man-eating whales to the simple magic of children's stories. (Bruno Bettelheim observes, for instance, that the child can sleep peacefully precisely *because* it has exorcized its worst inner fears by projecting them onto the baleful beasts of its bedtime stories. But we will return to this question of 'horror at a distance' in our discussion of Kant below.) What monsters reveal (*monstrare*) to us is nothing less than our craving to put a face on phobia. 'No matter how many times we exorcize them, blow them to bits, or banish them to outer space, they keep coming back for more. Our monsters are always trying to show us something, if we would only pay attention.'[10]

I think Beal is right to point up here a deep human tendency towards psychic transference and scapegoating. It is doubtless true that monsters provide us with images for our otherwise hazy sentiment of incipient doom; and viewed in this light, we can indeed see how Hollywood monster movies serve as vehicles for what Beal calls a ' public rite of exorcism in which our looming sense of unease is projected in the form of a monster and then blown away'. For even if there is some 'collateral damage' before the battle is over, the monster will be defeated in the end and the nation restored to safety. More specifically, in the turbulent wake of 9/11, such monster movies provide 'a sense of closure' – for a time at least.

This last proviso is, I believe, all important. Monsters are more than surrogate traumas. They also reveal the undecidable character of many of our neat divisions and borders. Like those medieval maps where still uncharted territories were marked out with drawings of hideous creatures, accompanied by such caveats as Lenox Globe's *hic sunt dracones* ('here reside dragons'!).[11] And just as our ancestors were cautioned *and* enticed by such admonitions, we today also find our monsters both fascinating and forbidding. When it comes to terrors stalking our unconscious, we still encounter multiple miscreants staking out dark landscapes. In short, the monsters of the past are never really past.

What is most original about Beal's thesis, however, is his exploration of a deep complicity between Gods and monsters. Religion and horror, he argues, have been symbolically allied in many religions. Why? Because both signal a perplexing experience of otherness which is 'awe-ful'. That is to say, a religious experience of radical alterity often appears terrible in its very unfamiliarity. So much so that the idea of the 'Holy' itself (*Das Heilige*) is explicitly linked by thinkers like Rudolf Otto and Mircea Eliade to an experience of wondrous horror – what the medievals called a *mysterium tremendum*. Or to return to examples from horror movies and literature, it is curious to note how films like Jordan's *Interview with a Vampire*, Merhinge's *Shadow of the Vampire* or Herzog's *Nosferatu* deal with heterodox inversions of divinities as demons, proposing the monstrous as a dreadful yet alluring disclosure of otherness. Thus we find that while Mary Shelley's *Frankenstein* (and its many literary and cinematic successors) explores the possibility of God as monster, vampire stories inspired by Bram

121

Stoker's *Dracula* tend to feature reversals of monsters as Gods. That there is interchangeability between Gods and monsters is not new of course. Figures of supernatural strangeness were often identified with the divine, and especially, adds Beal, 'with its more dreadful, maleficent aspects'. Indeed, it can be argued that horror before the monstrous is analogous to certain kinds of mystical experience, especially when they elicit 'a vertigo-like combination of dread and fascination'. Though this is surely giving a new twist to what St John Chrysostom called 'Holy Terror'.

It may be claimed, accordingly, that the popular culture of horror affords an alternative site for religious investigation.[12] And if it is true that New Age revivals of upbeat spirituality have been immensely popular in our time, the preoccupation with monsters – amplified by 9/11 – may be said to represent its downbeat equivalent. As if sweetness and light needed to be counterbalanced by a new focus on the darkness of the divinity. In short, while much New Age religion celebrates harmony, peace and self-questing, preternatural horror emphasizes our experience of 'rupture, fragmentation and insecurity'. Or as Beal explains, if the focus of the spiritual mainstream tends to be 'holistic' and 'cosmic', addressing our need for 'orientation within a meaningfully integrated and interconnected whole', the monsters of contemporary horror, by contrast, frequently recall the more 'chaotic, disorienting, and ungrounding dimensions of religion, envisioning an everyday life that is not without fear and trembling'.[13]

I agree with much of this analysis. But I have some reservations. In particular, I worry about the quasi-equivalency between light and horror. This smacks – to me at least – of the old Gnostic notion of God as a composite of good and evil – a notion which leads all too easily to a relativizing of ethical thinking: i.e. *deep down* we are all rapists, murderers, child molesters, SS torturers, etc. Well, no. Etty Hillesum was not Hitler. Mandelstam was not Stalin. Jesus was not Judas. And even though it is arguable that no human being is entirely innocent, it is important to be able to defend the claim that those slaughtered in Dachau, Rwanda, Srebernice or the Twin Towers were *not* identical with their slaughterers. So, while I fully endorse Beal's efforts to read our fascination with monsters symptomatically in terms of unconscious scapegoating and displacement mechanisms, I have to part company with him when he leans too closely towards Gnostic interpretations of religion as horror. For such interpretations all too often result in theodicy: the justification of evil as part of some overall divine plan. I do not think Beal would want to go down that road, but some of his conclusion are, to say the least, ambiguous. For instance:

'Our monsters open spaces in popular culture for negotiating ultimate questions . . . that resonate with a new and undeniable depth in this time of war and terror . . . Is (evil), as Van Hesling says in *Dracula*, rooted deep in all good?'[14]

In short, while agreeing with pleas for a more tolerant attitude to enemies, I think it is important to stop short of morally equating the terrorist perpetrators of 9/11 with the victims. For no matter how many monsters lurk within our collective unconscious, some people are more innocent than others. And some more guilty. At least some of the time. Monstrous *actions* matter as much as monstrous *fantasies*. And we are responsible for both.

Philosophical responses

In my graduate seminar on 9/11, I discussed two main philosophical arguments. The first was Jean Baudrillard's analysis of the Twin Towers and Terror. The second was Kant's commentary on the relationship between terror and the sublime in *The Critique of Judgment*.

Baudrillard's fatalist thesis

Was it an accident that the terrorists chose the Twin Towers as the primary target of attack? Why did the World Trade Center come to represent the apex of Western global power and wealth? Baudrillard's basic thesis is that the Twin Towers in New York epitomized the postmodern condition of capital. Contrary to the conventional view that the historical movement of capital develops from open competition towards monopoly, the suggestion here is that it actually reaches beyond monopoly into a 'tactical doubling of monopoly'. In short, duopoly is more final and effective than simple monopoly. Or if one prefers, when it comes to the economic culmination of capital and power, unitary systems need to be supplanted by binary systems. This is how Baudrillard argues his case:

> Power is absolute only if it is capable of diffraction into various equivalents, if it knows how to take off so as to put more on. This goes for brands of soap-suds as well as peaceful coexistence. You need two superpowers to keep the universe under control: a single empire would crumble of itself. And the equilibrium of terror alone

can allow a regulated opposition to be established . . . The matrix remains binary. It will never again be a matter of a duel or open competitive struggle, but of couples of simultaneous opposition.[15]

In this scenario, the fact that there are two towers at the NY World Trade Center takes on exemplary significance. This doubling is, Baudrillard insists, quite novel with respect to the modernist architecture of New York city which for decades had produced an urban scape of singular, staggered buildings rivalling each other according to a logic of 'competitive verticality'. The Chase Manhattan competed with the Rockefeller Center which in turn mimetically competed with the Empire State and so on. But the skyline of the pyramidal jungle, with every building trying to outdo the other, completely changed with the construction of the identical Twin Towers. Construing New York in this way as an architectural barometer of the historical evolution of the capitalist system, Baudrillard offers a startling summary of the symbolic function of the Towers. This new post-monopoly architecture, he observes, 'incarnates a system that is no longer competitive, but compatible, and where competition has disappeared for the benefit of the correlations'.[16] He continues his symptomatic reading thus:

> The fact that there are two of them *signifies* the end of all competition, the end of all original reference . . . For the sign to be sure, it has to duplicate itself . . . The two towers of the W.T.C. are the visible sign of the closure of the system in a vertigo of duplication, while the other skyscrapers are each of them the original moment of a (modernist) system constantly transcending itself in a perpetual crisis and self-challenge.[17]

Just as Andy Warhol's replication of faces marked the shift from the modernist avant-garde of innovation and originality to its postmodern parody, so too the replication of the Towers epitomized the move from modernist to postmodernist architecture: the dynamism of historical *evolution* terminating in a certain homeostasis of *involution*. As high as they are, the twinning of the towers spells the end of verticality.

> They ignore the other buildings, they are not of the same race, they no longer challenge them, nor compare themselves to them, they look one into the other as into a mirror and culminate in this prestige of

similitude. What they project is the idea of the model that they are one for the other, and their twin altitude presents no longer any value of transcendence.

In short, the double towers signify that the strategy of models has triumphed over the logic of rivalry and surpassing. And in this respect, it is significant that all reference to the outside world – the surface as façade, face, interior looking out on exterior – is absent, replaced by an intra-contemplating sufficiency of two. Like blind Siamese twins who talk only to themselves. 'There remains only a series closed on the number two, just as if architecture, in the image of the system, proceeded only from an unchangeable genetic code, a definitive model.'[18] The apex of auto-contemplation: 'l'égoisme à deux!'

*

But Baudrillard goes further. In a highly contentious essay, 'The Mind of Terrorism', written after 9/11, he extrapolates some disturbing implications of his doubling argument. The collapse of the Twin Towers was, he now claims, the 'Mother of all events' in that it symbolized the supreme *suicidal* act not just of the terrorists but of Western global capital itself. The image of the imploding Towers, he asserts, marked the self-collapse of the American Empire which had become so omnipotent and omnipresent that the only means of sublating it was for the terrorist virus to attack from within – in this case targeting the very heart of the Nation. The almost unanimous moral condemnation of this act across the globe masks, for Baudrillard, another unavowed but equally strong reaction: a secret 'jubilation in watching this world superpower being destroyed, or rather destroying itself in an act of beatific suicide'.[19]

Baudrillard goes on to make the controversial claim that we are all inhabited by 'a terrorist imagination' unbeknownst to ourselves; and that this was evinced in our fascination with the televised images of the burning towers – as if we were saying, 'they (the terrorists) did it, but we (secretly) wished it'! *Schadenfreude*. Without this tacit complicity, he insists, the event would not have had the resonance it did. And part of the terrorists' own symbolic strategy was that they could rely on this 'unspeakable collusion'.[20]

Baudrillard's reasoning here, as I see it, rests on the somewhat fatalist notion that the greater a power system becomes the more it provokes its own negation; as when a body generates a self-eroding cancer or virus within itself. So that the scene of the self-collapsing World Trade Center becomes the binary mirror image of the suicidal planes. A double self-destruction. Power corresponding to anti-power. Divinity (as in the Gnostic version) corresponding to the demon dark of its own unconscious. 'The West, in the guise of an omnipotent and morally absolute divinity, declares war on itself.'[21] Hence the logic – however shocking – behind the fact that the terrorists had lived banal American lives for several years, boarded typical American airliners in typical American cities, before rounding on the nerve centre of the body politic itself *from the inside*. The evil was shown to have been residing within the system itself. The collapse of the system was fatally predetermined all along.

But an added difficulty I have with Baudrillard's account here is that it seems to actually *justify* the act as an ineluctable counter-move within the binary game of absolute power. As though 9/11 marked the necessary return of the repressed principle of 'singularity' to a homogenous world system that had excluded it.[22] In this scenario, the terrorists become 'double agents' marking the return of the alienated monster within the body politic itself. The dividing line between outside and inside disappears. And this blurring of boundaries finds further confirmation in the viral spread of biochemical agents within the organs of centralized power – the Senate, Congress, Law Courts, media stations, etc. Terrorism, explains Baudrillard, occupies the heart of the culture which combats it, and the 'visible fracture which opposes the underdeveloped and exploited parts of the world to the West secretly realigns itself with the *internal* fracture of the dominant system'.

Now, in my view, Baudrillard simply compounds the error of his fatalist hypothesis when he concludes that while the system can cope with visible adversaries, it is helpless before this inner viral structure – as if the system of domination was secreting the seed of its own dissolution, its own 'anti-dispositif'. Terrorism is thus considered the inevitable 'shock wave' of a dialectical reversal. Having ostensibly banished evil and darkness from its Enlightened Modern Empire, the West is henceforth compelled to suffer the return of the repressed – with a postmodern vengeance. This is why – after three world wars in the twentieth century (including the Cold War) – the enemy has now taken on the phantasmatic guise of a toxin infiltrating the interstitial fissures of power within the system: a guise which the West is unable to counteract having grown oblivious to its genesis and raison d'être. And while Islam is, for Baudrillard, the crystallization of this phantasmal feedback, he insists that the binary conflict between terror and counter-terror is in fact in every one of us. The virus is everywhere. No one escapes. The system, devoid of effective enemies in the external world (the Taliban not counting as anything more than a convenient temporary target), finds itself at war with itself. Hence the emblematic function of the Twin Towers collapsing into themselves in a hail of smoke and ashes. Hence also the reason why suicide became the ultimate weapon of terrorism, as evidenced in Al Qaeda's boast: 'Our men desire to die as much as Americans desire to live'. Baudrillard wraps up his nihilist thesis, finally, by declaring that what is really at stake in all this is *death*. Death not only as it irrupts 'live' onto the TV screen, but as an absolute event of symbolic sacrifice.[23]

*

I personally find much that is fanciful, pretentious and objectionable in Baudrillard's account. It smacks too much of the Fukuyama thesis of the 'end of history' and represents that more cynical strand of postmodern thinking which all too often leads to paralysis and anomie. His conclusion that 'there is no solution' is untenable. But for all that, we may still concede that Baudrillard offers some useful insights. His focus on the Twin Towers as epitome of western capitalism, for instance, may shed some light on the compulsive character of the scenes broadcast across the TV screens of the entire world on 9/11. Far more so than the attack on the Pentagon (the epicentre of US military prestige), the attack on the WTC was perceived as a spectacular attack on the entire Western capitalist world. It had, as Baudrillard rightly surmises, a symbolic sacrificial charge. And that is perhaps the reason why it included such an intense double response – of compassion and complicity – from many non-US nations. The target was not confined to one building or one nation. The feeling of unity experienced by so many in the wake of the attack may actually have been amplified by the duality of the object targeted and the deep ambivalence of the response.

Nor, it could be argued, was it symbolically insignificant that the collapse of the split towers led in turn to an international split between US and THEM, between inside and outside, between what Baudrillard refers to, rather schismatically, as 'Christian' and 'Muslim'. Here we might briefly recall Baudrillard's remark that each power needs another adversarial power in order to procure 'an equilibrium of terror' in some sort of 'regulated opposition'. This is where, in my view, his reasoning regresses back to the Huntington caricature of a world cleft between East and West. A world-view that is also promoted, let us not forget, by Al Qaeda in its Jihad against the infidel West. But I want to ask – against the fatalist binary logics of Baudrillard, Huntington and Al Qaeda – if this *has* to be so. Are there not ways of critically responding to the apocalyptic scenario of splitting? Is it true that the West is irrevocably confined to a blind cul-de-sac of homeostatic capitalism? Or that the East is condemned to a rage of fanatic fundamentalism? Are we *really* so imprisoned in binary systems that no exit from the labyrinthine matrix is conceivable? If such be the case, there is no answer to our question: what is to be done? And that, I submit, is unacceptable.

Kant on sublime terror

Let me defer a more considered response to this issue for now, in order to look briefly at the second text explored in our seminar on 9/11 – namely, Kant's observations on the sublime and its relation to war and terror.

The sublime, for Kant, involves a 'representation of limitlessness'. Unlike the positive pleasure we feel on apprehending the beautiful, the sublime provokes a negative pleasure, combining a certain fascination with a certain repulsion. Moreover, as a contradictory pleasure, it arises only indirectly. 'Being brought about by the feeling of a momentary check to the vital forces followed at once by a discharge all the more powerful', writes Kant, 'it is an emotion that seems to be no sport, but dead earnest in the affairs of the imagination.'[24] As such, the feeling of the sublime is said to 'contravene the ends of our power of judgment'. It is, we are told, 'ill-adapted to our faculty of presentation'. Thus challenging our capacity both to know and to represent, it is even described by Kant as 'an outrage on the imagination': an outrage, moreover, which is 'judged all the more sublime on that account'.[25]

To rephrase this enigmatic account by Kant in the *Critique of Judgment*, we could say that the sublime is that which arises on the ashes of presentation (conceptual or sensible); it exposes itself like a photographic plate by virtue of inversion, its light emerging from its own darkness. With the sublime, the mind is incited to 'abandon sensibility' and admit that there is no adequate presentation for the event in question. But so doing, it acknowledges that it is, paradoxically, on the basis of the 'sensuous presentation' of this very inadequacy that it flares up in the first place. In fact, it is the experience of the annihilation of the external world (what Kant calls nature), and the threat which this poses to us as perceivers, which excites the sublime as an experience of our own subjective interiority. We become most aware of our liberty – and therefore our superiority to nature – at the very moment when nature threatens to humiliate our sensible faculties. We take our distance from the formless menace. We negate the negation, as it were. And the name for this double negation is *freedom*. The sublime, in sum, expresses our freedom from nature. Freed from objective reality we become free for our own subjectivity. Outer pain turns to inner pleasure.

So it seems that it is not any particular object in nature that is sublime. It is something *in us*, made manifest in our response to certain experiences of 'chaos, disorder and desolation' in nature. On the whole, explains Kant accordingly, the sublime reveals nothing final in nature itself, 'but only in the possible *employment* of our intuitions of it in inducing a feeling in our own selves of a finality quite independent of nature'. This is imagination withdrawing from the world into itself. It is the mind returning to its internal, hitherto unsuspected resources. Admittedly, it often projects this feeling of *interior* psychic power in response to adversity onto the *exterior* object which occasions this response in us. For sublimity, Kant repeats, 'does not reside in any of the things of nature, but only in our own mind'.[26]

It is in this specific sense that we might say that the feeling of awe and shock experienced by many who witnessed (largely on TV) the events of 9/11, might be called 'sublime'. This seemingly inappropriate appellation begins to seem less insensitive, however, when we read how Kant relates the sublime to terror and fear in paragraph 28 of the Third Critique. Here Kant identifies the depth of the sublime in terms of our *resistance* to something dreadful. It is, he says, our response to terror that is in fact sublime rather than the terror itself. Citing a series of terrifying events, from volcanoes and vertiginous heights to hurricanes and violence, Kant argues that:

> Provided our own position is secure, their aspect is all the more attractive for its fearfulness; and we readily call these objects sublime, because they raise the forces of the soul above the height of vulgar commonplace, and discover within us a power of resistance of quite another kind, which gives us courage to be able to measure ourselves against the seeming omnipotence of nature.[27]

In other words, it is because our mind discovers unsuspected depths within itself in the face of some immeasurable menace outside of us that we feel 'sublime'. And this very self-discovery presupposes that we have a certain security vis-à-vis the threat itself. As in Greek tragedy when we feel protected by the 'estrangement device' of stage or chorus. Or in horror movies or televised portrayals of violence where the electronic screen itself intervenes between us and destruction. Terror framed is terror defused.

The sublime may be understood, consequently, as an experience in the mode of the imaginary rather than of the real. If we were *literally* confronting terror we would collapse. But the mind which is helpless in nature becomes uncredibly bold once immunized by the vaccine of subjectivity. This is how Kant accounts for the complex dialectic:

> The irresistibility of the might of nature forces upon us the recognition of our physical helplessness as beings of nature, but at the same time reveals a faculty of estimating ourselves as independent of nature, and discovers a pre-eminence above nature that is the foundation of a self-preservation of quite another kind from that which may be assailed and brought into danger by external nature.[28]

This distanciation is, says Kant, what saves us from humiliation in our own person, 'even though as mortal men we have to submit to external violence'.[29] We are dealing with a kind of aesthetic dispassion or audacity before adversity triggered by our ability to somehow transcend the immediate danger – at least *in our minds*. What we call sublime, therefore, is precisely that which 'raises imagination to a presentation of those cases in which the mind can make itself sensible to the appropriate sublimity of the sphere of its own being, even above nature'.[30] And this claim is followed by Kant's all important qualification that 'this estimation of ourselves loses nothing by the fact that we must see ourselves safe in order to feel this soul-stirring delight'.[31]

To sum up this complex analysis, I would say that sublime composure before danger might be thought to stem either (a) from an aesthetic distance (as in fictional or theatrical accounts of terror); or (b) from a certain negation – 'resistance' in both Kant's and Freud's sense – in the very midst of terror. This latter attitude of courageous calm in the midst of horror is, Kant affirms, witnessed in the great soldier who keeps his nerve in spite of all – a fortitude aided and abetted on the battlefield by the regulation of violence by certain martial forms, laws and conventions. One thinks of the lines of flute players and drummers leading the infantry into enemy fire (as in Kubrick's *Barry Lyndon*), falling like skittles without cry or confusion. Smartly uniformed soldiers marching through the valley of death *as if* immune to their imminent destruction – their sublime indifference stemming from an uncanny detachment from the violence all around them as they evince an almost superhuman endurance of suffering. Under such circumstances, says Kant, even war is sublime.

> War itself, provided it is conducted with order and a sacred respect for the rights of civilians, has something sublime about it, and gives nations that carry it on in such a manner a stamp of mind only the more sublime the more numerous the dangers to which they are exposed, and which they are able to meet with fortitude.[32]

By contrast, Kant suggests, peace favours the soft-centred life of beauty. It fosters bourgeois mediocrity. He opines: 'a prolonged peace favors the predominance of a mere commercial spirit, and with it a debasing self-interest, cowardice, and effeminacy, and tends to degrade the character of a nation'.[33]

Political terror today

This Kantian account may be brought into more contemporary focus, I think, if we link it up with Hannah Arendt's analysis of Terror. In 'Ideology and Terror', Arendt identifies the subject of terror as one living in an aesthetic 'mood' of existential and epistemological 'dislocation'. A curious sense of sublime detachment, she notes, often attends this mood in those experiencing war or totalitarian coercion. The 'mood' induced by such Terror involves the following key characteristics: (1) flight from reality; (2) suspension of ordinary judgement and common sense; (3) fascination with the 'positive pain' of sublime self-destruction (Burke's phrase) linked to a yearning for total detachment; (4) a contradictory attitude of attraction and recoil; (5) an aesthetisizing of political reality; and, finally, (6) a conflation of truth and fiction (i.e. ideology). The mood, she insists, remains attached to 'dark, confused, uncertain and obscure' sentiments, provoked by experiences of awe and terror. But it also entails, paradoxically, a wrenching disengagement from our everyday cares and concerns: a curious fact in keeping with Kant's view that the sublime 'calls up a power in us of regarding as small the things we care about: goods, health and life'. This strange and estranging mood is invoked by Arendt in relation to phenomena regarded as 'monstrous, colossal, shapeless and formless', overflowing the given limits of imagination and defying our empirical intuition. Its relevance to the events of 9/11 is evident.

What is most intriguing about Arendt's analysis is that she attributes all of these characteristics to specific forms of *contemporary* politics – in particular, totalitarian and terroristic ideologies. In this way, Arendt gives a more topical spin to the Kantian association between terror and the sublime, anticipated by Burke's maxim that 'terror is in all cases whatsoever, either more openly or latently, the ruling principle of the sublime'.[34] Arendt's recontextualizing of the issue in relation to twentieth-century society gives the whole aesthetic analysis a very different charge. Now the sublime cocktail of 'negative pleasure/positive pain' takes on more disturbing connotations. The mood of disinterest vis-à-vis the everyday, caused by our divorce from the ordinary universe of common sense, shows potential signs of non-democracy. Our standing outside of ourselves can, we now realize, all too easily lead to self-alienation. Our indifference to the everyday preoccupations of concrete human affairs can slip into a certain social and political blindness. There is, in short, a price to pay.

To rephrase this shift in terms of the Kantian contrast between the beautiful and the sublime we could say something like this. If 'beauty is the symbol of morality' (Kant), the sublime is its opposite. For if the category of beauty induces democratic sentiments of universality and *sensus communis* – allied to the 'enlarged thinking' which comes from our capacity to imagine what it is like to be *others* or to engage in concrete moral action – the sublime draws us away from such democratic impulses into an unworldly inwardness. The sublime induces a freedom of indifference which can actually lead to political un-freedom – a sort of complicity with the impersonal administration of our universe by Party, Movement or State. Worst of all, suggests Arendt, the political sublime can destroy the contemporary citizen's capacity for distinguishing between the imaginary and the real.[35] An incapacitation which consorts with that perverse alliance of coercion and collusion which, for Arendt, is the hallmark of ideological terror.

*

The above accounts might, I suspect, shed some light on what was going on in the minds of the terrorists as they planned and executed their act of terror. But they might also, albeit in a very different register, help explain why so many millions of viewers sat transfixed before those TV images of towers collapsing on 9/11. The terror portrayed had, admittedly, nothing of the 'order' or 'respect for civilians' mentioned by Kant in his above description of the sublimity of war. But the manner of its portrayal in the world media could be said to have offered viewers a screen which vividly manifested the terror at the same time as it maintained the spectator at a safe distance. In such wise, television viewers were afforded a double experience of: (a) suffering 'as if' they were *present* to the terror (in modern America's first traumatic experience of alien Terror on its own soil); and (b) detachment by virtue of their real *absence* from the scene itself (as when Bush said to Congress, 'We are a Nation awakened to danger').

One hesitates to call this 'sublime' given the hideous nature of pain and loss involved. But when one considers Kant's insistence on the *negative* character of the experience as well as the repulsion mixed with the fixation, it is not entirely irrelevant. How else explain the compulsive repetitiveness of those incredible, unthinkable images, endlessly played out on TV? Or the addictive response of many viewers? Indeed the endless replication of the scene, together with the verbal repetition of media-speak ('This is *impossible* to describe', 'This is *unreal*', etc.) suggested that what was at issue was not just the transmission of information but an experience of something *too real* to be consumed in anything but an imaginary idiom. In sum, the media experience of 9/11 seems to have been less *cognitive* than *aesthetic*. Its reality was expressed by unreality.

Conclusion

So how does our critical survey of approaches to terror help us make sense of 9/11? The answer is by no means evident. But I will try, in conclusion, to outline a number of possibilities.

First, I believe that such analyses may help us recognize how mainstream media coverage of 9/11 actually covered over as much as it uncovered. As mentioned above, the almost obsessional repetitiveness of the visual and verbal responses of news programmes and talk-shows served to anaesthetize as much as to instruct the public. Indeed I was even reminded at times of Walter Benjamin's observation that a society governed by media images might one day be capable of watching its own destruction with a certain aesthetic frisson. The vicariousness of the television viewing was itself a guarantor of security and even a certain voyeurism. But these disturbing issues are not topics favoured by the mass media. The mass communications networks are reluctant to put themselves under the spotlight. And this disinclination to self-scrutiny is even more pronounced in times of fear. Critically interrogating how the media portray terror may in such circumstances appear inappropriate or, worse, unpatriotic.

The above analyses suggest that we may find more sophisticated and insightful ways of understanding terror in certain works of art or philosophy. Why? Because such disciplines are at an even further (Kant would say transcendental) remove from events than the media and so can sometimes afford us greater possibilities of reflecting upon, and facing up to, the uncanny phenomenon of attraction–recoil which the horrible can evoke. Hence my surmise that a critical analysis of Kant's observations on the 'negative pleasure' felt before the sublimity of war, or of Baudrillard's diagnosis of the doubling strategies of postmodern simulation and capital, might shed some light on the phenomenon of postmodern terror – especially as communicated through the mass media. Philosophical and artistic works are, I believe, capable of furnishing some extra, because indirect, insights into the enigma of horror. For both proffer an *unnatural* perspective on things – by virtue of style, genre and language. And this unnatural perspective is almost invariably absent from the all-too-naturalistic stance of most entertainment and news media which promise to bring us 'live' to the events themselves – with special reporters 'on the ground' dispatching the latest reports from the heat of battle. This is of course an illusion. The media are invariably *mediating* such events. But it is an illusion which hides itself, giving viewers the impression that they are witnessing things in a state of immediate reality (what Kant calls 'nature'). The advantage of art and philosophy is that they are 'critical' discourses (again in Kant's sense) which underscore the character of such illusion. And in so doing they may allow us to understand that every coverage of the unthinkable is always to some extent a cover-up. There is no unmediated presentation of events – however terrible – which does not involve some kind of framing, editing, emplotment, perspective or packaging.

The eye is never innocent; and even less so the eye of the media. That is, I believe, one of the primary truths disclosed by philosophical and artistic reflections on 9/11, and most especially by the exposure of the ways in which we try to show that which cannot, in reality, be shown. Genuine art and philosophy acknowledge the artifices inevitably involved in the portrayal of events. Which does not mean they give up on truth. On the contrary, they often bring it nearer. Certainly nearer than any news and entertainment medium that conceals its own mediating role – presuming to give us direct access to the 'things themselves'.

All this remains at the level of diagnosis, however. We have said nothing yet of the possibilities of prognosis that philosophical or artistic understanding might offer in the face of terror. I do think it is important that we say something about this. For I believe that our hermeneutic of suspicion should be supplemented where possible by a hermeneutic of affirmation. An account of the ineffably sublime character of terror (or the target of terror, capital) is suggestive. But it is not enough. The sublime, as Kant, Baudrillard and Arendt all concede, does not connect us to any kind of universal narrative empathy. Rather it draws us away from what Kant called 'aesthetic reflective judgement' and shatters our *sensus communis*. And if in the process the experience of sublime horror does serve to humiliate the rationalist and narcissistic pretensions of the ego – no bad thing – it still leaves us helpless before the basic question of how to respond ethically to the enigma of terror. As Noam Chomsky pertinently remarked on 9/11:

> The terrorist attacks were major atrocities . . . As to how to react we have a choice. We can express justified horror; we can seek to under-stand what may have led to the crimes, which means making an effort to enter the minds of the likely perpetrators.[36]

The analysis of the sublime does not, in a word, help us to empathize with our fellow humans. This might be best achieved, I would suggest, by returning to the three ways of responding to the monstrous outlined in our preceding chapter – namely, (a) *practical understanding*, (b) *working through* and (c) *pardon*. The greatest of these, and by far the most demanding, is pardon. How do we forgive our enemies? And how do enemies forgive themselves (and us)? Who has the power to forgive? And who the right? Is forgiveness of terror possible? And even if impossible, should we still attempt it? I have no answers to such questions. But I do suspect that the more we understand the evils and causes of terror – in the phronetic, narrative and hermeneutic senses outlined in Chapter 4 – and the more we work through the traumas of such terror, the closer we may get to making impossible pardon that little bit more possible. Pascal was right when he said, to understand is to forgive (*comprendre, c'est pardoner*). But is there anything more difficult?

I would suggest, finally, that it is not insignificant that some of the most insightful responses to 9/11 came from thinkers and artists. In the first category I would cite the reflections of Greisch, Derrida, Said, Chomsky and Beal, some of which are quoted in the previous notes.[37] In the latter category

I would mention the pieces by such writers as Salmon Rushdie, Susan Sontag, Joyce Carol Oates and Ian McEwan. The contribution by McEwan to *The Guardian* a few days after the event is to my mind one of the most cogent testimonies to the power of *narrative understanding*. 'Emotions have their narrative', writes McEwan. 'After the shock we move inevitably to the grief, and the sense that we are doing it more or less together is one tiny scrap of consolation.' To illustrate this, he narrates how many of us moved from the initial amazement and delirium before the visual impact of the televised scenes – 'the first plane disappearing into the side of the tower as cleanly as a posted letter; the couple jumping into the void, hand in hand', etc. – to a more personal, reflective empathy with the inner pain of particular victims. Like that of the San Francisco wife who phoned her sleeping husband from the burning tower to tell him (as he slept through the phone message) that she loved him. McEwan concludes: 'There is only love, and then oblivion. Love was all they had to set against the hatred of their murderers.'

But these testimonies compel us, in turn, to imagine ourselves into those very moments. To ask what we would have done or said had we been there? McEwan adds that if the hijackers themselves had asked this question and identified with the sufferers they could not have carried out their acts.

> It is hard to be cruel once you permit yourself to enter the mind of your victim. Imagining what it is like to be someone other than oneself is at the core of our humanity. It is the essence of compassion, and it is the beginning of morality. The hijackers used fanatical certainty, misplaced religious faith, and dehumanizing hatred to purge themselves of the human instinct for empathy. Among their crimes was a failure of the imagination. As for their victims in the planes and in the towers, in their terror they would not have felt it at the time, but those snatched and anguished assertions of love were their defiance.[38]

Such art breeds understanding.

*

If I began with Spinoza, let me end with Plato. In the *Crito*, Plato has Socrates recount the myth of Theseus and the Minotaur. Acknowledging that the monster of greed and violence has taken possession of the city, Theseus sets

out to slay the Minotaur. But Socrates declines that option. He argues instead
that the Monster is best resisted by the guiding principle: 'do not harm, no
matter what the circumstances'.[39] Socrates prefers to stay on in the city than
to become a murderer of its laws by escaping. Resolving to address the hidden
cause of the Monstrous, rather than simply slay the beast, Socrates confirms
his basic philosophy that it is 'better to suffer than to do wrong'. He says no
to the lure of sacrificial vengeance. He refuses to scapegoat.

Part II

6

HAMLET'S GHOSTS
From Shakespeare to Joyce

This chapter is about ghosts. Ghosts who haunted the unconscious of Shakespeare and, refusing to go away, reappeared as central figures in James Joyce's *Ulysses*. Both texts, I will argue, address the question of *memory*. They show how certain traumatic experiences resurface in 'sublimated' works of literary remembering. In short, my hypothesis is that what cannot be recalled in life, because no mourning is adequate to the sense of loss or rupture, may be either repressed (and repetitively acted out) or retrieved into poetic works. This act of creative return may itself take the form of a narrative of memory: a replay of the theme of memory in the text itself. Such, I will suggest, is the case in both *Hamlet* and *Ulysses*. Moreover, the fact that part of Joyce's novel – the National Library episode – is itself conceived as a literary reprise of Shakespeare's play, adds a further twist to this uncanny doubling of memory. Not surprisingly, we will be encountering many spectres, Doppelgängers and phantoms along the way.

Shakespeare's *Hamlet*

Mourning and memory

There is memory and there is memory.

First, there is so-called 'normal' memory. In cases of pain or loss, this kind of memory, we are told, can be recalled through a process of mourning and maturation. It takes time but it can be worked through.

Second, there is memory that refuses to be so recalled and resists such therapeutic reworking. Instead, it insists on returning to us in the guise of an unconscious repressed – some spectre or monster rearing up from the mists of time. This is what the French call a *revenant*: something that comes back precisely because it has been buried or concealed. The ghost of Hamlet's father, rising from the grave to summon his son, epitomizes this second category – memory that petrifies remembrance. This I call 'traumatic' or 'impossible' memory.[1]

*

The great irony of Shakepeare's *Hamlet* is that it is a play which opens with a ghost who enjoins the protagonist to remember something that cannot be remembered. From the opening scene we find ourselves embroiled in a play about the terrible impossibility – yet inescapability – of memory.

'Remember me', says King Hamlet to his son. Tell my story. Carry my memory, my legacy, my legitimacy, into the next generation, to my people, to my children and grandchildren? And why not? Should not every son remember his father? Especially when he was a glorious King, cut down while still in his prime? Is it not mandatory for any King – and certainly those in Shakespeare plays – to end their days confiding their secret stories to their sons, transferred with their benediction and their birthright? Of course. And was not young Hamlet born for this? To tell his father's story to the people of the union: the union of two nations, Denmark and Norway, sealed with the pearl won by his father in the famous duel with Fortinbras the Elder. (A duel fought, as is recalled by the gravedigger, the *same day* that young Prince Hamlet entered this world.) Was not Prince Hamlet born, then, to carry on his father's history and avenge his murder?

But there's a rub. First, we cannot be sure *who* speaks when the spectre speaks. Hamlet's friend Horatio, a scholar returned from Wittenburg, says 'tis but a fantasy'; or, worse, 'a guilty thing'. At best a ghost, one moment there, one moment gone, there and not there, present and absent, the past as present. And when the sepulchral spirit finally talks, after much coaxing, he claims he is a creature come, not back from heaven (as we would expect for such a noble father), but from *hell*: from 'sulphrous and tormenting flames'. He is indeed a 'questionable shape'.

*

But there's another rub. If we can't be sure *who* the ghost is, neither can we be sure *what* he is trying to say. He bids his son, 'Remember!' Yes. But *what is*

142

he to remember? His father's glories as illustrious monarch, faithful to his people, spouse and son? No. The irony is that the first thing father tells son is *what he cannot tell him*. Recall the actual words spoken in Act I, scene V:

> I am thy father's spirit,
> Doomed for a certain term to walk the night
> And for the days confined to fast in fires
> Till the foul crimes done in my days of nature
> Are burnt and purged away. But that I am forbid
> To tell the secrets of my prison house,
> I could a tale unfold whose lightest word
> Would harrow up thy soul . . .

In other words, the very secret that the father is bidding his son to *remember* is a 'tale' that the father is actually *forbidden* to tell! No wonder the young Prince is going to experience – like most other characters in the play – a crisis of memory.

But there are further problems. King Hamlet proceeds to command his son to prevent the 'royal bed of Denmark' from being 'a couch . . . of damned incest'. Here again the Prince is thrown into disarray, for his father immediately adds: 'do *not* contrive against thy mother aught'. In other words, Hamlet is confronted with another contradictory injunction. First: remember me/ remember me not. Second: intervene/don't intervene. The paralysis of memory is doubled as a paralysis of action.

*

Freud, as we know from his famous reading of the play in the *Interpretation of Dreams*, sees these paradoxes as symptomatic betrayals of Hamlet's Oedipus Complex. Memory is playing tricks because of Hamlet's repressed desire to destroy his father and possess his mother.[2] Lacan goes somewhat further in describing Hamlet's double injunctions as a 'tragedy of desire'.[3] Nicholas Abraham reads the whole crisis of memory as a symptom of the gap left in Hamlet by the untold secrets of those who came before him. What the 'phantom' objectifies, says Abraham, is the cavity carved within our unconscious 'by the concealment of some part of a love object's life'.[4] In an essay entitled 'The Phantom of Hamlet', Abraham adduces the following hypothesis:

The appearance of the Father's ghost at the start of the play objectifies the son's awareness–unawareness. Awareness–unawareness of what? Of his own uneasiness due to a circumstance not to be doubted: the late King must have taken a secret with him to the grave. Does the ghost appear in order to lift the state of unawareness? If that were the case, the ghost's objectification would have no more object than Hamlet's own dubious 'madness of doubt'. A ghost returns to haunt with the intent of lying: its would-be 'revelations' are false by nature.[5]

Abraham concludes that what audiences and critics have generally ignored for over four centuries is that the so-called 'secret' revealed by the ghost – that he has been murdered and so must be avenged – is itself but a subterfuge for another *more secret* secret: 'this one genuine and truthful, but resulting from an infamy which the father, unbeknown to his son, has on his conscience'.[6] Read from a psychoanalytic perspective, Hamlet provokes the *phantom effect* of a repressed generational secret encrypted in the spectre of Hamlet's father. The ghost is a symptom of blocked memory.

In this light, King Hamlet's 'Remember me!' seems to signal a double command: (1) to commemorate the ghost's memory by honouring his summons to avenge; and (2) to recall what 'foul crimes' the ghost-King actually committed in his own youth, if he could only tell them (which alas he is 'forbid'). This self-contradicting summons represents what we might best describe as a *tragedy of narrative memory*. Hamlet has a history to tell but cannot tell it. And he cannot tell it because he is not permitted to remember it.

Rights of memory

Hamlet, by this account, is a story about the simultaneous necessity and impossibility of stories. And without stories, there are no histories. For histories are a matter of narrated memories. Ophelia cannot tell her story until she goes mad (when she tells everything but is no longer herself: 'Here's rosemary for remembrance'). Claudius cannot tell his story, even in the confessional, and so it has to be acted out for him by the play within the play. Gertrude cannot tell her story because she is ignorant of it (she does not know that Claudius killed the King). Polonius and his fellow courtiers – Rosencrantz, Guildenstern, Osric – cannot tell their stories since they contrive only to serve others. But most dramatically, of course, Prince Hamlet cannot tell *his* story for as long as conscience makes a coward of him. Not, that is, until dying of

144

a fatal wound he begs his friend Horatio: 'absent thee from felicity awhile to tell my story'. All of which means that this is a play where no one actually tells their story, no one truly remembers. Until Prince Fortinbras arrives too late on the scene, and announces: 'I have some rights of memory in this kingdom/which now to claim my vantage doth invite me' (Act V, ii).

What exactly these rights of 'memory' are, Shakespeare never tells us. And if he could have told us the play would probably not have survived the first act. In other words, the play is about a cover-up, the concealment of a secret which the hero, Hamlet, is trying to uncover. And the way in which Hamlet seeks to do this is by having his story told after his demise. Only in that way may the disjunction of time, signalled by the anachronistic return of the Ghost, be finally addressed.[7] For the telling of the tale is an attempt to respond to the time being 'out of joint', to bring concordance back into discordance, to 'synthesize the heterogeneous'.[8] But the matter is not simple. The ghost is not about to yield his secret easily. Hamlet will have to pay a tragic price for the recovery of the deeply buried 'crime'.

*

As noted, numerous psychoanalysts over the years – drawn to the play like kittens to a ball of wool – have read between the lines and dared to try to tell the untold tale. For instance, as André Green and Nicholas Abraham would have it, the secret is that King Hamlet has done to King Fortinbras what Claudius does to both Hamlets: poison them to secure the rights of kingship.[9] The 'rights of memory' restored by young Fortinbras in the last act would refer, on this reading, to the final righting of the wrong committed against Fortinbras' own father by Hamlet's father. And in this view, the fact that King Hamlet's 'foul crime' occurred on Hamlet's birthday becomes far from adventitious. It becomes key to the plot, confirmed by the Prince's opening invocation of the 'dram of evil' – that 'vicious mole of nature in (particular men),/as in their birth, wherein they are not guilty,/ since nature cannot choose his origin . . .' (Act I, iv).

The task of remembrance, staged here by Shakespeare, proves more complex then than might at first appear. Indeed, were it less complex one wonders if Shakespeare would have succeeded in turning a standard revenge play into a tragic masterpiece. It's true 'the play's the thing in which (we'll) catch the conscience of the king'. But which king are we speaking of? King Hamlet or King Claudius? Who is the rightful king in this whole sorry history

145

of poison and betrayal? Who truly possesses the legitimate 'rights of memory'? And *who* speaks when the Ghost speaks?

So that we may ask if the real *crisis of memory* – with which the play opens and closes – is not itself a *crisis of legitimacy* which in turn expresses itself as a *crisis of identity*: the famous 'to be or not to be'?

It is because there's no quick solution to these puzzles that *Hamlet* the play survives to this day and Hamlet the prince is the most written about person in Western culture after Jesus and Napoleon.

Joyce's Hamlet

In 1907 Joyce delivered a series of lectures on *Hamlet* in Trieste. Much of the material was to subsequently find its way into the National Library sequence of *Ulysses*, where Joyce has Stephen expound on his theory of Prince Hamlet and his spectral father. Joyce's reading of *Hamlet* is deeply biographical. We have it on Richard Ellmann's authority that Stephen's pronouncements here (unlike many other episodes of the book) may be taken as Joyce's own.

Joyce's basic argument is that *Hamlet* is a literary sublimation of Shakespeare's traumatic incapacity to mourn the death of his only son, Hamnet. Hamnet died in 1596, aged eleven, just four years prior to the production of *Hamlet*; and Shakespeare's own father died just months before he wrote the play. The fact that Hamlet is the common name for both father and son in the play is, for Joyce, the most obvious sign of Shakespeare's personal implication in the drama. *Hamlet* is interpreted by Joyce, accordingly, as a work of impossible mourning expressing itself as a tragedy of impossible memory. It is a play, in other words, about Shakespeare's effort to sublimate his melancholic grief at the death of his own father and his own son. The ghost keeps returning because there is unfinished business between fathers and sons.

Stories and histories

The kernel of Joyce's reading is that Shakespeare identifies not only with Hamlet the son but also with Hamlet the father – and, by implication, the Ghost (whom Shakespeare actually played in several performances in 1601). If the play was completed and staged just months after Shakespeare's father's demise, it would appear evident that the author found himself struggling with the meaning of *fatherhood*: that is, both his relation to his father and his own fatherly relation to his deceased son, Hamnet.

In Joyce's account of this crisis of paternity – delivered by Stephen in the National Library – we find recurring references to 'fatherhood' as a 'mystical estate', a 'necessary evil' and 'a legal fiction' (since, when these authors wrote, no father could ever be certain he was the biological father of his son). This enigma is captured in the query: 'Who is the father of any son that any son should love him or he any son?'[10]

All fatherhood, we are told, is experienced as a 'sundering' with the son. And the son in turn is condemned to conflict: 'The son unborn mars beauty: born, he brings pain, divides affection, increases care. He is male: his growth is his father's decline, his youth his father's enemy'.[11] Whence, for Joyce, the ingenuity of a certain Christian theology which transforms the neurosis of paternity into a suprahistorical fantasy: an 'apostolic succession' where the 'Father was Himself His Own Son'.[12] The Trinity was devised, Stephen tells us, as a strategy to reconcile the primordial conflict between father and son: a conflict dramatically acted out in Hamlet's relationship to his own ghost father and stepfather (Claudius). Shakespeare's play, according to Stephen Dedalus, is one great imaginative effort to convert the pain of paternity into some fictional resolution. Divided between father and son, and no longer knowing his role as a subject in his own right, Shakespeare writes the play of himself in which the 'truth is midway'. 'He is the ghost and the prince. He is all in all.'[13]

Hamlet is thus about Shakespeare's own transition from son to father – 'the boy of act one is the mature man of act five'. Just as *Ulysses* is about Joyce's transition from Stephen to Bloom. This latter transition is, moreover, subtly witnessed in the indirect encounter between the two characters in the Library scene of *Ulysses*. A scene where Joyce, qua author, finds himself 'midway' between the two. (The 'Wandering Rocks' title of this section refers to Ulysses' legendary attempt to chart a middle course between Scylla and Charybdis.) As Declan Kiberd observes:

> In *Ulysses*, Joyce is Stephen at the start and Bloom at the end . . . The Artist, like God in the Trinity, is both father, son and ghost, creator of all including himself (or as Mulligan jokes, 'himself his own father'). The whole trajectory of the book is to bring Stephen, a surrogate for the youthful Joyce, into harmony with Bloom, a version of the mature man, so that in this way Joyce can become his own father.[14]

This is attempted through the mediating role of the ghost – the Spirit of the Trinity or Art – which mediates between father and son. In sum, just as God

147

created the play of Himself where he became (in Stephen's parody of the Sabellian Creed) 'the son consubstantial with the father . . . He who Himself begot, middler the Holy Ghost',[15] so too Shakespeare wrote the play of himself called Hamlet. And Joyce wrote the book of himself called Ulysses.

Both Hamlet and Ulysses may be read, consequently, as attempts to come to terms with the trauma of fatherhood. Both deal with an impossible mourning which could only find an outlet from melancholy in the sublimation of literature. For Shakespeare this trauma was provoked by the double death of his son and father, reworked as the impossible 'remember me' injunction issued by the Ghost to the Prince, and ultimately worked through into the cathartic mourning of the final Act. For Joyce, Ulysses seems to be a revisiting of the trauma occasioned by his estrangement from his own father, John Joyce, after he went into exile, and also by the birth of his own son, Giorgio, in a poorhouse in Trieste under the most miserable of circumstances. (The experience catapulted Joyce into a critical awakening to the nature of the father–son relationship he had avoided all his life.) Moreover, an especially brutal mugging in Rome in 1906, which left Joyce penniless and destitute, recalled an earlier mugging, several years previously in Dublin, when he found himself rescued by a Dublin Jew called Hunter: a father figure who resurfaced as the fictional Leopold Bloom in Ulysses.[16]

Between past and future

Little wonder then to find Joyce claiming that Ulysses is a story about father and son. Or more precisely, a story about a surrogate father, Bloom (mourning his dead son, Rudi) and a surrogate son, Stephen (trying to flee both his feckless father and the memory of his dead mother returning to haunt him: 'agenbite of inwit'). Bloom can no more deny the memory of his deceased son than Stephen can escape his 'mothers of memory'. Both endeavour to obviate the 'nightmare of history' in favour of a mystical trinitarian union between Father and Son through the mediating art of the Holy Ghost. The Library sequence in Ulysses may thus be seen as a replay not only of Hamlet but of a certain theology of biblical atonement. Ulysses opens, let us not forget, with a reference to a 'theological interpretation' of Hamlet as 'the son striving to be atoned with the father'.[17] But the best that Stephen and Bloom can achieve, after their conspicuous failure to commune in the Eccles Street encounter (described as the 'dry rocks of mathematical catechism') is to accept their lot with 'less envy than equanimity'.

Like Hamlet who finally accepts that the 'readiness is all' – embracing death and conceding Fortinbras' 'rights of memory' – so too Bloom and Stephen come to remember what they had forgotten. The midnight chimes of St George's church remind Bloom of his dead son Rudi. (Rudi had died almost eleven years previously having lived for only 'eleven days', echoing the 'eleven years' of Shakespeare's dead son, Hamnet.) The tolling bell summons Bloom to a reconciliation with this impossible memory. For not only did Bloom lose his son on that fatal day, he also lost his intimate relationship with his wife Molly, with whom he has not experienced 'complete' sex since. Bloom gives up the ghost as it were. He foreswears his paralysing jealousies and fantasies. A traveller at rest at last: 'childman weary, manchild in the womb'.[18]

*

For his part, Stephen is finally recalled to his reality as 'eldest surviving son of Simon Dedalus, of no fixed abode'.[19] Abandoning great expectations, which sustained his denial of reality, Stephen too comes to accept the past – the 'ineluctable modality' par excellence. At this point Joyce–Stephen, the struggling lost son, seems to become a father in his own right. His final mood of acquiescence echoes his earlier prediction in the Library discussion on Hamlet: 'in the future, the sister of the past, I may see myself as I sit here now but by reflection from that which I shall be'. His injunction: 'See this. Remember' may be read in this light as a rejoinder to the 'Remember me' of Hamlet's ghost. And a reminder too, as Kiberd puts it, that 'this is a backward glance with much hindsight'. Kiberd explains the temporal anomaly of the Library scene where Stephen announces his theory of Hamlet/Hamnet and crosses paths with Bloom for the first time in the novel:

> Written in 1918, but dealing with a day fourteen years earlier, this section includes lines which predict its future composition, implicitly uniting the young graduate of 1904 with the mature father and artist of 1918 . . . Already Stephen sets himself at an aesthetic distance from events.[20]

Joyce seems to be suggesting that the mid-life transition – between past and future – in his own literary career parallels a similar one in Shakespeare's. Hamlet, as Joyce notes, marks a key moment in Shakespeare's life as a writer. It is the work of a mid-life crisis which enabled the author to die unto himself, leaving behind – as Stephen seeks to do in the Library Scene – the bitter literary rivalries of his contemporaries in order to be reborn as a mature 'tragic' writer. This furnishes a new angle on the son-to-father mutation in that it signals a shift of writing styles within the author's own storytelling career. As Harold Bloom puts it, Hamlet had always been Shakespeare's idea of

> his play, and it seems no accident that the successful revision of Hamlet opened Shakespeare to the great tragedies that followed: Othello, King Lear, Macbeth, Antony and Cleopatra, Coriolanus. There is a savage triumphalism in Hamlet's nature, at least before Act V, and the prince's tragic apotheosis seems to have released a certain triumphalism in Shakespeare the poet-dramatist. Hamlet somehow has gotten it right in the high style of his death, and Shakespeare clearly at last has gotten Hamlet (and Hamlet) right, and has liberated himself into tragedy.[21]

So in answer to Kenneth Burke's query about how a work serves its author, we might say that Hamlet not only helped Shakespeare over his impossible grief for his son and father, but also enabled him to overcome his youthful mimetic rivalry with Marlowe and his other literary and fraternal peers. A similar 'working-through' of mid-life trauma may, likewise, have released Joyce from his obsessional jealousy with his old Irish rivals – Gogarty and Cosgrave who claimed that Nora cuckolded him – liberating him from youthful illusions into literature.

What both Shakespeare and Joyce teach us is that accepting the passage of time – the transition from filiality to paternity – enables 'ghostly' memory to resurface as genuine memory. Thus may emerge a mourned remembering – a work of poetic catharsis.

Questionable ghosts

Shakespeare, like Joyce, was banished from his hometown. 'Banishment from the heart, banishment from home, sounds uninterruptedly', as Stephen says in Ulysses. Shakespeare was betrayed by his wife Ann Hathaway who, according to Stephen's theory, slept with his brothers Richard and Edmund. Just as Bloom was betrayed by Molly who offered her 'adulterous rump' to Blazes Boylan and others, and just as Joyce himself believed he had been betrayed by his wife Nora who had allegedly 'gone with' his old Dublin rival, Vincent

Cosgrove. (Joyce's jealous fantasies in this regard led to a feverish exchange of letters between Joyce and Nora in the summer of 1909, forming the basis of the love triangle in Joyce's play *Exiles*.)[22]

It is undoubtedly on the matter of impossible mourning and the traumatic father–son dyad that Joyce found his most profound complicity with the bard of Stratford. In *Hamlet* we witness the collapse of the Law of the Father, symptomatically expressed in the endless 'repetitions' of murder: Fortinbras the father by Hamlet the father, Hamlet the father by Claudius the stepfather, Polonius the father by Hamlet the prospective son-in-law, Hamlet the son by Claudius the stepfather and Laertes the son. These uncanny repetitions all devolve from the double message of the undecidable ghost, mentioned above. For this is a ghost who *plays at* being the noble father – 'I am thy father's spirit ' – but comes across as *anything but*: namely, a 'guilty thing', 'grizzly' shape, 'perturbed spirit', mere 'fantasy' or 'a creature come from hell' (Act I, v). And if the Prince is traumatized by what he beholds, it is surely because his supposedly virtuous father returns with allusions to 'foul crimes' which have 'doomed him to walk the night', to 'fast in fires' and purge his secret sins in some fiendish 'prison house'. Indeed the Ghost's secrets are so horrendous that were he to disclose them to the Prince (which, as noted above, he is forbidden to do), they would 'harrow up' his soul and 'freeze [his] blood' (Act I, v). But even though the Ghost withholds such secrets, the Prince has seen enough to realize that the 'time is out of joint'. What he beholds is more than he can handle:

> Thou comest in such questionable shape
> That I will speak to thee. I'll call thee Hamlet,
> King, father, royal Dane. O, answer me!
> Let me not burst in ignorance, but tell
> Why (the sepulchre) . . .
> Hath oped his ponderous and marble jaws
> To cast thee up again?

Summoning up his courage, the Prince fires another battery of queries at the vizored spectre before him. His sense of horror is unmistakable. Though he wants to believe this is the spirit of his father, he cannot help construing it as something monstrous.

> What may this mean
> That thou, dead corpse, again in complete steel,
> Revisit thus the glimpses of the moon,

Making night hideous, and we fools of nature
So horridly to shake our disposition
With thoughts beyond the reaches of our souls?
Say, why is this? Wherefore? What shall we do?

(Act I, iv)

But Hamlet receives no answers to his questions. No more than Francisco in the opening act when he commands the Ghost to 'stand and unfold (him)self!' And no more than Horatio when he bids him five times to 'speak'. The Ghost will not speak to anyone but Hamlet; and when he does it is only to tell of secrets that cannot be told, crimes that cannot be revealed, and duties of vengeance that cannot be realized for the very reason that the identity of the Ghost who commands them remains utterly 'questionable' – and profoundly contradictory. The return of the paternal spectre confers not peace but the undeniable persuasion that there is something rotten in the state where he presided. The very question with which the act opens – 'Who goes there?' – remains unanswered as the Ghost departs. And we have little choice but to agree with Horatio when he declares, dumbfounded: 'O day and night, but this is wondrous strange'.

Is it any wonder then that if the king plays at being a king it will take a play to expose him? The play is indeed the thing in which we'll catch the conscience of the king.

Genealogy of father and son

Plays within plays

The father/son hypothesis is further corroborated by a review of Shakespeare's sources. Curiously, this confirmation comes less in terms of what Shakespeare borrowed from his historical material than in what he altered or left out. Though the first chronicler of the Hamlet story was Saxo Grammaticus in his twelfth-century Latin *Danish History*, it was the French retelling by Belleforest in volume five of his *Histoires Tragiques* which Shakespeare read. This version recounts how a certain Danish warrior Horwendil, having killed the King of Norway in a duel, wins the daughter of the King of Denmark, Gerutha, and fathers the child Amleth – meaning 'idiot' or 'tricky fool who fails'.[23] Now what is particularly striking about Shakespeare's reworking of his source is that he not only changes the names of father and son to form the synthetic name,

Hamlet, but he calls his own son, born to him by Ann Hathaway in 1585, Hamnet.

Moreover, the fact that in the original chronicle the father kills the King of Norway, thereby securing the crown of Denmark and the paternity of a royal Prince (Amleth), establishes a telling precedent for the suspicion that the infamous 'mole of nature' or hereditary sin that Hamlet associates with his own birth, may in fact refer to the original regicide (of the King of Norway by King Hamlet) which is hinted at several times in the play; though it is never actually *named*. The strongest hint, noted above, is the reminder that the duel of Hamlet the father with Fortinbras the father was fought on the very day that Hamlet was born – a direct link between the father's killing and the son's birth. And this hint is reinforced by other allusions throughout the play to some primal act of murder involving illicit poisoning. These allusions include: (a) the reference during the graveyard scene of Act V, i to the 'first murder'; (b) the poisoning of Gonzago in the play within the play; (c) the poisoned duelling rapier of the closing act echoing earlier references in the play to the duel between Fortinbras and King Hamlet fought out and refereed by the scheming Polonius some twenty years previously; and, most importantly, (d) the Ghost's own references to the fact that he is condemned for 'foul crimes' committed in his youth.

The legendary regicide which enabled the usurping Horwendil to procure the crown and wed Princess Gerutha in the original history, is nowhere explicitly stated in Shakespeare's play. But it haunts almost every scene like a repressed act returning to plague the actors of the next generation, condemning them in turn to an endless acting out of the primal scene of transgression. Claudius kills King Hamlet with poison (thereby doing to King Hamlet what King Hamlet presumably did to King Fortinbras in the rigged duel thirty years previously). Laertes kills Prince Hamlet with a poisoned sword. Claudius kills Gertrude with a poisoned chalice, admittedly intended for the Prince, and Hamlet kills Claudius with the same poisoned foil with which Laertes had struck him.

The ineluctable repetition of a suppressed memory also finds symptomatic expression in the fact that no one can properly mourn the dead king – Gertrude and Claudius have precipitously thrown off their mourning, and Hamlet himself is too late back from Wittenburg for the funeral which, we are told, was conducted with unseemly haste.

*

Deficit of mourning triggers fits of doubling. This is most obvious in the reiteration of the name, Hamlet, for both father and son, and in the return of the dead King as his own Ghost. But the whole 'double business' is replicated in numerous subplots. Laertes and Hamlet, to take an obvious example, are repeatedly described as mirrors of each other. This is dramatically evinced in the scene by the graveside where Hamlet and Laertes are presented as twin images: 'By the image of my cause I see the portraiture of his', says Hamlet of his *frère ennemi*. Or again, 'the bravery of his grief did put me into a towering passion' (Act V, ii). This mimetic rivalry reaches its apogee in the duel scene when Hamlet announces: 'I'll be your foil Laertes' (meaning both his sword *and* his mirror-self – 'foil' also denotes the silver lining of a mirror).

But the logic of mirroring is also witnessed in the encounter between Hamlet and his mother. Here the prince compares the two kings – Gertrude's respective husbands – as competing images: 'Look thee on this portrait/Now on this . . . This was your husband/This is your husband'. The fact that for Gertrude the two are indistinguishable says it all. The prevailing suspicion is that the Prince, not the Lady, doth protest too much! And that suspicion, perhaps, masks another. Namely, that Hamlet cannot properly mourn his father because of an unconscious wish to have done what Claudius did.

Then there is the famous play within the play which doubles, at the level of theatrical simulation (the poisoning of Gonzago), what Hamlet supposes the secret act of murder to be. Finally, there is the deathly duel of Act V which replicates the duel, invoked in Act I, between Hamlet's father and Fortinbras' father fought on the day of the Prince's birth. Such multiple microscenes of doubling produce in us, the audience, that feeling of the 'uncanny' which Freud famously linked with the return of the repressed.

Double business

Everyone in the play, as René Girard notes, is 'to double business bound'.[24] All are symptoms of an original forgetfulness that has blighted the kingdom. No character escapes the mimetic cycle of compulsive repetition and revenge, covered over with a rhetoric of 'seems' and ceremony. Until, that is, reality is confronted at the end of the play and young Fortinbras enters the scene to reclaim his ' rights of memory' to the kingdom.

This recovery, or rather un-covery, of the original cover-up is already prepared for, as noted, in the graveyard scene where Hamlet, who was unable to properly mourn his own father, comes to mourn his surrogate father, Yorick. A skull is thrown up by the gravediggers – 'like Cain's jawbone, that did the first murder'. But of course, Yorick is a foster father who seems to have managed, through play-acting and humour, to have escaped the mark of Cain, which condemns most other characters in the play to a cycle of fratricide. And in so doing he, the King's jester, proved capable of genuine paternity towards Hamlet – 'here hung those lips that I have kissed/I know not how oft'. Now he can be mourned as a father after the event (nachträglich).

In this grave scene, Hamlet confronts the real. He comes to acknowledge death. And this acceptance of separation and loss amounts to what Lacan and other psychoanalytic readers of the play call 'symbolic castration'. This exposure of the 'real' is symbolized not only in the exhuming of dead skulls – in particular that of Yorick – but in a whole metaphorics of vanity and ashes running through the exchanges between Hamlet and the gravediggers. These include jokes about how such mighty figures as Alexander and Caesar were finally 'turned to clay'; and perhaps most pointedly, Hamlet's command to the skull that it go to the 'Lady's chamber and, tell her, let her paint an inch thick/to this favour she must come'. The graveyard scene teaches Hamlet that no matter how much we cover over our earthly origins we must all undergo the 'fine revolution' which returns us to the 'base uses' of a 'sexton's spade'. Ornamental pomp and make-up count for nought.

But the biggest disclosure of the graveyard scene is that Hamlet was born on the very day his father fought the duel with King Fortinbras thirty years previously. This fact is recalled by the gravedigger since he, coincidentally, became a gravedigger that same day. So, the message seems to be that this gravedigger's uncovering of skulls reminds Hamlet of two forgotten facts of paternity: (a) the crucial role played by his foster father Yorick (whom he now belatedly mourns) and (b) the killing of Fortinbras by his actual father on the day of his birth. So we may reasonably suppose, may we not, that the body the gravedigger committed to the ground on that first day of his employment, coinciding with Hamlet's birthday, was the corpse of King Fortinbras? And may we not surmise, by extension, that it is to the recovery of his father's body that Fortinbras the younger refers in his closing allusion to his 'rights of memory in this kingdom'?

Only by passing through the guts of a beggar can Hamlet come to his own self. By mourning his surrogate father (Yorick), and then embracing his own death in Act V, Hamlet ultimately undergoes – after the passage of much time – the impossible mourning for his ghostly father. This is no doubt what

Nietzsche had in mind when he claimed that the greatness of Hamlet was that he gained an insight into the 'horrible truth'. An insight which set him free.[25]

Such mourning itself coincides, finally, with Fortinbras' claim to realize his own 'rights of memory', which include the rite of commemoration at his father's grave. Some four thousand lines after the ghost of King Hamlet bids his son to 'remember' we find another son remembering his deceased father with cathartic mourning. Fortinbras, Hamlet's princely double, completes the latter's insufficient mourning. And by mourning Hamlet in turn – instead of gloating at his demise – Fortinbras brings an end to the bitter cycle of repetition and revenge.

Beyond melancholy

Hamlet is thus transformed from a revenge tragedy, initially modelled on Kyd's Spanish Tragedy, into a play of tragic memory. It stages the working through of the immemorial until it yields peace. This transformation of melancholy – or what I call 'impossible memory' – into cathartic mourning is powerfully expressed in Hamlet's final acceptance of the sword of mortality. So much so that one has good reason to suspect that if the Ghost were to return in the final act he would be given short shrift by his son. Indeed, were this to happen, the mature and illusionless Prince would, logically, neither hear nor see the spectre. Why? Because his mourning would have been activated. Moreover, I would claim that it is Hamlet's passage from melancholy to mourning which enables him not only to face death but to preserve life – if not his own life then at least that of others after him. This is why Hamlet's parting words to Horatio are so crucial. He begs him to renounce suicide and instead to heal his (Hamlet's) 'wounded name' by living on to serve as his memorialist. 'Absent thee from felicity awhile', pleads the dying Prince, 'to tell my story'.

Conclusion

Against the standard view that Hamlet marks the 'majesty of melancholy', I prefer to read the play as a metamorphosis of melancholy into mourning. On this reading, we may surmise that Shakespeare himself moved beyond melancholy to mourning by writing this 'folio of himself' as a work of narrative art.[26] This hypothesis confirms our reading above of how Joyce wrote Ulysses as a similar mourning for a former self, sublimating his melancholy loss – of his 'mothers of memory' and 'faith and fatherland' – into the hitherto 'uncreated conscience of his race'. The traumatic impact of John Shakespeare's demise on William Shakespeare appears to find a parallel in the trauma of Joyce's mugging in Rome, which triggered the memory of an earlier humiliation in Dublin when the surrogate father, the Dublin Jew called Hunter, came to his rescue. Thus Joyce, like Shakespeare, accepted the loss of illusory ideals and embraced a condition of wise detachment. Joyce called it 'equanimity', Shakespeare 'readiness'.

What furnishes the singular quality of mourning – shared by both Shakespeare and Joyce – is, I believe, the act of transfiguration which turns a paralysed melancholic into a wise subject of action. That Shakespeare himself succeeded, on completing the play in 1601, in transmuting his own double loss – of father (John Shakespeare) and son (Hamnet Shakespeare) – doubtless deepens the poignancy of this drama of mourning. And perhaps it is this very identification of *author* (Shakespeare) with *actor* (Hamlet the son and Hamlet the ghost father) which gives us the *audience* the impression that, in Hazlitt's famous phrase, 'it is we who are Hamlet'.[27] This hermeneutic complicity between author, actor and audience holds the key, I submit, to the legendary power of *Hamlet*.

Oscar Wilde argued that thanks to Hamlet the world had grown sad. But this is a sadness, I would suggest, which, by the end of the play, has worked through the traumatized memory – which unremembered was obsessively repeated as melancholy – towards a catharsis of wisdom. This transition from melancholy to mourning is nowhere more succinctly stated than in Hamlet's 'Let be'. But letting be does not mean silence. Or certainly not straight off. The 'rest is silence', yes. But only *after* the tale is told. For if Horatio had not obeyed Hamlet's dying summons to tell his story, this drama would never have been recounted. If Horatio had not foresworn the sacrificial cycle of suicide and revenge, committing himself instead to the transmission of Hamlet's testimony, this tale of transition from death to rebirth, from melancholy to mourning, would never have graced the stages of the world.

In this sense, we may conclude that *Hamlet* is a story about storytelling. It is a play about saying the unsayable and remembering the immemorial in cursed spite of all. Thanks to it, we can harbour hope that even 'impossible' memory remains susceptible to the possibility of healing.

*

We will revisit the critical connection between melancholy, memory and the immemorial in our next two chapters.

APPENDIX:
FROM MELANCHOLY TO MOURNING
– PSYCHOANALYTIC READINGS

Jacques Lacan declared that 'from one end of the play to the other, all anyone talks about is mourning'.[28] This sentiment is echoed by Harold Bloom when he affirms that what is most universal about Hamlet is the 'quality and graciousness of his mourning'.[29] Bloom claims that the deepest mysteries of Hamlet's character are involved 'in his universal mourning and in his self-cure'.[30] And he sees the most crucial question of the play to be this: 'How ought we to characterize Hamlet's melancholia in the first four acts, and how do we explain his escape from it into a high place in Act V, a place at last entirely his own . . .?'[31] Bloom doesn't answer this question; but he convincingly argues that the legendary fascination of Hamlet revolves around 'mourning as a mode of revisionism', and even upon 'revision itself as a kind of mourning for Shakespeare's own earlier self'.[32] Now, this self-transformation of Shakespeare, who mourns not only his father and son but his own earlier self – he was thirty-six when he wrote the play – is of course acted out in the drama itself in the personage of the player prince who 'revisioning the self replaces the project of revenge'.[33] In other words, 'Hamlet is also Shakespeare's death, his dead son and his dead father. . . . Hamlet is Shakespeare's own consciousness'.[34] This very process of self-revision and self-overcoming is what makes *Hamlet* a play of the 'fiercest inwardness ever achieved in a literary work'.[35]

The danger of such a turn inward, however, is that Shakespeare/Hamlet might lapse into solipsistic melancholy. In that instance, the lost and then idealized object (in this instance Hamlet's over-revered father) might be internalized to the point that he suffers a pathological neurosis. Or to revisit Freud's definition of melancholy, it would be a refusal to let go of the lost object (such letting go being the proper work of mourning). Hamlet's descent into radical interiority is epitomized by the seven soliloquys and especially the most famous of all – 'To be or not to be' – where he rehearses his own prospective suicide. This move to subjective inwardness, in addition to his inability to *love* Ophelia, to *forgive* his mother or to *act* against Claudius, would all suggest symptoms of melancholic paralysis. But the play charts the movement *beyond* the temptation of such self-absorption through a series of epiphanies – the play within the play, the sea change effected by his visit to England, and most importantly the 'symbolic castration' of the graveyard exchange. All these lead to a final embrace of the *real* – the way things are, our mortality and finitude – expressed in the admission that the 'readiness is all'. And if Hamlet's final self-consciousness is still theatrical, it is: 'a different kind of theater, eerily transcendental and sublime, one in which the abyss between playing someone and being someone has been bridged'.[36] So examplary, in fact, is this sublimatory act that it may be taken as a lesson for modernity as a whole. If our Western culture is to overcome its current self-hatred it must become 'only more Hamlet-like'.[37]

Other psychoanalytical readings shed further light, in my view, on Hamlet's crisis of melancholy which is so masterfully analysed by Bloom. I have especially in mind the insights of post-Freudian critics like Lacan, Abraham, Green and Kristeva who speak of the strangeness of the Real and the challenge it poses to conventional notions of the unitary subject. Kristeva's analyses of the power of horror and the sublime (see Chapters 3 and 4 above) are deeply indebted to the Lacanian triad of the imaginary–symbolic–real. But Lacan's own take on the uncanniness of death can be best witnessed, for our purposes, in his intepretation of Hamlet as symptom of the contemporary crisis of desire. Although Lacan does not focus, as Joyce did, on the crisis of narrative provoked by the breakdown of the father–son relation, with its attendant crises of identity and legitimation, he does offer some fascinating observations on the play's obsession with doubles, ghosts and the unmourned dead.

Lacan traces this fit of doubling to a post-religious *lack of lack* – that is, a growing neglect of the Name of the Father out of fear of (symbolic) castration. 'The tragedy of Hamlet is a tragedy of desire', claims Lacan. And he goes on, somewhat sententiously, to offer this reading:

> I know of no commentator who has ever taken the trouble to make this remark,
> however hard it is to overlook once it has been formulated: from one end of *Hamlet*
> to the other, all anyone talks about is mourning.

He cites as prime evidence (a) Hamlet's return to find his father already buried without proper funeral rites and (b) Gertrude's remark that the cause of Hamlet's 'distemper' is 'his father's death and our overhasty marriage'. The entire play, on this reading, revolves around the 'relationship of the drama of desire to mourning'. The recurrence of the ghost is attributed to the insufficiency of mourning (played out again in Hamlet's hiding of Polonius' dead body in the castle thereby preventing a proper funeral rite). And this might explain, furthermore, the intimate link between 'the lack, skipping or refusal of something in the satisfaction of the dead' and 'the appearance of ghosts and spectres in the gap left by the omission of the significant rite'.[38] This insufficiency of mourning is exacerbated by the fact that for Hamlet, as for Oedipus – two dramatic heroes who captivate the imagination of contemporary psychoanalysis – there is an uncanny secret behind the crisis of mourning.

Lacan, and several of his followers, read the play accordingly as a process of successive *detachments* from objects of lure and illusion: what Lacan calls the 'little a objects' that stand in for the missing phallus. This process eventually leads to the moment of truth when Hamlet confronts the 'real' by meeting his own death – the ultimate act of detachment – and so finally succeeds in mourning. It is only with the decline of the Oedipal complex, argues Lacan, that the phallus (as stand-in for the original lost object) can be mourned. It is only when 'Hamlet's hour' finally arrives at the moment of death, that he can act and accept the 'hole in being' – the uncanny abyss of the *Real* anticipated by the empty grave of Act IV. Until then, Hamlet is unable to act, a paralysis most evident in his incapacity to avenge his father by striking at the phallic substitute, Claudius:

> It's a question of the phallus, and that's why he (Hamlet) will never be able to strike
> it, until the moment when he has made the complete sacrifice . . . of all narcissistic
> attachments, i.e., when he is mortally wounded and knows it.[39]

159

In this light, Lacan construes the entire drama as a critique of the power of the phallus – and its 'objets petit a' supplements – to draw agents into imaginary identifications with it to the point of psychotic splitting and doubling: the reign of ghosts. Hamlet's journey through the guts of a beggar is interpreted thus as a passage towards 'symbolic castration' via a progressive disillusionment with the various claims of the illusory fetish-phallus: (a) the Ghost's appeal to a fallacious paternal authority and vengeance; (b) Claudius' link to a 'divinity (that) doth hedge a king' (reinforced by the erotic desire of Gertrude); (c) Ophelia's incarnation of phallic substitution; (d) Laertes' rival phallic passion which represents the 'desire of the other' and sets the phallic signifier in motion.

Only when Hamlet undergoes symbolic castration in the hour of death, finally liberated from the desire of the other and its endless fetishistic signifiers, can Hamlet become his own subject and accept the 'real': namely, the truth that the phallus is 'nothing' and that the 'readiness (to accept this) is all'. Hamlet may well be a melancholic neurotic for most of the play; but when he dies, he dies 'cured'. It is then he realizes that the phallus does not exist – or, in Hamlet's own words, that 'the king is a thing – of nothing' (Act IV, ii). In short, it is only when Hamlet faces the true strangeness of death, and sees through the paralysing estrangement of the ghost (his father's returned double), that he is freed from illusory attachments to the phallus and from the mimetic cycles which hold him in thrall. But, sadly, Hamlet only comes into his own desire *posthumously*, when it is too late. Which is why his desire is tragic.

*

In an essay entitled 'The Phantom of Hamlet', Nicholas Abraham argues in a similar vein when he claims that what haunts Hamlet is an 'unspeakable' event which has been buried and entombed. He states the aim of Shakespeare's play thus:

> It is to spur the public to react unconsciously to the enigmas that remain and to backtrack toward an equally unstated yet no less imperative goal: breaking down the 'phantom' and eradicating its effect, the uneasy state of knowledge– nonknowledge responsible for the unconscious conflict and incongruous repetitions. The aim, in other words, is to cancel the secret buried in the unconscious and to display it in its initial openness.[40]

But how can such a secret be exposed given that the shame and guilt attached to it persist? 'Their exorcism leads necessarily not to the punishment, real or imagined, of the other, but to a higher wisdom about oneself and the world of humans at large'.[41] More explicitly still:

> Reducing the 'phantom' entails reducing the sin attached to someone else's secret and stating it in acceptable terms so as to defy, circumvent, or domesticate the phantom's (and our) resistances, its (and our) refusals, gaining acceptance for a higher degree of 'truth'.[42]

For his part, Abraham proceeds to write a fictional Sixth Act to the play in which Hamlet and Fortinbras become reconciled, acknowledge their respective fathers' secrets and restore to

Poland the kingdom which their fathers had stolen from it . . . even returning the usurped Pole, Polonius, to his native Poland for proper burial![43]

André Green adds an interesting gloss on the psychoanalytic reading of Hamlet in his Hamlet et Hamlet when he claims that the whole play is a theatrical uncovering of the buried, covered-up memory of murder. Theatrical representation itself becomes a form of proto-psychoanalytic representation or 'showing' of the primal scene which serves a therapeutic–cathartic role for audiences. This of course gives extra weight to Hamlet's throwaway line after his staging of the play within the play – 'The play's the thing in which I'll catch the conscience of the king'. The basic hypothesis is that drama can actually stage the unconscious and enable it to show/say what cannot otherwise be shown/said at a purely conscious, and therefore censored, level.[44]

Finally, Julia Kristeva adds her own elusive but suggestive gloss on the subject in Powers of Horror. What is original is her concentration on the role of the maternal rather than paternal signifier. She writes:

> Constructed on the one hand by the incestuous desire of (for) his mother and on the other by an overly brutal separation from her, the borderline patient (read here Hamlet), even though he may be a fortified castle, is nevertheless an empty castle. The absence, or the failure, of paternal function to establish a unitary bent between subject and object, produces this strange configuration: an encompassment that is stifling (the container compressing the ego) and, at the same time, draining (the want of an other, qua object, produces nullity in the place of the subject). The ego then plunges into a pursuit of identifications that could repair narcissism – identifications that the subject will experience as in-significant, 'empty', 'null', 'devitalized', 'puppet-like'. An empty castle, haunted by unappealing ghosts – 'powerless' outside, 'impossible' inside.[45]

*

What such psychoanalytic readings fail to appreciate, however, is that Hamlet's tragedy also comprises narrative catharsis. Denmark is saved from its 'rottenness', and the memory of Hamlet's struggle with phantoms lives on, thanks to the testimony of Horatio who absents himself from felicity to 'tell his story'. Thanks also, we should not forget, to his former rival, Fortinbras, who, equally liberated from the cycle of mimetic desire and revenge, ensures that Hamlet the son has the proper mourning and burial which Hamlet the father never received.

It seems to me that both Shakespeare and Joyce are aware of a healing power which escapes Lacan and his apocalyptic apostles of 'nothing': namely, the power of narrative memory and imagination. Hamlet, I would argue, can teach contemporary culture – crippled as it is with endless crises of identification and legitimation – that strangers can be allies as well as rivals, that sons can acknowledge the secrets of their fathers, and that some stories can save.

When one considers the vast number of contemporary tales – literary, cyber and cinematic – focusing on the collapse of the father–son relation (Magnolias, American Beauty, Star Wars, etc.) one appreciates that if the Hamlet narrative is indeed perennial it is especially pertinent to certain postmodern phenomena of paralysis, simulation and psychosis. Wherever the logic of doubling rules, the story of Hamlet needs to be told, again and again.

7

MELANCHOLY
Between gods and monsters

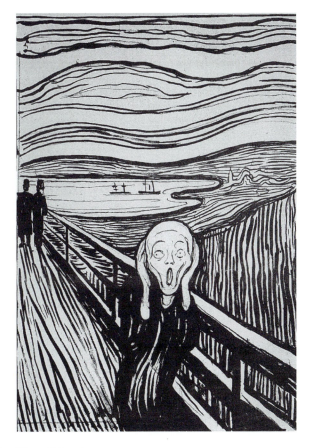

The Scream by Edvard Munch.
© National Gallery, Norway, 2000/ © Munch Ellingsen Gruppen, 2000. (Photo J. Lathion)

From its earliest beginnings, the Western tradition portrays the figure of melancholy in a double light – as god and monster.

On the one hand, we have the image of melancholy as a cruel Kronos devouring his own children and banishing his other victims to a netherworld of isolation and darkness. No doubt mindful of this ancient myth, Plato identifies melancholy with the lowest and most tyrannical soul of all (*Phaedrus*, 248e); and he unambiguously states that 'a man becomes a tyrant when . . . he is a drunkard, a voluptuary and a melancholic' (*Republic*, 573c).[1] This negative notion finds supplementary support in the classical medical theory of the 'four humours' – melancholic, phlegmatic, choleric and sanguinary. Here melancholy is associated with the disease of the black bile (*atra bilis/melas khole*): a biological fluid in the body with its corresponding 'temperament' or 'mental type', usually linked to instability or insanity. This characterization resurfaces, in still darker guise, in the medieval concept of idle sloth (*acedia*), that is, submission to despondency and despair. Here it is reviled as a demonic temptation as well as a diseased humour. And it finds more contemporary if secular expression in Freud's famous essay, 'Mourning and Melancholy', where the latter is described as a repressed aggression towards a lost object. Instead of undergoing the painful process of mourning the idealized loved one, the melancholic refuses to accept the reality of loss and turns the grief *inwards* instead. Melancholy thereby replaces the nothingness of a disenchanted world with a nothingness of self, sometimes to the point of suicide. But even Freud has to admit, in the final analysis, that he really 'understands nothing' of this pathological enigma.[2] Melancholy, it seems, brings us to the limits of reason.

But this is not the whole story. There is a significant counter-movement of thought on the subject. By this second account, melancholy is celebrated as

165

a condition of contemplative wisdom. Here we are presented with the noble face of Kronos – or Saturn in Latin – freed from the vicissitudes of the temporal world and providing a basis for deeper insight into the hidden truth of things. This positive reading corresponds, philosophically, with the ancient Aristotelian association of melancholy with inspired heroes (Ajax, Hercules and the wandering God, Belerophon) or wise men (Empedocles, Socrates and Plato himself). In his treatise, 'The Notion of Melancholy: Problem XXX, I', Aristotle began by asking 'Why is it that all those who have become eminent in philosophy or politics or poetry or the arts are clearly melancholics . . .?'.[3] Attributed thus to noble figures, melancholy was considered by some as the 'disease of heroes', carrying with it a certain 'nimbus of sinister sublimity' and even, at times, a kind of divine vision (theia mania).[4] As Panovsky and Klibansky observe in their momental study, Saturn and Melancholy:

> Thus it came about that, associated with the myths, the melancholic disposition began to be regarded as, in some degree, heroic; it was idealized still further when equated with 'frenzy' (mania), inasmuch as the 'humor melancholicus' began to figure as a source, however dangerous, of the highest spiritual exaltation, as soon as the notion of frenzy itself was interpreted (or rather, reinterpreted) in this way.[5]

Such an alliance between melancholy and visionary insight was to reappear at several junctures in the history of art and ideas, most decisively in the Renaissance humanist notion of melancolia generosa found in the work of Ficino. But it would reach its apogee in the modern existentialist and expressionist portrayals of angst as the ultimate mark of authentic existence. If Munch's Melancholy: On the Beach can be said to exemplify the alienating visage of dread, Rodin's Le Penseur represents the visionary–contemplative alternative.

The fact that the two representations of melancholy – abject and inspired – often differ only by a whisker's breadth is a telling symptom of the inner twinship that binds the opposing faces of this most enigmatic mood. Once again in this chapter, as in several others in this volume, we find ourselves confronting a limit experience on the edge of the sayable: a no man's land of dread where fantasies – of strangers, gods and monsters – proliferate. Melancholy touches on things which can be shown but not known.

The existentialist account

In what follows I will explore some salient figures in this legacy of ambivalence. I begin with Martin Heidegger's allusion to melancholy – or what he prefers to call *angst* – in the ancient myth of Saturn. In Section 42 of *Being and Time*, Heidegger rehearses the classic narrative. Saturn presided over the origin of the human being, consigning (a) its body to the earth (*humus*) from which it received its name (*homo*); (b) its spirit to the highest Olympian deity (Jupiter); and (c) its basic 'mood' to the figure of Care (*Sorge*) who shaped the first human from a mixture of earth and heaven. Thus, Heidegger surmises, each mortal remains a cleft creature with one eye on its terrestrial genesis, the other on its celestial aspirations. This split is what accounts for the specifically 'Saturnine' quality of our finite existence (*Dasein*), manifesting itself as a *temporal division* between life and death, between memory and promise. Because of it we find ourselves already *thrown* into the world and *projecting* ourselves into a 'not-yet'. As Heidegger puts it:

> The decision as to wherein the 'primordial' Being of this creature is to be seen, is left to Saturn, 'Time'. Thus the (mythological) characterisation of man's essence expressed in this fable, has brought to view in advance the kind of Being which dominates his *temporal sojourn in the world*, and does so through and through.[6]

In this Heideggerian account, melancholy is a response to the passing away of time, a typical existential reaction to the splitting of present into past and future. The God Saturn becomes the one who forges the link between our being and our temporality: a connection which Heidegger identifies with our experience of (a) 'dread' (*angst*) as a facing up to our own inner nothingness, and (b) 'care' (*Sorge*) as a 'being-free for one's own possibilities', that is, for one's own authentic future which is *not yet*.[7] In melancholic dread we experience 'nothing' and 'nowhere'. Or to be more precise, we encounter ourselves as a free temporal projection of possibilities culminating in our own death (the possibility of our non-being which is the impossibility of any further possibilities). But it is, strangely, this very experience which *individualizes* us and makes us authentic (*eigentlich*). 'Anxiety', writes Heidegger

> makes manifest in Dasein its . . . *Being-free for* the freedom of choosing itself and taking hold of itself. Anxiety brings Dasein face to face with

its *Being-free for* (*propensio in* . . .) the authenticity of its Being, and for this authenticity as a possibility which it always is.[8]

We thus find ourselves in a state of profound 'uncanniness' (*Unheimlichkeit*), of 'not-being-at-home' (*Nicht-zu-Hause-Sein*). The Saturnine mood delivers us from the tranquillized self-assurance of 'everyday publicness' and conformity into – ourselves alone.[9] Melancholy is that sweet 'sadness without cause' which, to quote Yeats, helps us 'wither into the truth'.

For Heidegger, as for other existentialist thinkers like Kierkegaard (*The Concept of Dread*), Guardini (*On Melancholy*) and Sartre (*Being and Nothingness*), the melancholic tendency to estrange us from the quotidian sway of illusion and anonymity is a precondition for authentic insight. And without such insight no genuine decision or responsibility is possible. Indeed, Guardini will argue that melancholy is much more than a psychiatric symptom of nerves and neurones. It issues, he insists, from the very ruptured 'depths of human nature' whose disquietude is a sign of the eternal.[10]

This existentialist view was not entirely new, of course. It was already intimated by Aristotle's and Ficino's association of melancholy with contemplative insight. But it also found another, somewhat unexpected, prefiguration in the *Anthropology* of the Enlightenment rationalist, Immanuel Kant. In a section of the *Anthropology* entitled 'On the Cognitive Faculties', Kant describes melancholy as a mixing of the real with the imaginary which – unlike 'mental illness' – can be addressed and redressed by a wise practice of philosophical reflection. The melancholic differs from the 'madman' in that he is *aware* that his imaginings are imaginings, whereas the latter is not. He is like someone half-dreaming who 'has the chimeras in his power'. For he knows that his imaginary creations are alterations of his 'inner sense' and not part of external reality. Indeed Kant considered himself to be a melancholic hypochondriac saved from psychic collapse by the self-preservative therapy of philosophizing![11] But for all its suggestiveness, Kant's account is too elliptical and elusive. It at no point positively affirms melancholy as a mark of authenticity, as the later existentialists would do.

The genealogical account

Taking my cue from the time-honoured link between melancholy and the ancient god Saturn, I will now take a closer look at how this particular figure arose and developed in Greco-Roman mythology. For it must be conceded that however much the enigma of melancholy has fascinated certain philosophers throughout the ages, it has never managed to escape entirely the more shadowy zones of myth and fantasy. Plato, after all, only managed a few disparaging remarks about its tyrannical impulses, while Aristotle took refuge in a largely medical analysis of the 'black bile', so dense and cryptic in places that some doubt it is written by Aristotle at all. Even Ficino, who tried to rehabilitate the notion of melancholy in his Renaissance treatise, *De Vita Triplici* (see below), never succeeded in offering more than a brief, quasi-mystical account of its paradoxes. And if it is true that the melancholic mood receives more sustained treatment in certain modern writers, here too the tone remains tentative and often confused. Existential analysis, as noted, opts for rather loose synonyms such as *angst*, *ennui*, dread, anxiety or depression, while the very founder of psychoanalysis will concede that he ultimately doesn't know what he means when he writes of melancholy! That is why, if we are to have a fuller picture of the mystery of melancholy than that offered by the cursory insights of philosophers, we need to look to the archives of the imaginary and symbolic unconscious. For it is in the images of mythology, religious portraiture, popular culture and art itself that melancholy will find more fulsome expression.

*

Most early myths depict Saturn as a god of time who could destroy or create. As destroyer we find multiple representations of Saturn as an ageing figure with a dark cloak over his head, a sickle or zodiac in his hand, frequently engaged in the act of devouring his own offspring. This sinister aspect of melancholy derives from the tale of Kronos – the original hellenic version of the Roman Saturn. And it is highly significant that Kronos was ultimately conflated with the Greek *chronos*, meaning 'time'.

Kronos swallowed his children when he realized that they would replace him and put an end to his eternal reign. Or to put it another way, Kronos refused to accept that one generation succeeds another. But one of his sons, Zeus, managed to escape. His mother (Rhea) replaced him with a stone wrapped in cloth which Kronos consumed in his stead. Zeus then proceeded to castrate his father, Kronos, dispatching him to the outer universe.[12]

It may be telling, moreover, that the act of castration occurs twice in the Kronos myth. Not only is Kronos castrated by his son, Zeus, but it happens that he himself had castrated his own father, Ouranos, with a scythe. And as legend has it – legends being famous for narrating unspeakable primal scenes

– it was from the emasculated genitals of Ouranos, cast into the waves of the sea, that Venus and the nymphs first arose. In short, sexual desire for female beauty was intimately linked, in our mythological unconscious, with an initial act of sundering and separation. Without castration there could be no sense of that lack, difference or otherness which is so indispensable to the workings of eros. Indeed, we find countless allusions to the amorous, venal and sometimes lecherous character of the melancholic throughout the ages.[13]

The identification of Kronos–Saturn with 'time' is more than a phonetic coincidence (*Kronos–chronos*). The melacholic is intimately related to the dread produced in mortals by the scythe of Time the Reaper – i.e. by that separation of all separations, death. The 'chronological' character of melancholy is thus captured in Kronos' threefold act of devouring, substitution and castration, each of which represents a fundamental aspect of time. Indeed another way to read this myth would be to emphasize the futility of Kronos' efforts to remain eternal by *reversing time*, drawing his progeny back into himself: an act of monstrous self-absorption punished by the inevitable passage of time as both substitution (one moment replacing another) and castration (the cutting of the illusion of phallic self-sufficiency). In other words, to the extent that Kronos destroys he is himself destroyed. Kronos is the destroyed destroyer, just as he is the castrated castrator.

This paradoxical character of the Kronos–Saturn figure is further underscored, moreover, by the fact that the experience of sundering can also give rise to *creativity*. The inaugural myths of castration lead not only to the survival and empowerment of the greatest Olympian deity – Zeus – but also to the birth of beauty and desire (Venus rising from waves bloodied by castrated genitals). In this reading, *cyclical time* which seeks to return to itself gives way to *chronological time* which acknowledges the ineluctability of historical transience and mortality. It is this virtue of wisdom, capable of accepting the ruptures of mortal existence, which lies at the root of the visual representations of Saturn as elderly sage and resigned sovereign.[14] Disenchanted with the narcissistic ideal of self-plenitude, the creative melancholic is one who re-experiences the world without illusion, that is, with eyes capable of seeing otherwise.

According to this Saturnine narrative, in sum, the artist is one who lets go of the ego in order to rediscover him- or herself anew. Working through melancholy towards a form of productive mourning, the artist becomes like a wise Olympian deity, a curious 'gaiety transfiguring all that dread' (Yeats).

*

This more upbeat legacy runs from certain ideas of classical antiquity up to the middle ages and early Renaissance, as witnessed in countless sculptures, frescoes, murals and portraits depicting *Melancolia* as a creative thinker, head on hand, calmly embracing death. This is the melancholic mind that authentically accepts its 'being-towards-death' (Heidegger). Or to use psychoanalytic language, it is the narcissistically wounded soul that has undergone 'symbolic castration' and acknowledged its incorrigible and ultimately insatiable condition as 'want-to-be' (*manque à être*). The melancholic moves from destruction to creation by accepting his/her own death. Darkness encountered and traversed becomes a source of new light, a 'black sun'. Hence the proliferation throughout the Western visual tradition of images of the castrated–castrating Kronos holding aloft a sickle, scythe or dragon of time biting its own tail.[15] Unless, these symbols suggest, we embrace our mortality as a limit-experience of irreversible loss, we cannot transform the disease of melancholy into healing insight.

The bifocal nature of the melancholic imagination is also evidenced in the visual symbols of Saturn as a circular movement of ascension and decline. This sometimes take the form of a Wheel of Fortune where the highest revolves into the lowest and vice versa. This rotation motif was frequently invoked in the late middle ages to suggest that the poor and suffering too can have their day. Thus we find images of cripples, prisoners and peasants (those closest to the earth/*humus*) parading through fields in the guise of 'Saturn's children'. This egalitarian idiom of social reversal – from lowest to highest – is itself linked to the Roman feast of Saturnalia in December when slaves were released and the population was permitted to engage in unrestrained merry-making and revelry, irrespective of rank or class. As Klibansky's catalogue of classic illustrations shows, Saturn easily alternates between earthbound, spade-bearing beggar and celestial, sceptre-wielding sovereign.[16]

The fact that Saturn was, in addition, the 'highest star' – the seventh and most distant of all planets in the ancient universe – provided further astrological motifs for the visual representation of the melancholic cycle of ascent and descent, elevation and fall. This is what in modern psychological parlance might be called the manic-depressive bipolarity of melancholy.[17] In other words, the respective representations of Saturn as heavenly deity or downtrodden peasant were typical of the ambiguity expressed towards the phenomenon of 'dread' in classical and late antiquity.

This ambivalence was later consolidated, it might be added, by Western Christendom which took over the dual readings of melancholy. Here we find it being associated, at best, with the meditative detachment of the hermit (St Jerome at prayer in his cave); or, at worst, with a sinful proclivity towards gloom, sloth and despair (the medieval vice of *acedia*). In both cases, we witness the moral–allegorical representations of time as (1) *salvation*, if one accepts mortality as the antidote to vanity; or (2) *damnation*, if one succumbs to the ravages of morbid despondency.

Melancholia generosa

It was not in fact until the triumph of Renaissance humanism that we find the medieval equivocation being replaced by a bold affirmation of the Saturnine mind – the famous *melancholia generosa* celebrated by Ficino and other Florentine literati. The big shift here was from the notion of melancholy as an objective physiological condition (Aristotle's treatise and the Galenic theory of humours) to a specific kind of *subjective mood*.[18] In his influential treatise, *De Vita Triplici*, Ficino marks this epistemological turn when he distinguishes between (a) those who make melancholy their enemy by clinging to the inauthentic banalities of the commonplace, and (b) those who transform it into a creative gift by detaching themselves from the world in order to become artists and intellectuals. Such a transformation produces new minds capable of dignity, freedom and self-expression – three cardinal virtues of Renaissance humanism. According to Ficino, Saturn serves as a dark monster wreaking destruction on those still caught up in vulgar sentiment; but he represents a blessing for those who follow the more 'sequestered and divine life' of Saturn himself. 'Men whose minds are truly withdrawn from the world are, to some extent, his kin and in him they find a friend.'[19] Those who experience Saturn as a benevolent rather than baneful influence are, by this reasoning, those 'who give themselves over with heart and soul to divine contemplation, which gains distinction from the example of Saturn himself'. 'Instead of earthly life, from which he is himself cut off', concludes Ficino, 'Saturn confers heavenly and eternal life on you'.[20]

Thus Ficino proposed to replace the ancient mistrust of the sinister demon with a curious glorification of him. Or as the adage of the Saturnine Florentines went, *aut Deus, aut daemon* (either God or demon). The choice was now *ours* – to embrace our Saturnine condition or to suppress it. The god Saturn, observes Klibansky, 'who had given up dominion for wisdom, and life in Olympus for an existence divided between the highest sphere of heaven

Melancholia I by Dürer. The Metropolitan Museum of Art

The Castration of Saturn.
By Maisie Bernard, after a thirteenth-century ink drawing

and the innermost depths of the earth, eventually became the chief patron of the Platonic Academy of Florence'.[21]

*

The move from a medical to a mystical model of melancholy, with its attendant notion of cosmic attunement, was to exert a deep influence on the Romantic cult of aesthetic imagination. Klibansky offers a useful account of this turn towards melancholic genius. The melancholic, he writes:

> should apply himself of his own accord to that activity which is the particular domain of the sublime star of speculation, and which the planet promotes just as powerfully as it hinders and harms the ordinary functions of body and soul — that is to say, to creative contemplation . . . As enemy and oppressor of all life in any way subject to the present world, Saturn generates melancholy; but as the friend and protector of a higher and purely intellectual existence he can also cure it . . . Ultimately the Saturnine man can do nothing better than embrace his fate and resign himself heart and soul to the will of his star.[22]

The romantics held accordingly that through an act of heroic abandonment, the melancholic could gain not only a heightened form of self-awareness but even, at times, genial states of illumination. The melancholic could swing into creative mania if instead of trying to combat dread, the creative mind surrendered to its call. But for Renaissance as for romantic modernity, art was there to provide form and measure to stem the excesses of manic elevation and prevent it from slipping into the excesses of 'lugubrious intoxication'.[23] Whether it concerned the last sonatas of Beethoven, Keats' odes to melancholic delight or Baudelaire's famous 'Saturnine book' in Les Fleurs du mal, it was a question of transmuting black sadness into song.

What art ultimately allows, according to this reading of the melancholic 'genius', is a certain 'sublimation' of the malady of life. One of the aims of such sublimation is to make the experience of unsayable loss more sayable. The task here is to cross over the limit of what the human psyche can bear to know and return with new words and images. Paul Ricoeur puts this well in Memory, History, Forgetfulness when he observes how art can turn the melancholic slide towards irresistible sadness into joy. For such joy, he notes, is the

174

'recompense for the renunciation of the lost object and the sign of one's reconciliation with one's internalized object'. Here we discover, as the very goal of artistic transfiguration, 'a happy memory, when the poetic image completes the work of mourning'.[24]

Dürer's *Melancholia I*

Nowhere, in my view, is this transition from the ancient to the modern representation of melancholy more graphically expressed than in Dürer's celebrated *Melancholia* I. Here we have the first auto-portrait of the Saturnine genius. Or if one prefers, the portrait of the artist as a melancholic man. All the accumulated resonances of the classical and Renaissance traditions are here congregated in a single charged image – an emblematic image forged at the crossroads between the old world and the new.

The crowned face of Melancholy is half in darkness, half in light. The dark signals both the influence of the black bile and the shadowy countenance of our earthly mortality, as the sun sets and night approaches. The light, by contrast, points to rebirth in the figure of the playful child. The drooping head, cheek on hand, captures the mutation of despair into insight, of weariness into wisdom – what Baudelaire would call the enigma of *la paresse féconde*. The purse and keys hanging from the winged figure's belt are emblematic of the power and riches of Saturn as ruler-king of the universe. And the geometrical instruments (hammer, set square, compass and mould-ing plane) serve as icons of the Renaissance scholar personifying the liberal arts. As do the bell, scales and hour glass, all instruments for measuring time – another use of applied geometry as one of the seven liberal arts.[25] Finally, the wreath and wings are probably an allusion to the Renaissance figure of the *homo literatus*.

Invoking the Wisdom of Solomon (xi, 21), Dürer once wrote: 'I will take measure, number and weight as my aim'. By this he meant that creative work cannot dispense with the tools God used to create the world in the first place. Dürer's winged *Melancholia* is committed both to mathematical measure and to sensory intuition (epitomized by the scholar's sleeping dog with its flair for hunting hidden bones!). In short, Dürer's engraving embodies the *mens contemplativa* which 'deworlds' us from our common concerns and points towards higher things. But it does so without forgetting the *vis imaginativa* which recalls our connection to the lower world of earthly memory and images. At best, the modern artist envisioned by Dürer is one who combines this double allegiance to light and dark, heaven and earth, freedom and necessity – someone capable of transforming the disease of melancholic dementia into the *melancholia generosa* of the artistic genius. Indeed, it is precisely in this proto-modern legacy of melancholy that we may situate Raphael's devotion to the Saturnine muse, Beethoven's Melancolia Quartet (*Opus 18, no. 6*) and Keats' evocation of the 'very temple of delight' where 'veiled melancholy has her sovran shrine' ('Ode to Melancholy'). Not to mention the prodigious cult of melancholy in the work of countless artists, figurative and abstract, inspired by existentialism: one thinks of Munch, Giacometti, Pollock, Rothko. And such melancholic mood swings are by no means absent from the whole postmodern fascination with the sublime, already analysed in Chapters 4 and 5 above.[26]

Conclusion

I close with a reflection of Julia Kristeva's which I believe accurately captures the complex and ambivalent legacy we have been probing and sounding in this chapter. Noting how the melancholic imagination struggles with the extremes of mania and despair, Kristeva claims that 'artistic creation both integrates and consumes them; works of art leading us thereby to establish less destructive, more pleasurable relations with ourselves and with others'.[27] If the melancholic imagination offers the possibility of putting the human experience of loss and rupture into images, of grappling with the void so as to turn monsters into gods, and aliens into angels, never was it more needed than today when the proliferating crises of identity – personal, ideological and cultural – expose an ever-widening abyss at the core of existence. The choice remains: succumb to our inner dark or turn it into song. Self-destruction or self-creation. The black sun can swing either way.

But how might we be guided in our choice? Kristeva suggests there are three ways: *religion, psychoanalysis* and *art*. The contemplative saint in his cave. The analysand ready – after transference and working-through – to live beyond illusion. The artist transfiguring the luminous dark. But I think, in light of our above discussion of the Saturnine legacy, we might add a fourth way: that of *philosophical understanding*. Such understanding could never be exhausted by a purely scientific account, for the depths opened up by melancholy cannot be reduced to imperatives of empirical exactitude and proof. But such understanding – closer once again to *phronesis* than to *theoria*, to *reflective judgement* than to *pure reason* – can yield many insights into the mountains and caverns of the mind, as philosophers from Aristotle and Ficino to Heidegger and Kristeva have shown. And one of the strongest virtues of melancholic understanding is, perhaps, that it knows its limits. It knows, in sum, where understanding surpasses itself and has recourse once more to religion, psychoanalysis or art.

8

THE IMMEMORIAL
A task of narrative

Hope is a memory of the future.
(Gabriel Marcel)

Narrative is, I have suggested in several chapters above, one of the most effective responses to the failings of memory. Not any kind of narrative mind you. There is narrative and narrative. For while some stories congeal and incarcerate, others loosen and emancipate. And it is important to know the difference. Once again, at the limits of the tellable, we encounter the need to discern between different modes of telling.

The famous 'talking cure' of psychotherapy provides a useful, if by no means uncontroversial, glimpse into this process of discernment. Many people seek out therapy not because they cannot tell stories but because they are telling the wrong ones. Or because they are telling the right ones in the wrong way, that is, in a manner that has become too narrow or oppressive. In such cases, a good therapy would start off by inviting the client to abandon his or her prefixed account of the past and to explore whether the Official Version of beginning–middle–end is the only one available. In other words, some sufferers of blocked or melancholic memory have, first, to become very bad storytellers – making their lives basically unreadable – if they are ever to begin to retell their lives again. Sometimes stories have to get worse to get better.

Dilemmas of remembrance

Let me try to spell this out in more detail. Narrative repetition of the past, when obsessional or coercive, needs to be undone so that another kind of narrative, more capable of addressing the true tasks of remembrance, can take

179

its place. As Freud recognized in 'Remembering, Repetition and Working Through', repetition is the worst kind of forgetting. It is a forgetting that has forgotten its own forgetting and so compels us to 'act out' our pain in a compulsive fashion. I suspect this is what Adam Phillips had in mind when he argued that in therapy 'life-stories fragment in the telling', so that the patient has to 'refuse himself the conventional satisfactions of narrative'.[1] In this way, a new kind of narrative, free from the sedation of repetitiveness, may emerge from the ashes of old stories. A bit like Marcel in Proust's *Search for Lost Time* having to undergo disillusionment, taking a distance from his habituated tales in order to be reborn as a Narrator able to serve as both 'author and reader of his own life'. Stifled memory dissolves finally before the 'reminiscences' and 'recognitions' of genuine memory.

Taking this cue from Proust we might agree with Phillips that one of the aims of psychoanalysis is to 'produce a story of the past – a reconstructed life-history – that makes the past available, as a resource to be thought about rather than a persecution to be endlessly re-enacted'.[2] For in melancholic repetition, the past has no future. Art and analysis seek to secure such a potential future for memory. How? By unfreezing repetition and rendering recovery of the past possible. In this sense both art and analysis might be seen as cathartic portals to genuine autobiography and, by extension, to genuine historical remembrance.

*

But some would argue that there are certain kinds of past experience that cannot and should not be remembered. This defence of the *immemorial* is found in several post-Holocaust commentators. One of the most articulate exponents of this view is Lawrence Langer in his award winning book, *Holocaust Testimonies: The Ruins of Memory*. Here the author suggests that the very 'inaccessibility' of past suffering may be a necessary defence against the will to reimagine the 'inner chaos' of the past, thereby resisting the attempt to integrate it into 'an outer public world'.[3] But, I find myself asking, if Holocaust survivors such as Primo Levi or Elie Wiesel had not recorded their memoirs of unspeakable loss, thus making remembrance possible for future generations, would not the Nazi attempt to wipe out the history of the Jews have triumphed? And is not the duty to retell the monstrosity of Auschwitz *again and again* not the best assurance, to cite Primo Levi, that it will 'never happen again?'

This question becomes even more vexed when the memorials to this past come from non-survivors whose record is largely fictional or literary. Great controversy, for example, surrounded the publication of Paul Celan's 'Death Fugue'. Michael Berstein captures the dilemma well when he describes the consequences of describing the experience of the death camps as a non-survivor in the first person. This act of 'imaginative ventriloquism', he notes, violates one of the major taboos of our time. And yet he – rightly in my view – defends Celan's poem.

> 'Death Fugue' demonstrates that poetry *can* imagine the unimagin-able, create a language for what is unsayable, and give memorable shape to catastrophic experiences that are not autobiographically grounded. The real 'scandal' . . . is its transgression of the sole almost universally agreed-upon taboo arising out of the Shoah: the injunction against anyone except a survivor presuming to represent directly the thoughts and feelings of prisoners in a death camp.[4]

But, I repeat, it is precisely the power of Celan's testimonial imagination which makes the memory so alive for countless readers today. Of course, no fictional retelling can ever presume to retrieve the depth and detail of the actual suffering of those who died. However, some testimonies can do better than others and the blanket condemnation of all literary narrative remembrances of the Holocaust is, it seems to me, purist and self-defeating. So in answer to Adorno's maxim that after Auschwitz no one can write poetry, I would reply that this would be, paradoxically, to consolidate the original SS resolution to ensure that no one ever told the story of genocide. Or more generally, in reponse to Coleridge's classic question – does the fact that literature 'excites us to artificial feelings' necessarily mean that it 'makes us callous to real ones?' – I would reply in the negative. In fact, I would argue that the opposite may, on occasion, be the case. For narrative testimony can sometimes give us such a deep empathic connection with the suffering of others that not only is their past honoured in the present but our own present is enlarged by this past. This exchange of testimonial memories – between past and present, Jew and non-Jew, native and alien, us and them – holds out possibilities of reconciliation. And recent experiences of truth tribunals in South Africa and Northern Ireland suggest that such possibilities are not entirely utopian.

The purism of silence should be prepared, in my view, to bow before the exigency of peace.

A narrative paradox

I am suggesting then that narrative imagination – in the guise of historical or literary testimony – may help prevent past traumas from becoming fixated in pathological forms of melancholy, amnesia or repetition. But what kinds of narrative imagination are we talking about here?

Let me try to clarify. The manifold of our life-stories is 'run through' and 'held together' by our historical imagination, which translates this manifold into a story. Such practice is, to use Kantian terms, both (a) *reproductive* in that it synthesizes and structures our past memories, and (b) *productive* in that 'the spontaneity of storytelling works as a retrieval of the contingent and passive links of our temporal experiences'.[5] Moreover, it is the privilege of a well-told story to be able to disclose, as Aristotle put it, 'universal' aspects of the human condition; and to do so in a way which a purely empirical history, bound to the contingent happenstance of experience, could not. That is why Aristotle held that narrative (*mythos–mimesis*) offers a more in-depth 'philosophical' understanding of the past than history, often issuing in 'practical wisdom' (*phronesis*). In this way, phronetic understanding informed by narrative can offer us a very special kind of insight unavailable in either (a) a mere chronicle of disparate events, or (b) a purely scientific account of abstract laws. More precisely, narrative imagination can conjoin the particular with the universal, enabling us via various 'plots' to relate forms of virtue to joy or pain.[6] It is, moreover, just this *ethical* capacity of narrative imagination which renders it all the more fitting to testimonial rememberings of the Holocaust and other historical horrors. This is why I believe that to declare such horrors too horrible to recall is to neglect our moral debt to the dead.

Genuine narrative is always 'on its way to the other'. Even poetry, as Celan reminds us, 'intends an other, needs this other'.[7] This narrative calling out to the other is related to what Habermas terms our 'interest for communication' – an interest which goes beyond a mere interest for facts or information. To engage in narrative history – as opposed to a purely statistical record – is to enlarge our sphere of communication and connection with others. And this is what makes every true historian someone who 'belongs' to the field that he/she studies. Consequently, as Ricoeur says:

> Every procedure of objectivation, of distanciation, of doubt, of suspi-
> cion, and in short, everything that makes history a form of inquiry
> is equally part of this interest for communication . . . Thanks to the

objective work of the historian, these values (i.e. what deserves to be remembered and recorded) are attached to the common treasure of mankind.[8]

More simply put, historical memory needs both empathic belonging and critical distance. The interest in retrieving the forgotten past finds its counterpart in a complementary ethical attitude of 'disinterestedness' in the past. This implies a readiness to suspect one's own condition of personal interest or prejudice, 'an aptitude to practice the *epoche*, the bracketing of one's own desires'. For thanks to this *epoche* 'the alterity of the other is preserved in its difference'.[9] Thus a dialectic may emerge between what is distant and what is close, what is foreign and what is familiar, between what we might call (a) the objective/universal and (b) the subjective/intersubjective attitudes to history. It is precisely this hermeneutic dialectic which brings history close to narrativity. As Ricoeur argues:

> The recognition of the values of the past in their difference opens the real to the possible. History, too, in this respect, belongs to the logic of narrative possibilities. It does so, however, not through fiction, but precisely by means of its 'true' stories. The 'true' stories of the past expose the potentialities of the present.[10]

This narrative paradox reveals history to be a field of 'imaginative variations'. It reveals the present as one variation amongst others and reminds us that the *actual* state of affairs is not the *only* one. Ricoeur is correct, I believe, when he concludes accordingly that if history opens us to the possible by opening us to the 'different', fiction, by opening us to the 'unreal', brings us back to what Aristotle called the 'essential'.[11]

Deconstructing memory

Not everyone agrees with this line of thinking, however. Several postmodern theorists have challenged the hermeneutic capacity to retell the historical past. They counter with a defence of the *immemorial*: that which refuses memory. To the fore here are thinkers like Lyotard and Derrida.

Derrida warns against the notion of 'reconcilation' as a premature restoration of a 'normal' past. Certain reconciliation and truth tribunals may, in their rush to forgiveness, not only betray the immemorial suffering of the dead victims but also engage in a facility of compulsive public mourning which Derrida puts down to the dominant sway in our time of a 'psychotherapeutic economy'.[12] Moreover, the temptation to resolve past horrors by means of some redemptive 'master narrative' of universal pardon often ignores those 'others' who are suppressed within this narrative or excluded from it altogether. For the very community (any community for that matter) which seeks to dispense such an amnesty is invariably plagued by 'gaps' in its own memory – 'haunted by the ghosts of those who were either colonized, expelled, or killed in its name'.[13] In critical response to this practice of exclusion and oblivion, deconstruction proposes to sensitize us to the 'faceless and nameless who have been buried beneath the weight of officially sanctioned history . . . to keep watch for a past which has never been present to us in the form of a Grand Narrative'.[14] This requires, the deconstructionists tell us, a special 'micrological' attention to those ghosts and spectres who have been exiled from the annals of official narrative history.

My response to this objection is, however, that no emancipation of forgotten memory would be conceivable without recourse to practices of hermeneutic memory and retrieval. Such practices need not always be guilty of repressive excisions. On the contrary, they may succeed, through a labour of critical reinterpretation, in (a) bringing forgotten ghosts back again (as *revenants*) and (b) giving them the future, in memory, that they have been robbed of in reality.

Horror and the ineffable

Lyotard develops the critique of historical remembrance when he argues that any judgement of history risks denying the heterogeneity and incommensurability of the opponent by absorbing it into the dominant language game of the judge. In defence of what he terms an 'agonistics of the differend', Lyotard repudiates the 'referentialist credulity' of standard historiography. Against this, he declares that history, like literature, must recognize that there is something that 'cannot be said', something 'incomparable' and irreducible to representation and reference. The ineffability of past horrors consigns them to silence. Traumatic events of history – which he compares to dementia or the sublime – are untranslatable into publicly shareable narrative memories. They belong to what Lyotard calls time 'immemorial'.[15]

The difficulty here again, however, is that in refusing historical trauma any reference or reality claims and in treating the whole issue of historical truth in such a deflationist fashion, Lyotard jeopardizes its radical political potential.[16] I have discussed this problem at some length elsewhere (On Stories, Parts 3 and 4); but it is crucial to return here to the precise context of Lyotard's defence of the 'immemorial'. I suspect that Lyotard's account of historical narrativity as a medley of incommensurable language games (or 'linguistic islets') ultimately issues in a form of nominalist relativism which endangers the very notion of memory itself. And I believe that it also renders virtually impossible the critical duty of historians to distinguish between truer and less true retellings of the past – a duty that is all too necessary, for example, in the 'negationist' controversy over the existence of death camps.

So, while I readily grant that if such a postmodern approach does well to remind us of the otherness and uniqueness of the past, I fear that it makes the past itself unnecessarily inaccessible to us. By indicting all narrative truth claims as violent integrations of unassimilable alterity, Lyotard tends to reduce historiography to a literalist science. It is here that Lyotard proposes his own alternative of 'paganism' as 'just gaming', that is, as a mode of reading without criteria or truth claims. 'Whereas the pious philosopher aims to speak the truth', quips Lyotard, 'the pagan uses ruses and trickery in order not to redefine the truth but to displace the rule of truth'.[17]

The limits of representation

The problem here, as I see it, is that there is no middle ground between the extremes of (a) an absolute dogmatism of history (the tyranny of master narratives); and (b) the anarchic serialism of micronarratives. The answer is surely not to abandon all criteriology of justice or truth in our adjudication of different language games (e.g. the Nazi and the non-Nazi), but to re-establish such criteriologies on a basis that is more critically attentive to the otherness of the weak and powerless. For all its radical intent, Lyotard's agonistics runs the danger of collapsing into an antagonistics of irreconcilable conflict and violence. And I would suggest that one of the consequences of the prolongation of limitless agonistic negotiation – even as a pagan ruse to trick the strong – is that it risks consolidating 'the faits accomplis of an injustice'.[18]

But there are further problems. It seems to me that the postmodern cult of the 'immemorial' amounts to a wholesale rejection of critical hermeneutics. Lyotard's equation of historical representation with totalizing oppression is simplistic. By identifying all truth claims to reference the past with an onto-theological politics of the powerful, Lyotard endorses an inordinately nihilistic attitude towards historical remembering. Almost everything becomes a language game of power. And so the only legitimate response becomes one of 'silence'. Or, at most, idiosyncratic experiments in differential 'phrasing' which seek to testify to the unrepresentable without succumbing to discourse as such. Thus, with respect to the Holocaust, Lyotard repudiates any attempt to translate this horror into the history of inhumanity and injustice – for that would be to reduce its uniqueness by comparing it to other historical atrocities such as the Armenian or Rwandan genocides or the liquidation of American Indians, etc. Any such efforts at historical representation or comparison pander, Lyotard believes, to the revisionists. Or, almost as bad, to those who wish to discuss the possibility of pardon and reconciliation. For Lyotard and certain other die-hard sceptics, any attempt to come to terms with the horror of the immemorial past is an abdication of justice. In the final analysis, no analysis of memory is possible. Only the immemorial is just.

But rather than reject all notions of 'representation' and 'reference' out of hand, would it not be wiser to problematize and redefine them? To repudiate absolutely every reality claim amounts surely to a ruinous dichotomy between a modern *positivism of fact* and a postmodern *apophatism of silence*. And that, I submit, is to caricature history and give up on it. To suggest that the only genuine response to the horror of the Holocaust is to bear witness to the impasse of the ineffable is to deny the victims their right to be remembered – a right which cannot be adequately respected, it seems to me, without some recourse (however minimal and problematic) to narrative images and representations. To be non-represented can also mean to be un-represented.[19] Which means that many historical injustices may actually remain ignored.

Let me take a stark example. If representation is, for Lyotard, a way of neglecting the horror of Auschwitz, the total refusal of representation may be another and arguably more harmful one. Not all narrative remembrances of the Holocaust – or other historical atrocities – are reducible to the repressive 'economy of speech'. Not every attempt to 'say it as it was' signals a collapse into logocentrism. Such either/or exclusivism, I am convinced, merely exacerbates a new binarism between (1) a post-ontological sphere of ineffability, which supposedly respects the radical otherness of the past, and (2) an ontological sphere of speech which invariably betrays otherness by translating it into the idioms of conscious synthesis and unity. As Lyotard puts it, 'by opposing discontinuity with synthesis, consciousness seems to be the very thing that throws down a challenge to alterity'.[20]

But by consigning the alterity of the past to the unpresentable void of prehistory, does not Lyotard himself rule out the possibility of historical remembrance (in anything but a negative sense)? The horrors of history thus become subject to the imperative of the immemorial. Historical narrative is outlawed. As though we were witnessing a postmodern version of Plato's absolute 'beyond' (*epekeina*). With this crucial difference: it is now evil rather than good that is being placed beyond speech.

A way between

My basic question, then, is this: does not Lyotard respond to the modern 'compulsion to communicate' with an equally compulsive *refusal* to communicate? Does he not, by setting up hermeneutic approaches to alterity (especially Habermas, Ricoeur and Gadamer) as universalist straw men, not end up espousing an obversely untenable extreme of isolationist privacy, bordering on a sort of philosophical autism? Between these caricatured extremes of modern communicability and postmodern incommunicablity, we would be wiser, I suggest, to continue our search for a 'way between' (*metaxy*). A path which enables us to walk at sea level, charting a careful itinerary between the bipolar swings of cognitive binarism.

Such a metaxological approach, already outlined in our introduction to *The God who May Be*, seeks an intermediary course between the simplistic polarities advanced by Lyotard: anti-essentialism versus essentialism, alterity versus consciousness, silence versus speech, ineffability versus representation, paganism versus globalism, micro-narratives versus master-narratives. It simply doesn't have to be like this. All or nothing. Historical memory is not a matter of black and white but of grey on grey. And that means that in approaching the past we need to deconstruct such binary dualisms so as to 'muddle through' with the help of a certain judicious mix of phronetic understanding, narrative imagination and hermeneutic judgement. In other words, rather than abandoning all possibilities of referencing historical 'reality' (the way it was), we might do better to explore new criteriological models of historical remembering. We claim that it is possible to recall past horrors without relapsing into the old 'modernist' error of cognitive positivism. Though we would not for a moment deny the extraordinary difficulties and complexities attached to such possibility. If for Lyotard the only alternative to sublime ineffability is essentialist totality, that is Lyotard's problem.[21] Not everything can be cut at the joints. Not everything can be split neatly in two. Absolutism – however finessed by postmodernism – invariably leads to binarism. There are other options.

Hermeneutics of self and other

The hermeneutic 'middle way' I am proposing here requires, amongst other things, a redefining of the historian as a narrative self. For bluntly put: if there is no self capable of responding to the lost 'others' of history, how can they be recalled in their 'otherness'?

The very notion of a narrative self has been challenged by certain post-modern declarations of the death of man. This line of thinking finds expression in the view that the human self is an epistemic construct of recent invention whose time has come, and gone. If the self survives as all, it does so, we are told, only in the altered guise of a rhetorical 'trope', 'desiring machine' or 'effect' of the signifier. As we proceed into the third millennium the human subject has become, in the eyes of some, little more than a postman circulating postcards in an endless communications network without sender or addressee. A shipwrecked navigator floating on the linguistic jetsam of differential anonymity.

One of the tasks of a new diacritical hermeneutics is the reinvention of a genuine narrative subject in the wake of the mortified narcissistic author. In several other works – *The Wake of Imagination*, *Poetics of Imagining* and *On Stories* – I have argued for the indispensable role of a post-metaphysical self in our postmodern culture. And I would reiterate my conviction here that once the masters of deconstruction have done their necessary work, it is important to retrieve the notion of a responsible narrator committed to the task of historical and personal remembrance. For even after deconstruction we must still suppose a human self who suffers and creates, a self capable of addressing the blocked memories and traumas of postmodern melancholy.[22]

The challenge, in other words, is to to envisage the existence of a narrative self prepared to work through the pain of the past in dialogue with its Others. This would operate as a memoried self who recognizes the limits of remembering while resisting the fetishism of the immemorial. A post-deconstructionist subject, if you will, able to carry out acts of semantic innovation (poetics) and just judgement (ethics). A narrative identity woven from its own histories and those of others.

That there are many puzzles and anxieties surrounding such a post-metaphysical self I do not deny. But I remain convinced that it is possible to continue to speak meaningfully of a narrative *ipse* in the framework of a hermeneutic conversation which takes on board the postmodern assaults on the sovereign cogito without dispensing with all notions of selfhood. To reiterate the recurring thesis of this book: without some sense of self there can be no sense of the *other-than-self*. Though this very notion of selfhood is one that can only be reached (*pace* Descartes and the Idealists) through the odessey of alterity. No account of selfhood dispenses with what the old Irish migrant monks called *circumnavigatio*: the path home through the detour of the world. And even Hamlet, as we saw above, needed Horatio to tell his story. The shortest route from self to self is always through the other.[23]

Conclusion

So, returning then to the debate on narrative remembrance I would say this by way of summary. Narrative testimony cannot be taken for granted. The common reduction of history to official stories, ideological antiquaries or cult commemorations proves just how easily memory is susceptible to abuse. At the more individual level, the almost obsessive need of certain therapies to recover 'long term repressed memories' in order to explain away pain and identify culprits who can make victims of us all, gives room for pause.[24] The cult of compulsory memory requires to be subjected to as much suspicion as its opposite – the cult of postmodern melancholy. For if the former leads to practices of excessive anamnesis, the latter slides towards the cynicism of anomie.

When it comes to history, there is no quick fix. Not everything in the past can be redeemed. And not everything in the past need remain frozen. But there is, I am persuaded, a middle way that invites us to reinvent modes of narrative remembering so that history, having been suitably problematized and deconstructed, can still hold out the hope (however difficult) of some kind of healing and reconciliation. I think this is what a Holocaust writer like Paul Celan actually indicates in works like 'The Meridian' or 'Death Fugue', mentioned at the outset. For such works insist on speaking 'on behalf of the other . . . perhaps an altogether other'.[25] They speak for now speechless witnesses in 'desperate conversation' with those no longer occupying our time and speech – but in conversation nonetheless. They speak in fragmentary voices which defy standard narrative continuity – but which narrate nonetheless. They may even speak in the voice of a first person narrator who testifies to disparate voices of the dead exceeding all efforts to identify them

– but they testify nonetheless. In short, even where narrative testimony can never measure up to the complexities and alterities of the past, it is important – ethically and poetically – to continue to remember. Or at least to keep on trying. I would go so far as to say that it is precisely when one is right up against the limits of the immemorial that one most experiences the moral obligation to bear witness to history, echoing the words of Beckett's unnameable narrator: 'I can't go on, I'll go on'.

The alternative, as I see it, is the expansion of the postmodern malady of melancholy without reprieve or redress. And that is unacceptable. It is precisely when confronted with the verdict that 'la mémoire est morte' that the narrative self owes it to the Other to retort: 'Vive la mémoire!'

9

GOD OR KHORA?

'The Container of the Uncontainable'.
From the Monastery of Khora, Istanbul, Turkey. (Photo by John Manoussakis)

God plays with creation
All that is play that the deity gives itself
(Angelus Silesius)

Another concept which defies reason and brings us to the very edge of hermeneutic understanding is *khora*. First invoked in Plato's *Timaeus*, this borderline concept has become a recurring stamping ground for several contemporary thinkers. The allusive and undecidable character of this name-less name – serving as a sort of Hellenic obverse of Exodus 3:15 – has provoked a number of intriguing readings, from the psychoanalytic interpretations of Kristeva and Žižek to the deconstructive ones of Caputo and Derrida. In what follows, we review some of these before advancing our own hypothesis that God and *Khora* are not so much diametrically opposed alternatives as supplementary partners in dialogue – what I call the 'third way of *posse*'.

Plato and khora

In the *Timaeus* 48e–53b, Plato enquires into the primordial origin from which all things come. In what must be one of the most intriguing passages in his entire oeuvre, Plato struggles to identify the fundamental condition of possibility of there being a world. He calls this *khora*, a virtually untranslatable term referring to a kind of placeless place from which everything that is derives. Deploying a number of allusive metaphors – nurse, mother, a perfume base, space, winnowing sieve, receptacle – Plato acknowledges how *khora* challenges our normal categories of rational understanding. He suggests that we might best approach it through a kind of *dream* consciousness. As soon as

193

he tries to put words on this unnameable stuff, Plato thus finds himself engaged in what we might call a hermeneutic poetics. He attempts to define *khora* as follows:

> It is the receptacle and, as it were, the nurse of all becoming and change . . . anything that is to receive in itself every kind of character must be devoid of all character. Manufacturers of scent contrive the same initial conditions when they make liquids which are to receive the scent as odourless as possible . . . In the same way that which is going to receive properly and uniformly all the likenesses of the intelligible and eternal things must itself be devoid of all character. Therefore we must not call the mother and receptacle of visible and sensible things either earth or air or fire or water . . . but we shall not be wrong if we describe it as invisible and formless, all embracing, possessed in a most puzzling way of intelligibility, yet very hard to grasp.
>
> (*Timaeus* 49–51)

Plato concludes this dense text by claiming that *khora* is a

> space which is eternal and indestructible, which provides a position for everything that comes to be, and which is apprehended without the senses by a sort of spurious reasoning and so is hard to believe in – we look at it indeed in a kind of dream . . .
>
> (*Timaeus* 52)[1]

But what exactly does Plato mean by this amorphous space which precedes all that appears in our world? Is it being? Is it God? Or both? Or *before* both? And which discipline is most adequate to address this elusive X? Cosmology? Ontology? Psychology? Theology? These are the sorts of questions which have been exercising a number of postmodern thinkers. In this chapter I propose to engage what I consider to be some of the most challenging of these readings.[2] My basic wager will be that *khora* is neither identical with God nor incompatible with God but marks an open site where the divine may dwell and heal.

Psychoanalysis and *khora*

Julia Kristeva offers a psychoanalytic interpretation of *khora*. Taking Plato's hints that it is pre-intelligible and pre-formal, she identifies *khora* as the primordial matrix of the unconscious. She describes it as a 'strange space' where certain 'drives hold sway': drives which have been discarded by the prohibition against the maternal body (hence the metaphors of mother and nurse). As such, khora infuses the signifying process of language with 'instability'; it threatens to return the conscious ego back to 'its source in the abominable limits from which, in order to be, the ego has broken away' – namely, the non-ego realm of archaic drive.[3]

Kristeva associates khora with what she calls the 'semiotic' processes of maternal organization. This preexists the 'symbolic' function of language itself – a function which she, following Lacan and Freud, identifies with the Law of the Father. For a human being to become an ego-self it must 'abject' this maternal matrix, henceforth considered off limits and taboo. The ego dismisses khora as irrational and confused, even horrifying. Khora is described by Kristeva as a womb or nurse in which 'elements are without identity, and without reason'. It is a 'place of a chaos which is and which becomes, preliminary to the constitution of the first measurable body'.[4]

The human subject, and indeed society itself, depend for their existence on the repression of this maternal 'body without borders'. And this repression results in the jettisoning of this space beyond the limits of the rational symbolic process of law and logos into a no man's land of abjection. In other words, if I am to become a subject the khora must become abject. Kelly Oliver explains:

> The abject is disgusting. It is what is on the border, what does not respect borders. It is neither one nor the other, undecidable . . . The abject is what threatens identity; it is neither good nor evil, subject nor object . . . but something that threatens these very distinctions.[5]

As such, it erodes the paternal logos of naming, bringing us to the very limit of what can be thought and said. 'It causes', says Kristeva , 'the Name to topple over into the unnameable that one imagines as femininity, non-language, or body'.[6]

In Revolution in Poetic Language, Kristeva attempts to describe khora in more technical – psychodynamic and linguistic – terms. She claims that the drives, understood as energy charges as well as psychical marks, express khora: 'a non-expressive totality formed by the drives and their stases in a motility that is as full of movement as it is regulated'. Here she explicitly invokes Plato's notion of khora to refer to what she calls 'an essentially mobile and extremely provisional articulation constituted by movements and their ephemeral stases'. And she then distinguishes this 'indeterminate *articulation* from a *disposition* that already depends on representation'. *Khora*, defined as rupture, is said to precede all criteria of 'evidence, verisimilitude, spatiality and temporality'.[7] In this enigmatic commentary, Kristeva proceeds to argue that all of our discourse is based on a paradoxical premise in that it 'moves with and against the *khora* in the sense that it simultaneously depends upon and refuses it'. And even though *khora* can be regulated and designated, it can never be clearly or distinctly posited. Consequently, even though we can locate *khora* and even give it a topology, we can never give it 'axiomatic form'.[8]

Blending Plato with Melanie Klein, Kristeva goes on to make the further claim that it is this same 'rhythmic space' of *khora*, devoid of thesis or position, which serves as precondition for our most basic kind of meaning (*signifiance*). Plato himself, she reminds us, 'leads us to such a process when he calls this receptacle or *khora* nourishing and maternal, not yet unified in an ordered whole because deity is absent from it'.[9] And yet, though deprived of the paternal properties of identity, unity and divinity, the *khora* 'is subject to a regulating process which is different from that of symbolic law but nevertheless effectuates discontinuities by temporarily articulating them and then starting over, again and again'.[10]

Khora thus emerges for Kristeva as a 'pre-verbal semiotic space'. A placeless place before language, law or cognition proper. Or to use Lacanian terms, *khora* is closer to the imaginary or the real than to the symbolic order. Qua psychosomatic modality of signifying, 'anterior to sign and syntax', it is not something that can be assumed by a knowing, constituted subject but rather governs the very connections 'between the body (in the process of constituting itself as a body proper), objects and the protagonists of family structure'.[11] Thus while the semiotic *khora* – as the site of pre-cognitive, pre-verbal drives – is 'on the path of destruction, aggressivity and death', it is also, insists Kristeva, the locus of a maternal 'ordering principle'. She explains the paradox thus: 'The semiotic *khora* is no more than the place where the subject is both generated and negated, the place where his unity succumbs before the process of charges and stases that produce him'.[12] And yet the very semiotic relations that make up the space of *khora* are only, Kristeva admits, properly attended to in '*dream* logic' (*Timaeus*, 52a); or in more accessible guise, in the semiotic rhythms of certain experimental literary texts. 'Indifferent to language, enigmatic and feminine', concludes Kristeva, 'this space underlying the written is rhythmic, unfettered, irreducible to its intelligible verbal translation; it is musical, anterior to judgement . . .'[13] In short, for Kristeva, as for Plato, khora brushes against the limits of logic and language.

*

Slavoj Žižek offers a more sinister take on this psychoanalytic reading when he develops the distinction between khora and symbolic law in the direction of a full apocalyptic scenario, inspired by Hegel and German Idealism. Žižek sees Hegel's notion of the pre-ontological 'night of the world', which precedes our constituted reality of subjects and objects, as a modern attempt to revisit the Platonic khora. He claims that in the entire history of philosophy, the 'first to approach this uncanny pre-ontological, not-yet-symbolized texture of relations was none other than Plato himself, who . . . feels compelled to presuppose a kind of matrix-receptacle of all determinate forms governed by its own contingent rules (khora)'.

Žižek insists, however, that it was the great breakthrough of German Idealism to outline the precise contours of this pre-ontological domain of the 'spectral Real': a domain which eludes the ontological constitution of reality.[14] While Kant identified this as the blind, uncanny X which preconditions the transcendental construction of our world, it was Shelling – ghosting Hegel – who took the dilemma by the horns, identifying the khora-zone as the 'divine madness' of the Ground of Existence itself, namely, that which 'in God himself is not yet God'.

On foot of this reading, khora emerges for Žižek as that obscure no-man's-land of monstrous drives and 'ghastly apparitions' which can never be grasped as such – only glimpsed in the moment of withdrawal.[15]

Deconstruction and khora

Although Kristeva and Žižek touch on the religious implications of khora they fail to tease them out. On occasion indeed, they appear almost to dismiss the issue out of hand by declaring khora to be so devoid of divinity as to precede any theological or religious consideration (linked, for them, to the paternal function of law and logos). By contrast, Jack Caputo does us the service of redressing this lacuna by raising the crucial question – God or khora? I want to concentrate here on Caputo's analysis of this quandary in *The Prayers and Tears of Jacques Derrida: Religion without Religion* (henceforth abbreviated as PT) and in related works.[16] Though this analysis is deeply indebted to Derrida, and

197

especially his 1996 essay entitled 'Khora',[17] there is, I will argue, something uniquely suggestive about Caputo's reading.

Caputo first discusses khora in the context of Derrida's distinction between the differance of deconstruction and the God of negative theology. This is how Caputo unpacks the distinction:

> However highly it is esteemed, differance is not God. Negative theology is always on the track of a 'hyperessentiality', of something hyper-present, hyper-real or sur-real, so really real that we are never satisfied simply to say that it is merely real. Differance, on the other hand, is less than real, not quite real, never gets as far as being or entity or presence, which is why it is emblematized by insubstantial quasi-beings like ashes and ghosts which flutter between existence and nonexistence, or with humble khora, say, rather than with the prestigious Platonic sun.
>
> (PT, p. 2)

Caputo concludes with this typically teasing inversion: Derrida's differance, he suggests, is but 'a quasi-transcendental anteriority, not a supereminent, transcendent ulteriority' (PT, p. 3). So far, so clear.

Later in this opening chapter of Prayers and Tears, entitled 'God is not Differance', Caputo adds this telling point: If God is higher than being, differance is lower than it. If God, like Plato's agathon, has gone beyond us, differance is more like Plato's khora in that it hasn't yet reached us. It is beneath us, before us, behind us: anterior rather than ulterior. This is how Caputo, paraphrasing Derrida, puts it: 'God does not merely exist; differance does not quite exist. God is ineffable the way Plato's agathon is ineffable, beyond being, whereas differance is like the atheological ineffability of Plato's khora, beneath being (Khora 30, On the Name, 96)' (PT, p. 10). In other words, unlike the God of theology, Khora is radically anonymous, amorphous, aleatory and errant – or as Derrida would say, 'destinerrant' (PT, p. 11).

In a subsequent section of the book entitled 'Three Ways to Avoid Speaking', Caputo clarifies this distinction when he revisits Derrida's landmark intervention in the negative theology debate, 'How not to Speak: Denials'.[18] The apophatic tradition of negative speaking – extending from the Greeks to Eckhart and Heidegger – begins with Plato. But Plato was divided. He pointed to two different 'tropics of negativity (Psy., 563)'. On the one hand, the famous Good beyond being (epekeina tes ousias) that so influenced the Christian neo-Platonic heritage of negative theology. On the other hand, infamous khora before being. Or as Derrida himself observes, khora is without being in that it 'eludes all anthropo-theological schemes, all history, all revelation, all truth' ('Khora' in On the Name).[19] Whereas one is obliged with khora, as with agathon, to unsay what one has said, the former differs from the latter in that it is not a form, or the Form of all Forms, but precedes both form and sensibility. It also differs from the Good in that it is not a fullness of presence and light but a dark bottomless 'abyss', a 'void of empty space'.[20] Neither sensible nor intelligible, khora is a third kind of thing, and is at most obliquely apprehensible through a hybrid reasoning. Reinterpreted by human language, khora can only be expressed in a series of tentative analogies or 'didactic' allusions. Hence Plato's metaphors of nurse, mother, matrix, imprint, receptacle etc. Hence also the invocation of such related notions as hyle (Aristotle, Husserl), extensio (Descartes) or magma (Castoriadis).

*

What interests Derrida and Caputo is not, however, how khora came to be said, albeit inexactly, within the language of logocentric metaphysics. It is rather how khora manages to escape this tradition of language. How it appears instead as an absolute stranger to it – or, to quote Caputo, as an 'outsider with no place to lay her/its head, in philosophy or in mythology, for it is the proper object of neither logos nor mythos' (PT, p. 35). Caputo claims that this second (more elusive and external) tropic of negativity is anterior to both being and non-being, the intelligible and the sensible, without being analogous to either. Citing Derrida on Plato's reading of khora, Caputo makes the following suggestive stab at a description of the indescribable:

> Khora is neither present nor absent, active nor passive, the Good nor evil, living nor nonliving (Timaeus 50c). Neither theomorphic nor anthropomorphic – but rather atheological and nonhuman – khora is not even a receptacle, which would also be something that is itself inscribed within it.
>
> (PT, p. 36)

This discourse, Caputo insists, even surpasses the language of symbol and metaphor. Why? Because it has nothing to do with a 'sensible likeness of something supersensible, a relationship that is itself within khora' (ibid.). For Caputo and Derrida in short, Khora has no meaning, no identity to fall back on. 'She/it receives all without becoming anything, which is why she/it can become the subject of neither a philosopheme nor a mytheme' ('Khora' in ON, p. 102). As Caputo cryptically surmises, 'khora is tout autre, very' (PT, p. 36).

Now while we might be tempted to think that the Platonic metaphors of matrix, mother and nurse in the Timaeus imply a certain act of nurturing beneficence, Caputo and Derrida are adamant that this is no normal mother. We are not dealing here with a recognizable family resemblance. Khora is altogether too indeterminate to engender anything.[21] And it is not a giver of gifts. One cannot say of khora, as one might say of God or the Good, that it 'gives'. It has no who. It does not care. Khora, Derrida tells us, is 'this "thing" that is nothing of that to which this "thing" nonetheless seems to give place (donner lieu) – without however, this "thing" ever giving anything (Psy., p. 568)'. For although one can say that khora 'gives place' to something, one must qualify this by saying that it does so 'without the least generosity, either divine or human (Foi, p. 86)'. Giving place, it seems, is simply a letting take place that has nothing to do with producing, creating or existing as such. One cannot even say that khora is, or is not; only that there is Khora (il y a khora). But this il y a, as Derrida again insists, 'gives nothing in giving place or in giving to think, whereby it will be risky to see in it the equivalent of an es gibt, of the es gibt which remains without a doubt implicated in every negative theology . . .' ('Khora' in ON, 96; see also Caputo, PT, p. 36).

In sharp contrast, therefore, to the neo-Platonic/Christian/metaphysical tradition of One-Good-God beyond being – and also in contrast to the Heideggerian gesture of Being (Es gibt Sein) – khora is a-theological and a-donational. It eschews the contemporary retrievals of transcendence and mystery – be it the Levinasian idea of infinity (otherwise than being), the Marionesque gesture of donation (God without being) or the Heideggerian principle of event (the gift of being). It is not even a third kind (genos) beyond the alternatives of being and non-being. No, it is not a 'kind' at all, but a radical singularity of which one might say – what is your name? (ON, p. 111). But then again khora cannot even possess a proper name. It is unnamable and unspeakable. Ineffable alterity. Tout autre par excellence. And yet, both Derrida and Caputo keep repeating, it is the very impossibility of speaking about khora that is also the necessity of speaking about it!

Revelation and khora

But how can we do so? How can we say anything at all about this pre-original khora? It seems impossible. And yet, it is (in Derrida's words) something that 'beyond all given philosophemes, has nevertheless left its trace in language' (*Psy.*, 569). As noted, Plato, for starters, hazarded a guess at this nameless thing by calling it *khora*, with its attendant exfoliation of metaphors. But *khora*, unlike the words God or the Good, is a word-trace that 'promises nothing' (*PT*, p. 37). In sharp contradistinction to the theological names deriving from the Good beyond being of Greek metaphysics or the Creator God of Judaeo-Christian revelation, *khora* suggests an altogether alternative site – one that is 'barren, radically nonhuman and atheological'. So that if this 'place' called *khora* can be said, like the God of negative theology, to indeed be *wholly other*, it is so in a manner utterly distinct from all theologies, apophatic or otherwise. Its desert is not a dark night of the soul waiting to be redeemed by light but a no-place that remains deserted. Just ashes and ashes, without ascensions into heaven. Abyss within abyss without elevation from the void. *Il y a la cendre*, to cite Caputo reciting Derrida.

So one is a little surprised to find Caputo suggesting at one point that there is at bottom a certain undecidability between God and *khora*. Having persuasively demonstrated the radical difference between the two – as exemplified by Levinasian hyperbole on the one hand and Derridean deconstruction on the other – we now have Caputo asking: 'What is the wholly other . . . God or *khora*? What do I love when I love my God, God or *khora*? How are we to decide? Do we have to choose?' (*PT*, p. 37). I suspect that Caputo thinks that we *don't* have to choose – since the issue remains radically undecidable. But I would like to disagree and suggest that we *do* whenever we opt to believe in God or not to believe. A religious belief, I submit, is hardly worthy of the name unless it calls for such choice (what Kierkegaard called the leap of faith). And Derrida himself, it seems, has little hesitation about declaring his own personal option, namely, for atheism. He candidly confesses that he 'rightly passes for an atheist'.

Moreover, Caputo also appears to allow for such choice when he claims that the antithesis between *khora* and God admits of no 'passage' between them. So we are back with a decisive difference, in spite of all. While the theist takes the high road towards the God/Good beyond being, the deconstructionist descends the low road to the uncompromising and inconsolable abyss. Whereas Dionysius and other mystical–apophatic theologians praise and pray to God, invoking his kenotic goodness and hyperousiological generosity, *khora* is a very different kettle of fish. It does not command praise. It does not call for prayer. It is neither good nor generous nor giving. No, *khora* is radical 'destinerrance'. And those who end up in its desert always end up lost. *Khora* does not care for us. And we do not care for khora. (Which does not, I hasten to add, prevent Caputo and Derrida, devotees of khora, from caring greatly about things and people, especially the downtrodden, underprivileged and suffering.)

Desert fathers and destinerrance

Fair enough. But if this be so – if 'destinerrance' is what khora does to us – is Caputo justified in claiming that Derrida is really on the side of the original desert fathers, the anchorites (or 'an-khora-ites' as he cleverly rechristens them) with their lean and hungry looks? Can he legitimately nominate, even in jest, the advocate of deconstructive khora as 'Saint Jacques, Derrida the Desert Father!'? For, unlike Derrida, the desert fathers did praise, dance and sing quite openly before their desert God. Anthony and Jerome, Simon and John Chrysostom, spent months in their caves – to be sure – but they also walked out into the light and magnified their Maker. To have done less would be despair. Or to put it in Kierkegaard's terms in *Fear and Trembling*, it would mean taking only the first step in the two steps of faith: the step of infinite resignation which gives up creation without taking the second step of wanting it back again. If Abraham had opted for endless 'destinerrance' over religious faith, he would never have ventured his leap of faith and received Isaac *back*. That is why I do not think it is quite right to equate Derrida with Kierkegaard as Caputo does (PT, p. 59).

I am asking, in short: can Caputo have it both ways? Can he claim on the one hand that Derrida takes the path of a-theological desertification and then reclaim him as a saintly anchorite father? Or, alternatively, can he refuse the two options altogether and declare the issue undecidable – God is both/and/neither/nor khora? Wouldn't that too be wanting it both ways? Not an option, I would suspect, for religious believers. (Though a perfectly consistent one for deconstructionists.)

It is not inconceivable that khora could inspire its own kind of belief (an-khora-itic albeit not theistic). It might well trigger its own kind of leap of faith (albeit not towards God). It might even be that God and khora are two different ways of approaching the same indescribable experience of the abyss. But the choice between the two is not insignificant. Which direction you leap in surely matters. For while the theistic leap construes our experience in the desert as 'a dark night of the soul' *on the way towards* God, the latter sees it as a night without end, a place where religious prayer, promise and praise are not applicable. Not, I imagine, a place the desert fathers would want to hang around for very long.

In the khora desert it is inevitable that one loses one's way. Isn't that precisely what the deconstructive commitment to 'destinerrance' means? But in the ankhorite wilderness – invoked by the original desert fathers and traversed by mystics like Silesius, Eckhart, Teresa and John of the Cross – the journey through desolation is made in the fervent hope that one will find a path to God, that the lost sheep will be gathered and brought home to the Father. (A prospect anathema to deconstructors, I presume.) There is a genuine difference between anchorite fathers and deconstructive sons. A healthy difference to be sure. But one that can't be magicked away in a soft-shoe shuffle of undecidability.

It boils down to this, as I see it: Deconstruction isn't just describing khora as one might describe a twilight or a storm at sea. It is describing it in the same way it describes différance or pharmakon or supplement or archi-writing. That is, it appears to express a marked preference for khora, and its allies, over its rivals. Not moral preference, granted; but in some minimal and irreducible sense, an evaluative preference nonetheless. As one reads Caputo one cannot help surmising that for him khora is – at bottom and when all metaphysical illusions are stripped away – the ways things are. It is a better, deeper way of viewing things than its theological or ontological rivals – God or Es gibt. For its advocates, khora seems, in the heel of the hunt, closer to the 'reality' of things than all non-khora alternatives. In that sense, yes, deconstruction does appear to take sides even when it is doing its most non-committal four-step of neither/nor/both/and. Deconstruction makes a preferential option for khora. Though it would not deny for a moment that non-khoraites can also be genuine questioners, who might find their way back to the no-place of différance – eventually.

From khora to the kingdom

But that is not the only disagreement I have with the deconstructionists. I have a deeper reservation about the nature of khora itself – if taken as the most archi-original and ineluctable site. Let me try to articulate my reservations here in the quasi-existential idioms of thinkers like Caputo and Kristeva, for whom a certain hermeneutics of lived facticity is almost invariably operative in contrast to the quasi-transcendental language of Derrida's account of khora. Phrasing the matter in terms of le vécu, therefore, I would suggest that if khora is indeed experienced by most of us as a place/no place we encounter sometime in our lives – perhaps even sometime every day of our lives – it is not, I think, the best place to spend our entire lives, or to encourage others to spend theirs. I am not talking here, I hasten to add, of Plato's purely cosmological notion of khora. Nor indeed of Kristeva's psycho-semiotic one. For neither of these, as I read them, see khora as an explicit player in the religious drama. No, I am speaking here of khora, as described by Caputo, in terms of a formless desert abyss, a no-place we experience in fear and trembling moments of uncertainty and loss, that dark night of waiting in the il y a without exit or response. I am referring to what Levinas terms the 'mute, absolutely indeterminate menace' of the 'there is' – the 'horror' of 'nocturnal space'. Indeed Levinas leaves us in no doubt as to the a-theistic nature of this experience: 'Rather than to a God, the notion of the there is leads us to the absence of God, the absence of any being . . . before the light comes'.[22]

I acknowledge this experience of khora as part and parcel of human existence. I do not deny that we all have some experience of khora/il y a as the 'horror of the night with "no exits" which does not answer . . .'[23] But I'm not sure I want to celebrate it as the best we can do. Or, at bottom, the place where the buck stops. And I certainly wouldn't want to recommend it as an ongoing modus vivendi for those who are suffering its darkness. If compelled to choose, I would personally opt for Levinas' move from the Il y a of irremissible existence to the illéité of ethical transcendence. While acknowledging, of course, that any genuine religious belief in transcendence is inextricably linked to a prereligious and atheistic experience of the an-khora-ite 'there is'.

But this is still heady stuff. What might khora be in more familiar terms? I imagine that for many non-philosophers, khora is experienced as misery, terror, loss and desolation. The insomniac dark. Might we not imagine khora accordingly – since even the unimaginable calls out for images – in terms of various examples drawn from the great narrative traditions? The Greek stories of Oedipus without eyes, Sisyphus in Hades, Prometheus in chains, Iphighenia in waiting? The biblical stories of tohu bohu before creation, Job in the pit, Jonah in the whale, Joseph at the bottom of the well, Naomi all tears, Jesus abandoned on the cross (crying out to the Father) or descended into hell? Or the fictional and dramatic accounts of Conrad's heart of darkness, Hamlet's stale and unprofitable world, Monte Cristo's prison cell, Primo Levi's death camp? Or more basically still, is khora not that pre-original abyss each of us encounters in fear and trembling when faced with the bottomless void of our existence?

Who would deny the *reality* of these kinds of *khora*-esque experiences? They may well be the *most* 'real' (at least in Lacan's sense) of human experiences, the most unspeakably traumatic 'limit experiences' of things that exceed our understanding. The most sublime of horrors. But again I have to say I would find it hard to make a preferential option for them, or counsel others to do likewise.

*

Caputo might well reply: that is not what I meant at all! Of course *khora* is unlivable. We know human kind cannot bear too much reality. We accept that people need to climb out of the *khora*-ite cave into the light of everyday consolations, pastimes and distractions (call it the 'They world', 'natural attitude', or any common religious belief in God as saving, healing, loving, benevolent grace). All we are saying is – give *khora* a chance. Because even though it may not be liveable it is what life is unavoidably and at bottom about! *Au fond, sans fond, il y a khora.* That is, I suspect, how Caputo would respond.

So let me try to be clearer here. I am *not* suggesting for a moment that we flee the shadow at the heart of existence. I am not saying we shouldn't face up to the terrors and indeterminacies of the world and do so in fear and trembling. On the contrary, if we do not acknowledge meaninglessness – how could we ever speak about it or go beyond it? As Camus rightly said, you must live the absurd in order to fight it. Agreed. But is that what Caputo is saying about *khora*? That we should confront it in order to struggle against it, or put an end to it as soon as we can? I get the impression rather that for most deconstructors, *khora* is ultimately more archi-ultimate than God or the Good or Being. Just as writing is more archi-ultimate than speech and *differance* is more archi-ultimate than presence. If *khora* is indeed being lost in the desert – the unillumined, undecidable, atheological dark of destinerrance – I'm not certain that deconstruction is reassuring us that this is just *temporary*. A passing moment of trial and transition. I don't hear deconstruction urging us to rise up from the *khora* dust so that (with a few more prayers and tears) we may soon find our Shepherd again and be guided towards the Kingdom.

One gets the *opposite* impression reading Caputo: that to accept being lost in destinerrance, *without* looking for meaning or healing, is really more steel-nerved and unblinking than seeking to be found. Not that Jack Caputo wouldn't have sympathy for those of us who can't take the cold of the desert night for too long, for those scared witless by the horrors of *toho bohu*. His heart, I have no doubt, would go out to those who need to put an end to fear and trembling by taking a leap of faith and getting their Isaac back, climbing down off the cross, opening the cell hatch, hankering for redemption and peace and calm. He would have every sympathy for those who pray the black void of depression will fade, the chalice pass – even if that means adding a little Prozac to their prayers. But he wouldn't buy into it. It is not for him, or the other hardy chevaliers of deconstruction. Higher than the children of faith are the knights of khora who brave the long day's journey into never-ending night. And never look back.

So my reading is patently different from deconstruction here. In my view, anchorite monks went to the desert to find God, not khora. They didn't make a mystery of loss or a virtue of the void. And if it is indeed true that they traversed emptiness and destitution it was faute de mieux. An unavoidable detour on the way to grace. They would have preferred, I am sure, to hit the land of milk and honey after the first dune. But since life is not like that, they had to learn the hard way on their way to the Kingdom. Losing life – yes – but in order to gain it. Renouncing their beloved, yes, killing their darlings, yes, sacrificing their Isaacs, yes, but believing all the while they would get them back again.

In the heel of the hunt, deconstruction does not appear neutral on the question of khora. If anything, it seems to reckon it is the place (or no-place) to be if you really want to get to the heart of things. It's what is really out there (in here) once we go beyond alibis and illusions, salves and solaces, Confiteors and consolations, and open our eyes.

It is hard, of course, to be sure about something as elusive as khora. So by way of conclusion, let me return to Caputo's bracing text for one final, closer look.

Towards a God who May Be

Caputo does indeed admit prayer into the unholy of unholies – the khora. But it is a very specific kind of prayer: a-theistic and a-theological. It is not, he insists, a 'Christian prayer, directed to the Trinity' (PT, p. 39). Deconstructive prayer – as in the prayers and tears of Jacques Derrida – is not addressed to God 'the saving name, the giver of all good gifts' (ibid.). It does not seek to keep itself 'safe from the abyss of khora' (ibid.). It does not look beyond that anonymous 'interval' within which all things find their place ('Khora', ON, p. 125). Here prayer is no 'desert guide' but an unconsoling and, as Caputo notes, 'slightly sinful' mode of address. Why? Because it addresses an alterity in each and every thing so terrifyingly sublime, so textually irreducible, that there is no exit (short of some quick back-flip into theology/ideology/logocentrism). Caputo fully endorses here Derrida's view that khora has very little to do with a theistic divinity and everything to do with the 'very spacing of de-construction' (ON, p. 80). Something like a 'surname for differance' (PT, p. 40).

What I find most problematic in Caputo's approach, in sum, is that it sets up deconstruction/differance/khora as an *alternative* to theology. Either khora or God. Either the Pseudo-Dionysius or Derrida. Or as Caputo cleverly rephrases the options in a later chapter: either the 'angelic doctor' from Aquino or the 'devilish deconstructor' from the Rue d'Ulm (PT, p. 168–9). On one side of the ring, Caputo lines up the idioms of paternal metaphysics – fusion, presence, union, circularity, totality, economy, sameness. On the other, he marshals his clearly preferred idioms of the 'more maternal simulacrum' of khora – 'aleatory gratuitousness and anarchic abandon' (ibid.). If you say thanks to God the giver, concedes Caputo, you do not say thanks to khora (ibid.). 'Il y a khora', he goes on to explain, 'but she/it does not generously "give" anything' and is not 'the gesture of a donor subject' (Khora, 37–38/ON, 100). Rather khora is the 'spacing within which an unlimited number of events take place, in her/its place' (ibid.).

This kind of alternativism, I conclude, risks turning theology (negative or positive) into a caricature and seems to assume that saintly doctors – like Aquinas after he had seen the light – were victims of some kind of ecclesiastical closure (PT, p. 60–1). Not all mystical experience is fusional, as Caputo seems to imply in such passages (but not, incidentally, in his earlier books on Eckhart and Aquinas). And not every notion of the Trinitarian God – not to mention Yahweh or Allah – is a fetish of presence or hyperessence. What of Eckhart's God beyond God, so inspiringly invoked by Caputo himself in other writings? What of Silesius' rose without why, so dear to Heidegger and Derrida? Or Cusanus' Possest as we explored it in *The God Who May Be*? Or, finally, the wonderfully ludic notion of the three persons dancing around an empty space in respective acts of dispossession – perichoresis, translated by the Latins as circumincessio: an event of loving letting-be graphically captured in Andrei Rublev's icon of the three angels? An interplay already prefigured in the wonderful verse of Zephaniah 3, 17: 'He will rejoice over you with happy song/He will renew you by his love/He will dance with shouts of joy for you/as on a day of festival'.

This is all a far cry, is it not, from the old metaphysical notions of pure self-identical presence: *ens causa sui, ipsum esse subsistens, actus purus non habens aliquid de potentialitate?* Hoary chestnuts which we should all be grateful to see cracked apart over open fires by the likes of Derrida and Caputo.

What I have been trying to point out here is how Caputo, and at times Derrida, has a tendency to set up a somewhat precipitous gulf between (a) divinity, equated with fusion/union/essence/presence; and (b) its deconstructive other, equated with *khora/differance/*writing*/pharmakon.* And while it is understandable why one should do this from a pedagogical point of view – we all need dramatic distinctions – is it not a little surprising coming from the finest masters of deconstruction? Is it not something of a compromise regarding the deconstructive finesse of both/and/neither/nor?

To avoid such polarizing gestures, we might remind ourselves that there are many degrees of latitude between the North Pole of God (qua pure hyperessence) and the South Pole of *khora* (qua anonymous abyss). My short list above – ranging from Eckhart to *perichoresis* – not to mention other approximations sketched in this volume, signal tentative, probing paths towards a 'between' way. There are, I am suggesting, more than just two options. And the third option I am adumbrating here would, I wager, liberate a space of chiasmic play between *khora* and *hyperousia*. A space for what in my final chapter below, and in my companion volume *The God Who May Be*, I call the possible God.

APPENDIX:
DERRIDA AND THE DOUBLE ABYSS

Am I fair to deconstruction? It is true that Caputo does, in certain other passages of PT, appear to offer a different take on the God–khora relation (without appearing to acknowledge it as different). In such passages, Caputo does seem to concede that khora may be an ally as much as an adversary of God. On one occasion, for instance, he even sees khora as a precondition of genuine theistic faith. Khora, he grants here, is 'a general condition of any "belief"'; adding: 'How could Derrida – for whom everything depends upon faith – rule out religious faith? Why would Derrida want to ban the name of God, a name he dearly loves?' (p. 59). Caputo even appears, in this particular passage, to equate Derrida's version of khora with Kierkegaard's version of theistic faith:

> Derrida does no more than follow Johannes de Silentio, Abraham's poet, from whose fear and trembling we learn that faith 'must never be a certainty' but passion, the 'highest passion that . . . still has the heart to push ahead' (DM 78/GD 80), which is the repetition forward and the marvel.
>
> (p. 59)

Indeed in a related text on khora in his *Deconstruction in a Nutshell*, Caputo even suggests that Judaeo-Christian faith may be closer to Derrida's 'bastard' khora than to the aristocratic super-being of Neoplatonism. It is worth asking, he says, 'where the hearts of the prophets and of Jesus would be – with the St. James's street aristocrats, the best and the brightest, or with the Dickensian down and outs'.[24] A fair point. But that is a change of tune, is it not, from the more prevalent register of either/or – either khora or God – rehearsed above?

How might we account for this shifting position? One hypothesis could be that Caputo is so keen to make connections between deconstruction and theology that he bends over backwards not to give in to his own urge to rush his fences and secure a premature synthesis. He wants at all costs to respect Derrida's right to declare himself an 'atheist'. As though Caputo, a crypto-theist, is desperately trying not to evangelize deconstruction by turning it into a crypto-theology. A case, perhaps, of the theist does resist too much. So that, by a curious irony, it is sometimes Derrida himself who seems *more* ready to build bridges (however provisional) between the abyssal khora and the saving God. Derrida, a self-declared atheist, has less difficulty throwing ropes, at certain moments, across the ostensible ravine separating the ungodly khora and God. (Not that Derrida has any difficulties cutting these cords too!) While making sure never to identify God directly with Khora, Derrida seems prepared at times to admit certain uncharted crossings.

There are some pertinent passages on this question in Derrida's 'Post-Scriptum' to *Derrida and Negative Theology*, subtitled 'Aporias, Ways and Voices'.[25] Most intriguing is Derrida's sympathetic commentary on the Christian mystic, Angelus Silesius: '"God" "is" the name of this bottomless collapse, of this endless desertification of language' (p. 301), he writes, 'a name which is, at the same time, interpreted by Silesius as "the divinity of God as gift"' (p. 300). Derrida then proceeds to relate this God of Silesius – a God whom he, Silesius, prays to give Himself to the prayer – to 'some khora (interval, place, spacing)' (p. 301). Everything, says Derrida, 'is played out here' (ibid.). And to Silesius' equation of the 'Place' (Ort) and the 'word' (Wort) – *Der Ort und's Wort ist Eins* – Derrida adjoins this telling reflection:

> It is not that in which is found a subject or an object. It is found in us . . . The here
> of eternity is situated there, already: already there, it situates this throwing or this
> throwing up . . . but first of all throwing that puts outside, that produces the outside
> and thus space . . .
>
> (p. 301)

Later in the same 'Post-Scriptum', Derrida displays a deep fascination with Silesius' approach to God's giving in terms of *Gelassenheit* and play. (The verse he is commenting reads: 'God plays with creation/All that is play that the deity gives itself' (ibid.).)

But before we lapse into ecumenical euphoria, Derrida puts an end to equivocation by appearing to draw a deep line – a gulf in fact – between the reading of place as God and as khora. As this statement of Derrida's position is crucial I quote the passage in full:

> *Der Ort is das Wort* (1: 205) indeed affirms the place as word of God. – Is this place
> created by God? Is it part of the play? Or else is it God himself? Or even what
> precedes, in order to make them possible, both God and his Play? In other words,

it remains to be known if this nonsensible (invisible and inaudible) place is opened
by God, by the name of God (which would again be some other thing, perhaps),
or if it is 'older' than the time of creation, than time itself, than history, narrative,
word, etc. It remains to be known (beyond knowing) if the place is opened by
appeal (response, the event that calls for the response, revelation, history, etc.), or
if it remains impassively foreign, like *Khora*, to everything that takes its place and
replaces itself and plays within this place, including what is named God.

(p. 314)

Derrida leaves us in little doubt that a choice is called for here between two rival,
incompatible and mutually exclusive notions of place. 'Do we have any choice? Why choose
between the two? Is it possible?' he asks rhetorically. To which he proffers the following
altogether non-rhetorical answer:

But it is true that these two 'places', these two experiences of place, these two
ways are no doubt of an absolute heterogeneity. One place excludes the other,
one (sur)passes the other, one does without the other, one is, absolutely, *without the
other.*

(p.315)

And so we have the antithesis:

On one side, on one way, a profound and abyssal eternity, fundamental but accessible
to the teleo-eschatological narrative and to a certain experience of historical (or
historial) revelation; on the other side, *on the other way,* the nontemporality of an
abyss without bottom or surface, an absolute impassibility (neither life nor death)
that gives rise to everything that it is not. In fact, two abysses.

(p. 315)

What we have here, in sum, is nothing less than the abyss of God facing off against the abyss
of *khora.*

As I read Derrida, deconstruction operates on the side of the latter – the nontemporal,
bottomless, impassible abyss, that does the work of *khora* and *differance.* To be sure, Derrida does
admit of a certain relation between these two abyssal 'places' in respect of an 'exemplarism'
of conjunction–disjunction which he explores in his analysis of the term 'without'. But this
highly complex notion cannot really distract from the fundamental opposition between the
two senses of 'place'. Nor does it abrogate Derrida's fundamental choice, as I see it, for *khora*
over God. A choice I admire for its bold radicality, but do not share.

To repeat: despite numerous cross-cuttings, there is a radical difference, in the final analysis,
between Derrida and Silesius. Silesius sees our experience of the place of play as 'one abyss
calling to the other' (echoing Psalm 41) – the void within us crying out to the unfathomable
deep of God. (Silesius: 'The abyss of my spirit always invokes with cries/The abyss of God:
say which may be deeper?') By contrast, Derrida construes the place as the 'indestructible
Khora . . . the very spacing of de-construction' (p. 318).

210

Where Silesius' God promises peace and healing, Derrida's *Khora* is 'gulf and chaos' (p. 321). The choice is, at bottom, between theism and atheism. The two are as inextricably linked as Siamese twins, granted; but they beat with different hearts. They may look alike, but they think different thoughts and signal different options.

'My faith comes forth from the crucible of doubt', confessed Dostoyevsky, the crucible serving the role of atheistic *khora*. But his faith does come forth; it surpasses and goes beyond the preconditioning crucible – rightly or wrongly, for better or worse. It does not remain indefinitely within the crucible. There is, after all, a fundamental decision to be made between reading the desert place as *khora* or as God. Even if that choice is never final or assured. For if the theist does choose God it is always in fear and trembling and can never be more than a hair's breadth from the underlying, undecidable abyss of *khora* – a common pre-original void from which faith issues and from which it is never definitively removed, to its dying day. Indeed, were it so definitively removed it would no longer be faith.

When God created the world he created it from nothing, chaos, *tohu bohu*, *khora*. That is why God and *khora*, like theism and atheism, are two sides of the same coin. And maybe in a strange way, occasionally hinted at by both Derrida and Caputo, they need each other. Perhaps. I conclude, then, with the suggestion that God and *Khora* may, on occasion, supplement rather than exclude one another. A suggestion which finds curious support in the fact that murals of the Mother of Christ in certain early Byzantine churches were inscribed with the name *khora tou akhoretou* – 'Container of the Uncontainable'.[26] If God without *khora* risks dogmatism, *khora* without the possibility of God risks desolation. Perhaps *khora* could be reinterpreted as the primordial matrix of the world which God needs to become flesh? The key word to the kingdom being, as always, *perhaps*.[27]

10

LAST GODS AND FINAL THINGS
Faith and philosophy

What do we mean when we use the word God? In that word is
contained everything we hope for.

(Augustine)

Of all the limit-experiences which challenge the scope of hermeneutic
interpretation, that of 'God' must rank amongst the most perplexing
and persistent. For centuries controversies raged about names for God. Some
religious movements, from Hebrew and Christian iconoclasticism to the
apophatic extremes of negative theology, forbade any attempt to represent the
divine. And certain philosophical schools expressed an equally scrupulous
reserve regarding our ability to know anything at all about God – an attitude
epitomized in the classic question: *Aut fides aut ratio* (either faith or reason)?
One view was that philosophical thinking was a mere 'handmaiden' to
monotheistic theology, and could at best serve to provide supplementary aids
to the great books of Revelation. Another view, particularly strong in the
late middle ages, held that there were in fact two truths at issue: one pertaining
to the worldly realm of ontology and science, the other reserved for the
higher, transcendent sphere of religious belief. As the adage went: *quasi sint duae
contrariae veritates.*

Faith or Reason?

The early Heidegger was surely mindful of such debates when he argued
that theology and philosophy are radically distinct disciplines. The former,
he declared, was based on the *positum* of Judaeo-Christian Revelation, while
the latter was committed to an agnostic questioning of all that is. That at least

213

was his position in 1927 when he delivered his famous lecture on 'Phenomenology and Theology'. Here he wrote:

> Theology is a positive science and as such is absolutely different from philosophy . . . The occurrence of revelation, which is passed down to faith and which accordingly occurs through faithfulness itself, discloses itself only to faith . . . Theology has a meaning and a value only if it functions as an ingredient of faith, of this particular kind of historical occurrence.[1]

The corollary thesis endorsed by Heidegger was that 'philosophical research is atheism'.[2] Indeed, it was Heidegger's firm conviction that the phenomenological method he developed in the 1920s resisted all forms of 'prophetism' and refused the temptation to provide ethical or evaluative 'guidelines for life'.[3] This persuasion was sustained throughout *Being and Time* (1927) where God hardly got a look in. And it even evolved into an 'aggressive atheism' in the 1930s when, as John Caputo informs us, Heidegger reinforced his rejection of his young theological leanings and deemed Christianity to be a 'decadent falling away from experience'.[4]

It was, however, in his controversial 1935 text, *Introduction to Metaphysics*, that Heidegger spelt out most clearly the opposition between philosophy and faith. He declared here that philosophy could not even begin to pose its inaugural question – Why is there something rather than nothing? – if it had recourse to theological answers, e.g. God created the world. The God of theology, he now insisted, does not feature in philosophy. And by the same token, as St Paul acknowledged from the other side of the fence, faith is a 'folly for philosophers'. The *logos* of St John has little or nothing to do with the *logos* of Heraclitus and Greek metaphysics. In fact, in the same text Heidegger delivered the uncompromising verdict that a Christian philosophy is a 'round square and a misunderstanding'.[5]

This antithetical relation between philosophy and theology was reiterated in several subsequent statements by Heidegger in the 1940s and 50s. We might cite, for example, his avowal to a group of Swiss theologians at the Academy of Hofgeismar in 1952 that even though he hailed from a theological background he firmly believed that 'faith has no need for the thinking of Being'; adding that if he, Heidegger, were ever to embark on such a thing as theology 'the word Being would not feature in it'.[6] Heidegger made a similar point to A. Noack in 1953, declaring that there is nothing in philosophy that could confirm the experience of religious grace. 'If I were addressed by faith', he said, 'I would abandon my vocation as a philosopher'.[7] In this scenario, Being can never be a predicate of God. And the God of faith has no real role in a philosophy of Being.[8]

Only a God

Nothing would seem more evident then: either God or Being? But never both at once; nor one in positive relation to the other. Things are not so simple, however. For while Heidegger does seem to advance an either/or view in the above statements, there are numerous other passages in which he appears to take a different view. I am thinking particularly of his enigmatic, but pointed, confession in the Der Spiegel interview, published after his death in 1976, that 'only a god can save us now' (Nur ein Gott kann uns noch retten). The passage in question reads as follows:

> Philosophy cannot produce an immediate effect which would change the present state of the world. This is not only true for philosophy but for all specifically human endeavours. Only a God can save us now. The only possibility remaining to us in thought and in poetry is to remain available for the manifestation of this God or for the absence of this God in our decline.
>
> (Der Spiegel, 31 May 1976)

But what kind of a 'God' is Heidegger talking about here? Is it the God of theology (Creation and Redemption)? The God of philosophy (Aristotle and Western metaphysics)? Or the God of the poets (Hölderlin, the German romantics and ancient tragedians)? I have argued elsewhere that it is in fact the last of these – the 'God' of the poets – that Heidegger has in mind when he makes his Der Spiegel statement. I do not propose to rehearse these arguments here. Only to probe the further question: how can a deity of poetic saying and thinking relate, if at all, to the eschatological God of Revelation?

*

What first needs to be established is that for Heidegger the God of poetics is essentially a deity that appears as a 'holy' dimension within a phenomenology of Being. This is made evident in a telling passage in The Letter on Humanism, addressed to Jean Beaufret in 1947.[9] And it is developed in a number of later texts where Heidegger speaks of 'the gods' as one of the four ontological dimensions of the 'Fourfold' (*Das Geviert*), alongside mortals, sky, and earth. Heidegger offers as examples of the Holy's radiance the creation and dedication of a temple, statue or tragic drama. In 'The Origin of the Art Work', he writes accordingly:

> To dedicate means to consecrate, in the sense that in setting up the work the holy is opened up as holy and the god is invoked into the openness of the presence. Praise belongs to dedication as doing honour to the dignity and splendour of the god. Dignity and splendour are not properties beside and behind which the god, too, stands as something distinct, but it is rather in the dignity, in the splendour that the god is present. In the reflected glory of this splendour there glows, i.e., there lightens itself, what we called the word.[10]

Here Christ and Apollo are brothers.

In such texts, there is clearly no question of resorting to a theological privileging of Monotheistic Revelation over Greek paganism. Indeed the opposite seems to be the case – namely, that for Heidegger's ontology, the Greek aesthetic of divinity is actually closer to the sacred presencing of Being than either (a) the God of Jacob, Isaac and the prophets, or (b) the divine *causa sui* of metaphysics before which (Heidegger claims) one can neither pray nor dance. As Caputo puts it, with characteristic aplomb, the 'saving god' of Heidegger has 'virtually nothing to do with the God whom Jesus called Abba or with the religion of the cross . . .'[11]

And yet, for all that, Heidegger does admit in certain passages of some form of relationship between ontology and theology. Although we have noted how Heidegger opposes philosophy to faith in the *Introduction to Metaphysics*, this does not prevent him from acknowledging, however obliquely, certain kinds of indirect rapport between the two. The first of these entails an 'as if' mode of what we might call methodological atheism whereby a believer can learn more about his or her faith by contrasting it with its alternative (i.e. philosophy). This would chime with Dostoyevsky's view that true faith comes forth from the crucible of doubt. And it would not be incompatible with Kierkegaard's claim that the religious leap of faith (by virtue of the absurd) is rendered all the more authentic by virtue of its traversal and ultimate surpassing of philosophical reasoning.

But there is a second, and to my mind more fruitful, form of indirect relationship between philosophical and theological reflection outlined by Heidegger. Rehearsing an old Thomist category, Heidegger makes the curious move of proposing an analogy of proper proportionality: *a is to b what c is to d. Dasein is to the sacredness of Being what the believer is to the God of Revelation.* Thus while careful to preserve the distinctness of the two approaches – philosophical and theological – Heidegger does appear to admit of a certain crossing-over between a new understanding of Being and of God.[12]

What will particularly concern us here are the implications of the analogy between (a) Heidegger's ontological rethinking of Being as the 'loving possible' (*Letter on Humanism*) and (b) our own efforts to rethink God as eschatological *posse* (*The God Who May Be*).[13]

The last god

The first thing to be noted is that every relation of analogy (proportional or otherwise) comports dissimilarities and similarities. Before discussing the similarities, I will briefly mention some divergences between ontological and eschatological approaches to the 'possible God'.

One of the major differences is the role of the *ethical*. Heidegger looks for salvation to those poets and thinkers who surpass the technological will-to-power of our times and dare to face the abyss. These rare figures, he believes, prepare us for a new event of Being (*Ereignis*) by renaming the 'holy'. The salvific poets consecrate the holy in the very midst of the unholy. But while exposing themselves to the danger of apocalypse, from whose ashes a new poetical 'god' may appear, there is nothing they, or we, can actually *do* about it. The readiness is all. No decision or intervention by mortals can alter the destiny of Being. Nothing can effect the arrival of the 'saving god'. There is no place, it seems, for ethical action.

*

This suspicion is confirmed by even a cursory reading of Heidegger's pronouncements on the 'last God' (*der letzte Gott*). Most relevant passages here are to be found in three volumes written in the late 1930s and published posthumously, namely *Beiträge zur Philosophie* (1936–8; GA 65), *Besinnung* (1938–9; GA 66) and *Die Geschichte des Seins* (1938–40; GA 69).[14] Heidegger declares that while it is entirely fitting that we ask 'whether God is fleeing us or not and whether we truly experience this?' (GA 66, p. 415), we should be wary of confusing such an experience with theological or metaphysical conceptions of God. The 'Last God' who commands Heidegger's attention in these works of the 'Turning' (Kehre) is radically 'opposed to the Gods of the past (die Gewesenen) and especially the Christian God' (GA 65, pp. 403, 283).[15] This deity, Heidegger insists, is far removed from any kind of 'Jewish-Christian apologetics' (GA 65, pp. 411, 289). It is indeed so ultimately 'unique in its uniqueness' (einzigste Einzigkeit) as to forbid any comparison whatsoever with the God of monotheism or any other confessional faith (ibid.)[16] To say it is a 'last' God is not to imply an ending but rather 'another beginning'. But this new commencement, which Heidegger promises holds 'immeasurable possibilities for our history', is only available to a small elite of luminaries. It is to be the preserve of a few 'great and secret individuals' (GA 65, p. 414), the prerogative of those who are retrieved from human communities and congregations into 'the pliancy of a reserved creating of seats' (GA 65, pp. 7–8, 6).

There is, it seems, a certain aristocratic hauteur in Heidegger's position here. Especially in his insistence that only a select coterie of poets and thinkers will be privy to the ultimate truth. Perhaps he was influenced by Nietzsche's Zarathustra? Perhaps not? Either way, the last judgement of Heidegger's last God has reserved seating only.

But there are other divergences between Heidegger's God and the God of Revelation. For instance, Heidegger claims that the Last God is a radically temporal phenomenon and has nothing to do with the biblical notion of the 'eternal' or with any 'eschatological attitude'. At one point, it is true, he does say that we are faced here with an 'eschatology of being' (GA 65, pp. 410, 288). But this unfolds within the horizons of a strictly finite ontology. Or as Heidegger puts it, the 'innermost finitude of be-ing reveals itself: in the hint of the last God' (GA 65, pp. 410, 288). Heidegger's God is utterly subordinate to the destiny of being.[17] Or to be more precise, it never appears in personal or interpersonal experience (Erlebnis) but only in the 'abysmal Space (abgrundigen Raum) of Being itself' (GA 65, p. 416). As such, it has little or nothing to do with the eschatology of an infinite personal God which – understood as healing and enabling posse – we seek to explore in The God who May Be.

What is more, the Last God is refractory to ethical or historical action in that it fills those it deigns to inspire with 'fear' (Erschrecken) and 'awe' (Scheu) (GA 65, p. 15). If anything, the terrifying destitution of God (Not den Gottes) (GA 66, p. 7) petrifies us. Before it we lapse into an attitude of passive silence

(*Erschweigung*). We experience *nothing*. And the experience leaves us speechless. In and through its very indigence (*Durftigeit*), this abysmal deity strikes us as 'alien' (*befremdend*), 'disturbing' (*entsetzlich*), 'inhuman' (*un-menschlich*) and – most curiously of all – as 'god-less' (*gott-los*) (GA 66, pp. 223, 69, 24).[18] For as Heidegger makes clearer in section XVIII of *Besinnung* entitled 'The Gods': it is only when the elect few face up to the godlessness of the abyss (*Abgrund*) of being that these few may once more become *capax dei* (*gottfähig*) (GA 66, p. 98). Paradoxically then, it is by facing down the de-divinization (*Entgötterung*) of divinity (*Gottschaft*), marked by our present age of fake sacralization (*Vergötterung*), that we can once again embark, in apocalyptic dismay and distress, upon a new divinization (*Götterung*) (GA 66, p. 239).

This quasi-prophetic call to a redivinizing of the sacred has, one suspects, far less to do with the biblical quest of Moses or Jesus for the kingdom than with a kind of New Age call for 'another initiation'. Such a call was first announced by the likes of Hölderlin, Schelling and Nietzsche. And it has been bolstered up in our own time by the rise of neo-Gnostic mysticisms. For Heidegger, Judaeo-Christian faith – indeed the philosophy and practice of religion in general – has exhausted the possibilities of God and left us with an empty space. And Heidegger seems to suggest that it is from this very emptiness and dereliction – from the very void of being where gods are absent – that the new gods will arise. But only, of course, for the cognoscenti who are awestruck enough to hearken. Ours is, whether we like it or not, an 'a-theistic' age. And one gets the impression that if we do not begin from that phenomenological given, we cannot even begin to listen to the voice of the 'last God'.[19] Heidegger's 'last God' is not destined for *homo religiosus* in the ordinary sense, but for a very select number of votaries bound to an esoteric truth and bold enough to withstand the shock waves of its irruption.

Heidegger's Last God inhabits a zone of unsayable indigence and distress. And it seems to me that such a space is far removed from eschatological hope in a God of eternal promise, kenotic giving or theophanic redemption (GA 66, pp. 252–3, 245). On the contrary, Heidegger reiterates his refrain that it is perhaps only an elect 'we' that may prove bold enough to exchange the religious God of transcendence for an abyssal God of abjection (GA 69, p. 119). This last of last gods is, arguably, closer to Plato's *khora* than to his 'Good beyond being' (*to agathon epekeina tes ousias*). It certainly has little to do with the God who declares love and promises justice. It is rather the very shock of the Last God's alienating and dehumanizing nothingness which disorients and 'overpowers' us (GA 65, pp. 415, 292). Recalcitrant to every kind of human desire or hope, this deity is unlike any God witnessed before. It would certainly be futile to go wandering the highways and byways looking for it like the Shulamite in the Song of Songs. For, Heidegger insists, 'one can never find the free place where God abides' (GA 69, p. 59).

Is this, then, a God before whom one can pray or praise? Is it a transfiguring God who calls us to act in order to transfigure our world? The answer must surely be no.[20] Heidegger leaves us in little doubt: 'Here no re-demption (Er-lösung) takes place' (GA 65, pp. 413, 290).

*

This attitude leads ultimately, I would argue, to extreme quietism. After the Turn, Heidegger is so hostile to any form of voluntary historical transformation – perhaps a reaction to his own disastrous engagement in Nazi politics in the 1930s – that all he can do is passively attest to the traces of fugitive gods and bemoan the contemporary 'missingness' of sacred names. Neither human will, nor divine will, can change anything. For both are pre-empted by the mission of Being. 'We now await a new god', as Caputo astutely comments, 'a new and unpredictable sending of the Holy's graciousness, which appears to be a function of being's sending, not of God's will'.[21] Nor, we might add, of *our* will. The only thing we can do is *not to will* anything to come to pass. Not even the coming of a Last God who now emerges as decidedly more 'pagan–poetic' than 'ethico-religious'.[22]

In light of the above, I find myself compelled to assume that Heidegger's poetic thinker does not sing or dance before the Last God, any more than he does before the *causa sui*. Nor does he affirm, or deny, the existence of God. He merely observes his 'lack' and patiently endures. 'I do not deny God. I state his absence', says Heidegger. 'My philosophy is a waiting for God.'[23] Waiting for Godot indeed. And not just in two Acts, where nothing happens twice – as was famously said of Beckett's play – but in a dark unpeopled scenario of endless passivity.

What if the truth were monstrous?

Heidegger was one of the most significant thinkers to alert us to our estrangement. Exposing the abyss at the heart of our post-religious society he opened the way, on foot of Nietzsche's 'death of God', for new modes of understanding the divine. My difficulty with the divinity proposed by

Heidegger is, however, its curiously non-personal and non-ethical character. By completely bypassing, for example, the Judaeo-Christian ethic of pardon and hospitality towards the stranger – so honoured by contemporary thinkers like Levinas, Derrida, Kristeva and Ricoeur – Heidegger espoused a certain nostalgia for primordial fusion and bedazzlement. While this can make for genial poetics – it certainly did for the Greeks and romantics – it runs the risk of blurring our capacity to discern in matters of moral responsibility and political justice. The problem is not that Heidegger ignores 'strangeness' – in fact he makes it central to his intellectual aesthetic – it is that he registers it as a sublimely overwhelming 'nothingness', far from the face of the other. A primordial sense of terror, anxiety and fear (*deinon*) accompanies Heidegger's account of *das Nichts*. Indeed in his inaugural lecture to the Freiburg University Faculties in July 1929, entitled 'What is Metaphysics?', Heidegger argued that this very experience is at the root of any genuine thinking:

> Only because the nothing is manifest in the ground of Dasein can the total strangeness (*die Befremdlichkeit*) of beings overwhelm us. Only when the strangeness of being oppresses us does it arouse and evoke wonder. Only on the ground of wonder – the revelation of the nothing – does the 'why?' loom before us.[24]

This passage can appear somewhat alarming, I submit, when juxtaposed with certain other pronouncements by Heidegger. One thinks, for example, of his invocation of the estranging wonder of primordial thought in the service of 'the spiritual existence of the Volk' (*geistig-volklichen Daseins*) in 'The Self-Assertion of the German University' (May, 1933), written just after Hitler came to power. In this lecture terms like *Fate*, *Volk* and *destiny* begin to assume an ominous cast when coupled with the proposal to transform the ancient Greek notion of astonishment 'into being completely exposed to . . . what is concealed and uncertain', thereby compelling us to accept 'what is inescapable'.[25] As one commentator asks:

> What does wonder have to do with *greatness*? Is there something ominous, something foreboding, which lurks within the folds of wonder? Is wonder dangerous? Does wonder hold the capacity to oppress, to limit freedom, and to suppress/censor discourse?[26]

Certainly Heidegger advocates an attitude of passive subjection to terror (*deinon*), awe (*die Scheu*) and astonishment (*das Erstaunen*) felt before the sway of the destiny of Being. The pathos of submission appropriate here is, he insists, 'connected with *paschein*, to suffer, endure, undergo, to be borne along by, to be determined by'.[27]

Now, I repeat, there is nothing particularly suspect in this claim when applied to poetic or ontological experience (we have no wish to scapegoat Heidegger). But as a model for political or ethical action it is less than inspiring. After all, what if John Sallis is right when, commenting on Heidegger, he asks: 'What if the truth were monstrous?'[28] It is clear in any case that for Heidegger it is not in any kind of personal or communal experience (*Erlebnis*) that the Last God appears but only in some 'abyssal space' which mortifies narrative and reduces us to silence.[29] The notion of an 'epiphany', where the divine appears in what is most humble and loving, is here displaced by that of 'kratophany' and 'hierophany', where the divine discloses itself as shock or splendour.[30]

*

I think one could trace interesting links between this whole Heideggerian problematic and the postmodern cult of painful–pleasurable *jouissance* before the blinding terror of the sublime. It was, as we saw in Chapters 4 and 5, the Kantian analysis of the sublime which most deeply influenced the writings of thinkers like Lyotard and Žižek on this issue. One of the basic dilemmas here was to establish how the transgressive experience of the sublime in terms of terror and abasement could be reconciled with any kind of discerning judgement (especially at an ethical or political level). For if in the experience of the sublime it is something 'inhuman' which gives the rule to the human self, as Kant suggested, then either the self is deprived of its autonomy or it is exposed to something more primordial which lies beyond the law. In the latter case, the human subject can only pretend to be autonomous to the extent that it conceals the fact that it derives from something strangely alien which is anything but benign. In this instance, as one astute commentator of Kant puts it, 'It is more often wildness, frenzy, the primitive, the ugly, the excremental, the senseless. Genius and madness become indistinguishable. And we seem hard put to discriminate between divine madness and mad madness.'[31] For an artist, poet or experimental thinker, such indiscrimination may not be a worry. But for someone hoping to discern in historical circumstances where such 'madness' is at issue, little comfort is to be offered.

Destiny, fate, and the saving God

Hubert Dreyfus, an expert Heidegger commentator, offers a qualified defence of Heidegger's stance by arguing that if the technological understanding of being is indeed our 'destiny', it does not have to be our 'fate'. I want to take up Dreyfus' useful distinction and see if it will alleviate some of my unease.

'Although the technological understanding of being governs the way things have to show up for us', Dreyfus observes, 'we can be open to a transformation of our current cultural clearing'.[32] But, I find myself asking, is it enough to be simply 'open'? Do we not also have to act, to intervene, to judge what kind of cultural – or political – transformation is actually occurring? Transformation is not in itself a guarantee of ethical improvement. Stalin transformed Russia. Hitler transformed Germany. Ezra Pound and Louis-Ferdinand Céline transformed modern literature. And all were deeply opposed to an ethic of democracy. Or, we may ask, is the transformation of our current cultural clearing simply one that occurs at the level of consciousness, not engagement – at the level of the *vita contemplativa* rather than the *vita activa*? Is this just a matter of a gestalt switch: a change of mind or heart but not necessarily of society as such? A question of turning Marx on his head and returning to the Hegelian preference for the ideal over the real?

Dreyfus would doubtless resist such a reading; yet he seems to point in this direction in certain passages. As when he writes, 'The danger – namely that we have a levelled and concealed understanding of Being – when grasped *as* the danger, becomes that which saves us: "The selfsame danger is, when it is *as* the danger, the saving power"'.[33] Are we to take this to mean that the 'saving power' that comes from having an ontological insight into the danger is the same as being open to the 'saving god'? Nothing more? Nothing less? I suspect the answer is yes. For Heidegger, the 'saving of man's essential nature' is the issue of 'keeping meditative thinking alive'.[34] For meditative thinking is here a matter of remaining '*receivers* of understandings of being',[35] rather than of responding to a summons from other human beings who suffer and die, seek justice and care. This is why I believe Dreyfus and certain other apologists of Heidegger underestimate the extent to which Heidegger remains captive to the metaphysical charm of *theoria*, though he purportedly critiques it in his destruction of western Platonism. And here I would agree with Jacques Taminiaux's thesis that Heidegger's eclipse of ethical praxis is a symptom of his residual obsession with speculative knowing, inherited from German idealism and, by extension, Platonic idealism.[36] Dreyfus' comments on

Heidegger's 'saving god' dilemma are telling in this context. 'Once one sees the problem', Dreyfus concludes, 'one also sees that there is not much one can do about it . . . One cannot legislate a new understanding of being'.[37] But we might ask, why not? Are the demands of historical justice and human rights not matters which must always be negotiated for in democratic institutions?

The Heideggerean change – or 'gestalt switch' – is here again cultural–ontological rather than practical–ethical. An analogy offered by Dreyfus is that of the Woodstock music festival.

> A hint of what such a new god might look like is offered by the music of the sixties. Bob Dylan, the Beatles, and other rock groups became for many the articulators of a new insight into what really mattered. This new awareness almost coalesced into a cultural paradigm in the Woodstock music festival of 1969, where people actually lived for a few days in an understanding of being in which mainline contemporary concerns with order, sobriety, wilful activity, and flexible, efficient control were made marginal and subservient to certain pagan practices, such as enjoyment of nature, dancing and Dionysian ecstasy, along with neglected Christian concerns with peace, tolerance and non-exclusive love of one's neighbour. Technology was not smashed or denigrated; rather, all the power of electronic communications was put at the service of the music, which focussed the above concerns.[38]

Dreyfus rounds off his utopian account as follows: 'If enough people had recognised in Woodstock what they most cared about and recognised that many others shared this recognition, a new understanding of being might have been focussed and stabilised'.[39]

Whatever sweet nostalgia is aroused at the memory of 'non-exclusive love of one's neighbour,' most advocates of a Heideggean 'saving god' might want more convincing examples than Woodstock when faced with the evidence of Heidegger's 1933 *Rectoratsrede* and subsequent affiliation with Nazism. Dreyfus, to be fair, goes on to acknowledge that Heidegger's biggest mistake was to confuse the 'saving god' with Hitler. But I believe he fails to appreciate how Heidegger's position offered no ethical coordinates for discriminating between one kind of ontological gestalt switch and another. Dreyfus does not appear to acknowledge that Heidegger's philosophy possessed insufficient critical resources to distinguish between just and unjust events of transformation, between a 'god' of peace and a 'god' of exotic violence. For it is one thing to claim that we are caught in an inevitable circle of interpretations, quite another to affirm the need to judge ethically *between* such competing interpretations.

*

Dreyfus does ultimately concede that Heidegger's philosophy is 'dangerous' to the extent that it professes that 'only a god – a charismatic figure or some other culturally renewing event – can save us from falling into contented nihilism'. He thus cautions us against a naive embrace of Heidegger's deity in so far as it 'exposes us to the risk of committing ourselves to some demonic event or movement that promises renewal'.[40] Here I am in full agreement with Dreyfus. Yet while dissenting from Heidegger's penchant for apocalyptic mysticism, Dreyfus appears to concur with the broad Heideggerean persuasion that ontological–cultural manifestations of the 'saving god' are more fundamental than ethical–practical ones. He thereby joins company, unbeknownst to himself, with those Heideggereans who fail to appreciate that waiting poetically for a 'saving god' is not enough. For if waiting for God is indeed a necessary condition for world-transformation, it is not a sufficient one. Poetic waiting needs to be supplemented by an ethics of action – one which answers to beings who suffer and struggle in the ordinary universe.

It is no accident, I think, that most criticism of the non-ethical character of Heidegger's deity comes from Jewish and Christian thinkers. Objections to Heidegger's sacrificial neo-paganism have been rehearsed by philosophers such as Levinas, Buber, Jonas, Ricoeur and Caputo. The criticism in almost all these cases is that Heidegger reduces the advent of 'God' to an event of Being (*Ereignis/Es gibt/Sein*), thereby ignoring the radical alterity and transcendence of the biblical deity. And in the process, these critics argue, God's ethical summons to change our world of alienation into a kingdom of justice is eclipsed. The divine good is subordinated to a sacred shining splendour. ('It is', says Heidegger typically, 'in the splendour that the god is present'.)[41] In sum, ethics is thus subordinated to aesthetics. Paul Ricoeur sums up this opposition succinctly in his Introductory Note to *Heidegger et la question de Dieu*:

> What has often astonished me in Heidegger is how he seems to have systematically eluded an encounter with the whole Hebraic mind. He

does sometimes reflect on the basis of the Gospels and Christian theology; but always in eschewing the Hebrew tradition which is the absolute other to Greek discourse. Heidegger obviates ethical thinking with its relations to the other and to justice as so often noted by Levinas. He summarily dismisses ethics as a thinking about value . . . and does not acknowledge its radical difference to ontological thought.[42]

Ricoeur concludes with a vigorous and I think appropriate challenge to the Heideggerian notion of divinity:

> Surely the task of rethinking the Christian tradition by means of a 'step back' requires that we recognise the radically Hebraic dimension of Christianity, which is rooted in Judaism before its encounter with the Greek tradition? Why reflect only on Hölderlin and not on Jeremiah and the Psalms?[43]

I have not yet encountered a convincing Heideggerian response to this question.

Possible gods

We noted above how analogies comport similarities as well as differences. This is also true of the analogy of proper proportionality which Heidegger proposes for another way of thinking (*ein anderes Denken*) about God in relation to being. Hitherto I have stressed the critical distinctions between Heidegger's ontological 'god' and the ethico-eschatological God of the Scriptures. In what remains I will sketch out some points of convergence, particularly around the notion of the 'loving possible'.

In spite of the above analysis, Heidegger did not always insist on a polar opposition between God and Being. In some later texts he entertained certain more congenial modes of convergence. The most suggestive is, perhaps, the analogical model outlined in the *Introduction to Metaphysics* noted above. But there are other tantalizing passages where similar modes of rapprochement are intimated. In *The Piety of Thinking*, an English translation collection of Heidegger's essays on religion, he speaks for instance of 'certain historical junctures which call for a correlative parallelism, intimate and non-indifferent, between the two modes of thought'.[44] While in *Poetry, Language and Thought* (another collection of English translations), Heidegger goes so far as to maintain that the 'default of God and the divinities' is not to be understood as an empty nothing but rather as a 'coming-into-presence' of the 'divine in the world of the Greeks, in prophetic Judaism or in the presencing of Jesus'.[45] This more inclusive approach – however exceptional – to the respective truth-revelations of Greek ontology and Judaeo-Christian faith leaves room for a less confrontational rapport between the 'saving god' of Being and the redeeming God of monotheism. And nowhere may this dialogue be more fruitfully explored, it seems to be, than on the terrain of the 'possible' where the 'loving potency' of Being comes into contact with the grace-giving *posse* of the Creator. Here both ontology and eschatology encounter the 'limit' of what can be thought and said – and dare make the impossible possible.

If, as we suggested in Chapter 5 of *The God Who May Be*, Heidegger has something crucial to teach us about the overcoming of the onto-theological prejudice against the possible, it is reasonable to assume that a renewed thinking about Being as 'loving possible' will also have innovative implications for our understanding of God. In short, the overcoming of metaphysics, qua onto-theology, may have something to contribute to a new theology as well as to a new ontology. There is no doubt in my mind that Heidegger's radical analysis of Being as *Das Vermögen des Mögens* – surpassing the traditional categories of both *possibilitas* and *potentia* and reversing the priority of actuality over possibility – has revolutionary lessons for a post-Heideggerian approach to God. For we find ourselves suddenly attentive to a whole variety of neglected thoughts about God, e.g. as one 'who may be' (Cusanus, Bruno, Boehme) or as one 'who is beyond being and non-being' (Dionysius, Eckhart, Tauler). Unthinkable thoughts ostracized as 'mystical' or 'heretical' by the mainstream orthodoxy find themselves back in the light of day. The retrieval of the forgetfulness of being discovers a parallel in the reversal of the forgetfulness of God as *posse*. For if Being can be reinterpreted as a loving can-be (*pouvoir-être*), might not God be reinterpeted as a loving may-be (*peut-être*)?[46] On this score at least, religious thinking owes much to Heidegger's intellectual daring. And we are also in his debt, I would add, for reminding us at a time when Holy Wars are still being waged in the name of One True God that monotheistic absolutism is not the only way to think about God.

The famous 'step back' from the metaphysics of will, manifest today in the planetary domination of technology, opens us to the 'possible future' (*die mögliche Ankunft*) of another way of existing. Whereas Heidegger reads this possibility as a postmodern dispensation of the destiny of Being, emerging from the dark night of modern forgetfulness, we read it rather as the promised coming of the Kingdom. Heidegger conceives of this future *topologically* as the lighting up of a new site (*topos*) for finite Dasein – a new way of being in the temporal-historical world. Our reading, by contrast, considers the future *eschatologically* as the transfiguring of our finite existence into an infinite no-time (*a-chronos*) and no-place (*u-topos*) which eye has not seen nor ear heard. Neither a finite earth nor a Platonic heaven – but, as Paul tells us, a 'new heaven and a new earth'. The impossible made possible.

Such an eschatological Kingdom is 'beyond Being' to the extent that it does not passively await the circular 'happening' of what-is – the event of the same origin returning in its end.[47] But it has not abandoned the hope that the God who makes the impossible possible may return to Being in hitherto unimagined ways. There is an ethical urgency to eschatological expectation. There is an awareness that if the 'possible advent' indeed comes as unpredictable surprise, like a thief in the night, it always comes through the face of the most vulnerable – the cry of 'the smallest of these', the widow, the orphaned, the anguished, the hungry, those who ask: 'Where are you?' To reply to this ethical call, it is crucial to be able to say I *am* here. And this *being present* here and now before the summons of the fragile other, requires that the *eschaton* still-to-come already intersects, however enigmatically and epiphanically, with the ontological order of being as loving possible. Were this not so, the word God would no longer contain, in Augustine's phrase, 'everything we hope for'.

But these are enigmas which receive further exploration in our companion volume, *The God Who May Be*. For now, let me end with the words of poet, Emily Dickinson:

> I dwell in Possibility –
> A fairer House than Prose –
> More numerous of Windows –
> Superior – for Doors –
>
> Of Chambers as the Cedars –
> Impregnable of Eye –
> And for an Everlasting Roof –
> The Gambrels of the Sky –
>
> Of Visitors – the fairest –
> For Occupation – This –
> The spreading wide my narrow Hands
> To gather Paradise –

CONCLUSION

This book has been exploring questions of ultimacy in our contemporary culture. How do we make sense of what defies common sense? How do we interpret those limit situations of death, deity, sublimity, trauma or terror which seem to shatter reason and leave us speechless? We touched on several challenges: the enigma of good and evil in a post-religious age pervaded by sentiments of undecidability and indeterminacy; the obsession of our media with aliens and scapegoats as symptoms of deep crises of identity and legitimation; the difficulty of formulating judgements about repressed horrors which return to haunt us in the guise of 'uncanny' phantoms, simulations and doubles; the quest for a God who might save a civilization afflicted with apocalyptic fears; the task of doing justice to strangers.

In my efforts to respond to these issues I have endeavoured to outline a hermeneutics of our contemporary cultural unconscious. This has meant exploring diverse ways in which human ideas, images and narratives have tried to say the unsayable. To this end I have sought to develop a diacritical hermeneutics of alterity. For if the deconstruction of the cogito was a necessary correction to the modern idolatry of the ego, it needs to be supplemented by a critique of the postmodern obsession with absolutist ideas of exteriority and otherness. The suspicion of 'sameness', I have been arguing, requires to be suspected in turn lest it lead to a new idolatry: that of the immemorial, ineffable Other. And it is with this in mind that I have been making hermeneutic soundings and chartings of the limits of ultimacy. The threat to a genuine relation to others comes in fetishizing the Other as much as it does in glorifying the Ego. Both extremes undermine our practical understanding of ourselves-as-others. For each ignores that strangers are both *within* us and *beyond* us.

Between such extremities, I have sought to map a middle path, and have done so under the general rubric of 'narrative imagination'. Working to this end, my wager has been twofold: (a) that we are *beings at the limit* and (b) that we are *beings who narrate*.

By the former I mean that human existence is always hovering about those frontiers that mark the passage between same and other, real and imaginary, known and unknown. Indelibly marked by finitude, the human self has never ceased to ponder its boundaries or to imagine what lies beyond – namely, those strangers, gods and monsters that populate its fantasies. And that is why I have chosen as my guide Hermes (and his hermeneutic method): god of voyagers, interpreter of dreams, night porter and passenger of thresholds.

One of the main hypotheses of this volume has been that our contemporary world of doubling and undecidability has blurred our intellectual boundaries and evacuated the frontier-posts which monitor passage back and forth. In a post-metaphysical age there are no longer clear maps as to who or what lies beyond the reaches of human finitude. There is no credible authority to sanction passports and verify identities. No bad thing in itself, but disquieting if taken too far. For sometimes it seems as if Jacob's ladder had been stood upside down and the messengers didn't quite know in which direction they were heading any more. Or, to borrow another analogy, it feels as though we had reached another period of not knowing, similar to that at the close of the Middle Ages when new worlds sprang up in all directions, rendering existing charts redundant. Now, as we hover between modern and post-modern worlds, we encounter once again the demand for new cartographies. At Land's End once more, we require novel mappings of uncharted realms, lest we slip over the edge into the abyss of the unknowable. The familiar dragons and demons have been replaced with different ones, of course. More weaponized like Kurtz's commandoes, Ripley's aliens, or Al Qaeda's hijacked planes. But no less terrifying for that. And no less challenging. Strangers, gods and monsters will always be with us. There will always be limits to what we can say or tell. But rarely has the call for new paths of interpretation and action been more urgent. The more we know the less we need to understand.

For all our sentiments of disorientation, however, we have not forfeited the capacity to narrate. The hermeneutic self is still resolved to travel with Hamlet to those countries 'from whose bourne no traveller returns' and tell the story; to relate the impossible tale; to put a face on the vizored ghost. Even in our world of fuzzy edges, many continue to wrestle with gods until they yield their names, to talk to strangers and reckon with monsters. In short, to say the unsayable as if it were somehow sayable. Aware all the while that if there are definite limits to what can be said, the resolve to try to say something is indispensable to both ethics and poetics. That is why we ultimately prefer a hermeneutic revision of Jacob's ladder – allowing messengers back and forth – to the ultimatum of the unbridgeable abyss separating us (Lazarus) from them (Dives) by virtue of some irrevocable rupture.

And so to my second wager – that the human self has a narrative identity based on the multiple stories it recounts to and receives from others. In this sense I argue that our very existence is narrative, for the task of every finite being is to make some sense of what surpasses its limits – that strange, transcendent otherness which haunts and obsesses us, from without and from within. That is why I believe that storytelling invariably involves some kind of hermeneutic interpretation. We know there is no immediate access to a transparent, unitary ego. We acknowledge that there are only mediations and detours after which the self may, at best, return to itself enlarged and enriched. We accept that we are narrative beings because the shortest road from self to self is through the other. And that even the shortest route takes time.

To assume our intrinsically hermeneutic nature, as interpreting selves, is in turn to recall our fragility and fallibility. We all have a sense of an ending. And one of the reasons our lives are in quest of narratives is because we know that our existence, like the stories we tell, will come to an end. The limit experience of death is the most sure sign of our finitude. Moreover, it is precisely *because* we are beings who know that we will die that we keep on telling stories, struggling to represent something of the unpresentable, to hazard interpretations of the puzzles and aporias that surround us. Resolving to recover, in spite of the odds, the 'yes of joy in the sorrow of the finite'.[1]

Our hermeneutic revisitings of such figures as Saturn, Melancholia, Hamlet, Dedalus, Ripley or Willard – to cite just some examples – suggested that the uncanny experience of estrangement need not always mean a paralysing collapse before 'horror'. Any more than it signals, for that matter, a sublime act of elation. Beyond the excesses of melancholy and mania, we have traced some alternative responses to the enigmas of otherness. There are, we have indicated, certain narrative footbridges which may help us negotiate both the dizzy peaks of alterity and the subterranean chasms of abjection. Paths where we might at last walk at sea level. And what the stories of Saturnine artists – from Dürer and Shakespeare to Joyce and Coppola – reveal is that strangeness need not always estrange us to the point of dehumanisation. If we can only echo Prospero's words to Caliban: 'this thing of darkness

I acknowledge mine' (when it *is* mine). And if we can accept, in all humility and hope, that nothing is the end of us.

It may well be that we find more of ourselves than we lose in befriending those monsters that are ultimately neither *fremd* nor foe, embracing the strangers in ourselves and others. For such mindfulness brings peace and transfigures fear.

And when it comes to Gods – the greatest of these – we have just this to say in conclusion. Belief in God as a transcendent alterity does not have to deny that the divine Other may take the form of different others. For just as Being, in Aristotle's formula, manifests itself in diverse ways, is this not also true for God? Faith in an Absolute might best avoid the trap of absolutism – source of so many wars and injustices – by embracing a hermeneutics of religious pluralism.[2] For thus might we endeavour to judge between different kinds of selves and different kinds of others, while avoiding the twin temptations of judgementalism and (its opposite) relativism. A diacritical hermeneutics of discernment, committed to the dialogue of self-and-other, wagers that it is still possible for us to struggle for a greater philosophical understanding of Others and, so doing, do them more justice.

*

This book concludes our trilogy on Philosophy at the Limit. To its companion volumes, *The God Who May Be* and *On Stories*, it tenders its own chosen testimonies to those strangers, gods and monsters that keep us company on the sinuous paths through postmodernity and beyond.

NOTES

INTRODUCTION: STRANGERS, GODS AND MONSTERS

1 See our discussion in *On Stories*, Routledge, London and New York, 2002, pp. 119–21, 180–1, of the postmodern theories of monsters advanced by Michel Foucault in 'The Order of Discourse' in R. Yang (ed.) *Untying the Text*, Routledge, London, 1981, and by Andrew Gibson in 'Narrative and Monstrosity', Chapter 7 of *Toward a Postmodern Theory of Narrative*, Edinburgh University Press, Edinburgh, 1999. See also Claude Lévi-Strauss' fascinating analysis of monster myths as 'machines for the suppression of time' (and its contradictions) in *Structural Anthropology*, Basic Books, New York, 1963, especially the chapters entitled 'The Structural Study of Myth' and 'The Effectiveness of Symbols'. The basic thesis here is that monsters serve as hybrid creatures operating in terms of structural binary oppositions between Nature (born from one, from the earth, from chaos) and Culture (born from two, human parents, society). By telling stories about monsters we provide symbolic resolutions to enigmas – those of our origins, time, birth and death – which cannot be solved at the level of our everyday historical experience. In short, monster myths offer imaginary answers to real problems. They signal the triumph of the structural over the empirical, mind over matter.

2 Anthony Storr, *Feet of Clay: A Study of Gurus*, HarperCollins, London and New York, 1997, p. 160.

3 Julia Kristeva, 'Strangers to Ourselves' in *States of Mind: Dialogues on the European Mind*, University of New York Press, New York, 1995, pp. 13f.

4 Such de-alienation is, of course, not just a matter of critiquing the 'imaginary' or 'symbolique' of alterity – unravelling the multiple and often covert narratives of its strangers, gods and monsters. It also involves a critique of the material world of economics and politics in which we live out our daily existence: a world where the gap between the income held by the richest and poorest 20 per cent continues to increase dramatically and where 90 per cent of international capital is now used for non-productive speculation rather than trade or long-term investment (N. Chomsky, *Secrets, Lies and Democracy*, Common Courage Press, New York, 1994). But this very distinction between superstructural (cultural–ideological) and infrastructural (material–economic)

domains is itself increasingly blurred by the subsuming of the whole economic and monetary order into networks of virtual exchange and communication (see H. Dreyfus, *On the Internet*, Routledge, London, 2001). A case in point is the Enron Venture Capitalism scandal which shook the US in 2002 involving multiple listed companies, debt equity swaps, associated general partnerships, intermediary credit transfers, 'creative accounting' and other financial 'simulations' which played on the credulousness of investors, employees, government and the public generally before eventually 'imploding' and losing credibility. A case, in short, of the postmodern emperor of capital wearing no clothes – i.e. of the imaginary outstripping the real to the point of no return.

5   Jean Greisch, 'L'épiphanie, un regard philosophique' in *Transversalités*, no. 78, April–June, Paris, 2001.

6   Cited by Denis Donoghue, *Adam's Curse*, Notre Dame University Press, 2001, p. 70. Tate is speaking here about Dante in particular.

7   Plato, *Symposium*, 221d. The emblematic relationship between Socrates and monstrosity has been touched on by John Sallis, who argues that for Plato there is 'a bit of monstrosity' hidden in every philosophy which exceeds nature in the pathos of wonder ('. . . A Wonder That One Could Never Aspire to Surpass' in *The Path of Archaic Thinking*. ed. Kenneth Maly, SUNY, Albany, New York, 1995, p. 253).

8   Hannah Arendt in 'Philosophy and Politics' (*Social Research*, vol. 57, no. 1, 1999) and Jacques Taminiaux in *The Thracian Maid and the Professional Thinker: Arendt and Heidegger*, SUNY, Albany, New York, 1997, make some intriguing comments on the ambivalent role of *thamazein* in the genesis of philosophizing, and in particular on the paradox that the pathos of 'wonder' as a source of metaphysical reasoning is itself something that 'befalls' or 'overcomes' us and that is thus beyond our ken and control, stemming from and culminating in 'speechlessness'. Another recent thinker to advert to the paradoxical mix of mythos and logos in Plato is William Desmond, *Perplexity and Ultimacy*, SUNY, Albany, New York, 1995, for example p. 34:

> Logos in *aporia*, logos at an impasse: these are constitutive for the Platonic sense of philosophical thinking. It is as if the wonder that is said to be the originating pathos of the philosopher reappears after he has done his best job in giving a determinate logos. The indeterminate perplexity reappears, wonder resurrects itself, in a different sense of being at a loss, now at the limit of logos itself.

Indeed from this perspective it is telling that Thaumas is related to a river whose nature begins and ends on the borders of the unspeakable. See also Charles Griswold, *Self-Knowledge in Plato's Phaedrus*, Yale University Press, New Haven, 1986, where he notes that Socrates' reflection on the need for a 'rational account' of strange, portentous and monstrous things (*teratologon* and *atopiai* such as Chimaeras, Hippocentaurs, Pegasuses, Gorgons, etc.) leads ultimately to the invocation of the Typhon motif in the *Phaedrus* – a motif which raises the enigma of the rapport between 'complex hubristic madness on the one side, and simplistic sophrosyne on the other; between unintelligible and ungovernable eros and law-abiding reasonableness . . .' (p. 42). I am indebted to my doctoral student, David Bollert, for bringing many of the above references and comments to my attention.

9 These and analogous passages from Plato's *Parmenides* are commented by Emmanuel Levinas in *Totality and Infinity*, Duquesne University Press, Pittsburgh, 1969, p. 50 and by Robert Bernasconi in 'The Alterity of the Stranger and the Experience of the Alien' in *The Face of the Other and the Trace of God*, ed. Jeffrey Bloechl, Fordham UP, New York, 2000, pp. 64f.

10 E. Levinas, *Totality and Infinity*, p. 50.

11 J. Derrida analyses the Levinasian rupture between thought and language in 'Violence and Metaphysics', *Writing and Difference*, University of Chicago Press, 1978, pp. 114ff. On this point, see also Bernasconi, op. cit. pp. 74ff. There is also the question of Levinas' Judaic belief in this regard – for example, his statement in *Difficult Freedom: Essays in Judaism*, trans. S. Hand, Johns Hopkins University Press, Baltimore, 1990, p. 15: 'For a Jew, Incarnation is neither possible nor necessary'. Commented by D. Donoghue, *Adam's Curse*, p. 57.

12 J. Derrida, *Writing and Difference*, pp. 111f. It is telling that in commenting Levinas' efforts to think infinity positively, Derrida himself resorts to the term used in *The Sophist* to describe non-being (méon) – aphtheggon te auto kai arréton kai alogon (238e).

13 See Paul Ricoeur, *Hermeneutics and the Human Sciences*, Cambridge University Press, 1981 and Jack Caputo, *More Radical Hermeneutics*, Indiana University Press, Bloomington, 2000, pp. 156f.

14 J. Caputo, ibid., p. 70.

15 J. Caputo, ibid., p. 71. For Maurice Blanchot there is an unbridgeable, uncrossable gulf separating me from the other: see M. Blanchot, *Friendship*, trans. Elizabeth Rottenberg, Stanford University Press, Stanford, 1997, pp. 290ff. Blanchot's position is commented on at length by Derrida, *Politics of Friendship*, trans. George Collins, Verso, London, 1997 and by J. Caputo, op. cit., pp. 60–83.

16 J. Derrida, *Politics of Friendship*, pp. 68, 232 and J. Caputo, op. cit., p. 83.

17 Rudiger Bubner, 'Phenomenology and Hermeneutics' in *Modern German Theology*, Cambridge: Cambridge University Press, 1981, p. 45. I am grateful to Chris Lawn for introducing me to this work. For other useful efforts to examine the critical boundaries and borders of hermeneutics, in addition to the recent work of Ricoeur, Caputo and Sallis, see Patrick Bourgeois, *Philosophy at the Boundary of Reason: Ethics and Postmodernity*, SUNY, Albany, 2001 and Jean Greisch, *Le Cogito herméneutique*, Vrin, Paris, 2000.

1 STRANGERS AND SCAPEGOATS

1 See Georges Bataille, *Theory of Religion*, Zone Books, New York, 2000, pp. 45–96.

2 See Regina Schwartz's critique of the exploitation of certain biblical narratives for the purposes of territorial aggression, ethnic violence and national division, *The Curse of Cain: The Violent Legacy of Monotheism*, Chicago University Press, Chicago, 1997.

3 Lorenzo Lorenzi, *Devils in Art, From the Middle Ages to the Renaissance*, trans. M. Roberts, Cantro Di della Edifirmi Srl, Florence, 1999, p. 50.

4 Ibid., p.66.

5 Ibid., p.73.

6 Ibid., p.22.

7 Ibid., p.21.

8 Mircea Eliade, *The Sacred and the Profane: The Nature of Religion*, Harcourt Brace and Company, New York, 1959, p. 30.

9 Timothy Beal, Introduction, *Religion and its Monsters*, Routledge, London and New York, 2001. Beal defines monsters as 'paradoxical personifications of *otherness within strangeness*' and determines in this fine work to 'learn something from religion by getting to know its monsters'.

10 Ibid.

11 Ibid.

12 Rudolph Otto, *The Idea of the Holy: An Inquiry into the Non-Rational Factor in the Idea of the Divine and Its Relation to the Rational*, Oxford University Press, New York, 1950, p. 28. I am grateful to Tim Beal for this reference and discussion.

13 T. Beal, Introduction to *Religion and its Monsters*.

14 Ibid.

15 Rudolph Bultmann, *Theology of the New Testament*, SCM Press, London, 1952.

16 Jürgen Moltmann, *The Theology of Hope*, SCM Press, London, 1967.

17 G. Bataille, *Theory of Religion*, Zone Books, New York, 2000, p. 67. For Bataille, sacrifice marks the triumph of the mythical over the real (p. 45). It resolves the 'antinomy of life and death by means of a reversal', thus establishing the primacy of the 'unreality' of the divine. Sacrifice negates all that is useful in the real order of work, production and preservation in favour of a magical return to 'lost intimacy' and 'immanence' (pp. 49–50). 'The divine', explains Bataille, 'was initially grasped in terms of intimacy (of violence, of the scream, of being in eruption, blind and unintelligible, of the dark and malefic sacred)' (p. 73). This was characterized by an act of violent destruction, before which separate individuals could only experience anxiety or horror. Sacrifice subsumed the individual into the fire of fusion. As such it inaugurated an order of the 'sacred' which filled mortals with a sense of impotent horror. 'The horror is ambiguous', explains Bataille. 'Undoubtedly, what is sacred attracts and possesses an incomparable value, but at the same time it appears vertiginously dangerous for that clear and profane world where mankind situates its privileged domain' (p. 36). Sacrifice calls for the violent negation of individuals as such, consuming them as flame consumes wood (p. 53). It is epitomized by the contagious communion of the 'festival' whose music, dance, inebriation and sexual orgy promise the fusion of a 'spectacular letting loose' (p. 54). While the sacrificial function of the festival keeps violence within the group, the externalizing of this violence to define one group over against another leads to scapegoating and war (pp. 57f). Sacrificial violence, for Bataille, is thus construed as being originally *internal* to the community, leading eventually to the sacrifice of the sovereign (representing the people as a whole) or the chosen child or slave (representing the sovereign) (p. 61). Whereas the malefic and beneficient aspects of the sacred were initially confused, as dualist and metaphysical religions developed the 'divine becomes rational and moral' (i.e. pure); and, in the process, reflective consciousness relegates the malefic sacred to the realm of the profane (p. 72). Henceforth, the divine is linked with purity and the profane with impurity: the former, equated with

mind, is called good; the latter, equated with matter, is called evil. But this increasing exclusion of sacrificial violence, now considered impure, brings about a weakening of the moral divine in favour of evil (p. 81). The divinity then remains divine only through that which it condemns and repudiates – i.e. the evil of violence (p. 84). See also the recent research on Inca child sacrifice in the Andes in *National Geographic*, 196, no. 2, 1999, 36–55.

18 *Beowulf*, translated and introduced by Seamus Heaney, Norton, New York and London, 2000, p. xiv.

19 See our *On Stories*, Routledge, London and New York, 2002, pp. 94–5, 175.

20 See also the illuminating analyses by Paul Ricoeur and Northrop Frye of the *pharmakos* (sacrificial victim) in the Greek myth of Prometheus as discussed in our *The Wake of Imagination*, Hutchinson, London, 1988 (reprinted by Routledge), pp. 82–4.

21 See Mircea Eliade, *Myths, Dreams and Mysteries*, Fontana, London, 1968; and our own analysis of the modern relevance of ancient 'sacrificial' myths in *Myth and Motherland* (Field Day Publications, Derry, 1984, republished in *Ireland's Field Day*, Hutchinson, London, 1985 and, in somewhat expanded fashion, in our *Postnationalist Ireland*, Routledge, London and New York, 1997, pp. 108–21), and in 'Myth and Martyrdom I–II' in our *Transitions: Narratives in Modern Irish Culture*, Wolfhound Press, Dublin, 1988, pp. 224–8, republished in the new and extended edition, *Reimagining Ireland*, Wolfhound, Dublin, 2002. See finally our study of the relevance of the Girard thesis to the contemporary invocation of sacrificial myths by the IRA in Northern Ireland, 'Terrorisme et Sacrifice: Le cas de l'Irlande du Nord', *Esprit*, April 1979.

22 E. Levinas, *Totality and Infinity*, Duquesne University Press, Pittsburgh, 1969, and R. Girard, *The Scapegoat*, The Johns Hopkins University Press, Baltimore, MD, 1986.

23 S. Heaney, Introduction to *Beowulf*, p. xix.

24 Girard, *The Scapegoat*. If such be the case, it would no doubt be an unconscious motivation on Girard's part. But this cannot serve as an alibi by Girard's own standards. As he clearly states, to seek recourse in the unconscious is to lapse into something 'even more mythical than myth itself'. Girard is, as we have seen, quite adept at detecting such unconscious motives in Sophocles, Guillaume de Machaut, and other authors of persecution narratives. Indeed, at one point he even suggests that those most practiced in the art of denouncing others' motives are often practitioners of a similar strategy. He approaches here a moment of confessional lucidity:

> I have spoken of naive persecutors and I might well have spoken of unconscious ones . . . Being imprisoned in a system permits us to speak of a persecutionary unconscious, and the proof of its existence is that even those most able to discover others' scapegoats in our day – and God knows we've all become past masters in the art – are the last to discover their own.
>
> (Ibid.)

Does this not apply to Girard himself? Might the expert inquisitor of scapegoating not also be prone to its obsessions? Might he not be at least partially captive to a new and more sophisticated labyrinth of condemnation? In sum, is not Girard's own critique of alienating ideologies of persecution itself subject to critique? Does it not, in that sense, deconstruct itself?

Girard concedes as much, I think, in the following passage from *The Scapegoat*, laced as it is with irony:

> In order to fathom the enormity of the mystery one must interrogate oneself. Each one of us is obliged to ask where he stands in relation to scapegoats. Personally I seem unable to recognize it in myself, and I am sure, dear reader, you will respond likewise. We have, you and I, only legitimate enmities. And yet the world is brimming with scapegoats. The lie of persecution is even more rife and duplicitous today than in the days of Guillaume de Machaut.
>
> (*The Scapegoat*, p. 62)

Thus Girard, the grand inquisitor of myths, redeems himself, I believe, to the extent that he turns the mirror back on himself.

25 Edward Said, *Orientalism* and Partha Mitter, *Maligned Monsters: A History of European Reactions to Indian Art*, University of Chicago Press, London and Chicago, 1992.

26 T. Beal, Introduction to *Religion and its Monsters*.

27 Ibid.

28 Ibid.

29 R. Girard, *The Scapegoat*. This appendix is an emended version of part of a paper entitled 'Le mythe comme bouc émissaire chez Girard', delivered at the René Girard conference at Cerisy, Normandy, in 1984, subsequently published in *Violence et Vérité*, ed. P. Dumouchel and J.-P. Dupuy, Grasset, Paris, 1985 and, in English, as 'Myth and Sacrificial Scapegoats: On René Girard' in our *Poetics of Modernity: Toward a Hermeneutic Imagination*, Humanities Press, New Jersey, 1995, pp. 136–47.

30 Girard, *Things Hidden since the Foundation of the World*, Athlone Press, London, 1987, p. 38.

31 Ibid., pp. 114–39.

32 Girard, *The Scapegoat*, p. 38.

33 Ibid., pp. 3–39.

34 Ibid., p. 40.

35 Ibid.

36 Ibid.

37 Ibid., p. 41.

38 Ibid., p. 52.

39 Ibid., pp. 57, 62. The New Age thinker, Joseph Campbell, for one, has much to say about messianic monsters in *The Power of Myth*, a best-selling book and enormously influential television series. The following passage, it seems to me, serves as cautionary reminder of the need for some kind of ethical decision:

> By monster I mean some horrendous presence or apparition that explodes all your standards for harmony, order and ethical conduct . . . That's God in the role of destroyer. Such experiences go past ethical judgments. Ethics is wiped out . . . God is horrific.
>
> (*The Power of Myth*, Doubleday, New York, 1988, p. 222)

See our discussion of this passage in Chapter 4. There we note how we do not need to go to the extremes of gnostic New Ageism to identify a moral confusion on this issue, since it is also evidenced in several post-structuralist and postmodern apostles of the Sublime.

40 *The Way of Chuang Tzu: A Personal and Spiritual Interpretation of the Classic Philsopher of Taoism* by Thomas Merton, Burns and Oats, Kent, 1965.

41 Cited in Martha Nussbaum *et al. For Love of Country: Debating the Limits of Patriotism*, Beacon Press, Boston, 1996, p. vii.

42 Thich Nhat Hanh, *Anger: Wisdom for Cooling the Flames*, Riverhead Books, New York, 2001, p. 70. Other recent works to explore the emerging biblical–Buddhist dialogue include *Benedict's Dharma: Buddhists Reflect on the Rule of Saint Benedict*, ed. Patrick Henry, Riverhead Books, New York, 2001 and Joseph S. O'Leary, *Religious Pluralism and Christian Truth*, Edinburgh University Press, 1996, especially Chapters 1 and 5. The works of John Main, Bede Griffith, Robert Magliola, Tony de Melo and Thomas Keating also move in this direction from a more contemplative perspective. I am grateful to four practitioners of this dialogue, Sally and Emma Fitzpatrick, Peggy McLoughlin and the late Mícheál O'Regan for bringing the importance of this 'way between' to my attention.

2 RIGHTS OF SACRIFICE

1 See R. Kearney, *On Stories*, Routledge, London and New York, 2002, especially Part Three.

2 Stephen Mulhall, *On Film*, Routledge, London and New York, 2002.

3 This is another way of describing what Heidegger and Freud identify, in their different ways, as the 'uncanny' (*das Unheimlich*): that which 'invades one's sense of personal, social or cosmic security – the feeling of being at home in oneself' (T. Beal, *Religion and its Monsters*). We will be revisiting this crucial theme of the uncanny in several chapters below.

4 S. Mulhall, *On Film*.

5 Ibid., Chapter 1.

6 Ibid.

7 Ibid.

8 Ibid.

9 Ibid.

10 Stanley Cavell, *The Claim of Reason*, Oxford University Press, Oxford, 1979, pp. 418–19. I am grateful to Stephen Mulhall's *On Film* for this quotation and several others.

11   In his turn, Kurtz the man, became a monster. He fused the moral and the immoral. Action, pure action, is the aim of any warrior for Kurtz. War is about action without thought, without hesitation and that is the new morality. Kurtz has, in a way, embraced the Nietschean Will to Power in its most horrific form.

      (Anthony Sculimbrini, 'Invitations to the Monstrous', Graduate Paper, Boston College, unpublished, 2001, pp. 9f)

I am also grateful to Joshua McKimber and Joshua Mills-Knutsen, two other graduate students in my BC graduate seminar, 'Strangers, Gods and Monsters', for their presentations on the subject.

12 The Dalai Lama, *The Good Heart*, Rider, London, 1996, pp. 88, 98. Would Theseus (Willard) have slain the Minotaur (Kurtz) if he had observed this verse? Or taken this more explicit Buddhist tale to heart:

> When one is thinking about devils, it is important not to have a notion of some independent, autonomous external force 'out there' existing as a kind of absolute negative force. The term should be related more to the negative tendencies and impulses that lie within each of us.

One finds similar teachings on the non-judgemental attitude to evil and the need to embrace negative energies in Thich Nhat Hanh, *Essential Writings*, Riverhead Books, New York, 2001, *Bouddha et Jesus*, Le Relié, France, 2001, pp. 136ff. and *Anger: Wisdom for Cooling the Flames*, Riverhead Books, New York, 2001, especially the chapter, 'No Enemies', which includes the following typical observation:

> Human beings are not our enemy. Our enemy is not the other person. Our enemy is the violence, ignorance, and injustice in us and in the other person. When we are armed with compassion and understanding, we fight not against other people, but against the tendency to invade, to dominate, and to exploit. We don't kill others, but we will not let them dominate and exploit us or other people. You have to protect yourself. You are not stupid. You are very intelligent, and you have insight. Being compassionate does not mean allowing other people to do violence to themselves or to you. Being compassionate means being intelligent. Non-violent action that springs from love can only be intelligent action.
>
> (pp. 128–9)

See also *Benedict's Dharma: Buddhists Reflect on the Rule of Saint Benedict*, ed. Patrick Henry, Riverhead Books, New York, 2001, e.g. the section 'Freedom in the Mind's Mirror' which suggests how 'our enemy teaches us patience and is therefore someone to be greatly valued' (p. 15). What Buddhism shares with the biblical ethic of forgiveness here is a desire to move from sacrificial violence to compassion, as already counselled in Psalm 51: 'Have mercy on me, O God, in your goodness; in the greatness of your compassion wipe out my offence . . . For you are not pleased with sacrifices; should I offer a holocaust you would not accept it.' I am grateful to Peggy McLoughlin, Emma Fitzpatrick, Sally Kearney, Joseph O'Leary and James and Patricia Leydon-Mahony for bringing these and similar texts to my attention. One of the main challenges arising from this Buddhist–biblical dialogue on enemies is, it seems to me, to outline a hermeneutic of pardon which might invite us to judge without judgementalism, to decide without decisionism (or absolutism) and to discern without discrimination. This will entail, where possible and appropriate, the critical conversion of the monstrous into monsters, of monsters into enemies, of enemies into strangers, and eventually of strangers into ourselves understood as strangers-to-ourselves: a position which ultimately points towards the goal of 'no enemies' or 'love your enemies'. With each step, we seek to move from the more abstract towards the more lived experience of alienation and estrangement, while not for a moment denying the everyday reality of evil and injustice and the need to resist evil-doing and evil-doers. A similar move from the abstract – the monstrous – to the more singular experience of justice and injustice will be applied to the equally abstracted and emblematic notions of 'Terror', 'The Sublime', 'Evil', 'The Devil', etc. in other chapters of this volume. On the complex question of pardon and critical understanding, see especially the conclusions to Chapters 4 (including note 61), 5, 7 and 9.

13 T.S. Eliot, *The Three Voices of Poetry*, Cambridge University Press, Cambridge, 1943. See the fascinating discussion of this passage by Denis Donoghue in *Words Alone*, Yale University Press, New Haven, 2000, pp. 27f and Mark P. Hederman, *The Haunted Inkwell*, Columba Press, Dublin, 2001, p. 14.

14 See Pema Chodron, *Start Where You Are*, Shambhala Books, Boston and London, 1994.

15 F. Nietzsche, *Beyond Good and Evil*, Random House, New York, 1966, section 146. I am grateful to Timothy Beal for bringing this quotation to my attention.

3 ALIENS AND OTHERS

1 I. Kant, *Perpetual Peace and Other Essays*, trans. T. Humphrey, Hackett, Cambridge, 1983.

2 Emile Benveniste, *Indo-European Language and Society*, trans. J. Lallot, London, Faber, 1973, pp. 71–82. See, for example, p. 71:

> The primitive notion conveyed by hostis is that of equality by compensation:
> a *hostis* is one who repays my gift with a counter-gift. Thus, like its Gothic
> counterpart *gasts*, the Latin *hostis* at one period denoted the guest. The classical
> meaning 'enemy' must have been developed when reciprocal relations
> between clans were succeeded by the exclusive relations of *civitas* to *civitas*
> (cf. Gr. *xenos* 'guest'+'stranger').

I am also grateful to Aidan O'Malley's discussions on this subject.

3 J. Derrida, *De L'hospitalité*, Calmann-Lévy, Paris, 1997.

4 Ibid., p. 53.

5 Ibid., p.44.

6 Ibid., p.45. Joshua Mills-Knutsen offers an illuminating illustration of this Derridean position in 'Kearney Contra Derrida: A Reading of "Aliens and Others" Both With and Against Of Hospitality' (unpublished). Speaking of Derrida's question 'Who is the foreigner?' he writes:

> I contend that for the purposes of ethics this question cannot be answered
> with a simple ontological outlook in which the Other is simply not 'me'. Just
> as I can be a foreigner when I travel, I can be in the political position of Other

when viewed in light of a politically stronger Self. Take the national narrative of the United States in which the Pilgrims come to the shores of a new world and encounter the Pequot tribe. Who is the Other? Who is the Stranger? Who is the foreigner? Common sense might dictate that the Pilgrim is the stranger in a strange land, relying upon the hospitality of the Pequot; after all it is the Pequot's land (in a western/capitalist conception). However, when I read the narrative of those happenings (as a European male) it is the Pequot who is different, and as Kearney explains, it is the Pequot who becomes the scapegoated other around which national identity is determined. So the Pequot is the Other, perhaps because I am more pilgrim than Pequot, but more than likely because the Pequot is no more. In this political engagement between Pequot and Pilgrim, by virtue of advanced weaponry, immunity to smallpox as well as other social and economic factors that favored the pilgrims, the Pequot is the Other.

Mills-Knutsen goes on to argue that what leads to the extinction of the Pequot, following Derridean logic, is the struggle for the power of hospitality.

> Hospitality is always bound to a power of welcoming and shunning. The struggle between the Pequot and pilgrim, in terms of hospitality can be seen as a struggle over the question, 'Whose house is it anyway?' As soon as we embark on this path of delineation between self and other, host and guest, same and different, we are doomed to tyranny, either of the Other or of us.

Derrida's text on hospitality offers, Mills-Knutsen contends, a way out of 'this cycle of binary exclusion'.

7 Ibid., p. 29.

8 Ibid., p. 69.

9 J. Derrida, 'Hospitality, Justice and Responsibility' in *Questioning Ethics*, ed. R. Kearney and M. Dooley, Routledge, London, 1998, pp. 66–83. The problem with this kind of deconstructive non-judgementalism is that it underestimates the intrinsic contingency of otherness (in addition to the contingency of selfhood which it readily exposes) – that is, the fact that in practice the other may be benign or malign, a radical transcendence or a projection of my unconscious desires and fears, or a mixture of both at once. The persecuting 'other' who tortures me is not the same as the benevolent 'other' who saves me from such torture and cares for me. But in spite of this, Derrida's analysis of hospitality does serve to remind us of the critical 'Foreigner Question', noted above. For the question 'who is this foreigner?' is a question posed not only by the self about the stranger, but by the stranger about the self! In other words, the question of the stranger is also the question of the stranger: the question of Oedipus to the King, of the Eleatic *xenos* to Parmenides, of Paul to the Elders. The question of the foreigner thus comes to upset the fixed identity of host and guest, asking instead which is which? *Whose home is this anyway?* To return to our discussion of note 6 above, we realize that for the Pequot natives of Massachusetts in 1620 this was a very real question: were the Plymouth

Pilgrims visiting them as 'guests' or replacing them as 'hosts'? Whose land was this to be hospitable with? Who was the real stranger here? And for whom? The native in his own homeland can become a foreigner in another's. And this very reversibility of host and guest, citizen and stranger, self and other, challenges the fixed binarism of ontological substances and invites every citizen to question his or her own sovereignty. Foreigners are named as foreigners by a sovereign state according to the laws and logic of that state. The citizen host imposes on the foreigner 'translation into his own language and that's the first act of violence' (Derrida, *Of Hospitality: Anne Dufourmantelle Invites Jacques Derrida to Respond*, trans. Rachel Bowlby, Stanford University Press, Stanford, 2000, pp. 4–21). Indeed it is because of this inherent violence in the laws and practices of ordinary hospitality that Derrida is drawn to a more Levinasian notion of absolute or 'hyperbolic' hospitality where the self seeks to transcend all the laws of hospitality (naming, identifying, certifying, legislating for the other-as-guest) in the name of an unconditional and ultimately impossible hospitality. And that is why the step (*pas*) to absolute hospitality is in fact a destruction of the laws of hospitality – a paradox captured in Derrida's pun, *pas d'hospitalité!* In absolute hospitality the very ability to say 'this is my home', 'you are my guest', is obliterated. 'Absolute hospitality commands a break with hospitality by right, with law or justice as rights' (ibid., p. 25). Again I am indebted to Joshua Mills-Knutsen's essay 'Kearney Contra Derrida' for several of these quotations and observations. The most important lesson, I believe, that we can draw from Derrida's analysis is that the exclusivist binary oppositions of 'us' (sameness) and 'them' (otherness) need to be challenged so that the 'Foreigner Question' becomes not only 'Who is this foreigner?' but 'Who am I for this foreigner?' And by extension 'Whose home is this anyway?' Such radical interrogations might encourage us to query the hard and fast categorizations of creed, class, ethnicity, gender and national sovereignty which are the source of so much injustice and discrimination.

10 J. Caputo, *The Prayers and Tears of Jacques Derrida*, p. 73; see also M. Dooley, 'The Politics of Exodus: Derrida, Kierkegaard and Levinas on "Hospitality"' in *International Kierkegaard Commentary: Works of Love*, ed. R. Perkins, Mercer University Press, Macon, 1999.

11 Emmanuel Levinas, *Otherwise than Being or Beyond Essence*, trans. A. Lingis, Kluwer, Dordrecht and London, 1991, p. 75.

12 Ibid., pp. 49, 92; and E. Levinas, *Of God Who Comes to Mind*, trans. B. Bergo, Stanford University Press, Stanford, 1998, p. 72.

13 Levinas, *Otherwise than Being*, pp. 82, 48, 101. I am grateful to my doctoral student, Thomas Casey, for pointing several of these passages out to me. Casey offers the following pertinent critique:

> It does not make much sense to us that a person should risk so much exposure without at least a limited hope that their wager may carry some reward. If the person does not receive some sign that their self-exposure will lead to support and recognition, then the encounter with other people simply becomes an excruciating apprenticeship in suffering. Thus subjectivity is not only stretched but twisted out of recognition, to the extent of annihilation. If that is what self-emptying entails, then there may be little left

in the wake of face to face relationships except a deep and merciless wound. Yet Levinas' conception of subjectivity promotes this uncritical willingness to become the object of such destructive cruelty and barbarism.

To which Casey objects: 'The very fact that I question suffering . . . can be an effort to ascend towards goodness by judging suffering as something that falls terribly short of the good beyond Being' ('The Humble and Humiliated Subject in Levinas' Philosophy', unpublished doctoral thesis, University College Dublin, 2001, pp. 235–6).

14 Simon Critchley, *Very Little . . . Almost Nothing: Death, Philosophy, Literature*, Routledge, London, 1997, p. 80.

15 Linda Colley, *Britons: Forging the Nation, 1797–1837*, Yale University Press, New Haven, 1992 and 'Britishness and Otherness' in *Journal of British Studies*, no. 31, 1992. See also on this same point, Charles Taylor, 'Nationalism and Modernity' in *The Morality of Nationalism*, ed. Robert McKim and Jeff McMahan, Oxford University Press, Oxford, 1997, p. 46:

> The modern context of nationalism is also what turns its search for dignity outward. No human identity is purely inwardly formed. The other always plays some role. But it can be just as a foil, a contrast, a way of defining what we're not, for better or for worse. So the aboriginals of the newly 'discovered' world figured for post-Columbian Europeans. The 'savage', the other of civilization, provided a way for Europeans to define themselves, both favorably (applying 'civilized' to themselves in self-congratulation) and sometimes unfavorably (Europeans as corrupted in contrast to the 'noble savage'). This kind of other reference requires no interaction. Indeed, the less interaction the better, or else the stereotype may be resisted.

16 Ibid., p. 226.

17 Cited by J. Kristeva, *Etrangers à nous-mêmes*, Fayard, Paris, 1988 (translated as *Strangers to Ourselves*, Harvester, London, 1991), p. 237 and p. 233. Kristeva notes how in 1793, many 'foreigners' were offered French citizenship – including Jeremy Bentham, George Washington, Thomas Paine, John Hamilton, James Madison and Anacharsis Cloots – amidst a general enthusiasm for a new 'universal Republic' of enlightenment cosmopolitanism, which declared the very word 'foreigner' a 'barbarian' term! '"l'étranger", expression barbare dont nous commençons à rougir', wrote Cloots, 'et dont nous laissons la jouissance à ces hordes féroces . . .' (cited in Kristeva, p. 241). On 14 March 1794, Cloots was guillotined with other Hebertists who considered it more important to be a 'citizen of the world' than a 'citizen of France', receiving this xenophobic rebuke from Robespierre: 'Oui, les puissances étrangères ont au milieu de nous leurs espions . . . Cloots est prussien!' (cited in Kristeva, p. 242). See also Rousseau on the relationship between the Patriot and Stranger: 'Tout patriote est dur aux étrangers . . . Ils ne sont rien à ses yeux. L'essentiel est d'être bon avec ceux avec qui l'on vit' (cited in Kristeva, p. 212). Hegel had an even more fundamental distrust of the 'stranger' as that negative dimension of cultural disunity and antagonism that requires to be in turn negated in the dialectic of mind so as to bring about the ultimate unifying synthesis of

absolute consciousness. In contrast to such distrust of what is foreign, alien and different, Kristeva quotes Montestquieu's *Les Pensées* on the virtue of cosmopolitan generousity: 'Si je savais quelque chose utile à ma patrie et qui fut préjudiciable à l'Europe, ou bien qui fut utile à l'Europe et préjudiciable au Genre humain, je la regarderais comme un crime' (Kristeva, p. 213). This quote could serve as exergue for our own ethic of the alien as much as for Kristeva's.

18 Kristeva, *Etrangers à nous-mêmes*, p. 219: Kristeva has few illusions about how difficult it was for the 'stranger' to question and challenge the covert codes of the tribe or Volk without being condemned as a saboteur of the domestic national consensus: 'Hélas! Elle ne résiste pas toujours aux tentatives dogmatiques de ceux qui – économiquement ou idéologiquement déçus – reconstituent leur 'propre' et leur 'identité' à coups de reject des autres' (p. 219).

19 Sigmund Freud, 'The "Uncanny"' in *New Literary History*, vol. 7, no. 3, 1976, p. 623. See also the insightful commentary on this essay by Hélène Cixous, 'Fiction and its Phantoms' in the same issue of *New Literary History*, pp. 525–48; and our own application of the Freudian category of the 'uncanny' to a reading of the poetry of Seamus Heaney, 'Heaney and Homecoming' in *Transitions: Narratives in Modern Irish Culture*, Wolfhound Press, Dublin/St Martin's Press, New York, 1988, especially the Appendix 'Heaney, Heidegger and Freud – The Paradox of the Homely', pp. 113–22.

20 Freud, 'The Uncanny', p. 622.

21 Ibid., p. 624.

22 Ibid., pp. 630–1.

23 Ibid., p. 634.

24 Kristeva, *Etrangers à nous-mêmes*, p. 250 (my translation).

25 I. Kant, *Essay on Perpetual Peace* (1795), cited and commented by Kristeva, op. cit. pp. 253–4.

26 Kant, cited Kristeva, ibid., p. 253

27 Kristeva, p. 268. Kristeva makes the additional point on pp. 194–5 that it is often in societies which give priority to the cosmopolitan 'Rights of Man' over the more restricted national 'Rights of the Citizen', thereby ostensibly dissolving the category of 'strangers', that the notion of 'strangeness' (*étrangeté*) may find another lease of life in the positive respect for the private, and even the secret, in an overall social world constructed as an alliance of singularities. She asks (p. 289):

> Peut-être s'agit-il, en définitif d'étendre à la notion d'étranger le droit au respect de notre propre étrangeté et, en somme, du 'privé', qui garantit la liberté des démocraties? L'accès des étrangers au droit politique se fera dans la foulée de cette évolution, et nécessairement, avec des garanties juridiques adéquates . . .

28 Ibid., p. 269 (my translation).

29 Ibid., p. 269. Kristeva follows Freud in describing our initial experience of the 'uncanny' as a threat of depersonalization and annihilation issuing from a feeling of being lost in a murky zone of indistinction between ourselves and the other.

Face à l'étranger que je refuse et auquel je m'identifie à la fois, je perds mes limites, je n'ai plus de contenant, les souvenirs des experiences où l'on m'avait laissée tomber me submergent, je perds contenance. Je me sens 'perdue', 'vague', 'brumeuse'. Multiples sont les avariantes de l'inquiétante étrangeté: toutes réitèrent ma difficulté à me placer par rapport à l'autre, et refont le trajet de l'identification-projection qui gît au fondement de mon accession à l'autonomie.

(p. 276)

Freud located the emergence of the 'uncanny' there where the limits between the imaginary and the real collapse and certain repressed memories surge up in the guise of doubles, automatons, dead people or the female sex (Freud offers a curiously eclectic list). He also goes on to suggest that one of the best ways to deal with this unsettling experience of the uncanny is to resort to 'fiction' – fairy tales, novels, fantastic stories – where the world of artifice removes the anxiety we feel at no longer being able to distinguish between real and imaginary doubles, thereby allowing the repressed to return without fear or threat. Kristeva offers a helpful gloss on the Freudian analysis of the uncanny as a dissolution of our conscious defences, constructed on conflicts between self and other (the stranger) whereby the self maintains an ambivalent relation to the stranger as the one with whom one identifies and whom one also fears. 'Le choc de l'autre', she writes, 'l'identification du moi avec ce bon ou mauvais autre qui viole les limites fragiles du moi incertain, seraient donc à la source d'une inquiétante étrangeté dont l'aspect excessif, représenté en littérature, ne saurait cacher la permanence dans la dynamique psychique "normale"' (p. 278). The aim is not therefore to deny or suppress the symptoms provoked by the 'uncanny' but to face them, understand them and where possible appease or sublimate them. Indeed one must be wary of removing the 'uncanny' altogether, for someone without any experience of the strange/alien/other would be a suitable candidate for psychotic acting-out in a sort of megalomania without limits. 'L'étrangeté est pour les "sujets", le souverain l'ignore' (p. 281).

30 Commented by Kristeva, *Etrangers à nous-mêmes*, pp. 279ff. See our analysis of Heideggerian dread in the opening part of Chapter 7. Kristeva's proposed solution to the essential 'uncanniness' of our existence, predicated on the split between our conscious and unconscious, seems to involve opting for irony and humour over fear and terror: 'S'inquiéter ou sourire, tel est le choix lorsque l'étrange nous assaille; il dépend de notre familiarité avec nos propres fantômes' (p. 282).

31 Kristeva, ibid., p. 284. Kristeva poses, finally, the challenging question about the intimate rapport between our own unconscious repressed fears and the age-old hostility towards strangers/aliens outside of ourselves. While admitting that is is rare for the self to experience the same terrifying anguish towards a human stranger that we feel towards our 'returned repressed' (i.e. death, evil powers, the female sex and so on), it is still probable that political xenophobia expressed towards others carries some aspect of 'cette transe de jubilation effrayée' that Freud called *unheimlich* and the Greeks *xenos*. Kristeva concludes (p. 283):

> Dans le rejet fasciné que suscite en nous l'étranger, il y a une part
> d'inquiétante étrangeté au sens de la dépersonnalisation que Freud y a
> découverte et qui renoue avec nos désirs et nos peurs infantiles de l'autre –
> l'autre de la mort, l'autre de la femme, l'autre de la pulsion immaîtrisable.

And it is precisely because the stranger is within us in this manner, that when we flee or fight the foreigner, we are in fact fighting with our own unconscious – 'cet "impropre" de notre "propre" impossible' (p. 283). And perhaps one of the reasons that Freud did not include foreigners and strangers in his own list of 'uncanny' candidates, was to better educate us in the difficult art of locating 'strangeness' within ourselves, rather than hunting for it outside. Kristeva celebrates the Freudian courage 'de nous dire désintégrés pour ne pas intégrer les étrangers et encore moins les poursuivre, mais pour les accueillir dans cette inquiétante étrangeté qui est autant la leur que la nôtre' (p. 284). The aim therefore is to analyse strangeness in analysing ourselves.

> A decouvrir notre troublante altérité, car c'est bien elle qui fait irruption face
> à ce 'démon', à cette menace, à cette inquiétude qu'engendre l'apparition
> projective de l'autre au sein de ce que nous persistons à maintenir comme un
> 'nous' propre et solide. A reconnaître notre inquiétante étrangeté, nous n'en
> souffrirons ni n'en jouirons de dehors. L'étranger est en moi, donc nous
> sommes tous des étrangés. Si je suis étranger, il n'y a pas d'étrangers.
>
> (Ibid.)

The ethics of psychoanalysis thus implies a corresponding politcs: 'il s'agirait d'un cosmopolitisme de type nouveau qui, transversal aux gouvernements, aux économies et aux marchés, oeuvre pour une humanité dont la solidarité est fondée sur la conscience de son inconscient . . .' (ibid.). What a psychoanalytic ethic of otherness teaches us is that each self is inhabited by difference and that this difference is the ultimate condition of our being-with-others. Kristeva pursues further political implications of this psyco-analytic ethic of alterity and difference in subsequent works, for example, Nations Without Nationalism, Columbia University Press, 1993 and Crisis of the European Subject, Other Press, New York, 2000.

32 Levinas, Totality and Infinity, Dusquesne University Press, Pittsburgh, 1969, p. 65; see also the excellent commentary by R. Bernasconi, 'The Alterity of the Stranger and the Experience of the Alien' in The Face of the Other and the Trace of God, ed. Jeffrey Bloechl, Fordham UP, New York, 2000, pp. 66f.

33 E. Husserl, Cartesian Meditations, trans. D. Cairns, The Hague, Martinus Nijhoff, 1970, pp. 109–15.

34 Levinas, Totality and Infinity, p. 67. Derrida gives a very different reading of Husserl's Fifth Cartesian Meditation in 'Violence and Metaphysics' when he suggests that Husserl's notion of mediated otherness is in fact a way of guaranteeing the alterity of the other vis-à-vis the constituting subjectivity of the ego. Or as Bernasconi sums up this subtle argument:

> The Other cannot be the Other of the Same except by being itself the same, that is, an ego . . . To make the Other immediate is to reduce the Other to the Same so that it is not the Other, and to make the Other absolutely other is either to say something nonsensical or to oppose the Other to the Same and so fail to establish genuine otherness. Otherness is maintained only in the contradiction *alter ego* which states that 'the absolute of alterity is the same'.
>
> ('The Alterity of the Stranger', p. 72)

Or as Derrida himself puts it, 'it is impossible to encounter the alter ego . . . to respect it in experience and language, if this other, in its alterity, does not appear for an ego' (*Writing and Difference*, University of Chicago Press, Chicago, IL, 1978, p. 123). But curiously, while Derrida thus retrieves and defends Husserl's phenomenological notion of the alter ego, he then seems to dispense with the *hermeneutic* necessity of mediation within the interpretive circle of language and *logos* (ibid., pp. 127–8).

35 See my more detailed discussion of this theme in *The God Who May Be* (Indiana University Press, Bloomington, 2001), especially the opening chapter, 'Toward a Phenomenology of the Persona', pp. 9–19. See also here again Derrida, 'Violence and Metaphysics' (etc.) when he argues that Levinas' critique of the phenomenological relation of self and other is in fact self-contradictory, presupposing the very terms he criticizes. Perhaps Levinas offers some kind of response to Derrida's argument when he defines 'substitution' as a way in which 'the other is in me and in the midst of my very identification' ('Otherwise than Being', p. 125). The 'self' (*le soi*) is now redefined by Levinas, in opposition to the ego (*le moi*), as a stranger in myself, 'contested in one's own identity' (ibid., p. 92) – a sort of ethical equivalent of Rimbaud's 'I is an other'. Levinas seems to be borrowing here Ricoeur's hermeneutic distinction between the 'moi' and the 'soi', by way of restoring some kind of relation between same and other. But as Bernasconi points out, Levinas' notion of substitution as a taking responsibility for the Other can also sound like 'paternalism, or perhaps identification' ('The Alterity of the Stranger', pp. 78–9). Bernasconi also offers a lucid analysis of Bernardt Waldenfels' reading of Levinas in 'The Other and the Foreign' (*Philosophy and Social Criticism*, 21, nos 5–6, 1995 and 'Experience of the Alien in Husserl's Phenomenology', *Research in Phenomenology*, 20, 1990). Waldenfels bases his reading on Husserl's paradoxical description of the experience of the Other in *Cartesian Meditations* (p. 114) as a 'verifiable accessibility of what is originally inaccessible'. Like Bernasconi and Ricoeur, he criticizes Levinas for his lack of attention to 'concrete others' in his almost exclusive emphasis on an abstract Other – a lacuna which leaves Levinas open to charges of failing to adress issues of sexism, ethnocentrism and, in relation to Israel, the question of the Palestinian 'other'. Drawing from Ricoeur's hermeneutic distinction between (1) the 'ownness' of *ipse*-selfhood, which contrasts to 'alienness or foreignness' (*étrangeté*/*Fremdtheit*), and (2) the 'sameness' of *idem*-identity, which contrasts to mere 'diversity' (*diversité*/*Verschiedenheit*), Waldenfels then proceeds to make the useful distinction between 'the relational', whereby a self distinguishes itself in open relation (*Bezug*) with an other, and 'the relative' where the Other is defined reductively in my terms (e.g. as an other 'for me' or 'for us'). The alien, he concludes accordingly, should be understood not just in contrast to the ego but also as an excess or

transcendence. In this manner, Waldenfels confirms and expands the hermeneutic rapport between the Other as other-than-self and the Other-as-Alien in its own right. He thus appears to reinforce Ricoeur's point that the ethical movement of the Other toward the self needs to be supplemented by a genetic–phenomenological move from self towards the Other. It might then be possible to speak of a 'relational alterity' of the stranger in contrast to the 'relative alterity' of the stranger proposed in Plato's *Sophist*, and brought to its most extreme logical conclusion in Hegel's *Phenomenology*.

36 Paul Ricoeur, *Autrement: Lecture d'Autrement qu'être ou au-delà de l'essence d'Emmanuel Levinas*, Presses Universitaires de France, Paris, 1997, p. 9. See Ricoeur's further challenge to Levinas' rejection of narrative memory and history in this later work, pp. 12–14, 38–9. In the following passage (pp. 24–5), Ricoeur is especially trenchant in his critique of Levinas' anti-theological emphasis on the 'traumatism of persecution' in *Autrement qu'être*:

> Bref, il faut que ce soit par sa 'méchanceté même' (p. 175) que la 'haine persécutrice' (ibid.) signifie le 'subir par autrui' de l'injonction à l'enseigne du Bien. Je ne sais si les lecteurs ont mesuré l'énormité du paradoxe consistant à faire dire par la méchanceté le degré d'extrême passivité de la condition éthique. C'est à l'outrage, comble de l'injustice, qu'il est demandé de signifier l'appel à la bienveillance: 'C'est de par la condition d'otage qu'il peut y avoir dans le monde pitié, compassion, pardon et proximité' (p. 186). Ce n'est pas tout; il faut encore que le 'traumatisme de la persécution' (p. 178) signifie l'irrémissibilité de l'accusation' (ibid.), bref, la culpabilité sans bornes . . . Il y a là comme un crescendo: persécution, outrage, expiation, 'accusation absolue, antérieure à la liberté' (p. 187). N'est-ce pas l'aveu que l'éthique déconnectée de l'ontologie est sans lanagage direct, propre, approprié? . . . La détresse du discours est encore aggravée par le déni et le rejet de toute solution 'théologique', apaisante ou consolante' (p. 184). Le texte de Levinas est à cet égard violemment antithéologique . . .

37 See Thomas Brockelman's lucid commentary on critiques of the self offered by such neo-Lacanians as Richard Boothby and Slavoj Žižek, *The Frame and the Mirror: On Collage and the Postmodern*, Northwestern University Press, Evanston, IL, 2001, pp. 129–44.

38 See Ricoeur, *La Mémoire, L'Histoire, L'Oubli*, Editions du Seuil, Paris, 2000; Jean Greisch, *L'Age herméneutique de la raison*, Editions du Cerf, Paris, 1985 and *Le Cogito herméneutique*, Vrin, Paris, 2000; Hans-Georg Gadamer, *Truth and Method*, Sheed and Ward, London, 1975.

39 See P. Ricoeur, *Oneself as Another*, Chicago University Press, Chicago, 1992, p. 355. Here Ricoeur, *pace* Levinas, advocates a certain equivocalness of the status of the other as source of moral conscience. The philosopher cannot say, concludes Ricoeur:

> whether this Other, source of the injunction, is another person whom I can look in the face or who can stare at me, or my ancestors for whom there is no representation, to so great an extent does my debt to them constitute my very self, or God – living God, absent God – or an empty place. With this aporia of the Other, philosophical discourse comes to an end.

In his commentary of Ricoeur's notion of the moral self, Guy de Petitdemange sees conscience as the most pivotal example of passivity before otherness, alongside the body and intersubjective relations: 'il y a pour Ricoeur une passivité "hors pair", la plus intérieure à soi, s'énonçant du plus loin et à la verticale, la voix de la conscience' ('La Notion du Sujet' in *Paul Ricoeur: Morale, Histoire, Religion*, no. 390 of *Magazine Littéraire*, September, 2000, p. 61). He develops his commentary of the Ricoeur–Levinas debate as follows, p. 61:

> A propos d'autrui , Ricoeur engage une discussion longue et souvent vive avec Levinas et il faut lui savoir gré de cette distinction. Chez celui-ci, il refuse l'hyperbole, l'excès, un paroxysme 'encore jamais atteint' ('Chaque visage est un Sinaï qui interdit le meurtre'), qui arrive à son comble avec la notion de substitution, coeur de son maître-ouvrage, Autrement qu'être. L'excès tient à deux choses liées: l'autre a 'l'initiative exclusive de l'assignation du soi à la responsabilité'; or, l'auto-assignation est 'le thème central de nos trois études'; et il résulte de cela 'l'hypothèse scandaleuse' d'un autre devenu 'maître de justice' et même 'l'offenseur' appelant à l'acte moral ultime, l'expiation. Ricoeur ne nie pas d'évidentes proximités avec Levinas, mais il met en cause l'hyperbole de la séparation du côté du même, donc du moi, bien moins situation de guerre avec autrui que presqu'autisme. L'amitié, la capacité d'accueil, le dialogue, sa spontanéité bienveillante, la réciprocité dans la reconnaissance et le fait même qu'autrui compte sur moi contesteraient la thèse intitiale de Levinas d'un moi totalement enfermé en lui, clos, clôturé, dans une asymétrie insurmontable, que l'autre, en l'arrachant à sa suffisance, pulvérise et n'en fait plus qu'un soi ayant en charge le monde et l'histoire qui l'accusent et l'écrasent, paralysent.

40 See E. Husserl's fifth meditation in *Cartesian Meditations* and Derrida's debt to this same meditation as admitted in *Questioning Ethics*, 'Hospitality, Justice and Responsibility', pp. 71–2. The model I am proposing here as an alternative 'third way' to the extremes of Levinasian expropriation and Hegelian–Husserlian appropriation, is a hermeneutic melange of ethics and ontology. I am trying to negotiate a new dialogue between ethos and logos – to disclose a chiasmus of asymmetry and reciprocity. Such a hermeneutic between-space (*mi-lieu*) would explore, for example, how hospitality to the other needs hermeneutic judgements in order to discern who the other is in concrete historical situations (a Gestapo officer or innocent victim). In sum, we need to compare, contrast and adjudicate between different kinds of other if we are to properly care for others and for their good. Thus while we may agree with Levinas that our *ethical* response to the other is primary in the order of responsibility, we would stress that my hermeneutic discernment of the character of the other is primary in the order of judgement and communication. Rather than opt for one form of absolute priority here it is wiser, I suggest, to speak of a critical balance – however difficult – between two equiprimordial primacies. Not either/or but both/and.

4 EVIL, MONSTROSITY AND THE SUBLIME

1 René Girard, *The Scapegoat*, The Johns Hopkins University Press, Baltimore, 1986. See our elaboration of this thesis in Chapter 1.

2 P. Ricoeur, 'Evil: A Challenge to Philosophy and Theology' in *Figuring the Sacred: Religion, Narrative and Imagination*, Fortress Press, Indianapolis, 1995, p. 250. Lawrence Langer notes a similar dialectic in the 'split' testimonies of certain Holocaust survivors who speak of divided selves – one self that 'does' and the other that is 'done to' (Lawrence Langer, *Holocaust Testimonies*, Yale University Press, New Haven and London, 1991, p. 47).

3 Ibid., p. 252. See also Ricoeur's classic hermeneutic account of the genealogy of evil in *Symbolism of Evil*, Beacon Press, Boston, 1967.

4 P. Ricoeur, 'Evil: A Challenge to Philosophy and Theology', p. 254.

5 Ibid., p. 257.

6 William Desmond, *Beyond Hegel and Dialectic: Speculation, Cult and Comedy*, SUNY, Albany, New York, 1992, p. 231f. See his general and very insightful discussion of evil in Chapter 4, entitled 'Dialectic and Evil: On the Idiocy of the Monstrous':

> True understanding ought to bring us to the limit of this intimacy (of horror), not talk its way around it or away from it. This intimacy of horror is something at the limit of sense or meaning, and our response to it is itself at the limit of sense and meaning. We ought not to fake our metaphysical helplessness with the bustle of pseudo-explanatory discourse. That is why all I can do is put down my head, crushed under the burden of something that in the end it would be obscene to try to rationalize.
>
> (p. 231)

Then citing Dostoyevsky's famous example of the the evil suffered by a child, Desmond describes it as an 'obscene surd', an obscenity that no rationalization will ever do away with. And as such this 'sinisterness of evil' horrifies us like a 'night of emptiness . . . a destructuring indeterminacy, a negative otherness that resists total recuperation in the logic of dialectical concepts' (p. 232). But while acknowledging thus that the alterity of evil brings us to the limit of reason, Desmond still insists that we have a moral obligation to try to think about it further, both imaginatively and intellectually, even if no concept or image is ever adaquate to its estranging horror (see also note 57 below).

7 Dionysius, *Mystical Theology* iii (1033 c) from *Pseudo-Dionysius: The Complete Works*, Classics of Western Spirituality, trans. Colm Luibheid, SPCK, London, 1987.

8 J. Derrida, 'Comment ne Pas Parler' in *Psyché: Inventions de l'autre*, Galilée, Paris, 1987, p. 571. The translation is my own. It seems to me that Heidegger is skirting similar zones of indistinction and privation when he declares that the 'Last God' appears only in some mystical 'abysmal space' which reduces us to silence (*Beitrage Zur Philosophie*, GA 65, Klostermann, Frankfurt, 1992, p. 416).

9 I. Kant, *Religion within the Limits of Reason Alone*, Harper Torchbooks, New York, 1960, p. 38. See also Ricoeur, 'Evil', op. cit. pp. 258–9.

10 Berel Lang, 'The Representation of Limits' in *Probing the Limits of Representation*, edited by Saul Friedlander, Harvard University Press, Cambridge, MA, 1992.

11 Peter Haidu, 'The Dialectics of Unspeakability' in *Probing the Limits of Representation*, p. 284. Jacques Derrida also comments on this disturbing collusion between violence and the sacred-mystical institution of law in 'Force of Law: The 'Mystical Foundation of Authority' in *Deconstruction and the Possibility of Justice*, ed. D. Cornell *et al.*, Routledge, London and New York, 1992, pp. 3–37.

12 Ibid., p. 284. Levinas, *Du Sacré au Saint*, Editions de Minuit, Paris, 1977. See also Timothy Beal, *Religion and its Monsters*, Routledge, New York and London, 2001, discussed in Chapter 1.

13 Ibid., p. 288.

14 Ibid., p. 292.

15 Julia Kristeva, *Powers of Horror: An Essay in Abjection*, Columbia University Press, New York, 1982, p. 11.

16 Ibid., pp. 11–12. The way in which most aesthetic or religious movements try to deal with this defiance is, Kristeva believes, to 'sublimate' the abjection by trying to find a name for it. In the case of the symptom (e.g. psychic breakdown), I am invaded and pervaded by the abject, I myself become abject. In the case of sublimation, by contrast, I somehow manage to give a quasi-presentation of the unpresentable. I insist on naming what cannot be named. Rather like Conrad in *Heart of Darkness* when he relates the experience and final words of Kurtz: 'The horror, the horror!'

17 I. Kant, *The Critique of Judgment*, Hackett, Indianapolis, 1987, p.99.

18 The sublime, Kristeva explains, 'is something added that expands us, overstrains us, and causes us to be both here, as dejects, and there, as others' (*Powers of Horror*, p. 12).

19 Ibid., p. 15.

20 Ibid., p. 16.

21 Ibid., p. 18. At times, Kristeva appears to succumb, like Lacan and Žižek, to extreme vacillations between a *via negativa* of unnamable transcendence and a *via abjecta* of descent into *das Ding* – occasionally blurring the line between the two. In *Powers of Horror* she claims that civilization as we know it is but a surface film over the horror of the *il y a*; and she goes on to argue that literature and art are rooted on the 'fragile border' where identities only barely exist, emerging as borderline, fuzzy, double, altered, uncanny, abject. Literature is thus redefined as the 'sublime point at which the abject collapses in a burst of beauty that overwhelms us – and 'that cancels our existence' (Céline) (p. 210). This helps explain, she says, our fascination (along with our revulsion) for that 'nocturnal power' of horror which takes the place of the sacred which, in her words, 'has left us without leaving us alone' (p. 208). On this reading, the 'communitarian mystery' of love of self and others is always underlaid by an 'abyss of abjection'; and the role of postmodern writers and analysts is to X-ray and expose this omnipresent apocalyptic void, revealing in turn how Judaeo-Christian monotheism which bolsters western culture is nothing less than the 'fulfillment of religion as sacred horror' (p. 210). The purpose of Kristeva's psychoanalytic reading is identified accordingly as a work of 'dis-appointment, of frustration and hollowing', laying bare the horror which the orderly veneer of civilization seeks to push aside by 'purifying' and 'systematizing' (ibid.). She concludes on this apocalyptic note:

For abjection, when all is said and done, is the other facet of religious, moral and ideological codes on which rest the sleep of individuals and the breathing spells of societies. Such codes are abjection's purification and repression. But the return of their repressed make up our 'apocalypse' . . .

(p. 209)

In subsequent works, however, Kristeva shows signs of wishing to go beyond this apocalyptic vision. She seems to resist the postmodern cult of the hysterical sublime, replacing the nihilistically and incurably 'split subject' of mainstream Lacanianism with a 'subject in process' capable of recreating itself as a healing and poetic stranger-to-itself. Here we might recall her conclusion to *Strangers to Ourselves*, cited in our opening chapter, that the choice facing each postmodern self when confronted with the 'strange' (*l'étrange*) is to collapse in anguish or to smile (*s'inquiéter ou sourire*): a choice which ultimately depends, she reminds us, on how 'familiar we have become with our proper ghosts' (*Etrangers à Nous-Mêmes*, p. 282). Or as she rephrases it in *Crisis of the European Subject*, Other Press, New York, 2000, pp. 167–9, the most important thing for us wandering postmodern subjects is to accept that we are 'hybrid monsters at the crossroads', citizens of a 'nomadic humanity' who are never fully at home (*heimlich*) in any native land: 'Giant or dwarf, the monster who struggles out of (us) takes pleasure in being content with itself'.

22 Jean-François Lyotard, 'The Sublime and the Avant-Garde' in *The Inhuman*, Stanford University Press, Stanford, California, 1988, pp. 89–90. In his postmodern reading of Augustine (*The Confession of Augustine*, Stanford University Press, Stanford, California, 2000), Lyotard even compares the Christian saint's experience of the absolute Other to an unspeakable experience of anal rape, so incommensurable and incomprehensible is the divine alterity which penetrates him to his very core: 'Thou went more inside me than my inmost part' (p. 9); '. . . with what stunning sensual exultation . . . is enacted the rape perpetrated by the Other. This ravishment is also undergone in surprise, there is no need to get to one's feet, to confront the Other head on, to experience the delights of torment – rather the contrary' (p. 23); '. . . a mad joy proceeds from the sexual . . . the cut is primal' (p. 36); or finally and most graphically:

> The majestic one takes the schoolboy like a woman, opens him, turns him inside out, turns his closest intimacy into his shrine, *penetrale meum*, his shrine in me. The absolute, absolutely irrelative, outside space and time, so absolutely far – there he is for one moment lodged in the most intimate part of this man. Limits are reversed, the inside and the outside, the before and the after . . .
>
> (p. 53)

In short, the sublime is interpreted by Lyotard as a transgression of natural limits and categories.

23 Ibid., p. 92.

24 Ibid., p. 95. Lyotard is citing Barnett Newman. See our more elaborate development of Kant's treatment of the sublime in Chapter 5.

25 Ibid., p. 96.

26 J.-F. Lyotard, *Lessons on the Analytic of the Sublime*, Stanford University Press, Stanford, 1994, p. 53; Thomas Brockelman, 'Kant and Collage: Judgment, Avant-Gardism, and the Sublime', in *The Frame and the Mirror: On Collage and the Postmodern*, Northwestern University Press, Evanston, Illinois, 2001, pp. 96ff.

27 J.-F. Lyotard, *The Postmodern Condition*, Minnesota Univeristy Press, Minneapolis, 1985, p. 76.

28 Brockelman, *The Frame and the Mirror*, p. 98.

29 J.-F. Lyotard, 'The Sublime and the Avant-Garde', p. 97.

30 Ibid., p. 100.

31 Ibid., p. 99.

32 Ibid., p. 101.

33 Ibid., p. 104.

34 Ibid., p. 105.

35 On this point see T. Brockelman's excellent observation, *The Frame and The Mirror*, pp. 98–9:

> Lyotard's reconstruction is interesting because it corresponds to an actual mode of self-understanding, one that has indeed proven powerful within the cultures of modernism and postmodernism. Certainly, Duchamp, about whom Lyotard has written considerably, demands to be understood in relationship to such a sublime principle, as does Warhol. Indeed, Lyotard's understanding is essential for understanding the quality of avant-gardism that is often called its 'negativity' – the quality that leads to the restless dissatisfied 'progress' of art in the period of classical avant-gardism. The category of the sublime seems perfect for describing those 'shock' effects that have been so essential to the development of historical avant-gardism. But if that's *all* that's going on in avant-gardism, then it would seem that the argument for any neo-avant-gardism today (which is, after all, what Lyotard intends to advocate) must be pretty weak . . . the effectiveness of avant-gardist shock today has diminished to nothing in a culture where outrageousness is itself a basis for commodification, where the very *ethos* of shock has been co-opted by the capitalist economy. When Mondrian is 'perfect' for coffee mugs and Warhol a small industry, an avant-gardism of the sublime loses any real effectiveness. But the experience of shock doesn't and can't add anything to our self-understanding. Insofar as it reduces to an aesthetics of the sublime, Lyotard's position is, by definition, a formula for a *narcissistic* avant-gardism. That is, it depends upon the progressive purgation from art of every remainder of the 'external', every dependence of the subject upon an other. Thus, if aesthetic avant-gardism is indeed reducible to a strategy of shock, it is really indefensible today.

36 J.-F. Lyotard, *The Postmodern Condition*, Minnesota University Press, Minneapolis, 1984, pp. 79ff.

37 For a more sympathetic reading of Lyotard's post-Holocaust aesthetics of the sublime, see Geoffrey Hartman, 'The Book of Destruction' in *Probing the Limits of Representation*, pp. 320ff. See also Lyotard's other and sometimes more elaborate and complex analyses of the sublime in 'After the Sublime, the State of Aesthetics' in *The Inhuman*, pp. 135–44; 'L'intérêt du Sublime' in *Du Sublime*, Editions Belin, Paris, 1988, pp. 149–78. See also the helpful commentaries on Lyotard's treatment of the sublime by Bill Readings, *Introducing Lyotard: Art and Politics*, Routledge, London, 1991, pp. 72–4 and Geoffrey Bennington, *Lyotard: Writing the Event*, Manchester University Press, Manchester, 1988, pp. 104ff, 165–9, 177f.

38 J.-F. Lyotard, 'The Sublime and the Avant-Garde', p. 98. One should also note here Lyotard's attempt to link ethical considerations with the unspeakability of the Shoah in *Heidegger and the Jews*, University of Minnesota Press, Minneapolis, 1990. We comment on this attempt in our essay, 'Narrative and the Ethics of Remembrance' in *Questioning Ethics*, ed. R. Kearney and M. Dooley, Routledge, London and New York, 1999, pp. 27–31. On the relationship between monstrosity and the aesthetics of the sublime see also Derrida, *The Truth in Painting*, Chicago University Press, Chicago, 1987, pp. 142–3, 349–51. For an illuminating account of the more religious implications of the Kantian sublime, see Clayton Crockett, *A Theology of the Sublime*, Routledge, London and New York, 2001, especially pp. 37–50, 99–110.

39 Slavoj Žižek, *The Plague of Fantasies*, Verso, London, 1997, pp. 218–29.

40 S. Žižek, 'The Unconscious Law' in *The Plague of Fantasies*, p. 219.

41 Ibid. Jean-Luc Marion gives a very different 'theological' reading of the 'monstrous nature of the Kantian sublime' in 'The Saturated Phenomenon', *Phenomenology and the 'Theological Turn': The French Debate*, Fordham University Press, New York, 2000, p. 214. Here he suggests that the fact that the sublime is, for Kant, a 'monstrosity' whose very 'unlimitedness' defies any analogy or horizon and contradicts the 'purpose of our faculty of judgment' (*Critique of Judgment*, Para 23), implies that the notion of a 'saturated phenomenon' exceeding all our powers of intentional adequation can be extended, eventually to the point of embracing an intentionless intution of the absolute Other, God.

42 See Gilles Deleuze, another radical postmodern theorist, on this subject:

> By establishing THE LAW as an ultimate ground . . . the object of the law is by definition unknowable and elusive. Clearly THE LAW, as defined by its pure form, without substance or object of any determination whatsoever, is such that no one knows nor can know what it is. It operates without making itself known. It defines a realm of transgression where one is already guilty and where one oversteps the bounds without knowing what they are . . .
>
> (Gilles Deleuze, *Coldness and Cruelty*, Zone Books, New York, 1991, pp. 82–3. See Žižek's psychoanalytic commentary on this, op cit., pp. 225–7.)

43 Žižek, op. cit., p. 227.

44 Ibid. See here Lacan's challenging reading of Exodus 3:15:

> I would like to know whom or what he (Moses) faced on Sinai and on
> Horeb. But after all, since he couldn't bear the brilliance of the face of him
> who said 'I am who I am', we will simply say at this point that the burning
> bush was Moses's Thing (das Ding), and leave it there.
>
> (The Ethics of Psychoanalysis, 1992, p. 172)

For a discussion on Lacan and Levinas on the theme of divine alterity see John
Manoussakis, 'Spelling Desire with two Ls: Levinas and Lacan' in JPSC: Journal for
Psychoanalysis of Society and Culture, vol. 7, no. 1, Spring 2002, pp. 16–23.

45 Ibid., p. 229.

46 Ibid., pp. 229–30. See, from a very different philosophical viewpoint, William Desmond's
reading of Kant's notion of 'genius' , 'terror' and 'transgression' in the Third Critique. In
spite of the difference of perspective, Desmond's conclusion is remarkably similar to the
postmoderns on certain points, e.g.:

> If we say something other gives the rule to the self, then either there is an
> inward otherness of selfhood which is beyond complete autonomy, or the
> self is a manifestation of something more primordial, and what is primordial
> is not itself lawlike and ordered and regular: the primoridal is beyond the law
> . . . when self proclaims its complete autonomy, it is only masking from itself
> its issue from something that is not reasonable, or intelligible, or morally
> benign. . . . More often it is wildness, frenzy, the primitive, the ugly, the
> excremental, the senseless. Genius and madness become indistinguisable.
> And we seem hard put to discriminate between divine madness and mad
> madness.
>
> ('Kant and the Terror of Genius' in Kant's Aesthetics,
> Walter de Gruyter, Berlin and New York, 1998, p. 614)

Unlike Žižek and fellow devotees of the equivocal sublime, Desmond is clearly uneasy
before such indiscrimination. Desmond offers an alternative to the Kantian–Hegelian–
Žižekian reading of sublime terror and monstrosity in 'Dialectic and Evil: On the Idiocy
of the Monstrous' in Beyond Hegel and Dialectic, SUNY, Albany, New York, 1992, pp.
189–250. For other original readings of the sublime, particularly as applied to art and
politics, see Paul Crowther, The Kantian Sublime: From Morality to Art, Clarendon Press,
Oxford, 1989, and The Contemporary Sublime: Sensibilities of Transcendence and Shock, Academy
Editions, London, 1995; and Luke Gibbons, Edmund Burke and Ireland: Aesthetics, Politics and the
Colonial Sublime, Cambridge University Press, Cambridge, 2003.

47 S. Žižek, Enjoy your Symptoms: Jacques Lacan in Hollywood and Out, Routledge, London and New
York, 1992, p. 123.

48 M. Brockelman, The Frame and the Mirror, p. 127. Brockleman continues his astute
commentary thus:

This symptom erupts as a kind of revenge of the modern against itself, wherever it seems that modern representation has extended to everything, where it seems that 'everything is under control'. It demands acknowledgment of the 'blind spot' in the most complete and universal representation, exacting the price of an 'undead' monstrosity for the repression of this truth/antitruth of the modern. Žižek's posthumanism – emergent both in popular culture and the politics of totalitarianism – provides a powerful tool for analysing all of those modes in which the contemporary social/political world is shaped by a peculiar fascination with/horror of the Other.

Brockelman criticizes Žižek, however, for dispensing with any kind of representational space for a hermeneutic mapping of the postmodern subject. In his insistence upon the total 'unrepresentability' of the excessive energies of the split or ex-centric subject, Žižek is in effect ruling out any possibility of interpreting the primary processes of the unconscious in terms other than those of pathological 'effects' or symptoms (which indicate *that* it exists but not how, why or what it is). In answer to Žižek's uncompromising scepticism, not to say nihilistic cynicism, Brockelman proposes some notion of oneiric poetics – based liberally on Freud's interpretation of the dream as 'another stage' with an 'unplumbable' spot or hole: 'a navel, as it were, that is its point of contact with the unknown' (*The Interpretation of Dreams*, p. 111n). Such a hermeneutics of the unconscious subject would enable us to concede that while the postmodern disappearance of the space of the Real marks the sundering of representational universality from the space of the subject, it does not 'leave the subject entirely without a field of representation' (p. 13). The remaining space is 'the field in which a kind of representational practice remains viable' qua conscious–unconscious site of dreams. This heterogeneous space of dreams, suggests Brockelman, provides a model for a 'nonpathological posthumanism' for it opens up a specific interpretation of the subject as both irrepresentable (sublime) *and* representable (beauty).

> This space is boundless, one never hits or perceives its limit, one never finds something that *doesn't belong or can't fit* in this space. But on the other hand, the space of the dream *is* structured and thus limited. The structure of dream space works like an equation for an infinite curve: radically heterogeneous to the phenomenon that it describes and yet determinative of it.
>
> (p. 132)

Brockelman goes on to explore possible readings of the 'posthumanist self' based on Freud's insistence that the meaning of a dream be understood not as a picture (e.g. some realist or naturalist correspondence) but as a picture puzzle or rebus where each discrete element may be read as a syllable or word which cannot be simply seen or intuited (qua unifying signified) but has to be figured out (as a complex interplay of signifiers). Taking an analogy from art, Picasso's *Man with a Hat*, where each element can be read in a variety of ways – as glass or face, as shoulder or guitar, etc. – Brockelman concludes that:

> The double signification denies any possibility that you might simply look
> through it, taking its reference as its meaning. The very nature of the signifying
> material demands that you always 'look again' and keep looking indefinitely
> at the painting's signifiers . . . The interpretive 'movement' associated with art
> here is precisely the opposite of what it is in every traditional ladder of the
> beautiful. Not the signified but the signifer controls development.
>
> (p. 136–7)

But we thus look again indefinitely not to disappear entirely into some *jouissance* of monstrous excess, but to rediscover ourselves as more flexible and mobile 'posthumanist' selves. In this way, Brockleman seeks to thematize a heterogeneous space of subjectivity in which a 'new model of both activity and self-understanding emerges' (p. 142). I fully endorse this search for a new '*practice and ethos*' (p. 144) issuing from the crisis of modernity as it faces into the delerious ex-centricities of postmodernity, shedding the old humanist illusions, but clinging to the hope that new modes of protest and emancipation may be disclosed and enacted.

49 Žižek, *The Plague of Fantasies*, p. 228.

50 Ibid., p. 229.

51 See also here Levinas' description of the 'there is' as radically godless in his early essay 'There is: Existence without Existents', first published in 1946 as a section of *De l'existence à l'existant* (Vrin, Paris), and reprinted in *The Levinas Reader*, ed. S. Hand, Blackwell, London, 1989. Levinas talks of the godless 'there is' or *il y a* as a 'mute, absolutely indeterminate menace' (p. 32). See our critical discussion of this subject in the Conclusion to this volume.

52 Joseph Campbell, *The Power of Myth*, Doubleday, New York, 1988, p. 222.

53 See my discussion of this question in Chapter 1 of this volume; and in our essay, 'Others and Aliens: Between Good and Evil' in *Evil after Postmodernism*, ed. Jennifer Geddes, Routledge, London and New York, 2001; see also our conclusion to 'Desire of God' in *Of God, The Gift and Postmodernism*, ed. J.D. Caputo and M. Scanlon, Indiana University Press, Minneapolis, 1999.

54 P. Ricoeur, 'Evil', p. 259.

55 P. Ricoeur, 'Life in Quest of Narrative' in *On Paul Ricoeur: Narrative and Interpretation*, ed. David Wood, Routledge, London, 1991, p. 23.

56 William Desmond, *Beyond Hegel and Dialectic*, pp. 233–4.

57 Ibid. Desmond criticizes the tendency of speculative metaphysics and dialectics to explain away the story of suffering (e.g. the story of Jesus for Hegel) as a mere 'representation' which must be sublated into an abstract concept which takes the harm out of it and subsumes its singular otherness and strangeness into the universality of absolute spirit. Desmond retorts: 'Despite any rational comfort we may glean from dialectics, does the mystery of iniquity still remain a mystery?' (pp. 234–5). Speculative rationalization is doomed to fail for the very claim to 'sublate' the other carries within itself the trace of this otherness which will not go away:

> [A] 'Trojan horse that threatens the viability of all claims to absolute self-
> sufficiency that pure thinking makes on its own behalf. The other of thought

is within the thought that tries to think itself, not as the completely appropriated other, but as a recalcitrant inward otherness that shakes dialectic from within.

(p. 240)

Desmond concludes accordingly that evil is precisely a *'breaking otherness* that breaches and iredeemably wounds the self-sufficient closure of thought thinking itself' (p. 241); and he responds with the claim that 'philosophy can be honest about its strangeness, ponder its otherness' (p. 237).

58 See P. Ricoeur, 'Memory and Forgetting' in *Questioning Ethics*, pp. 5–12, and *La Mémoire, L'Histoire, L'Oubli*, Editions du Seuil, Paris, 2000, pp. 574–93. See also S. Freud, 'Remembering, Repeating, and Working-Through' in *The Standard Edition of the Complete Psychological Works of Sigmund Freud*, Hogarth Press, London, 1955, vol. 12.

59 W. Desmond, *Beyond Hegel and Dialectic*, pp. 238–9.

60 Ibid., p. 239: 'Like the cry from the heart, there cannot be a systematic science of forgiveness, for forgiveness is an act of assent whose most important concrete reality is its thisness as a this'. In defiance of the speculative will to pure philosophical conceptuality, and wishing (as we do) to also eschew the counter-extreme of blind irrationalism, I would endorse here Desmond's recourse to a certain 'metaphorical' – and I would add narrative – language in order to try to speak and think about ostensibly impossible phenomena like evil, grace or forgiveness.

61 On this vexed issue of the possibility and impossibility of pardon see the recent work of Paul Ricoeur, Jacques Derrida and John D. Caputo. In *Questioning God* (Indiana University Press, Bloomington, 2001, ed. J. Caputo, M. Dooley and M. Scanlon), we find a fascinating series of exchanges on the question of forgiving the unforgiveable; see especially the Introduction and opening essays by Derrida, Robert Gibbs, John Milbank and Mark Dooley. Jacques Derrida develops several of these arguments in *On Cosmopolitanism and Forgiveness* (Routledge, London and New York, 2001), pp. 25–60, and cautions against rhetorical reconciliations and overhasty strategies of psychotherapeutic economy (p. 50):

> I believe it is necessary to distinguish between forgiveness and the process of reconciliation, this reconstitution of a health or a 'normality', as necessary and desirable as it would appear through amnesties, the 'work of mourning', etc. A 'finalized' forgiveness is not forgiveness; it is only a political strategy or psychotherapeutic economy.

Derrida does concede, however, that he is 'torn' between such a 'hyperbolic' ethical vision of the impossibility of pure forgiveness, and what he calls 'the reality of a society at work in pragmatic processes of reconciliation' (p. 51). These two poles of pure and pragmatic forgiveness are, he concludes, irreducible to one another yet indissociable. See also Paul Ricoeur's intriguing analysis of 'Le Pardon Difficile' in *La Mémoire, L'Histoire, L'Oubli*, pp. 593–658. Where Derrida speaks of the *impossibility* of pardon, Ricoeur prefers to speak of the *quasi-impossibility* or *difficulty* of pardon.

62 See S. Žižek, *The Plague of Fantasies*, cited in Chapter 2 above, and *On Belief*, Routledge, London and New York, 2001. See J.-F. Lyotard, 'After the Sublime: The State of Aesthetics' and '*L'intérêt du Sublime*', cited in note 31 of Chapter 2 above.

63 J. Derrida, *The Truth in Painting*, Chicago University Press, Chicago, 1987, pp. 108–9, 142–3 and 349–51. For a useful application of Derrida's notion of the monstrous to contemporary writing, see Andrew Gibson, 'Narrative and Monstrosity' in *Towards a Postmodern Theory of Narrative*, Edinburgh University Press, 1996, pp. 261ff.

64 E. Levinas, 'There is: Existence without Existents', first published in 1946 as a section of *De l'existence à l'existant* (Vrin, Paris) and reprinted in *The Levinas Reader*, ed. S. Hand, Blackwell, London, 1989, pp. 32–3. See our extended discussion of this point in Chapter 3, 'God or Khora?' above, note 21.

65 J. Derrida, *On The Name*, ed. and trans. by T. Dutoit, Stanford University Press, Stanford, California, 1995, p. 74.

66 J. Derrida, 'Hospitality, Justice and Responsibility' in *Questioning Ethics*, ed. R. Kearney and M. Dooley, Routledge, London and New York, 1999, pp. 70–1.

67 Simon Critchley, 'On Derrida's *Specters of Marx*', in *Philosophy and Social Criticism*, vol. 21, no. 3, 1995, p. 19. In *Ethics–Politics–Subjectivity* (Routledge, London and New York, 1999, p. 199), Critchley explicitly writes: 'I would like to answer the question directly now by saying that nothing prevents the face of the other being *das Ding*'. See also here Critchley's development of this line of argument in 'The Original Traumatism: Levinas and Psychoanalysis' in *Questioning Ethics*, pp. 230–42 and W.J. Richardson's intriguing exploration of similar issues in 'The Irresponsible Subject' in *Ethics as First Philosophy: The Significance of Emmanuel Levinas for Philosophy, Literature and Religion*, ed. A. Peperzak, Routledge, New York and London, pp. 122–31. It must be acknowledged that there is a deep ambiguity, if not contradiction, in Levinas' reading of the relationship between language and otherness. On the one hand, he sees the other as a radical saying that can never be said, narrated, imaged, remembered or named without betrayal – 'a past that can never become graspable or identifiable', an origin that cannot be treated within the 'horizons of phenomenology' (Adriaan Peperzak, 'From Intentionality to Responsibility: On Levinas's Philosophy of Language' in *The Question of the Other*, ed. A.B. Dallery and C.E. Scott, SUNY Press, Albany, New York, 1989, p. 17). Here we are concerned with an alterity so other that it is utterly unsayable, like some kind of divine *das Ding* – a position that almost, God forbid, concurs with Lacan's view that the 'I am what I am' of the burning bush is 'Moses's *das Ding*' (*The Ethics of Psychoanalysis*, Routledge, London, 1992, p. 174). See also John Manoussakis' analysis in 'Spelling Desire with two Ls: Levinas and Lacan' (in JPSC: *Journal for Psychoanalysis of Society and Culture*, Spring 2002). On the other hand, however, we find Levinas claiming that the Other is the very leaven of language and discourse, an approach which approximates at times to the quasi-hermeneutic formula that all saying is said by someone to someone else – e.g. 'a discourse always is said by someone to one or more others' (ibid., p. 11). It is as if Levinas could not ultimately choose between Lacan and Ricoeur! I am grateful to three graduate scholars in Boston College, John Manoussakis, Brian Treanor and Mark Goodman, for illuminating discussions of this Levinasian paradox of language. See also Jean Greisch's insightful comments on Heidegger's original notion of il y a (*Es Gibt*) in *L'Arbre de vie et l'arbre du savoir*, pp. 39–43.

68 Joseph O'Leary, 'Where All the Ladders Start: Apophasis as Awareness', forthcoming
    2002. O'Leary extends the critique of sublime terror to include certain extreme forms of
    'negative theology' which he sees as insufficiently attentive to the carnality and charity
    of the divine: 'Very Hellenistic is the language in which Marion evokes the encounter
    with God: "Terror attests, in the mode of the forbidden, the insistent and unbearable
    excess of the intuition of God"'. There may be such tremors in the text of Dionysius,
    though they are more evident in Gregory of Nyssa, who borrows from Enneads 1 6,4
    the phrase thambos kai ekplexis, 'stupor and panic' (In Canticum), which seems to evoke an
    archaic Greek world. Scripture does have awesome cosmic theophanies that inspire fear
    and trembling (e.g. Job chapters 38–41), but usually it inflects this primordial basis in
    an ethical and eschatological sense. The 'terror of the Lord' in parallel with the 'glory of
    his majesty' (Isaiah 2:10) in scenes of divine judgement. In the Hellenistically tinged
    cult of mystical vertigo there is a risk that the dynamic whereby Scripture subjects the
    primeval sacred terror to a sober, covenantal 'fear of the Lord' will be overcome. At best,
    concludes O'Leary, the methods of negative theology and deconstruction should be
    seen as so many 'skilful means', as in Eckhart or certain Buddhist masters, to save us
    from false abstractions and return us to the 'fragility of our own flesh'. Perhaps, he
    surmises, 'it is time for the religions to practice a new kind of negative theology by lying
    down, with Yeats, "where all the ladders start,/In the foul rag and bone shop of the
    heart"'. Our invocation of Jacob's ladder as a metaphor for our diacritical hermeneutics
    at several points throughout this volume and The God who May Be does well to recall this
    starting point at every turn. For a more elaborate account of the theological vocabulary
    of divine 'terror' from Gregory, Chrysostom and Augustine to Otto, Barth and Marion,
    see O'Leary, ibid., note 88. O'Leary's own preference, similar to my own in chapter 2
    of The God Who May Be (pp. 35–7) is for a neo-Eckhartian approach to the question of
    divine transcendence. Eckhart, he suggests, might be read in a new way as

    > transcending names and forms in order to come closer to the phenomena,
    > to what is nearest to hand . . . His radical aphairesis of God-language could
    > be an expression of down to earth realism, serving to keep free the relation
    > to the living God. His quest of the naked essence of divinity could be only a
    > hyperbolic way of expressing impatience with abstract conceptions that
    > prevent access to the presence of the divine here and now.

    I find myself in almost complete agreement with O'Leary's hermeneutic rereading of
    biblical, theological and deconstructive approachs to divine transcendence in dialogue
    with Asian, and especially Buddhist, teaching.
69 J. Derrida, Shibboleth, in S. Budick and G. Hartman (eds), Midrash and Literature, Yale
    University Press, New Haven, 1986, p. 342. See also here Joseph Campbell on the
    rapport between God and monstrosity, The Power of Myth, Doubleday, New York, 1988,
    p. 222; and our discussion of this question in 'Others and Aliens: Between Good and
    Evil' in Evil after Postmodernism, ed. Jennifer Geddes, Routledge, London and New York,
    2001, and our conclusion to 'Desire of God' in Of God, The Gift and Postmodernism, ed. J.D.
    Caputo and M. Scanlon, Indiana University Press, Bloomington, 1999, with a reply by

Derrida and Caputo, republished in a revised version entitled 'Desiring God' in *The God who May Be*, Indiana University Press, Bloomington, 1999.

5 ON TERROR

1 The term *understand* is important here. For if *imagining* the event was all too possible – thanks to the compulsive repetition of TV images of planes slicing into towers and towers collapsing; and if *knowing* was, at least in the immediate wake of the event, all too impossible; a question arising for philosophy remains, how might we attempt to understand this terrible and terrifying phenomenon? Or as Larry King put it, in more colloquial terms than those of Spinoza: 'How can we cover the unthinkable?' I am grateful to my friend and fellow philosopher, Jean Greisch, for the Spinoza citation and for his illuminating reflections on 9/11, 'The Great Game of Life and Fundamental Ethics'. In this paper, delivered at Boston College on 8 October, 2001 (*Transversalités*, vol. 81, January 2002), Greisch asks how certain works of dramatic art – in particular Sophocles' *Antigone* and Ionesco's *Tueur sans Gages* – may help us to understand something (however faltering, minimal and oblique) about the terror of 9/11. Is there any phronetic wisdom to be gleaned from these literary explorations of the enigmas of violence and evil? And what might thinkers like Spinoza, Kant, Heidegger, Taylor or Nussbaum be able to add to such wisdom? He ends by echoing Kant's famous question in the *Essay on Radical Evil*, 'What can we hope?' Although my examples are different, I share much of the spirit of Greisch's 'literary-hermeneutic' approach. See also the symposium 'Art of Darkness: Three writers speak of evil' featuring Kathleen Norris, Joyce Carol Oates and Nathan Englander in *Boston College Magazine*, vol. 62, no. 1, Winter 2002, pp. 20–8.

2 Edward Said, 'The Clash of Ignorance' in *Z Magazine*, September, 2001. Samuel Huntington later published a full-length book on the subject entitled *The Clash of Civilizations and the Remaking of the World Order* (2001), where he expanded on his prediction that twenty-first-century global conflict would not be waged between nation-states but between general 'civilizations' defined by shared cultures, values and religions and transgressing the boundaries of sovereign nations. Of the eight major civilizations, Huntington predicts that the most violent clash will occur between the Christian West and the Muslim nations of the East stretching from Africa and the Middle East as far as Indonesia. While I do not deny that this scenario may indeed be the preferred view of Bin Laden and certain generals in the Pentagon, I would support Said's argument that we should do everything to combat such monolithic models of schismatic thinking to the extent that they deny the complex realities of difference, diversity and dissent within every civilization, no matter how hegemonic or totalizing it may presume to be. The curious irony is that the most enthusiastic beneficiary of the Huntington thesis is the Al Qaeda itself. Said concludes that the Huntington thesis is an ideological distortion that wants to make 'civilizations' and 'identities' into what they are not: shut-down, sealed-off entities that have been purged of the myriad currents and countercurrents that animate human history, and that over centuries have made it possible for that history not only to contain wars of religion and imperial conquest but also to be one of

exchange, cross-fertilization and sharing. This far less visible history is ignored in the rush to highlight the ludicrously compressed and constricted warfare that 'the clash of civilizations' argues is the reality.

The hasty attempts to draw unambiguous lines in the sand, in the immediate wake of 9/11 – between US and THEM, West and Islam, etc. – not only denies the disorderliness of reality but also masks the 'interconnectedness of ordinary lives', 'ours' as well as 'theirs'. It often takes writers like Conrad, for instance, to remind us that the 'heart of darkness' we think is located way out there is also often to be found in the midst of the 'civilized' world itself. It was also Conrad, Said adds, who in *The Secret Agent* (1907) so brilliantly described 'terrorism's affinity for abstractions like "pure science" (and by extension for "Islam" and "the West"), as well as the terrorist's ultimate moral degradation'.

3 Alan Wolfe adds: 'By insisting that we are not at war with Islam, Mr Bush deprives Mr Bin Laden of the religious battle he so intensely desires' ('The God of a Diverse People' in *The New York Times Op-Ed*, 14 October, 2001).

4 Jean Greisch, 'The Great Game of Life'.

5 Michel Foucault, *Madness and Civilization: A History of Insanity in the Age of Reason*, Random House, New York, 1965.

6 Considering this wide variety of monsters and their enduring ability to provoke terror in us, the museum's curator, Nick Capasso, wrote:

> Monsters are everywhere, and always have been. These terrible and wonderful beings, since the dawn of human consciousness, have lurked at the edges and stood front and center in all our far-flung cultures. Their ubiquity and longevity are based on their power and adaptability as symbols and metaphors for a great number of things, all centered upon anxiety. Whenever we are *bothered, nervous, frightened, uncertain, threatened, alienated, oppressed, repressed, confined, irrational, guilty, ill, flawed, sad,* or *angry* monsters can appear. They are part and parcel of our condition, our imagination, our spirituality, our arts, and they won't go away – ever. We need them too much, and hence we are ever finding them, creating them, carrying them with us, and surrounding ourselves with them. They are legion.
>
> (Nick Capasso, Introduction to *Terrors and Wonders: Monsters in Contemporary Art*, DeCordova Museum Publications, Lincoln, Massachusetts, 2001, p. 7)

7 Ibid., p. 9: 'A world-view circumscribed by order, taxonomy, and the normative is constantly called into question by beings that resist classification and have no real limits or boundaries – the children of chaos.'

8 Ibid., p. 9.

9 Ibid., p. 10.

10 Timothy Beal, 'Our Monsters, Ourselves', *Chronicle of Higher Education*, 11 September, 2001.

11 Ibid. Beal writes wittily of monsters inhabiting those places 'where our well-established sense of the order of things touches chaos, where our toes curl over the edge of the abyss

... where our boundlessly confident, ever-expanding consciousness shudders and freezes in its tracks'. Here, he claims, we come up against 'the edges of secure knowledge, the limits of conscious reach, the boundaries of human expansion'.

12 Ibid. 'Supernatural horror literature and movies frequently explore how gods and monsters relate – change places, even – in culture and in our imaginations.'

13 Ibid.

14 Ibid. More precisely:

> In the aftermath of September 11, Americans are all too familiar with the ways religious discourse can serve political rhetoric in making monsters out of others, imbuing them with diabolical power and construing our war against them as a holy war of absolute good against absolute evil. The questions raised by horror culture can introduce ambiguity into this cultural mix, undermining attempts to boil things down to a battle between us versus them, good versus evil. They invite us to discover our monsters in ourselves and ourselves in our monsters.
>
> (p. 14)

This goes in a similar direction to Jacques Derrida's response to 9/11 and its aftermath, when he declares, in our New York Dialogue of 10 October, that 'in this war, no one is innocent'. 'On Terror, God and Deconstruction: Dialogue between Derrida and Kearney' in *Traversing the Imaginary*, ed. J. Manoussakis and P. Gratton, Rowman and Littlefield, Maryland, 2003.

15 Jean Baudrillard, from 'Simulations' in *Continental Aesthetics*, ed. R. Kearney and D. Rasmussen, Blackwell, Oxford, 2001, p. 423.

16 Ibid.

17 Ibid.

18 Ibid.

19 J. Baudrillard, 'L'esprit du Terrorisme', *Le Monde*, 2 November, 2001.

20 Ibid.

21 Ibid.

22 Ibid. Baudrillard writes:

> Le terrorisme est l'acte qui restitue une singularité irréductible au coeur d'un système d'échange généralisé. Toutes les singularités (les espèces, les individus, les cultures) qui ont payé de leur mort l'installation d'une circulation mondiale régie par une seule puissance se vengent aujourd'hui par ce transfert terroriste de situation ... Le terrorisme, comme le virus, est partout. Il y a une perfusion mondiale du terrorisme, qui est comme l'ombre portée de tout système de domination, prêt partout à se réveiller comme un agent double.
>
> (Ibid., p. 3)

Baudrillard's argument, it could be said, finds some support in the way in which the 'image' of Bin Laden, as rediscovered double secret agent, became not only a media obsession but the occasion of mass consumer commodities from Bin Laden mugs, posters and T-shirts (with 'Happy Hunting', 'Dead Meat' and 'Wanted Dead or Alive' on them) to anti-Bin Laden toilet paper at $19 a roll, which went into mass production as early as 13 September with the following inscriptions under the image of the bearded turbaned enemy: 'Fight the War even in your bathroom with XTC XWipes ... Wipe away the heartache.' As Houston University historian, Clifford Egan, remarked, because Americans didn't know who the real Bin Laden was, it was necessary in waging a shadow war to have an image of somebody out there to symbolize the threat and rally the populace. (Reported by Kevin Merida in The Washington Post, 6 October, 2001.)

23 Ibid., p. 6. Baudrillard's argument proceeds as follows:

> Ne jamais attaquer le système en termes de rapports de forces. Ça, c'est l'imaginaire (révolutionnaire) qu'impose le système lui-même, qui ne survit que d'amener sans cesse ceux qui l'attaquent à se battre sur le terrain de la réalité, qui est pour toujours le sien. Mais déplacer la lutte dans la sphère symbolique, où la règle est celle du défi, de la réversion, de la surenchère. Telle qu'à la mort il ne puisse être répondu que par une mort égale ou supérieure. Défier le système par un don auquel il ne peut pas répondre sinon par sa propre mort et son propre effondrement.
>
> (Ibid.)

Or again:

> La tactique du modèle terroriste est de provoquer un excès de réalité et de faire s'effondrer le système sous cet excès de réalité. Toute la dérision de la situation en même temps que la violence mobilisée du pouvoir se retournent contre lui, car les actes terroristes sont à la fois le miroir exorbitant de sa propre violence et le modèle d'une violence symbolique qui lui est interdite, de la seule violence qu'il ne puisse exercer: celle de sa propre mort. C'est pourquoi toute la puissance visible ne peut rien contre la mort infime, mais symbolique, de quelques individus.

In short, in addition to deploying the 'real' weapons of the system – knives, arms, credit cards, planes, technology – the terrorists of 9/11 also used the far more powerful weaponry of symbolic warfare, namely, sacrificial death. And we might add paranoia – each American looks to his/her other 'normal' neighbour and asks: is this typically well behaved person a 'potential terrorist'? This latter weapon of hysterical phobia is what Baudrillard calls 'mental terrorism'. Baudrillard compares this sacrificial and mental terrorism to chaos theory, where an initial localized event (e.g. the flapping of a butterfly's wings) can provoke incalculable, exponential consequences. This is how the 'image' of the collapsing towers functioned, like a 'primitive scene' that would be played out again and again in the Western subconscious. The event of 9/11 became an image, a 'theatre of cruelty' par excellence, a compulsive and obsessional image-event which signalled the advent of a new postmodern truth: that reality becomes fiction and that both rival each other in the quest for the most unimaginable of images! The unprecedented power of the 9/11 event is, according to Baudrillard, due to its uncanny conflation of the real and the imaginary (it was both at once), conscripting as it did the 'white magic' of electronic vision (TV) and the 'black magic' of terrorism. This 'spectacle of terrorism', concludes Baudrillard, provokes an 'immoral fascination' that makes both critical interpretation and meaningful political action impossible. Even the media cannot be blamed, for it too is part of the system ('There is no good or bad use of the media', claims Baudrillard). In this scenario of systemic doubling, good and bad, just and unjust, democracy and dictatorship become utterly 'reversible' – inter-changeable. Apocalypse is indeed now, 'the terrorist attack corresponding to the precedence of the event over all models of interpretation' (ibid.). These conclusions I cannot accept, for they spell not only pessimism but paralysis – a sort of postmodern theodicy without God.

24 Immanuel Kant, The Critique of Judgment, extract from 'The Analytic of the Sublime', Para 23, in Continental Aesthetics: An Anthology, ed. R. Kearney and D. Rasmussen, Blackwell, Oxford, 2001, p. 24.

25 Ibid.

26 Ibid., p. 27.

27 Ibid., p. 26.

28 Ibid.

29 Ibid.

30 Ibid.

31 Ibid.

32 Ibid.

33 Ibid., p. 27.

34 Edmund Burke, A Philosophical Inquiry into the Origin of our Ideas of the Sublime and the Beautiful, Notre Dame University Press, Notre Dame, 1986, p. 58. I am indebted to Michael Halberstam for this and other references in my discussion of Arendt and the sublime, see in particular his article, 'Hannah Arendt on the Totalitarian Sublime and Its Promise of Freedom' in Hannah Arendt in Jerusalem, ed. Steven Aschheim, University of California Press, London and Berkeley, pp. 105ff.

35 See Michael Halberstam, op. cit., p. 118. Arendt herself uses the term terror to refer to both the literal terrorization of society by a certain political movement or event, and also as a complex sentiment of existential dislocation, characterized by a paradoxical response of horrible humiliation and enthusiastic collusion on behalf of the 'subjects of terror'. See H. Arendt, 'Ideology and Terror' in The Origins of Totalitarianism, Harcourt Brace, New York, 1979. On the more specific issue of our response to 'Terror' resulting in a collapse of the real into the imaginary, see also the trenchant remarks of Susan Sontag to 9/11 ('Ne Soyons pas Stupides Ensemble', Le Monde, 26 September, 2001):

Mais ceux qui occupent des functions officielles ... ont decidé – avec la complicité volontaire des principaux médias – qu'on ne demanderait pas au public de porter une trop grande part du fardeau de la réalité. Les platitudes satisfaites et unanimement applaudies du Congrès d'une partie soviétique semblaient méprisables. L'unaminité de la rhétorique moralisatrice, destinée à masquer la réalité, débitée par les responsables américains et les médias au cours de ces derniers jours est indigne d'une démocratie adulte. Les responsables américains . . . nous ont fait savoir qu'ils considèrent que leur tâche n'est qu'une manipulation: donner confiance et gérer la douleur. La politique d'une démocratie – qui entraîne des désacccords et qui encourage la sincérité – a été remplacée par la psychothérapie. Souffrons ensemble. Mais ne soyons pas stupides ensemble. Un peu de conscience historique peut nous aider à comprendre ce qui s'est exactement passé, et ce qui peut continuer à se passer.

36 Chomsky adds:

If we choose the latter course (i.e. to try to understand) we can do no better, I think, than to listen to the words of Robert Fisk, whose direct knowledge and insight into affairs of the region is unmatched after many years of distinguished reporting. Describing 'The wickedness and awesome cruelty of a crushed and humiliated people', he writes that 'this is not the war of democracy versus terror that the world will be asked to believe in the coming days. It is also about American missiles smashing into Palestinian homes and US helicopters firing missiles into a Lebanese ambulance in 1996 and American shells crashing into a village called Qana and about a Lebanese militia – paid and uniformed by America's Israeli ally – hacking and raping and murdering their way through refugee camps.' And much more. Again, we have a choice: we may try to understand, or refuse to do so, contributing to the likelihood that much worse lies ahead.

(From Noam Chomsky, Open Letter circulated on Internet, 18 September, 2001. See also Chomsky, 9–11, Seven Stories Press, New York, 2001.)

37 Apart from those already cited above see also our dialogue with Jacques Derrida on the events of 9/11, recorded in New York University on 10 October, 2001 and published in *Traversing the Imaginary*, ed. J. Manoussakis and P. Gratton, Rowman and Littlefield, Maryland, 2003. See also the illuminating discussion of the events by two other French philosophers, Paul Ricoeur and Stanislas Breton, in 'Décrypter la Violence Terroriste' in *La Croix*, 25 October, 2001, pp. 14–15, where such issues as violent and non-violent resistance, Just War, Monotheism and the Western Crisis of democracy are debated. The key point issuing from this exchange is the need to 'understand' as well as to 'judge'. See also Thich Nhat Hanh's and the Dalai Lama's Buddhist reflections on 9/11 excerpted in *The Sunday Tribune*, Dublin, September, 2001:

All violence is injustice – the only antidote to violence is compassion. And what is compassion made of? It is made of understanding . . . To understand, we must find paths of communication so that we can listen to those who desperately are calling out for our understanding – because such an act of violence (as 11 September) is a desperate call for attention and for help.

38 Ian McEwan, the *Guardian* (UK), 15 September, 2001. I am grateful to my friends, Michael and Cathy Fitzgerald, for bringing this text to my attention.

39 See here Jeremiah Conway's illuminating article, 'Socrates and the Minotaur: Following the Thread of Myth in Plato's Dialogues', *Teaching Philosophy*, September 1993, vol.16, no. 3, pp. 193–203. I am grateful to my graduate student, Carlos Bohorquez, for bringing this essay to my attention. Conway argues that the Minotaur itself is not the real threat: 'the original threat is the greed, self-promotion, fear and revenge that led Minos to possess what belonged to the gods; these forces, not the Minotaur, are the real danger and responsible for creating the monster in the first place' (p. 199). Conway concludes that 'The role of Theseus (which the Athenians are busy celebrating) is a story of heroism built on forgetfulness. In killing the Minotaur, Theseus mistook the image of danger for the source of danger itself' (p. 200). Theseus was unmindful of the surrounding circumstances and deeper sources of evil. He forgot his own family's complicity with the creation of the Monster and that his own actions would make him just as monstrous as the Minotaur (ibid.). By contrast, Socrates' heroic refusal to engage in revenge and violence, 'repairs the forgetfulness of Theseus and restores to the myth precisely those dimensions that Theseus (and the Athenians who model themselves after him) overlooked. The hero's journey for Socrates is learning to do no harm, a ridding from the soul the desire for revenge. Though he sees Athens and its laws have become mis-shapen into a devouring Minotaur, Socrates will not slay it' (ibid.). In this manner, Plato is suggesting that philosophical understanding may help to guide Socrates out of the labyrinth of popular opinion and myth, which holds that one should answer one wrong with another wrong. 'The thread of philosophy' is thus offered by Plato to the Athenian audience as an alternative to the received propaganda of blood-cycles: 'love of truth' (*philein-sophia*) is proposed as an alternative to the sword.

6 HAMLET'S GHOSTS:
FROM SHAKESPEARE TO JOYCE

1 On the spectral return of repressed memories, often resulting in compulsive acts of repetition, see Sigmund Freud, 'Remembering, Repeating and Working-through', *The Standard Edition of the Complete Psychological Works of Sigmund Freud*, vol. 12, London, Hogarth Press, 1955, and 'The Uncanny', *The Standard Edition*, vol. 17. See also Paul Ricoeur on 'impeded memory' (*La mémoire empêchée*) in *La Mémoire, l'histoire, l'oubli*, Editions du Seuil, Paris, 2000, pp. 83–97; and his concise summary of this position in 'Memory and Forgetting' in *Questioning Ethics*, ed. R. Kearney and M. Dooley, Routledge, London and New York, 1999, pp. 5–12.

2 S. Freud, *The Interpretation of Dreams*, Pelican, New York, 1983, pp. 365–8, 575–6.

3 Jacques Lacan, 'Desire and the Interpretation of Desire in Hamlet' in *Literature and*

Psychoanalysis, ed. Shoshana Felman, The Johns Hopkins University Press, Baltimore and London, 1982, pp. 11–52. For an elaboration of Lacan's thesis see the Appendix to this chapter, pp. 158–61 and 'Hamlet' in *Dictionnaire de la Psychanalyse*, ed. Roland Chemama, Larousse, Paris, 1993, pp. 60–2.

4 Nicholas Abraham,'Notes on the Phantom: A Complement to Freud's Metapsychology' in *Diacritics*, vol. 18, no. 4, 1988, p. 171. See also p. 172: 'What comes back to haunt are the tombs of others . . . the burial of an unspeakable fact within the love-object'.

5 Nicholas Abraham, 'The Phantom of Hamlet or the Sixth Act' in *Diacritics*, vol. 18, no. 4, 1988, p. 188.

6 Ibid., p. 189. See also J.P. Muller, 'Psychosis and Mourning in Lacan's *Hamlet*' in *New Literary History*, vol. 12, 1980.

7 See Jacques Derrida's remarks on this 'out of joint' phenomenon in *Hamlet* in *Spectres of Marx: The State of the Debt, the Work of Mourning and the New International*, trans. Peggy Kamuf, Routledge, New York and London, 1994, p. xx. Derrida speaks here of a 'spectral moment' that no longer belongs to time understood as a linear sequence of present moments – past, present, future. 'Furtive and untimely, the apparition of the spectre does not belong to that time, it does not give time, not that one: "Enter the ghost, exit the ghost, re-enter the ghost"' (*Hamlet*). This spectral moment, which Derrida sees as intrinsic to the ontology of time itself, appears to us as a 'trace' which comes 'to disjoin or dis-adjust the identity to itself of the living present as well as of any effectivity. There is then *some spirits*. Spirits. And *one must* reckon with them' (p. xx).

8 Paul Ricoeur, 'Life in Quest of Narrative' in *On Paul Ricoeur: Narrative and Interpretation*, ed. David Wood, Routledge, London and New York, 1991, and *Time and Narrative*, Chicago University Press, Chicago, vols 1–3, 1984–7.

9 See André Green, op. cit. and Nicholas Abraham, op. cit. See notes 3–6 above.

10 J. Joyce, *Ulysses*, Penguin, London and New York, 1968, p. 207.

11 Ibid., pp. 207–8.

12 Ibid., p. 208.

13 Ibid.

14 See Declan Kiberd, Note to *Ulysses: Annotated Student's Edition*, Penguin, London and New York, 1992, p. 1013. Just as Joyce sought to become his own father by writing *Ulysses*, so too Shakespeare sought to become his own father (as Ghost) of his own son (Prince Hamlet) in *Hamlet*. These and related father–son parallels are recalled at various points throughout the novel. To mention just one curious minor detail, Shakespeare's son Hamnet was 11 when he died and Bloom recalls in his final bedtime reverie that it was also almost 11 years since his son, Rudi, had died. Harold Bloom has no doubts about these Joyce/Shakespeare correspondences; see his extraordinary essay 'Hamlet' in *Shakespeare: The Invention of the Human*, Riverhead Books, New York, 1998, p. 390. 'For him (Joyce/Stephen), Hamlet the Dane and Hamnet Shakespeare are twins, and the ghostly Shakespeare is therefore the father of his most notorious character.'

15 Joyce, *Ulysses*, p. 197

16 Richard Ellmann leaves us in little doubt about this Hunter/Bloom connection in his Appendix ('*Ulysses*: A Short Story') to the 1968 Penguin edition, pp. 705f. The Hunter in question, he explains, refers to a 'dark-complexioned Dublin Jew . . . rumoured to be a

cuckold whom Joyce had met twice in Dublin'. Joyce revealed to his brother Stanislaus in a letter of November 13, 1906, that this same Hunter is to be the central character of his new story *Ulysses* begun in that year. Ellmann writes:

> On the night of 22 June 1904 Joyce (not yet committed either to Nora or to monogamy) made overtures to a girl on the street without realizing, perhaps, that she had another companion. The official escort came forward and left him, after a skirmish, with 'black eye, sprained wrist, sprained ankle, cut chin, cut hand'. Next day Joyce lamented to a friend, 'For one role at least I seem unfit – that of man of honour'. He did not mention what in retrospect evidently became the most impressive aspect of the fracas: he was dusted off and taken home by a man called Alfred Hunter in what he was to call 'orthodox Samaritan fashion'. This was the Hunter about whom the short story 'Ulysses' was to be projected.

On this relation between the paternal figures Bloom/Hunter, see Giorgio Melchiori, 'The Genesis of Ulysses' in *Joyce in Rome*, ed. G. Melchiori, Bulzoni Editore, Rome, 1984, p. 37.

17 Joyce, *Ulysses*, p. 25.
18 Ibid., p. 658.
19 *Ulysses*, p. 656.
20 Declan Kiberd, op. cit., p. 1013. Most writers, it must be said, respond in some way to the poetic injunction – tell it but do not tell it exactly as it was. This call to fictional remembrance can be interpreted in different ways, of course. On the one hand, there is the Beckettian view that 'silence is our mother tongue'; and that all forms of remembering (apart from involuntary memory à la Proust) are distortions, stories we invent to ward off the 'suffering of being'. Hence Beckett's resolve to dismantle the narrative form, paring his stories down until they become 'residua' or 'no-texts' – anti-novels. Seamus Heaney offers a recent and ironic variation on this same tune when he writes: 'Whatever you say say nothing'. The best stories are the stories *never told* – hence Heaney's corollary counsel to 'govern the tongue', to write poetry rather than fiction. Against this, there is the Joycean tradition that says: tell everything! – a tradition that produces *Finnegans Wake* (the text of 'allmen') rather than Beckett's *No's Knife* (the text of 'noman'). This Joycean impulse celebrates the fictional re-creation of history in its entirety, working to the refrain of the garrulous washerwomen by the Liffey: 'mememormee, mememormee!' See Part 2 of *On Stories*, Routledge, 2002, a companion volume to the present work in our trilogy on narrative imagination entitled 'Philosophy at the Limit'. For a particularly insightful account of Joyce's unresolved memory of the immemorial Irish Famine, see also Kevin Whelan, *The Killing Snows: The Famine in History and Memory*, Cork University Press, Cork, 2002.
21 Harold Bloom, op. cit., p. 414.
22 On Joyce's 'cuckold-bawd' obsession, which finds parallels in both Leopold Bloom and in Joyce's Shakespeare (as related by Stephen in the National Library sequence), see our 'A Tale of Two Cities – Joyce in Rome and Trieste' in *Reimagining Ireland*, Wolfhound Press,

Dublin, 2002. See also the insightful comments of René Girard on this question, note 24 below.

23 Harold Bloom, op. cit., p. 390. Bloom also offers the curious suggestion that Shakepeare may have named his son Hamnet as a sort of 'talisman of family restoration, taking Amleth as a model of persistence in the quest for familial honor and a vindication of the relation between fathers and sons' (p. 399).

24 René Girard offers an illuminating reading of Hamlet's tragic imprisonment in the doubling mechanism of mimetic desire in Shakespeare: Les feux de l'envie, Grasset, Paris, 1990, especially the two essays 'La vengeance abâtardie d'Hamlet', pp. 331–53 and 'Croyez-vous vous-même à votre théorie?', which analyses Joyce's theory of Hamlet in Ulysses, pp. 313–30. Girard reads both Hamlet and Ulysses as literary attempts to go beyond the stifling logic of mimetic rivalry, revenge and sexual betrayal – a logic which he attributes to the 'originary traumatism', shared by both Joyce and Shakespeare, of the 'cuckold bawd' experience (Ann Hathaway's alleged betrayal with Shakespeare's brothers; Nora's alleged betrayal with Joyce's Dublin friend, Cosgrave, and the journalist from Trieste, etc.). In the same manner, Girard reads Hamlet itself as a critical parody of the revenge play, pointing to the destabilizing revelation at the play's outset that the one to be avenged – King Hamlet – is no innocent victim but someone who is now purging his own 'foul crimes' in purgatory. In short, the fact that the assassinated victim was himself an assassin under-mines the whole revenge–sacrifice mechanism. The exposure of this inner mechanism, argues Girard, reveals Claudius to be just one more loop in a chain of revenge murders which the young Hamlet will simply continue if he murders Claudius as he is commanded to do by the ghost. The revelation is expressed in a crisis of indifferentiation where each character looses his identity and becomes the mirror image of the other.

This inability to distinguish one murderer from the next is perhaps best epitomized in the dramatic boudoir scene where Hamlet presents his mother with two portraits – one of his father, the other of Claudius – only to show, in spite of himself, that there is more of a symmetry between the two brothers than he wishes to admit. The alarming symmetry is further revealed by Gertrude's inability to distinguish between the two. It is not the Lady that doth protest too much, however, but Hamlet himself who is becoming increasingly aware of how 'undifferentiated' his father and his uncle actually were. The interchangeability of those caught in the revenge cycle – what Girard calls the 'crisis of indifferentiation' – is also evident in the scene by the graveside where Hamlet and Laertes are presented as twin images of each other. In short, for Girard, Hamlet is a play which reenacts and subverts the sacrificial logic of mimetic violence at the heart not only of society but, at a more symbolic and originary level, of theatrical culture itself. It serves as a play within a play exposing the hidden structures of theatrical pretence and cover-up. Like the mousetrap play within the play, Hamlet too tries to 'catch the conscience of the king' – and of the rest of us as well. In this respect, concludes Girard, Hamlet should be read as a profoundly moral and Christian play which endeavours to expose the long repressed truth of the repetitive sacrificial logic upon which most human societies, and not just Denmark, are founded.

From a very different – and more secular humanist angle – see Harold Bloom's interesting take on the doubling mechanism of the play: 'Two Hamlet's confront each other, with virtually nothing in common except their names. The Ghost expects Hamlet to be a version of himself, even as young Fortinbras is a reprint of old Fortinbras' (H. Bloom, op. cit., p. 387). On whether Hamlet is a Christian or a secular tragedy see also Søren Kierkegaard, 'A Side-glance at Shakespeare's Hamlet', Appendix to *Stages On Life's Way*, ed. and trans. Hong and Hong, Princeton University Press, New Jersey, 1988, pp. 452–4; and G.W.F. Hegel, section on the 'Romantic Arts' in *Lectures on Aesthetics*, trans. T.M. Knox, pp. 1225–32. See our 'Kierkegaard and Hamlet' in *The New Kierkegaard*, ed. Elsbet Jepstrup, Indiana University Press, Bloomington, 2003.

25 Harold Bloom recalls Nietzsche's insistence that Hamlet possessed 'true knowledge' which is nothing other than 'the abyss between mundane reality and the Dionysian rapture of an endlessly on-going consciousness' (op. cit., p. 421).

26 Ibid., p. 431:

> When Shakespeare broke away from Marlovian cartooning, and so became Shakespeare, he prepared the abyss of Hamlet for himself. Not less than everything in himself, Hamlet also knows himself to be nothing in himself. He can and does repair to that nothing at sea, and he returns disinterested . . .

Stephen Dedalus undergoes a similar emancipation from the mimetic rivalry of his Dublin literary peers in *Ulysses*: see René Girard, 'Croyez-vous vous-même à votre théorie?', op. cit. See note 24 above.

27 Ibid., p. 413.

28 J. Lacan, 'Desire and the Interpretation of Desire in *Hamlet*', p. 39. For a complimentary commentary of this psychoanalytic take on Hamlet, see John P. Muller, 'Psychosis and Mourning in Lacan's *Hamlet*' in *New Literary History*, vol. 12, no. 1, Fall 1980, pp. 147–65. Muller's conclusion supports the Lacanian reading of *Hamlet* in terms of the desire/mourning dyad (p. 164):

> (Hamlet) is unable to strike the King (Claudius), for the King embodies the phallus, the signifier of the Queen's desire and . . . .in the classical psycho-analytic view also the signifier of his own Oedipal desire. All the while he is subject to the desire of others, as they determine his staying or leaving or returning or duelling. Once dead, Ophelia becomes the impossible object again desired by Hamlet, particularly in rivalrous mourning with her brother. His jealous identification with martial Laertes leads him to welcome the duel, wherein the final action takes place, eventuating in mass death. To the end we see the subject in dependence on the signifier of the phallus and the law of the Other – the law of language – from whose inexorability Hamlet is liberated only at the moment of death, for it is only then that narcissistic attachment to the phallus (in fear of castration) and subjection to the desire of others (whose desire is signified by the phallus) fades. The tragedy of Hamlet is indeed the tragedy of desire.

29 H. Bloom, op. cit., p. 413.

30 Ibid., p. 429.

31 Ibid., p. 430. Bloom holds that *Hamlet* is the 'most persistent and personal' of all Shakespeare's thirty-nine plays and the one that he 'never stopped rewriting . . . from the early version, circa 1587–9, almost down to his retreat back to Stratford' (p. 391). Bloom pursues his thesis as follows, relating the play directly to Shakespeare's personal and professional biography (p. 400):

> Shakespeare chose to make a revisionary return to his own origins as a dramatist (in Hamlet), perhaps in commemoration of his son Hamnet's death. There is a profoundly elegiac temper to the matured *Hamlet*, which may have received its final revisions after the death of Shakespeare's father, in September, 1601. A mourning for Hamnet and for John Shakespeare may reverberate in Horatio's (and the audience's mourning for Hamlet) . . . when he wrote *Hamlet* he seems to have realized that a spiritual culmination was upon him, and all his gifts seemed to fuse together, as he turned to a more considerable revisionary labor than he attempted before or after.

32 Ibid., p. 400.

33 Ibid., p. 400.

34 Ibid., p. 406–7.

35 Ibid., p. 401.

36 Ibid., p. 411.

37 Ibid., p. 419.

38 Lacan, op. cit., p. 39.

39 Ibid., p. 51.

40 N. Abraham, 'The Phantom of Hamlet', p. 189.

41 Ibid.

42 Ibid.

43 Ibid.

44 André Green, *Hamlet et Hamlet: Une Interprétation Psychoanalytique de la Représentation*, Balland, Paris, 1982.

45 Julia Kristeva, *Powers of Horror*, Columbia University Press, New York, 1982, p. 49.

7 MELANCHOLY: BETWEEN GODS AND MONSTERS

1 For these references to Plato and melancholy see R. Klibansky, E. Panofsky and F. Saxl, *Saturn and Melancholy: Studies in the History of Natural Philosophy, Religion and Art*, Nelson, London, 1961, p. 17.

2 Sigmund Freud, 'Mourning and Melancholy' from *The Pelican Freud Library*, vol. 2, *On Metapsychology: The Theory of Psychoanalysis*, ed. Angela Richards, Penguin, London, 1984, pp. 251–68.

3 Aristotle, 'The Notion of Melancholy: Problem XXX, I' printed in a bilingual edition in R. Klibansky, E. Panofsky and F. Saxl, *Saturn and Melancholy*, pp. 18–29. This text is also

extracted in a critical anthology and commentary by Jennifer Raden, *The Nature of Melancholy: From Aristotle to Kristeva*, Oxford University Press, Oxford, 2000. In addition to other theorists of melancholy (e.g. Avicenna, Kant, Ficino, Freud and Klein), this useful collection also contains some fascinating passages from writers and poets such as Goethe, Keats and Baudelaire. The editor's Introduction, 'From Melancholic States to Clinical Depression', offers an instructive and informative overview of this complex enigma.

4 Ibid., p. 16.

5 Ibid., p. 16. See also p. 17:

> It was Aristotelian natural philosophy which first brought about the union between the purely medical notion of melancholy and the Platonic conception of frenzy. This union found expression in what for the Greeks was the paradoxical thesis that not only the tragic heroes, like Ajax, Heracles and Bellerophon, but all really outstanding men, whether in the realm of the arts or in those of poetry, philosophy or statesmanship – even Socrates and Plato – were melancholics.

6 M. Heidegger, *Being and Time*, trans. J. Macquarrie and E. Robinson, Blackwell, Oxford, 1973, p. 243.

7 Ibid. See also Heidegger, 'What is Metaphysics?' in *Heidegger: Basic Writings*, ed. David Krell, London, Routledge and Kegan Paul, 1979, pp. 9–108, in particular, pp. 102–3:

> In anxiety there occurs a shrinking back before . . . that is surely not any sort of flight but rather a kind of bewildered calm. This 'back before' takes its departure from the nothing. The nothing itself does not attract; it is essentially repelling . . . (and) as the repelling gesture toward the retreating whole of beings, it discloses these beings in their full but heretofore concealed strangeness as what is radically other – with respect to the nothing. In the clear night of the nothing of anxiety the original openness of beings as such arises: that they are beings – and not nothing.

Or again, p. 103:

> Holding itself out into the nothing, Dasein is in each case already beyond beings as a whole. This being beyond beings we call 'transcendence'. If in the ground of its essence Dasein were not transcending, which now means, if it were not in advance holding itself out into the nothing, then it could never be related to beings nor even to itself. Without the original revelation of the nothing, no selfhood and no freedom.

8 Heidegger, *Being and Time*, p. 232.

9 Ibid., p. 233.

10 Romano Guardini, *De la Mélancolie*, Editions du Seuil, Paris, 1953, pp. 63–4:

Cette aspiration vers l'absolu s'unit chez le mélancolique à la certitude profonde qu'elle est vaine. La disposition d'esprit mélancolique est sensible aux valeurs, au bien suprême. Mais c'est comme si, précisément, cette exigence se retournait contre elle-même. Car elle va de pair avec le sentiment qu'elle est impossible à satisfaire ... L'impossibilité réside déjà dans la manière dont l'absolu est désiré: dans une impatience qui veut être trop vite satisfaite, dans une exigence d'immédiat qui ne voit pas les instances intermédiaires et s'engage dans un chemin extravagant pour le rejoindre. En tout cas, l'aspiration à la plénitude de la valeur et de la vie, à la beauté infinie, qui s'unit dans les profondeurs de l'être au sentiment de la fugacité des choses, du manquement, de la partie perdue, à la tristesse, à la désolation et à l'inquiétude qui s'insinuent dans l'âme et que rien n'apaise: telle est la mélancolie. Elle est comme une atmosphère qui baigne tout, comme un fluide qui pénètre tout, comme une amertume profonde et, en même temps, une douceur mêlée à tout.

See similar sentiments expressed in more mythological-literary terms in Claude Mettra's *Saturne ou l'herbe des âmes*, Seghers, Paris, 1981.

11 Kant, 'On the Cognitive Faculties', *Anthropology from a Pragmatic Point of View* (1793), in J. Radden, *The Nature of Melancholy: From Aristotle to Kristeva*, pp. 199ff. See also the illuminating study 'Kant's Hypochondria' by Susan Meld Shell in *The Embodiment of Reason*, University of Chicago Press, Chicago and London, 1996, pp. 265–305. Shell explores the ambivalent zone of 'melancholic hypochondria' opened up by Kant's startling admission that 'between insanity and healthy (understanding) sense there is no clear division, for hypochondria fills out the middle' (XV: 2:18).

12 See R. Klibansky, E. Panofsky and F. Saxl, *Saturn and Melancholy*, Illustrations 6 and 47.

13 On the castration of Ouranos by Kronos and its relation to the ancient problematic of desire and melancholy, see Pascal Guignard, *Le Sexe et l'effroi*, Gallimard, Paris, 1994, p. 349. See also Guignard's fascinating analysis of Seneca and Lucretius on melancholy and desire in classical Rome, pp. 243–4.

14 See Klibanski *et al.*, Illustration plates 10 and 13.

15 Ibid., Illustration plates 16, 47, 38 and 47.

16 Ibid., Illustration plates 23–6, 30, 38–9 and 57.

17 Ludwig Binswanger, *Mélancolie et Manie*, translated from the German, *Melancholie und Manie* (1960) by J.-M. Azorin and Y. Totoyan, Presses Universitaires de France, Paris, 1987.

18 In addition to the Heidegger and Guardini cited above, see J.-P. Sartre, *Being and Nothingness*, especially Part I, Chapter I, section I, translated from the French *L'Etre et le Néant* (1943) by Hazel Barnes, Philosophical Library, New York, 1956, pp. 21–40; and Søren Kierkegaard, *Sickness unto Death*, trans. W. Lowrie, Princeton University Press, Princeton, NJ, 1968, and *The Concept of Dread*, trans. W. Lowrie, Princeton University Press, Princeton, NJ, 1957. For an illuminating account of the genealogy and development of the existentialist notion of melancholy, especially as it pertains to Kierkegaard, see Harvie Ferguson, *Melancholy and the Critique of Modernity: Søren Kierkegaard's Religious Psychology*, Routledge, London and New York, 1995.

19 Marsilio Ficino, *De Vita Triplici*, pp. 111, 22; quoted in Klibansky *et al.*, *Saturn and Melancholy*, p. 241f.

20 Ficino, ibid., II, 15.

21 Klibansky, Panovsky and Saxl, *Saturn and Melancholy*, p. 273.

22 Ibid., p. 271.

23 See J. Kristeva, *The Black Sun: On Depression and Melancholy*, Columbia University Press, New York, 1989; and 'On Melancholic Imagination' in *Postmodernism and Continental Philosophy*, ed. Hugh J. Silverman and D. Welton, SUNY Press, New York, 1988. See also *Abjection, Melancholia and Love: The Work of Julia Kristeva*, ed. John Fletcher and Andrew Benjamin, Routledge, London and New York, 1990.

24 Paul Ricoeur, *La Mémoire, l'histoire, l'oubli*, Éditions du Seuil, Paris, 2000, pp. 91–5. Commenting on the 'sublimating' tradition of lyric poetry running from the Renaissance – especially Milton and Shakespeare – up to Keats and Baudelaire, Ricoeur notes a recurring 'éloge d'une humeur contrastée et, si l'on peut dire, dialectique où *Delight* répond à *Melancholy* sous les auspices de la beauté': Ricoeur speaks accordingly of the importance of recognizing in this notion of sublimated melancholy 'sa profondeur énigmatique que n'épuise aucune nosologie' (p. 93). Walter Benjamin deals with similar territory but from a somewhat more pessimistic and allegorical perspective in his famous study of the German *Trauerspiel*: see Max Pensky, *Melancholy Dialectics: Walter Benjamin and the Play of Mourning*, The University of Massachusetts Press, Amherst, 1993.

25 Klibansky *et al.*, *Saturn and Melancholy*, pp. 316–43. See also Ricoeur's comment that Dürer's *Melancholia I* provides us with an artistic and therefore somehow transformative representation of the true vanity of the real. Speaking of the instruments and symbols of the liberal arts scattered all around the melancholic figure, Ricoeur writes:

> La vanité du savoir est ainsi incorporée à la figure désoeuvrée. Cette fusion entre la géométrie cédant à la mélancolie et la mélancolie perdue dans une rêveuse géométrie donne à *Melencolia I* son énigmatique puissance: la vérité elle-même serait-elle triste, selon l'adage de l'Ecclésiaste?
>
> (p. 92)

And he adds, in a note:

> Il est vrai que la figure centrale a des ailes, mais repliées, que des *putti* l'égaient: suggestion de sublimation? Une couronne qui ceint la tête et surtout le nombre Quatre – le 'carré magique' des mathématiques médicales – paraissent faire antidote.
>
> (p. 92)

26 See our discussion of the postmodern cult of the sublime in Lyotard, Žižek, Kristeva and Baudrillard in Chapters 4 and 5.

27 J. Kristeva, 'On Melancholic Imagination', p. 21.

8 THE IMMEMORIAL: A TASK OF NARRATIVE

1 Adam Phillips, 'The Telling of Selves' in *On Flirtation*, Faber and Faber, London and Boston, 1994, p. 68. I am indebted to Phillips for much of my opening analysis.

2 Ibid., p. 69. See also here Ciarán Benson, *The Cultural Psychology of the Self*, Routledge, London and New York, 2001, especially part 1, chapter 3, 'Placing oneself in Personal Time: The Narrative Structure of Self'; Jerry Bruner, 'The Autobiographical Process', *Current Sociology*, vol. 43, no. 2/3, Autumn 1995. See our own discussion of narrative self-identity as both an historical and personal task in Part 2 of *On Stories*, Routledge, London and New York, 2002.

3 Lawrence Langer, *Holocaust Testimonies: Memory in Ruins*, Yale University Press, New Haven, 1991, p. 82. See also our extended discussion of Langer's thesis on the limits of memory in *On Stories*, pp. 47–8, 64–6.

4 Michael André Bernstein, 'Paul Celan: Radiance That Will Not Comfort' in *Five Portraits: Modernity and Imagination in Twentieth-Century German Writing*, Northwestern University Press, Evanston, IL, 2000, p. 104.

5 Paul Ricoeur, 'Can Fictional Narratives be True?' in *Analecta Husserliana*, ed. A.-T. Tymienecka, Dordrecht, Reidel, vol. 14, 1983, pp. 12f.

6 For an elaboration of this see P. Ricoeur, 'Life in Quest of Narrative', pp. 22ff., and our own previous studies, 'Narrative Imagination' in *Poetics of Modernity*, Humanities Press, New Jersey, 1995, 'Narrative Imagination – The Ethical Challenge', *Poetics of Imagining*, Fordham University Press, New York, 1998, and 'Narrative Matters', Part 4 of *On Stories*, pp. 125–56.

7 See Bernstein, op. cit. Bernstein quotes Krzysztof Zierek here who writes that the other, for Celan, 'does not appear merely as a theme, an image or a series of images in the poem, but, conversely, all aspects of the poem, its imagery, meaning, rhythm, point toward the other' (p. 113). On a more general, less controversial, level one might note that narrative imagination can also allow an attentiveness – both poetical and ethical – to the otherwise forgotten histories and stories of others. See for example, the following evocative passage in Robert McLiam Wilson's novel, *Eureka Street*:

> The merest hour of the merest day of the merest of Belfast's citizens would be impossible to render in all its grandeur and all its beauty. In cities the stories are jumbled and jangled. The narratives meet. They clash, they converge or convert. They are a Babel of prose. And in the end, after generations and generations of the thousands and hundreds of thousands, the city itself begins to absorb narrative like a sponge, like paper absorbs ink. The past and the present is written there. The citizenry cannot fail to write there. Their testimony is involuntary and complete. And sometimes, late at night, when most sleep, as now, the city seems to pause and sigh. It seems to exhale that narrative, to give it off like the stored ground-heat of a summer day. On such nights, you cross a city street and for a few golden minutes there are no cars and the hum of distant traffic fades and you look at the material around you, the pavements and street-lamps and windows, and if you listen gently,

you might hear the ghosts of stories whispered. And there is magic in this, an impalpable magic, quickly gone. It is at these times that you feel you are in the presence of something greater than yourself. And you are. For as you look around the perimeter of our illuminated vision, you can see the buildings and streets in which a dark hundred thousand, a million, ten million stories as vivid and complex as our own reside. It doesn't get more divine than that.

(*Eureka Street*, Secker and Warburg, London, 1996, pp. 215–16)

For an analysis of the powerful role played by stories in the construction of a collective identity – literary, social, political – see R.F. Foster's masterly work, *The Irish Story: Telling Tales and Making it up in Ireland*, Allen Lane, The Penguin Press, London, 2001.

8 Ricoeur, 'Can Fictional Narratives be True?', p. 13 and also *La mémoire, l'histoire, l'oubli*, Editions du Seuil, Paris, 2000.

9 Ricoeur, 'Can Fictional Narratives be True?' p. 16.

10 Ibid.

11 Ibid.

12 J. Derrida, *On Cosmopolitanism and Forgiveness*, Routledge, London and New York, 2001, p. 50f; also 'On Forgiveness', in *Questioning God*, ed. J. Caputo, M. Dooley and M. Scanlon, Indiana University Press, Bloomington and Indianapolis, 2001, pp. 56–66.

13 Dooley, 'The Catastrophe of Memory' in *Questioning God*, pp. 127f.

14 Ibid.

15 J.-F. Lyotard, *Heidegger and the 'Jews'*, Minnesota University Press, Minneapolis, 1988, pp. 9f; also 'The Sign of History' in *The Differend*, Manchester University Press, Manchester, 1988, pp. 165ff; *Political Writings*, University College London Press, London, 1993, p. 64. I am indebted to Mariana Papastephanou for her analysis of these and other passages, 'Linguistic Archipelago and Its History', in *Metaphilosophy*, Summer 2002.

16 Mariana Papastephanou, op. cit.

17 Bill Readings, *Introducing Lyotard*, p. 73 and J.-F. Lyotard, *Postmodern Fables*, University of Minnesota Press, Minneapolis, 1997.

18 M. Papastephanou, op. cit.

19 Ibid., p. 17:

> Non-represented can also mean unknown or forgotten, never wronged in the consciousness of the strong, the third party, the judge, or the wrong-doers themselves. Those who have been wronged in that way have no other means to demand justice but to articulate the wrong. The only ruse and trickery they can perform in our postmodern times is mimesis, to imitate the strong, to pretend that they are like them.

20 Lyotard, *The Inhuman*, Polity Press, Cambridge, 1991, p. 60. On Lyotard's notion of the 'unrepresentable sublime' see also Jack Caputo's typically insightful comments in *More Radical Hermeneutics*, Indiana University Press, Bloomington, 2000, pp. 143, 178–9. See also Joseph O'Leary's critical insight on the relationship between language and silence:

Silence signifies wisdom only when words have preceded and is compassionate only when words follow. Silence is deep only when rooted in an authentic existence: Vimalakirti's silence would have had no power if he had not lived a bodhisattva life of wisdom and compassion.

('"Where All the Ladders Start": Apophasis as Awareness',

Archivio di Filosofia, Rome, 2002)

O'Leary is drawing from both Asian and theological sources to make the point that silence is not absolute but always relative to language, as apophasis is to kataphasis. O'Leary thus proposes to demystify certain extreme absolutist formulations of negative theology in favour of phenomenological and hermeneutic bridgings between silence and speech.

21 M. Papastephanou, op. cit., pp. 20–1:

The true rupture will be effected when the *real* of *really* without inverted commas will no longer signify, or attract the charge of, positivism or logocentrism, but will connote other accounts of the real, alternative and richer than those imposed by the hegemony of a correspondence theory of truth. In that case, vigilance shall not need to manifest itself, for its power will be in the mute, i.e. unthematized, undisputed acceptance of its significance in all forms of research. The identification of ontology with inescapable logocentrism and positivism and the latters' elevation beyond history to a trans-temporal albeit an-archical parameter of representation mirrors the awe our era still feels, and perhaps feels more strongly now due to technology and telecommunication, with regard to traditional and truncating interpretations of reality. Before shifting the emphasis from traditional historiography to the search for more just forms, our '*conception*' of '*reality*' must be '*redefined*'. If our determination to dispense with positivism is genuine, representation will cease to be incriminated wholesale.

I am very much in agreement with Papastrephanou's critical reading of Lyotard but I part company with her final endorsement of 'creative nihilism'.

22 See here the insightful essay by Pascal Bruckner, *La mélancolie démocratique: Comment vivre sans ennemis*, Editions du Seuil, Paris, 2000. See also here Joseph O'Leary's critique of absolute indetermination in favour of a self beyond ego. Drawing from Henri Corbin's remark that the absolute needs to absolve itself of its own indetermination in order to enter a relation to the human, O'Leary surmises that this scheme might be applied

to the identity of the human person, reborn after the dissolution of ego just as God is reborn after the 'death of God'. Corbin admits that the false everyday ego is dissolved, but only in favour of the . . . integral person.

('"Where all the Ladders Start": Apophasis as Awareness',

forthcoming 2002)

Our own hermeneutic notion of a narrative self also goes in this direction.

23 See P. Ricoeur, Studies 5 to 10, *Oneself as Another*, University of Chicago Press, Chicago, 1992, and my own commentaries on the notions of narrative selfhood and hermeneutic imagination in *Poetics of Imagining* (Chapters 6 to 8), *Poetics of Modernity* (Chapters 5 to 7), *The Wake of Imagination*, Routledge, New York and London, 1992 (especially Conclusion) and *On Stories*, Routledge, London and New York, 2002 (Parts 2 and 4). By contrast, see the defences of the immemorial against such a hermeneutic position in Michel Henry, 'Speech and Religion', *Phenomenology and the 'Theological Turn'*, Fordham University Press, New York, 2000, pp. 230ff (which champions the notion of the 'immemorial self'), and Emmanuel Levinas, *Otherwise than Being*, Nijhoff, The Hague, 1981 (which defends the notion of the 'immemorial' other, in tune with Lyotard, Derrida and Caputo). For a critical take on the memorial/immemorial dialectic in terms of a double critique of 'too much' memory and 'too little', see P. Ricoeur, *La Mémoire, l'histoire, l'oubli*, Editions du Seuil, Paris, 2000.

24 Walter Reich, 'The Monster in the Mist: Are Long Buried Memories of Child Abuse Reliable?' in *The New York Times Review of Books*, May 1994. See our discussion of this controversy in 'Narrative and the Ethics of Remembrance' in *Questioning Ethics*, ed. M. Dooley and R. Kearney, Routledge, London and New York, 1999, pp. 22ff.

25 Michael Bernstein, op. cit., p. 112.

9 GOD OR *KHORA*?

1 Plato, *Timaeus and Critias*, trans. H. Lee, Penguin, London, 1965.

2 There are several other powerful contemporary commentaries of Plato's *khora* in both analytic and continental philosophy, in particular John Sallis, *Chorology: On Beginning in Plato's Timaeus*, Indiana University Press, Bloomington, Minneapolis, 1998. Unfortunately this latter study, which sheds much light on the discussions below, was brought to my attention after the completion of the current analysis. In future editions I would want to take this illuminating work into account.

3 See Julia Kristeva's *Powers of Horror*, Columbia University Press, New York, 1982, pp. 13–14.

4 J. Kristeva, 'Le sujet en procès' in *Polylogue*, Editions du Seuil, Paris, 1977, p. 57. See here the lucid and insightful commentary of Kelly Oliver, *Subjectivity without Subjects: From Abject Fathers to Desiring Mothers*, Rowan and Littlefield, Maryland, 1999, pp. 58–60, 74.

5 Kelly Oliver, *Subjectivity without Subjects*, p. 60.

6 J. Kristeva, *Tales of Love*, Columbia University Press, New York, 1987, p. 235. Kelly Oliver describes this ambivalence clearly:

> Maternity [says Kristeva] is a bridge between nature and culture, between the drives and the symbolic. The other's body is the 'pivot of sociality', at once the guarantee and a threat to its stability . . . The mother's body guarantees the continuation of the species and yet her questionable identity threatens the symbolic unity. Thus, maternity is impossible for the symbolic. Kristeva defines the maternal as 'the ambivalent principle that is bound to the species, on the one hand, and on the other stems from an identity catastrophe' . . .
>
> (*Subjectivity without Subjects*, p. 74)

7 J. Kristeva, *Revolution and Poetic Language*, excerpted in *The Kristeva Reader*, ed. Toril Moi, Blackwell, London, 1986, p. 93. See also the subsequent discussions of *khora* on pp. 94–8, 108–9, 115–17.

8 Ibid., p. 94.

9 Ibid.

10 Ibid.

11 Ibid.

12 Ibid.

13 Ibid., p. 97.

14 Slavoj Žižek, *The Ticklish Subject*, Verso, London, 1999, pp. 54–5.

15 Ibid., p. 55.

16 J. Caputo, *The Prayers and Tears of Jacques Derrida: Religion without Religion*, Indiana University Press, Bloomington and Indianapolis, 1997. See also Caputo's chapter, 'Khora: Being Serious with Plato' in *Deconstruction in a Nutshell: A Conversation with Jacques Derrida*, Fordham University Press, New York, 1997. In an essay entitled 'Dark Hearts', Jack Caputo has this to say about his debt to the great American Heideggerian, Bill Richardson:

> If, as Heidegger says, thinking is thanking, then one can offer a work of thought as a bit of gratitude. Derrida, on the other hand, repeats the warning of the circle of the gift according to which, in all gift-giving, something is always returned to the giver. The giver always gets a pay back, a return on the investment, if only (or especially) in the most oblique, the most indirect form, of gratitude. Therefore, the purest gift-gifting demands ingratitude, which does not pay the giver back and therefore pay off and nullify his generosity. Since I am in the highest degree the beneficiary of William Richardson's work and friendship, and more grateful than I am permitted to say, I have undertaken to protect his generosity with a certain ingratitude, precisely understood, with an utterly ungrateful bit of disagreement, not only with him, but also with Heidegger, to whom I have accumulated a life-long debt. So I offer what follows in the spirit of the deepest and most loyal ingratitude, cognizant always of the unworthiness of my ungift, which comes in response to what in a simpler world I would call the richness of the contribution that William Richardson has made to philosophy in America.
>
> (J. Caputo, 'Dark Hearts: Heidegger, Richardson and Evil' in *From Phenomenology to Thought, Errancy and Desire*, ed. B.E. Babich, Kluwer, Netherlands, 1995, p. 267)

Replace the names Richardson for Caputo – and Derrida for Heidegger – in the above citation, and you will have a reasonable idea of my own 'loyal ingratitude' to Jack Caputo in this chapter. Or as Nietzsche put it, in more graphic terms, the best way to thank a mentor is to be a thorn in his flesh. For a similar reading of the deconstructive approach to *khora* see James Olthuis, 'The Test of *Khora*: *Grâce à Dieu*' in *Religion with/out Religion*, ed. James Olthuis, Routledge, London and New York, 2002, pp. 110–19.

17 J. Derrida, 'Khora' in On the Name, trans. D. Wood, J.P. Leavey and I. McLeod, Stanford University Press, Stanford, California, 1995, pp. 89–127.

18 J. Derrida, Psyché: Inventions de l'autre, Galilée, Paris, 1987, pp. 563–70. See p. 570, where Derrida outlines the difference between khora and the God of negative theology:

> Le passage par la négativité du discours au sujet de la khora n'est ni un dernier mot ni la médiation au service d'une dialectique, une élévation vers un sens positif ou propre, un Bien ou un Dieu. Il ne s'agit pas ici de théologie négative, il n'y a là référence ni à un événement, ni à un don, ni à un ordre, ni à une promesse, même si . . . l'absence de promesse ou d'ordre, le caractère désertique, radicalement anhumain et athéologique de ce 'lieu' nous oblige à parler, à nous référer à lui d'une certaine et unique façon, comme à ce tout-autre qui ne serait même pas transcendant, absolument éloigné, ni d'ailleurs immanent ou proche. Non que nous soyons obligés d'en parler, mais si, mus par un devoir qui ne vient pas d'elle, nous la pensons et en parlons, alors il faut respecter la singularité de cette référence. Bien qu'il ne soit rien, ce référent paraît irréductible et irréductiblement autre: on ne peut pas l'inventer. Mais comme il reste étranger à l'ordre de la présence et de l'absence, tout se passe comme si on ne pouvait que l'inventer dans son altérité même, au moment de l'adresse.

Unlike the Judaeo-Christian or eschatological dialogue between human persons and a personal God, Derrida insists that 'cette adresse n'est pas une prière, une célébration ou une louange. Elle ne parle pas à Toi.' What occurs at the level of negative or trinitarian theology concerns questions of history, influences and events which, for Derrida, remain 'des significations étrangères à la khora' (p. 570).

19 J. Derrida, 'Khora' in On the Name, p. 125. For another perspicuous commentary on this subject, see James Olthuis, 'The Test of Khora: Grâce à Dieu' in Religion with/out Religion.

20 J. Caputo, Deconstruction in a Nutshell, p. 86.

21 Ibid., p. 90. Following Derrida's analysis of khora in On the Name, Caputo goes on to offer the following key descriptions:

> Khora is indifferent to every determination . . . let us say abysmally indifferent . . . (It is) a hyperessential sub-reality, an almost unreal, indeterminate indeterminacy which seems rather to fail words, to fall short of word or meaning . . . defection, less than meaning, essence and being.'
>
> (pp. 95–6)

Khora is that '"something" without thing', in Derrida's phrase, which takes place as the 'very spacing of de-construction' (On the Name, p. 80) – it is that 'incomparable, unmetaphorisable, desert-like place without properties or genus' (Deconstruction in a Nutshell, p. 97); 'an uncircumventable, achronic "preorigin" not to be confused with the Eternal, Originary "Truth"' (p. 98). In fact, because it is formless and nameless, khora appears to us as a mise-en-abîme – 'a play of reflections in a black pool', which precontains, as an-archic quasi-condition, 'all the oppositions that are inscribed in it' (p. 99) – e.g. being and non-being, the intelligible and the sensible – and we could perhaps add, God and godlessness. Or as Derrida himself puts it, khora is 'the relation of the interval or the spacing to what is lodged in it to be received in it' (On the Name, p. 125). Like Différance, of which it is a 'sur-name', khora is described by Caputo as 'an open-ended and porous receptacle of the uncontainable, of innumerable and incalculable effects, as an un-principle, an an-arche' (105). To see khora as the quasi-condition of both God and godlessness, as Derrida sometimes seems to do, does not sit easily however with Caputo's tendency to oppose God and khora as alternatives – 'God or khora?' There appear to be three ways in which khora may be related to God: (1) as undecidable and neutral quasi-condition of both theism and atheism; (2) as the atheistic 'real' which is pre-originary and prior to theistic figuration; and (3) as proto-theistic quasi-condition of faith in messianic justice and a kingdom of democracy-to-come. The three readings might be summarized as khora-open-to-God (neither for nor against), khora-against-God and khora-for-God. Both Caputo and Derrida appear to vacillate between these three positions, though the most consistent Derridean reading would seem to be the first.

22 E. Levinas, 'There is: Existence without Existents', first published in 1946 as a section of De l'existence à l'existant (Vrin, Paris) and reprinted in The Levinas Reader, ed. S. Hand, Blackwell, London, 1989, pp. 32–3. Elsewhere in this same passage, which first outlines his original and highly influential notion of the there is/il y a, Levinas writes:

> Night and the silence of nothingness. This impersonal, anonymous, yet inextinguishable 'consummation' of being, which murmurs in the depths of nothingness itself we shall designate by the term there is . . . The anonymous current of being invades, submerges every subject, person or thing . . . We could say that the night is the very experience of the there is, if the term experience were not inapplicable to a situation which involves the total exclusion of light.
>
> (p. 30)

In terms reminiscent of the deconstructive notion of khora, Levinas goes on to explain the inextricable link between the there is and darkness:

> When the forms of things are dissolved in the night, the darkness of the night . . . invades like a presence. In the night, where we are riven to it, we are not dealing with anything. But this nothing is not that of pure nothingness. There is no longer this or that; there is not 'something' . . . It is immediately there. There is no discourse. Nothing responds to us but this silence; the voice of this silence is understood and frightens us like the silence of those infinite spaces.
>
> (p. 30)

But in so far as the there is is an impersonal form, like it rains, or it is warm, its anonymity serves to de-subjectivize and de-personalize the human self. 'What we call the I', says

Levinas, 'is itself submerged by the night, invaded, depersonalized, stifled by it' (p. 31). So, without actually invoking the aboriginal notion of *khora*, Levinas' *Il y a* bears many of its traces qua dark and undifferentiated 'background of existence' (p. 32). But Levinas, like Derrida and Caputo after him, will add certain existential aspects to this pre-conditioning, anonymous, nocturnal space: 'It makes things appear to us, in a night, like the monotonous presence that bears down on us in insomnia' (p. 32). And this bearing down takes the form, for Levinas, not just of fear and trembling but of horror itself: 'Horror is somehow a movement which will strip consciousness of its very "subjectivity" . . . In horror . . . the subject is depersonalized' (p. 33). But this horror is exacerbated by the fact that the *there is* has no exits. It is more horrifying than death, indeed, for unlike death, it offers no escape. As the ludic event of the night, the *il y a* is, concludes Levinas:

> Like the density of the void, like a murmur of silence. . . . Darkness is the very play of existence which would play itself out even if there were nothing. It is to express just this paradoxical existence that we have introduced the term 'there is'.
>
> (p. 35)

Levinas' notion of the *there is* was to exert a deep influence on subsequent thinkers, informing not only Blanchot's concept of 'disaster' but also Derrida's and Caputo's reading of *khora*. Sean Hand offers a concise account of this enigmatic and elusive phenomenon:

> 'There is' is anonymous and impersonal being in general . . . It exists prior even to nothingness, the rumbling within silence that one hears when putting a shell to one's ear, the horrifying silence confronting the vigilant insomniac who is and is not an 'I'.
>
> (Introduction to 'There Is', *The Levinas Reader*, p. 29)

The *il y a* recurs throughout Levinas' oeuvre – *Time and the Other*, *Totality and Infinity*, *Difficult Freedom* – receiving this final formulation in Levinas' last major publication, *Autrement qu'être ou au-delà de l'essence*, Nijhoff, The Hague, 1974, p. 207:

> Mais l'essence imperturbable, égale et indifférente à toute responsabilité que, désormais, elle englobe, vire comme, dans l'insomnie, de cette neutralité et de cette égalité, en monotonie, en anonymat, en insignifiance, en bourdon-nement incessant que rien ne peut plus arrêter et qui absorbe toute signification, jusqu'à celle dont ce remue-ménage est une modalité. L'essence s'étirant indéfiniment, sans retenue, sans interruption possible . . . sans répit, sans suspension possible – c'est l'il y a horrifiant derrière toute finalité propre du moi thématisant.

23 E. Levinas, 'There is', op. cit., p. 34.
24 Caputo, *Deconstruction in a Nutshell*, p. 97.

25 Derrida, 'Post-Scriptum' in *Derrida and Negative Theology*, ed. H. Coward and T. Foshay, SUNY Press, Albany, 1992.

26 See for example, the Monastery of the *Khora* in Istanbul. I am grateful to John Manoussakis for bringing this to my attention. (See his essay '*Khora*: the Hermeneutics of Hyphenation' in *Revista Portuguesa de Filosofia*, vol. 58, 2002, pp. 93–100.) If we were to distinguish between two kinds of *khora* – one which negates God (like the *Il y a*) and the other which embraces God (like the Madonna as 'container of the uncontainable') – we might take some guidance from the crucial distinction made by the apophatic Neoplatonist, Damascius, between two kinds of 'nothing'. Speaking of the Ineffable beyond the One (which cannot be conceived though the One can), he writes:

> Or, si cela n'est rien, il faut que le rien soit de deux sortes: celui qui est meilleur que l'un et celui qui est en deçà: si donc nous nous avançons dans le vide en parlant ainsi, c'est qu'il y a aussi deux façons de marcher dans le vide, l'une en tombant dans l'indicible, l'autre dans ce qui n'est en aucune façon ni sous aucun rapport; indicible, sans doute, est également ce néant-ci, comme Platon lui aussi le dit, mais il l'est selon le pire, tandis que celui-là l'est selon le meilleur.

(Trans. Westerink and Combes, ed. Bude,
Paris, 1986, vol. 1, pp. 7–8)

I am grateful to Joseph. S. O'Leary for this quotation and also for his original reading of *Khora* in *Religious Pluralism and Christian Truth*, Edinburgh University Press, Edinburgh 1996, pp. 125, 176–7. O'Leary argues that the variability of religious discourse espouses the originary *khora*. It conceives the truth of God as heterogeneous origin, as the non-truth of woman. Here *khora* is compared to a Buddhist emptiness or a Christian kenosis of fixed identity – a milieu in which nothing exists except in relation but in which an ultimate reality announces itself. In Derridean language, one might say that *khora* releases divine originarity, dissolving the God-foundation in rhythms and waves of *différance*. But O'Leary insists that divine transcendence cannot be absorbed into *différance*. Derrida has 'a questioning openness to otherness, even divine otherness, but it is empty of concrete theological content, except perhaps his despairing messianism which is an idea of justice'. According to O'Leary, Derrida does not want theologians to identify his *khora* or Heidegger's originary *Ereignis* with the Holy Spirit. But O'Leary himself holds that an exploration of *khora* could remain in waiting for the God who 'dawns on chaos' (Shelley), since *khora* is intrinsic to the very texture of reality. Both God and *khora*, he suggests, could be passed through the mill of Buddhist emptiness so that *khora* could be attuned to a sense of ultimacy and allow the name and personal face of God as at least a skilful means of evoking ultimacy. Even if for the biblical religions the personal presence and will of God go beyond any impersonal concepts of ultimacy and cannot be reduced to mere 'skilful means'.

27 See our own analysis of the 'possible' and 'perhaps' in *Poétique du Possible*, Beauchesne, Paris, 1984, and more recently in *The God who May Be*, Indiana University Press, Bloomington, 2001, especially the chapter entitled 'Possibilising God'. See also J. Derrida's intriguing

analysis of the notion of 'perhaps' in 'Loving in Friendship: Perhaps – the Noun and the Adverb' in *Politics of Friendship*, trans. G. Collins, Verso, London and New York, 1997, pp. 26–49, and in 'Comme si c'était possible, "Within such Limits" . . .' in *Revue Internationale de Philosophie*, vol. 3, no. 205, 1998, pp. 497–529. It must be conceded, however, that in spite of our endeavours (and Derrida's) to build bridges between our eschatological position and that of deconstruction, Derrida makes it clear that what he understands by khora is not susceptible to a *khora* (mother)–logos (father) analogy. See 'Comment ne pas parler' in *Psyché*, p. 570:

> Même quand Platon semble la comparer à une 'mère' ou à une 'nourrice', cette *khora* toujours vierge en vérite ne fait pas couple avec le 'père' auquel Platon 'compare' le paradigme; elle n'engendre pas les formes sensibles qui s'inscrivent en elles et que Platon 'compare' à un enfant.

See also the longer passage from the same text cited above in note 18.

10 LAST GODS AND FINAL THINGS: FAITH AND PHILOSOPHY

1 Martin Heidegger, 'Phenomenology and Theology' in *The Piety of Thinking: Essays by Martin Heidegger*, ed. and trans. J.G. Hart and J.C. Maraldo, Indiana University Press, Bloomington, 1976, pp. 7, 10–11.

2 M. Heidegger, *History of the Concept of Time: Prolegomena*, trans. T. Kisiel, Indiana University Press, Bloomington, 1992, p. 80. This series of lectures was delivered at Marburg in 1925 and is considered by many to be the first and to some extent 'unexpurgated' version of *Being and Time*.

3 Ibid.

4 See J. Caputo's revealing account of Heidegger's move from early theistic interests to a position of 'methodological atheism' and ultimately to a frankly 'aggressive atheism' in the late twenties, 'Heidegger and Theology', *The Cambridge Companion to Heidegger*, ed. C. Guignon, Cambridge University Press, Cambridge, 1993, pp. 277–8:

> If (Heidegger) had begun as an ultraconservative Catholic, and if he had after 1917 become deeply involved in a dialogue with liberal Protestant historical theology, he was after 1928 deeply antagonistic to Christianity in general and to the Catholicism of Freiburg in particular, and he gives indications of having become personally atheistic . . . He would not accept the young Jesuits who came to Freiburg as his doctoral students and he treated other Catholic students like Max Müller exceedingly badly. When their dissertations were submitted . . . Heidegger treated them with disdain . . . When Martin Honecker died unexpectedly in 1941, Heidegger succeeded in having the Chair (of Catholic Philosophy) abolished, the very one to which he himself had aspired a quarter of a century earlier . . . his position during the thirties was that Christianity was a decadent falling away from the primordiality of experience.

5 M. Heidegger, *An Introduction to Metaphysics*, trans. R. Mannheim, Yale University Press, New Haven, 1959, p. 107.

6 Reported by Jean Beaufret in *La Quinzaine Littéraire*, no. 196, 1974, p. 3. See our discussion of this theme in our *Poétique du Possible*, Editions Beauchesne, Paris, 1984, pp. 252ff.

7 M. Heidegger, *The Piety of Thinking*, pp. 34, 36. See also our *Poétique du Possible*, p. 253, notes 2 and 3.

8 M. Heidegger, Address to students in the University of Zurich, November 1951. See *The Piety of Thinking*, p. 65.

9 M. Heidegger, *Letter On Humanism*, trans. F. Capuzzi and J. Gray, in *Basic Writings*, ed. D. Krell, Harper and Row, New York, 1977, pp. 193–242.

10 'The Origin of the Art Work' in *Poetry, Language and Thought*, trans. A. Hofstadter, Harper and Rowe, New York, 1971, p. 44. For Heidegger this poetic 'naming of the holy' epitomized the original Greek *mythos* of aesthetic experience where the gods showed themselves as part of a larger cosmic-ontological *poeisis*. See our development of this theme in our essay, 'Heidegger's Gods' in *Poetics of Modernity*, Humanities Press, New Jersey, 1995, pp. 50–64.

11 J. Caputo, 'Heidegger and Theology', p. 283.

12 See Heidegger's famous preface to *An Introduction to Metaphysics*, originally published in 1935 and published in English translation in 1959 (see note 5 above).

13 See our *The God Who May Be*, Indiana University Press, Bloomington, 2001, as well as *Poétique du Possible*, and 'Heidegger et le Dieu du Possible' in *Heidegger et la question de Dieu*, ed. R. Kearney and J. O'Leary, Grasset, Paris, 1980.

14 The full citations of these three works are *Beiträge zur Philosophie (Vom Ereignis)*, *Gesamtausgabe* 65, Frankfurt, 1989; *Besinnung*, *Gesamtausgabe* 66, Frankfurt, 1997; and *Die Geschichte des Seyns*, *Gesamtausgabe* 69, Frankfurt, 1998. These volumes are henceforth referred to in the text in the abbreviated form of GA 65, 66 and 69 respectively. The theme of the 'last God' which recurs in these three works has been astutely analysed by Jean Greisch in a number of pioneering studies, notably 'La Pauvreté du "Dernier Dieu" de Heidegger' in *Post-Theism: Reframing the Judaeo-Christian Tradition*, ed. H. Krop, A. Molendijk and H. de Vries, Peeters, Leuven, 2000, pp. 397–420; 'La *Gesamtausgabe* de Heidegger (1997–1998): de "l'ontologie" à la Penseé de l'Ereignis' in *Revue des Sciences Philosophiques et Théologiques*, vol. 84, Vrin, Paris, 2000, pp. 299–325. I am greatly indebted to Jean Greisch's research for many of the citations and comments which follow.

15 See Jean Greisch's perspicacious discussion of this passage in 'La Pauvreté du "dernier Dieu" de Heidegger', p. 399. See also D. Crownefield, 'The Question of God. Thinking after Heidegger', *Philosophy Today*, Spring 1996, pp. 47–54.

16 See commentary by Greisch, ibid., p. 402.

17 Jeff Prudhomme, 'The Passing-By of the Ultimate God: The Theological Assessment of Modernity in Heidegger's *Beiträge zur Philosophie*' in the *Journal of the American Academy of Religion*, vol. 61, no. 3, 1993, pp. 443–54. See J. Greisch on this subordination of the eschatological and personal God of confessional faith to the ontology of Heidegger's 'Last God' in 'La *Gesamtausgabe* de Heidegger (1997–1998)', p. 318:

> Heidegger affirme qu'il s'agit de tout à fait autre chose que d'une 'attitude eschatologique' (p. 245) au sens judéo-chrétien du terme. Mais suffit-il

d'affirmer que 'toute "eschatologie" vit de la foi en la certitude de l'état nouveau' (p. 245) et de souligner qu'à cette prétendue certitude s'oppose l'incertitude essentielle qui marque les avancées et les secousses de l'histoire destinale de l'être? Ce qui est sûr en tout cas, c'est que 'l'attente', qui n'en est pas une, du 'dernier Dieu' ne relève pas d'une foi religieuse et que son avènement n'est pas une 'théophanie' (p. 252).

Greisch goes on to conclude: 'Heidegger s'attache à montrer que la pensée post-métaphysique . . . est étrangère à toute vision du monde "religieuse" ou 'théologique' (p. 323).

18 See J. Greisch's suggestive commentaries, ibid., p. 320: 'La pauvreté s'y associe avec les notions d'Abîme, de Néant et de Silence (p. 106). Cela montre que la *Vielspurigkeit* qui caractérise la pensée de l'être se réfracte dans l'idée de pauvreté . . . une pauvreté qui n'a rien d'une kénose'; and also in 'La Pauvreté du "Dernier Dieu"', pp. 406–7. See also William Richardson's instructive summary of Heidegger's Last God in 'Whose Phenomenology?' (presented at Boston University Colloquium on Phenomenology and Theology, 2000). All through the *Beiträge*, says Richardson,

> Heidegger refers again and again to the divine . . . in the sense of a god, or gods – of the flight of the gods of the Greeks, the death of Christianity, the arrival of gods still to come – even the 'godding' (the 'very' being or 'presencing') of the gods – and finally the 'last,' the 'ultimate' god . . . the essential ingredients are as follows: (a) That the contemporary world is a godless one is a given. The plurality of the gods that have flown need not be taken as a polytheism so much as a sign of the manifold finitude and transiency of possible appearances of god. (b) The ultimate god is not last in a series but ultimate in the sense of signifying the most extreme form of the divine, representing thereby the heterogeneity of experiences by which the divine may appear. (c) This god is not identified with be-ing or *Ereignis*, but is in need of both in order to relate to humans and share some intimacy with them. (d) Dependent on be-ing, this god is profoundly finite, capable of manifesting itself, not through divine revelation in any sense the Judaeo-Christianity gives to that term, but through signs in passing that are detectable only after the fact. (e) Yet such a god enjoys a kind of eternity, not in the metaphysical sense of that 'which endlessly lasts,' but rather as that which can withdraw in any given instance in order to return once again – that which can return, not as [merely] similar (*Gleiche*), but as what transforms into the new, the one-only be-ing, such that in this manifestness it is at first not recognized as the same (*Selbe*).

Richardson concludes, 'Believers will find this, at best, a rather impoverished god . . .'

19 Heidegger (GA 66, p. 238):

> A-theism does not consist in the negation or loss of a God but in the absence of the grounding of the divinity of God. This is why the perpetuation of

a habitual divine cult and its consolations and elevations can still be an atheism, as well as the replacement of the cult by the excitation of the lived experience and the effervescence of emotion.

20 See Greisch, 'La Pauvreté du 'Dernier Dieu', pp. 416–18. On Heidegger's preference for 'sacred' extremity and excess over everyday action and charity, see Michael A. Bernstein's illuminating chapter 'Martin Heidegger: Judgement Terminal and Interminable' in *Five Portraits: Modernity and the Imagination in Twentieth-Century German Writing*, Northwestern University Press, Evanston, Illinois, 2000, pp. 71–3 and 75–7. For example p. 73:

> Heidegger more typically characterizes (Dasein's) advent as a unique moment of apotheosis, ecstasy, and epiphany, best expressed in his own distinctively elevated, hieratic, and ceremonial repetitive language. Real human existence could be thought of as almost the exact inverse of Heideggerean Dasein, and it is the defense of that unheroic, heterogeneous life . . . that is the real answer to Heidegger's fascination with the glamour of daring and authenticity.

Bernstein concludes that Heidegger is 'Europe's last, unwavering metaphysician of calamity' for whom the 'darkness of modernity and nihilism had spread over the globe . . .' (p. 77).

21 J. Caputo, 'Heidegger and Theology', pp. 282–3.

22 Ibid., p. 282.

23 Quoted in *The Partisan Review*, 1948.

24 'What is Metaphysics?' in *Basic Writings*, ed. D.F. Krell, Harper, San Francisco, 1977, p. 111.

25 M. Heidegger, 'The Self-Assertion of the German University' in *The Heidegger Controversy*, ed. R. Wolin, The MIT Press, Cambridge, Mass., 1998, pp. 32–3.

26 These questions are posed by David Bollert, 'The Theme of Wonder in Heidegger's Thought', doctoral thesis at Boston College, 2002. I am grateful to David Bollert for his informative treatment of this subject.

27 M. Heidegger, *What is Philosophy?*, trans. W. Kluback and J.T. Wilde, Connecticut College University Press, New Haven, 1958, pp. 82–3.

28 J. Sallis, 'Deformatives: Essentially Other than Truth' in *Commemorations: Reading Heidegger*, ed. J. Sallis, Indiana University Press, Bloomington, 1993, p. 29.

29 M. Heidegger, *Beiträge zur Philosophie*, GA 65, Klosterman, Frankfurt, 1992, p. 416.

30 Jean Greisch, 'L'éphiphanie, un regard philosophique', *Transversalité*, no. 78, Paris, April–June 2001.

31 William Desmond, 'Kant and the Terror of Genius' in *Kant's Aesthetics*, ed. Walter de Gruyter, Berlin and New York, 1998, p. 614.

32 H. Dreyfus, 'Heidegger on the Connection between Nihilism, Art, Technology and Politics' in *The Cambridge Companion to Heidegger*, ed. C. Guignon, pp. 306–15.

33 Ibid., p. 308.

34 M. Heidegger, *Discourse on Thinking*, trans. J. Anderson and E. Freund, Harper and Rowe, New York, 1966, p. 56.

35 H. Dreyfus, op. cit., p. 309.

36 J. Taminiaux, *Poetics, Speculation, Judgment: The Shadow of the Work of Art from Kant to Phenomenology*, SUNY Press, Albany, New York, 1993.

37 Dreyfus, op. cit., p. 310.

38 Ibid., p. 301.

39 Ibid.

40 Ibid., p. 314.

41 Heidegger, 'The Origin of the Art Work', p. 44. See also Wolin's critique of Heidegger's ontology of the 'flown gods' – 'we are too late for the gods and too early for Being' – when he claims that 'the theory of *Seinsgeschick* functions as an elaborate mechanism of denial' (*The Politics of Being*, Columbia University Press, NY, 1990, p.160).

42 See Paul Ricoeur, 'Note Introductive' in *Heidegger et la Question de Dieu*.

43 See the contrasting reading by George Kovacs, *The Question of God in Heidegger's Phenomenology*, Northwestern University Press, Evanston, Illinois, 1990. Kovacs argues that Heidegger's post-metaphysical thinking about Being leads to a 'truly divine notion of God'. For an excellent overview of the theological and the philosophical debates surrounding Heidegger's notion of divinity and god see Dominique Janicaud, *Heidegger en France*, vol. 1, Albin Michel, Paris, 2001, pp. 478–89.

44 Heidegger, *The Piety of Thinking*, op. cit., cited in our *Poétique du Possible*, p. 253, note 3.

45 Heidegger, *Poetry, Language, Thought*, op. cit., cited in *Poétique du Possible*, p. 554, note 4.

46 See our discussion of the contrast between the eschatological *Peut-être* and the ontological *Pouvoir-être* in *Poétique du Possible*, Parts 2 to 4; and in our chapters 'Possibilizing God' and 'A Poetics of the Possible' in our *The God who May Be*, Indiana University Press, Bloomington, 2001.

47 See *Poétique du Possible*, p. 254, note 6. See also the recent reflections by thinkers such as Derrida, Marion and Caputo on the relationship between the divine and the possible/impossible, especially in *God, The Gift and Postmodernity*, ed. J. Caputo and M. Scanlon, Indiana University Press, Bloomington, 1999.

CONCLUSION

1 Paul Ricoeur, *L'Homme Faillible*, Aubier, Paris, 1960 (English translation, *Fallible Man*, Regnery, Chicago, 1965, p.156). I am indebted to my friend and Erasmus exchange partner of many years, Jean Greisch, for his discussion of these issues of finitude and narrativity in the philosophies of Paul Ricoeur, Wilhelm Schapp, Jean Nabert, Franz Rosenzweig and others in his pioneering book, *L'Arbre de Vie et l'Arbre du Savoir*, Editions du Cerf, Paris, 2000, pp. 28–32. See also his recent companion volumes, *Paul Ricoeur: l'itinérance du sens*, Editions Millon, Grenoble, 2001, *Le Cogito Herméneutique*, Vrin, Paris, 2000, and *Le Buisson Ardent et les Lumières de la Raison*, Cerf, Paris, 2002.

2 In addition to the recent hermeneutic studies of religion by Greisch and Ricoeur already cited (in particular *Thinking Biblically*, with André LeCocque, University of Chicago Press, Chicago, 1998), see also here Joseph S. O'Leary, *Religious Pluralism and Christian Truth*,

Edinburgh University Press, Edinburgh, 1996; Hent De Vries, *Philosophy and the Turn to Religion*, The Johns Hopkins University Press, Baltimore and London, 1999; Mark Dooley, *A Passion for the Impossible*, SUNY, Albany, 2002; John D. Caputo, *On Religion*, Routledge, London and New York, 2001; Mark P. Hederman, *Kissing the Dark*, Columba Press, Dublin, 1999; James Olthuis (ed.), *Religion With/out Religion*, Routledge, London and New York, 2002; and Stanislas Breton, *The Word and Cross*, Fordham University Press, New York, 2001.

NAME INDEX